THE SIMPLEST GAME

D0976502

ALBANY COUNTY PUBLIC LIBRARY
Serving the Laramie Plains since 1887

Laramie, Wyoming 82070

PRESENTED BY

Friends of the Library

OTHER BOOKS BY PAUL GARDNER

Sports Illustrated Soccer (*with Phil Woosnam*)
Pelé: The Master and His Method
Nice Guys Finish Last: Sport and American Life

THE SIMPLEST GAME

The Intelligent Fan's Guide to the World of Soccer

Paul Gardner

With a Foreword by Pelé

Collier Books
Macmillan Publishing Company   *New York*

Maxwell Macmillan Canada   *Toronto*

Maxwell Macmillan International
New York   Oxford   Singapore   Sydney

ALBANY COUNTY
PUBLIC LIBRARY
LARAMIE, WYOMING

Copyright © 1976, 1994 by Paul Gardner

All rights reserved. No part of this book may be reproduced or transmitted in any form or by any means, electronic or mechanical, including photocopying, recording, or by any information storage and retrieval system, without permission in writing from the Publisher.

Collier Books
Macmillan Publishing Company
866 Third Avenue
New York, NY 10022

Maxwell Macmillan Canada, Inc.
1200 Eglinton Avenue East
Suite 200
Don Mills, Ontario M3C 3N1

Macmillan Publishing Company is part of the Maxwell Communication Group of Companies.

Library of Congress Cataloging-in-Publication Data
Gardner, Paul, 1930–
    The simplest game : the intelligent fan's guide to the world of soccer / Paul Gardner.—[2nd ed.]
        p.   cm.
    ISBN 0-02-043225-9
    1. Soccer.   2. Soccer—History.   I. Title.
GV943.G28
796.334—dc20   1994   93-2157
CIP

The Laws of Soccer are reproduced on pages 251–278 by permission of the Fédération Internationale de Football Association.

Macmillan books are available at special discounts for bulk purchases for sales promotions, premiums, fund-raising, or educational use. For details, contact:

Special Sales Director
Macmillan Publishing Company
866 Third Avenue
New York, NY 10022

First Collier Books Edition 1994

10   9   8   7   6   5   4   3   2

Printed in the United States of America

For the Tahuichi spirit—
and the boys who bring it to life

Rules of the Simplest Game was the title of one of the earliest sets of soccer rules, drawn up by J. C. Thring of Uppingham School in 1862.

Contents

Foreword

The title of my autobiography is *My Life and the Beautiful Game.*
Soccer, The Beautiful Game. Paul Gardner calls it The Simplest
Game, and perhaps that's the same thing. The simple beauty, the
beautiful simplicity that has made soccer the world's favorite sport.
   The United States has done things in its own way, in its own time.
For decades it resisted the call of soccer. But things have changed
over the past thirty years. Soccer has been growing steadily here, and
now I believe that its success in this country is inevitable. I see it taking its place, alongside baseball and basketball and football, as a major
sport.
   In 1975 I came to this country to play for the New York Cosmos. I
was excited by the opportunity to bring the joys of soccer to the
Americans. Everything pointed to a smooth triumph for pro soccer:
the thriving, growing North American Soccer League, large crowds, a
national television contract, worldwide interest in what was going on.
   Probably I should have been suspicious. One of the beauties, the
mysteries, of soccer is that things are never quite what they seem.
Certainly, I knew from my playing experience that it is the most
unpredictable of sports—that is part of its fascination. Suddenly,
things went badly wrong. In 1984, the league collapsed. Soccer, said
the pessimists, was finished.
   Yet here we are, a mere ten years later, with the United States
about to stage the most popular sports event in the world. A soccer
event. The World Cup, soccer's dazzling showcase.
   No, soccer did not die in 1984. The NASL had planted seeds every-

where, and the sport was now delighting kids—boys and girls—all over this huge country. In the ten years since the death of the league, the sport has gone on growing irresistibly at the youth level.

Today there are millions of kids and millions of parents and relations and friends involved in soccer in the United States. The beautiful game has taken root in this beautiful country. All the time that I and so many others have spent meeting with youth groups and giving instructional clinics over the past twenty years ago has not been lost.

I'm talking, of course, about the practical side of soccer, what we do on the field. But there is another side to the sport, another whole world of soccer. This is the world that Paul Gardner is writing about in this book. It is the story of the development of the game, of its great events, its great players, the story of all the marvelous things that have happened in the past and are happening today to make soccer the sport that it is. That, too, is a beautiful world, and from it Paul Gardner has created a vivid picture of the fascination and excitement of the constantly changing world of soccer.

The Simplest Game is not meant to teach you how to play the sport, or how to watch it, or how to coach it. Yet, when you have read all that Paul Gardner has to say, I think you will have a new and deeper understanding of soccer. An understanding of what we need to do to teach our youngsters the true, deep beauty of this game.

Whether you are an interested parent or a player or a coach or a referee or simply a spectator, *The Simplest Game* will help you to get more enjoyment from the sport of soccer.

Pelé

Acknowledgments

Special thanks to Lawrie Mifflin for getting the whole thing moving, to Mike Woitalla for all sorts of crucial help with a whole range of soccer matters, and to editor Rick Wolff for what was needed: stern—but always sensible and sensitive—attention to detail.

Thanks also to Peter Casanas, Keene Curtis, Sergio Di Cesare, Michael Gamarra, Lyn Fairhurst, Brian Glanville, Sunil Gulati, Ted Howard, Gordon Jago, Paul Kennedy, Andrea Masala, Julio Mazzei, John Sanacore, Graham Turner, George Vecsey, and Eric Weil; and to David Bloomfield of the Football Association, Terry Murphy of Arsenal F.C., Gordon Taylor of the Professional Footballers' Association, and Guido Tognoni and Andreas Herren of FIFA.

Introduction to the Second Edition

Things looked pretty rosy for soccer in the United States when this book first appeared in 1976. The sport was spreading explosively at the youth level, and a familiar phrase attached itself to soccer: fastest-growing. It was the fastest-growing youth sport, the fastest-growing high school sport, the fastest-growing college sport.

On top of all that, there was Pelé. The World's Greatest Player had just arrived to join the New York Cosmos. That, it seemed, added respectability and credibility to the North American Soccer League. Only a national television contract was missing. Surely, soccer was about to become the fastest-growing professional sport in the United States.

For a while, yes. The TV deal came in 1979, with a two-year contract from ABC. That same year, the NASL had twenty-four teams. Then it all began to fall apart. ABC did not renew in 1981, and the NASL's shrinkage began. Within two years it was down to twelve clubs. At the end of the 1984 season, which was played with only nine clubs, the curtain came down.

The NASL was gone—guilty, according to the postmortems, of everything from avarice and arrogance to shortsightedness and stupidity.

But if there was no room for soccer at the top, down among the nation's kids it was jumping. It was still the fastest-growing youth sport, and now a whole new adventure was opening up that promised to send the numbers to dizzying new heights: Soccer was catching on rapidly as a sport for girls.

The swelling tide of kids has changed the lives of millions of American parents who have been swept into the phenomenon, many of them pressed into service as novice coaches and referees. Soccer goalposts, which once cowered apologetically in the shadow of football posts at high schools, now stand triumphantly on their own in suburban fields all over America.

The growth has been spectacular, but it certainly has not been a carefully planned growth. Everything has happened too massively, too quickly.

True, the defunct NASL had made white suburbia the target of its missionary work, sending out coaches and players to give talks and clinics at high schools and youth clubs. There was planning in that, but it was financial, not soccer, planning. The NASL was trying to create the ticket buyers of the future, not necessarily the players. In the early years of pell-mell growth, the accent was always on numbers. There was strength in those constantly growing totals, they were the incontestable statistical proof that soccer was becoming a force to be reckoned with. Quantity ruled. Quality? That was left to look after itself.

Those attitudes have changed very little during the past decade. Numbers is still the name of the game. But now the numbers are needed not so much to prove that soccer exists, as to attract sponsors. No doubt that is a logical formula, but it is still a financial formula. More than ever, quantity rules, to the point where the numbers are stretched to include just about anyone who has even looked at a soccer ball. Research by SICA—the Soccer Industry Council of America—claimed to reveal that 14.6 million Americans played soccer "at least once" in 1991.

It is highly questionable whether anyone who plays soccer only once in a year can be counted as being involved in the sport, but the relentless advance of the numbers has no time for such niceties.

The significance of the figures is not to be sought in soccer terms. It lies in the fact that 27 percent of the participants come from households with an annual income of over $50,000, or in the fact that 39 percent of the participants are female. That is the sort of thing that interests the sponsors and the marketers.

The game itself, the sport as played on the field—how has that been faring? Has anyone been bothering about that? Not too much. Neither within the United States nor in the world soccer community. In the eighteen years since this book was first published, soccer has become a billion-dollar worldwide industry—a prolific soccer goose that has been laying golden eggs for nearly two decades. Only now, in the past couple of years, has there come a widespread acceptance that something has gone wrong. The supply of golden eggs is threatened because no one has been paying attention to the health of the goose.

The sport itself, what the players do on the field, has become overburdened with money. Games have become too important to allow soccer to be played with freedom, with personality, with enjoyment, with skill. These essential qualities have been slowly draining from the sport. Caution and fear have replaced them.

The quality of the game of soccer has been suffering. Who is to blame? At the same time, no one and everyone. Nobody really foresaw that as soccer got richer it would get duller. The connection was not a logical one. Yet that is what happened. The frustrating thing is that it took so long for a reaction to set in.

It is to be hoped that soccer has now taken stock of its position, and is on the way back to full health. The Fédération Internationale de Football Association (FIFA), the sport's worldwide governing body, is leading the way after years of inertia. There does seem to be a worldwide demand for better, more exciting soccer—a point that is crucial to the future of the sport in the United States.

A new drive is on for resumed growth at the top, for the formation of a new pro league. And a new stimulus is at hand. In 1975, it was the arrival of Pelé. In 1994 it is the staging of the World Cup. The mere fact that the United States is hosting the tournament shows how far the sport has come in this country. The absence of a pro league underlines how far it has to go.

World Cup USA '94 will no doubt be a huge success. Will it, as FIFA insists that it must, create an atmosphere of enthusiasm for soccer in which a pro league can flourish? Or will it be a transient success?

A pro league can only be based on high-quality soccer. Especially is that true in the United States, where soccer—for the first time in its worldwide history—is having to grow in the face of stiff competition from other well-organized, long-established pro sports.

In this book, after traveling through the development of the game worldwide, we arrive, in the final chapter, at the current situation here in the United States. The World Cup is upon us, the pro league is supposed to follow. It is the theme of this final chapter that soccer in this country has made, and continues to make, grave errors in its assessment of what is needed to get a pro league off the ground.

I have already mentioned that there has been a lack of attention to the quality, as opposed to the quantity, of soccer in this country. But even where the nature of the sport itself has been addressed, the judgments passed on what constitutes "high-quality soccer" have been alarmingly faulty.

The errors are grave enough to undermine the possibility of a successful pro league. They are correctable. But time is not on soccer's side.

New York, August 1993

Introduction to the First Edition

It has often occurred to me that sport, like sex, is an activity that should be either performed or watched—but not written about. Both lose a great deal in the telling. Such thoughts I chase from my mind as quickly as I can. I do, after all, make my living writing about sports. But there is something to it, I'll admit. Too often we writers are the pornographers of sport: We sensationalize, we titillate, we expose, we try to create again the excitement of a moment. But how often do we come to grips with the real nature, the essence, of sports?

I am wondering, at this moment, about soccer. What is soccer? And I am forced to the conclusion that I am not sure. Not exactly the best way to start a book on the subject, but trying to define soccer is like Mark Twain giving up smoking—easy, he'd done it hundreds of times. And so with soccer, there are dozens of definitions and none of them really works.

It is, we are told, simply twenty-two men kicking a ball around. Yet to the aesthete it is an art form, an athletic ballet. To the spiritually inclined it is a sort of religion. To the sociologist it is an escape from the boredom of everyday life. To the Marxist it is a capitalist trap for holding down revolution. To the cynical it is a big business, to the psychologist it is a catharsis, to the social worker it is a way of keeping kids out of trouble, to the uninterested it is a bore. And so on, and so on.

I suppose each one of these tells us something about soccer, but even the sum of them falls lamentably short of the whole picture. The mind of the novelist does better. Listen to J. B. Priestley describing the game in his mythical northern English city, Bruddersford:

To say that these men paid their shillings to watch twenty-two hirelings kick a ball is merely to say that a violin is wood and catgut, that Hamlet is so much paper and ink. For a shilling the Bruddersford United A.F.C. offered you Conflict and Art; it turned you into a critic, happy in your judgment of fine points, ready in a second to estimate the worth of a well-judged pass, a run down the touchline, a lightning shot, a clearance kick by back or goalkeeper; it turned you into a partisan, holding your breath when the ball came sailing into your own goalmouth, ecstatic when your forwards raced away towards the opposite goal, elated, downcast, bitter, triumphant by turns at the fortunes of your side, watching the ball shape Iliads and Odysseys for you; and what is more, it turned you into a member of a new community, all brothers together for an hour and a half, for not only had you escaped from the clanking machinery of this lesser life, from work, wages, rent, doles, sick pay, insurance cards, nagging wives, ailing children, bad bosses, idle workmen, but you had escaped with most of your mates and your neighbours, with half the town, and there you were, cheering together, thumping one another on the shoulders, swapping judgments like lords of the earth, having pushed your way through a turnstile into another and altogether more splendid kind of life, hurtling with Conflict and yet passionate and beautiful in its Art. Moreover, it offered you more than a shilling's worth of material for talk during the rest of the week.*

That is getting nearer to the heart of the matter, because there is a suggestion of soccer as a living thing, something that survives after the game is over, something that is vivid enough to brighten the memory for years, so that we can all say of some soccer game "I remember...."

• • •

Thinking there might be a heavy fog, or an accident, or perhaps a strike—well, so many things can upset railroad timetables—I got up at 5:00 A.M. to catch a train hours earlier than I really needed to. So I got into London around nine o'clock, leaving me some five hours to dispose of before I had to be at the stadium.

This was 1953, and in those days London on Cup final day was like a

* *The Good Companions* (New York: Harper, 1929).

town under benevolent siege. There always seemed to be at least one northern team represented (that year it was Blackpool and Bolton, both from the north), and the supporters arrived in boisterous little knots, drifting about the streets trying somehow to make a dent in the apathy of the big city. In the narrow streets that used to surround Euston Station, these working-class fans—they could have been Priestley's Bruddersfordians—were instantly at home, absorbed without trouble into the cheap boardinghouses and the sleazy little cafés, where their broad Lancashire accents badgered the waitresses endlessly, "Give us anoother coop o' tea, lass," and they talked about soccer. Not intelligently, but with the blind partisanship that had caused them to come all those miles to this heathen city, and to deck themselves out with huge rosettes and scarves and hats and even whole suits in their club colors.

"It's Stan's year, lads, it's Stan's year, I bloody know it. I bloody told you so when we beat 'uddersfield, I bloody knew it then, and I'll tell you now, bloody Bolton aren't gonna stop him. Who've they bloody got? Banks? He's a big ox, Stan'll make 'im look bloody daft, he'll wish he'd stayed home with the missus. . . . How about anoother coop here, lass?"

Solid agreement from all his Blackpool mates. They had a London newspaper in which one of the writers had picked Bolton—"What the bloody 'ell does 'e know about it?"—the very idea, a London writer daring to give opinions about northern teams.

I sat for a while, a middle-class interloper, listening to them tear Bolton apart until it hardly seemed worthwhile playing the game. As it happened, I agreed with them. I had no ties to either team, but I wanted Blackpool to win. Just because of Stan.

I had first seen Stanley Matthews play maybe ten years earlier, and I had never missed an opportunity to see him again. He had shown me, as he must have shown tens of thousands of others, just how superb a game soccer could be. Any game with Stan in it was likely to be a magical occasion. His nickname, said the papers, was the Wizard of the Dribble. In the papers, maybe, but never on the terraces. There it was always just plain Stan. "Come on, Stan, show 'im, Stan." And Stan, stooping, balding, his face a blank but always slightly drawn—the only thing about him that suggested anything approaching effort—would show them.

At his feet, the ball was at home, comfortably nestling in absolute security, caressed with soft little touches as Stan shuffled his bowed legs toward yet another hapless fullback. Watch the ball, not the man, is considered the defender's golden rule, and you would see them with a mesmerized, almost frightened concentration on the ball as Stan approached. But how could you not watch a man whose seductive body movements seemed to telegraph his every move? Surely no one could lean that far to his left, unless he were actually going to take a step in that direction? And so the fullback would move, had to move, and all was lost. In one smooth burst Stan would straighten up and sail away to his right, leaving the fullback staring at nothing but air, or falling onto his back as he tried to turn while off-balance.

Then the roar for Matthews as he headed for the goal line, the ball always just that calculated distance ahead of him where he could get to it but an opponent could not. Matthews was not a speedster, but I doubt whether anyone has ever been faster over those first few yards after he had beaten his man. There was never any hope of the fullback, even if he was still on his feet, catching Matthews. Usually another defender would come running across to cover, but this was just what Stan wanted. A player coming at full speed to tackle a moving Matthews had the most impossible of tasks. He had to get to the ball at once, and as his foot came in, Stan would pull the ball back and cut inside, or he would push it forward, what looked like just a few tantalizing inches beyond the tackler's outstretched foot, which he would step over as though it didn't exist, and complete his enchanted path to the goal line.

There the ball would be pulled sharply back and sent arcing into the penalty area where it would arrive like some gently falling bomb, always out of reach of the goalkeeper, always within reach of the attacking forwards surging in to meet it.

Inevitably, the torment of having to face Matthews invited rough tactics, and Stan was kicked and fouled more than most. The resilient, wiry body bore it all, and the stoic, rather sad face remained as blank as ever. He never had to be cautioned by a referee and, to my knowledge, when he retired at age 50, he had never retaliated, in a thirty-three-year-long career.

What I and most of England—except Bolton—wanted to see was Stan being presented with a Cup-winner's medal, just about the only honor in the game that he had never won. This was Matthews's third final in six years: Twice before, in 1948 and 1951, Blackpool had been beaten and Matthews had walked off the field a loser. Now he was thirty-eight years old and this must surely be his last chance.

The Blackpool fans had it all worked out; it would be 3–1 Blackpool when the final whistle went and I left them happily plotting Bolton's downfall among the empty teacups and the greasy plates. Pick another café and you'd have found the same Lancashire accents, wearing black and white, and telling you that Blackpool could put a hundred bloody Matthewses on the field if they liked, it was goals that counted, and "our Nat" scores goals, laddie—how many has Stan scored lately? And there was a lot of truth in that, too.

I walked into the West End, a different world this, of large, smart stores, one where little groups of fans stood out as foreign elements, and defiantly made all the more noise because of it. By one o'clock I was impatient. "You are advised to take up your position by not later than 2:30 P.M.," said my ticket, which left me ninety minutes to make a twenty-minute subway journey. But you never knew, there might be a delay of some sort, an accident. . . . By 1:30 I was at Wembley Stadium, proffering my ticket at the turnstile, holding my breath in case it was rejected as counterfeit (I had no reason to think it was; I had obtained it in the most respectable way, but you never know . . .).

My seat, I decided, was not a good one, too far to one end, giving an excellent view of one goal but a long-range look at the other. The stadium was already a third full, maybe 30,000 people, most of them gathered behind the two goals. Between them the famous Wembley turf, rich, green and glowing like a massive emerald carpet. A treacherous carpet, though, one that did strange things to players' legs. There always seemed to be cramps and pulled muscles and twisted knees at a Wembley final.

Community singing came next. Led by a military band standing in the middle of the field we sang popular songs and music-hall numbers until, with the stadium almost full and only fifteen minutes left, we were ready for sterner stuff—"Land of Hope and Glory," and then the traditional "Abide with Me," a solid working-class hymn sung with a fervor it would never command in any chapel. There is no real ending to "Abide with Me" at Wembley; the last note slides into a sustained cheer as banners wave and rattles rattle, a cheer that turns suddenly to an amorphous deafening roar of relief and expectation from 100,000 throats as the two teams walk sedately side by side onto the field.

More frustrating preliminaries. The new Queen Elizabeth, crowned earlier that same year, came onto the field to meet the teams—"As if she bloody cares, one lot's the same as t'other to her," said a Blackpool neighbor as the pinnacle of Britain's aristocracy and the nobility of its working classes met for a fleeting moment.

Then . . . a whistle, and an ever-changing mosaic of orange shirts and white shirts on the green, all commanded by the movements of a small light brown ball. Within two minutes, tragedy for Blackpool. Nat Lofthouse, our Nat, got the ball some 20 yards out and shot, an unimpressive effort that looked almost like a miskick. The ball spun across in front of the Blackpool goalkeeper, Farm, who went for it much too late . . . and went in.

While the Bolton fans rejoiced, poor Farm stood in dejected agony, engulfed by the noise his error had caused. Wembley nerves, I thought, something everyone knew about but something you didn't talk about for fear of inviting the worst. At least there was plenty of time left for Blackpool to reply. But within minutes the powerful Lofthouse was steaming through again, and this time his shot was hit perfectly, a searing drive that had the Bolton supporters yelling "Goal!" the instant it left his foot. Again, Farm hardly moved as the ball rocketed past him, only to crash against the goalpost with a solid smack that seemed to echo around the stadium in a moment of quiet as Blackpool's fans were mutely awaiting the worst and Bolton's were drawing breath for the final triumphant yell. Blackpool were reprieved with their head on the block, but Farm looked anything but happy. "Go easy on 'im, Nat, the poor bugger's shell-shocked!" crowed a Bolton voice.

Then it was Blackpool's turn to roar. Down at the other end, where I couldn't really see what was going on, Stan Mortensen ("the other Stan" on the Blackpool team) got the ball in the net. A mistake by the Bolton goalie, they said, so at least the Wembley nerves were striking impartially. But before halftime, Farm had let through another shot he should have saved, and Bolton went to the locker room leading 2–1, having looked much the better team.

Matthews? He had done little, but then the same could be said of all the other Blackpool forwards. I hoped for better things in the second half, when he would be attacking the goal in front of me. Soon after the restart, Wembley's major jinx struck. Bell, the Bolton left half-back, was injured. In those days there was no such thing as substitution, so Bell, barely able to run, was left on the field as a limping passenger in the rather optimistic hope that he might prove a slight nuisance to the Blackpool defenders. Within ten minutes he had done the impossible, leaping high to meet a center from the right to head Bolton's third goal. Even now, playing against only ten fit men, Blackpool were floundering. They were getting more of the ball, certainly, but their attacks were halfhearted affairs, quickly snuffed out by the Bolton defense.

With some twenty minutes left and their team apparently home and dry, the Bolton fans were in full voice, shouting cheerfully, "Coom on the ten men!" yelling derisively every time a Blackpool attack broke down.

But it was not the noise of the crowd that was to decide the game that afternoon. It was to be the genius of Stanley Matthews. The pressure on the Bolton defense mounted and always the ball was finding its way to Stan's feet, out on the right wing. I could see him cutting and corkscrewing his way through the left flank of the Bolton defense, stopping, accelerating, twisting to avoid desperate tackles, and now it was the Blackpool fans who roared, grasping feverishly at the hope that Stan was destined to get his medal after all, that he must bring off the miracle.

Another incredible Matthews run, going past defender after defender, an early center, beautifully judged to lure the goalkeeper out, and in the race for the ball it was Stan Mortensen who got there first to score. Bolton 3, Blackpool 2—one more goal (and it would be Blackpool's, for Bolton was in deep trouble, burned out as an attacking force) would send the game into overtime. But how many minutes were left? "Plenty of time, lad, plenty," said my Blackpool neighbor, but the minutes ticked away and despite all the Matthews magic, the trail of dazed defenders he was leaving after him every time he got the ball and the terrible tangles he was causing in the Bolton ranks, the crucial goal would not come.

I calculated there couldn't have been more than a minute or two left when Mudie, the Blackpool inside left, was brought down directly in front of the Bolton goal, some 20 yards out. Back came every Bolton player into his own penalty area to defend against the free kick. A wall of white shirts blocked off one side of the goal while goalie Hanson, crouching and rubbing his hands together, guarded the other half. Mortensen, one of the hardest kickers of a dead ball I had ever seen, aimed his shot at the top corner farthest away from Hanson. Either he had spotted a gap in that human wall or he gambled that someone would move out of the way of his ferocious drive.

Whichever, his shot flashed into the top of the goal, straight and unstoppable. All Hanson could do was to turn and watch as the ball bulged the netting and fell to the grass inside the goal. We were all on our feet now, Wembley Stadium nothing but noise as the late afternoon sun seemed to pick out the orange Blackpool shirts with a suggestively triumphant glow.

Time didn't matter now; the game would go into overtime and

Blackpool, running riot against a demoralized Bolton, would be the winner. There was less than a minute to go and the ball had found its way back to Matthews, lurking out on the wing, just inside the Bolton half. With the ease of a skater, Matthews was away on another flexuous run, inside one defender, then past his fullback, racing for the goal line. Barrass, the Bolton center half—and a good one—was drawn out of the middle to cope with the danger. The fatal error. Cutting in, Matthews ran the ball straight at Barrass until, just when it seemed the two must collide, there was that diabolical pivot, that almost ninety-degree turn on the run. The move did not get Matthews past Barrass, but that wasn't the idea; all Stan wanted now, having drawn Barrass out to the edge of the penalty area, was room to get the ball into the middle, and he created the space he needed with that one masterful swerve.

Matthews's center was the final perfect touch. Did he look up to see where he was putting it, or was it just a sixth sense, a soccer sense, that told him what to do? All I saw was the ball flashing low across the face of the Bolton goal, and I remember thinking, maybe saying, "Christ, no, Stan," certain that it must be intercepted by a Bolton defender. But Barrass, the key man, was out of position, and the ball ran through, untouched, until Perry, the Blackpool left winger met it at the far post and hit it, firm and low, into the goal.

With under a minute left, Blackpool were the sure winners, and from the roar even the Bolton fans must have been cheering, not for the goal, but for the man who had turned the game around, who had treated us all to one of soccer's greatest games. The roar was for Stan.

• • •

I would like to think that a day like that brings together all the things that make soccer what it is, that by describing what I saw and felt I have in some way defined the sport. But have I? Was that the real Cup final that I experienced, or is there another reality, the one explained by Danny Blanchflower, captain of Tottenham Hotspur, winners in the 1962 final:

> In truth we are all brainwashed about the Cup final. A player hears and reads a great deal about it before he ever gets there. He hears about the "Majestic" twin towers of Wembley Stadium ... the "Hallowed" green turf ... the "Royal" greeting ... the crowd singing "Abide with Me" ... it all sounds like some distant religious ceremony that takes place every year in the promised

land at the end of the football season. The reality of it can never live up to the dream. The dream is not for the player. It is for the fan, the worshipper without whom there would be no professional game at all. It is for the lover of the game who doesn't really know what it's like out there on the field, and never will know. It is as he imagines it, a football heaven.

There is more than one way of looking at the Cup final because it is a special event, an occasion in which pageantry and intensely subjective qualities like emotion and excitement figure so prominently.

These are qualities that will vary greatly in intensity from individual to individual, qualities that can apply just as easily to any other sport. Nevertheless, this idea of different people deriving different satisfactions from the same event brings us closer to the heart of soccer: its fluidity, its freedom of form, a freedom that allows it to be all things to all men. Soccer can be played in a host of different ways, each of them meaning something special to someone, each of them satisfying something different among the myriad sensations that give man pleasure.

Why should it be soccer, more than any other sport, that has this protean ability to take on so many different shapes yet still remain recognizably the same sport, to be molded and reshaped to please the whims and fancies of Italians and Scots and Turks and Brazilians?

Here I have a confession to make. After years of denying that there is anything like a mystique attached to soccer, I have changed my mind. There is a unique quality (mystique, though, is too strong a term) to soccer, and it is the obvious one: the fact that it is played without using the hands. This sets it apart from virtually every other sporting activity, and gives soccer its freedom, makes it such a pliable sport. It is free of the overwhelming influence of the hands, which inevitably come to dominate any ball game in which they are used. In soccer, things are more complicated. The ball cannot be held and manipulated with a few easy, familiar hand movements like catching and throwing. It can only be controlled, a technique that may mean using the head or the chest or the thigh or the feet—the whole body comes into play with the feet, so to speak, calling the tune.

If it begins to sound as though I am describing a dance, rather than soccer, this is no coincidence. Are not both among the most widespread of man's physical recreations, both of them formalized yet full of improvisations, both of them showing national and regional variations?

Yes, soccer is a sort of dance, with the ball as a playful, slightly reluctant partner. And knowing that, would one expect the Brazilians with their sambas and their marimbas to play the sport in the same way as, say, the Scots with their reels and bagpipes? British soccer, says the Brazilian anthropologist Gilberto Freyre, is Apollonian, and "whereas the Apollonians have control over themselves, Brazilian football is a dance full of irrational surprises and Dionysiac variations."

It never does to stretch analogies too far, but this one lures to my mind two appropriate examples. I can't resist thinking of the England team that won the 1966 World Cup in Freyre's "Apollonian" terms. Here was a team that seemed to have complete control over itself. For many of us, it had too much control. It was disciplined to play unspectacular soccer, defending methodically and attacking cautiously with the probing patience of a skilled surgeon. Never once did the team lose its self-possession and abandon itself to all-out attack.

Bobby Moore and Jackie Charlton, the two cool, unemotional center backs, typified the approach. Their job was to defend and not to put a foot wrong, and they looked capable of doing it for days at a stretch. Charlton with his long neck ("the giraffe," foreign journalists called him) heading away the high balls, Moore using his massive legs to break up ground attacks with superbly timed tackles. In front of them roamed little Nobby Stiles, his front teeth left safely in the locker room as he played the destroyer's role, attaching himself with grim persistence to the opponent's star forward, yelling gummy abuse at friend and foe alike.

None of these three was required to do much in the way of attacking. That was done in the traditional English way, testing the opposing goalkeeper and fullbacks with long, high balls into the middle, hoping for an error. The mistakes came, and England won the World Cup because they took advantage of them and made so few of their own. Unimaginative they certainly were, and predictable, too—the inevitable price for their Apollonian control?

Four years later in Mexico it was Brazil that won the World Cup, and the contrast between their team and that of England in 1966 could hardly have been greater. The English press, always quick to criticize foreign goalkeepers, decided that the Brazilian Felix was the worst they had ever seen on a World Cup team. An absurd judgment, but even had it been true the Brazilians would not have been too concerned. They readily admitted their weakness in defense. Their strength was in attack. They were there to score goals. If their defense gave one up, well, they would simply score two at the other end. They did it all so beautifully because they had players like Pelé and Jairzinho and Tostão and Rivelino, who could fill the game with "irrational surprises and Dionysiac variations."

Mostly the ball was on the ground, tapped about with bewildering speed and skill between these agile, evasive Brazilians, stopping suddenly, accelerating again, pushing the ball into gaps between defenders, gaps that only they could espy, all of it accomplished with a wonderfully light-footed, rhythmic grace.

Against England there was Tostão, close-dribbling into the penalty area, turning suddenly to chip the ball into the middle where Pelé paused just long enough to draw two defenders, then flicked the ball casually away with the outside of his right foot, direct to Jairzinho who drove it into the net.

This was the same Jairzinho who had waltzed, jinked, and twisted his way past a line of defenders to score an unforgettable goal against Czechoslovakia four days earlier. The Brazilians had scored four times in that game, but it is the goal they didn't score that hangs in the memory: The ball was at midfield, neither goal in any danger. Viktor, the Czech goalkeeper, did what many goalkeepers do under those circumstances—he wandered out toward the edge of his penalty area.

In a flash all was changed. Pelé had the ball and in one lightning, instinctive motion saw Viktor—some 50 yards away—out of his goal, and released a sort of half shot, half lob. Viktor was slow to see the danger until, at the very last moment he scrambled desperately back toward his goal posts as the ball floated just over his head ... and wide. Pelé never did accomplish his oft-stated ambition to score a goal from the halfway line, but he never came closer than that. No other player, I am sure, could have sensed that situation so quickly and acted in the flash that it took Pelé to make his move. It was soccer at its most inspired. At its most Dionysiac.

The Cup final, the World Cup, these are the big occasions in soccer, and I am distorting the picture by trying to understand soccer solely in these terms. It is time to take a look at the lower levels of the sport, for one of soccer's greatest strengths has always been that everywhere it has gone it has quickly become a game of the people, the common man's sport.

The strongest of bonds has always existed between the fans and the players, the bond of a common background, a shared view of life. They grew up as next-door neighbors, even with the local club as their neighbor, the stadium nestling awkwardly between rows of working-class houses.

I always felt this intimacy particularly strongly whenever I went to watch the Rangers in what was then my hometown, Stafford. They were not, in those far-off days, very good—pretty awful, really, I suppose—but they were "our lads" and we used to turn out, a few thousand of us on Saturday afternoons, to see them do their worst. They regularly did their worst, but I don't think many of us were really very disappointed. We didn't go looking for heroics; we just wanted two hours of live action, a chance to shout abuse or encouragement and to talk soccer with each other, or even with the players if we could draw their attention away from the game for long enough.

Watching soccer at the Marston Road ground was like that, a social occasion without formalities or pretensions. Considering the surroundings, it could hardly have been otherwise, for Marston Road was not exactly a jewel among soccer grounds. At the beginning of the season there was a rectangle of reasonably healthy-looking grass, marked with spidery white lines, but that never seemed to last too long. The abiding image is of a strip of mud down the middle of the field, flanked by struggling patches of grass. Reading E. M. Forster's *Where Angels Fear to Tread* many years after I had left Stafford, I came across this: "a square piece of ground which, though not quite mud, is at the same time not exactly grass." Forster was describing a decaying Italian villa, but it was the Marston Road ground that suddenly stood before me.

If it rained and we wanted shelter there was, on one side of the field, a dark, brooding shedlike structure with a low roof that leaked, and over which the ball was forever being kicked. Just as regularly, as we waited for it to be reclaimed, would come the cries: "Never mind the ball, get on with the game." That was anybody's line, the first one to shout it got the laugh. It was the same with "Yours are the ones in blue, Alf," whenever a player misdirected a pass.

One afternoon the joke went around that a party of prisoners from Stafford jail was being allowed to watch the game . . . as part of their punishment. That was about as close as we came to original wit at Marston Road, but I still treasure one remark, muttered almost sotto voce by an elderly man standing next to me, as a Ranger player, not paying attention to the game, was caught yards offside—"Look at 'im, bloody mushrooming."

Most of the soccer in the world is played in an atmosphere like that.

There is a human scale to it that, despite the crudity and the harshness, makes the sport something warm and familiar. It is vibrant and hardy, because it touches people's lives, not just once or twice a year, but every day. It is part of their existence, it is in their blood, and they feel for it as they would feel for a lovable, troublesome, sometimes exasperating member of their own family.

The affection explains the comic: the English player who, when the game ball bounced into the river, jumped into a canoe to retrieve it and was swept a mile downstream. In the meantime they found another ball, and by the time he had made his way back, his ten-man team had lost the game.

The troublesomeness explains the tragicomedy: the Italian who, upset by the things the fans shouted at him, decided he was not tough enough to continue as a referee and quit to become a Franciscan monk.

And the exasperation explains the tragedy: the French fan who could not bear his team's 0–2 loss to another local team and shot a rival fan twice, once for each goal.

Obviously, what lies behind each of these stories is some sort of passion. Love, hate, fear, jealousy, joy—it is impossible to imagine any sport without them. The question is, does soccer generate more passion than other sports? I think it does. Partly because it is so much closer to the lives of its followers than other sports, partly because of its worldwide appeal that makes it a vehicle for nationalistic fervor, and partly because of the nature of the sport itself.

Soccer is a sport in which low scoring is the rule. During a game there is a constant building up and letting down of emotions—expectations are frustrated far more often than they are rewarded. The scoring of a goal, the one goal that could decide the game, means the joyful, explosive release of dammed-up hopes for one group of fans, utter despair for the other.

I have been trying to define soccer, but it remains teasingly beyond definition, as elusive as the soccer ball itself. Yes, yes, I've given the flavor of the ingredients: a free-flowing ball game, a dance, a sport of the people, the passions, the frustration, the grace, the power, the humor ... but the final mixture, the final proportions, that is something that each must create for himself.

When I want to reduce soccer to a single occasion, I think not of the Matthews Cup final, or indeed of any big game, or even of the lads of Stafford Rangers. I think of a hot, sultry summer's day in Sicily, some ten years ago. I had spent the afternoon among the glories of the cathedral at Monreale, but my mood of satisfaction and enchantment was broken by the bus ride back to Palermo.

The heat, the noise, the crowds, the fumes—as we entered the city, I knew I was going to faint. I brusquely pushed my way to the door, lurched off the bus, and stood for a moment or two watching it roar off in a cloud of gray dust. I had no idea where I was, but I was going to walk for a while until I felt better, then catch another bus.

I remember very little of the street. There were buildings, I suppose, some stores, then, after a few hundred yards, a gap that led to an open space where I could hear and see boys playing soccer. I walked over and sat down against the wall of a little hut, the only shade around. The boys seemed to be about twelve years old and there were, I eventually worked out, sixteen of them—they were difficult to count for the movement was constant. A whirl of sixteen little bodies chasing a battered lopsided ball would rush past me in one direction, then come roaring back in the other, giving off shouts and dust in about equal proportions.

The goals, I remember, were marked by little piles of rocks, except that one of the piles had an upright stick wedged into it, a stick that would periodically topple to the ground, at which point the game had to be stopped while it was resurrected. The other important thing about the game was the far touchline, which ran along the top of a railroad cutting. Anyone kicking the ball over that not only had to go down and get it but also had to sit out of the game for five minutes. This I discovered from a boy so banished who came and sat next to me.

"American?"

"No, English."

"Ah . . . you know Bobby Charlton?"

The international language, the names of soccer's stars; we talked about the sport for a couple of minutes, when he jumped up and rushed back into the game, convincing everyone his five minutes were up, turning to me for support, because *l'inglese* had a wristwatch.

His name was Salvatore, and he was the undisputed star of the game; his skinny little legs with their incongruously large black shoes were everywhere, and he was a source of mixed wonderment and amusement to his friends. A hefty swing of his leg sent the ball spinning wildly off the edge of his foot, straight up in the air; never stopping for a moment, he ran around in a tight little circle looking for the ball until it dropped, like a padded thunderbolt, right on top of his head. One of the other boys who had been watching this brief scene suddenly spun around and I could see his face, pulled tightly closed, his eyes wrinkled up, his mouth stretched and compressed into a thin grinning line, his hands dropped helplessly at his sides. He made not a sound, but I have never seen such a wonderful portrait of pure joy.

I stayed on to watch that marvelous little game until the shadows grew bigger than the players and it was time for everyone to go home. I was walked to the bus stop and put safely aboard amid promises to return, cries of Bobby Charlton, and predictions that Italy would win the World Cup. And that was it. Italy did not win the World Cup, and I never did return to that dusty patch of waste ground on the outskirts of Palermo. Or perhaps I did, for I have relived that evening many times, a golden evening spent under the spell of soccer.

New York, 1976

THE SIMPLEST GAME

CHAPTER 1

Beginnings

Soccer people like to claim that the word *football* should really be applied only to soccer. What else would you call a game played with the feet and with a ball? Logical enough, but the argument is flawed. The word *football* came into use in England in the mid-fourteenth century to describe a game played not *with* the feet but *on* foot, in order to distinguish it from pastimes that were played on horseback.

In those early forms of football, the participants kicked the ball, handled it, ran with it, and generally moved it about in any way that they could—indeed, the most notable feature of the contests was an absence of rules. It was not until 1863 that a definite division was established between a game played with the feet (soccer) and a game played primarily with the hands (rugby). Until then *football* was neither soccer nor rugby but a brawling mixture of the two.

Trying to work out who first played football, and where, and when, is really rather a fruitless occupation. The basic elements—kicking, throwing, running—have been among man's natural urges since the world began. Games built around these movements have sprung up at different times and in different cultures throughout history. Some of the games we have records of and some, no doubt the vast majority, we do not.

Huang-Ti, a Chinese emperor of 1697 B.C., is supposed to have invented *tsu-chu*, a team game played with the feet and with a leather ball stuffed with cork and hair—possibly an early form of true soccer. A thousand years later the Japanese had a similar game called *kemari*, which may have been their own invention, or may have been their version of *tsu-chu*.

So it could have been the Chinese or the Japanese who started football, except that their game appears to have died out and there is nothing to link it with the modern sports. If the Chinese were not the originators, then perhaps it was the ancient Egyptians, in whose tombs were placed balls that *could* have been used for football. Or perhaps the Berbers of the seventh century B.C. were the first with their *koura*, a game that apparently served as a fertility rite to encourage abundant crops, but again, *koura* seems to have dwindled away to nothing.

The athletic-minded ancient Greeks had a ball game, *episkiros*, which was played on an area marked by boundary lines and involved both kicking and throwing the ball. We think we know what happened to this one: The theory is that the Romans, who were experts at borrowing Greek ideas and debasing them, took it over and turned it into a much rougher affair that they called *harpastum*. It was popular with Roman legionaries, and it is a reasonable assumption that they took it to England during the years of Roman occupation between A.D. 43 and 407. There is a legend that in A.D. 276 the residents of the town of Derby beat a team of legionaries at a *harpastum*/football-type game.

Which, however tenuously, gets us to England, the country that for the next fifteen hundred years is the scene of all the major developments in the history of soccer. It is more than likely that when the Romans arrived in England, the Britons were already playing their own version of football. Something like the *koura* of the Berbers, games associated with fertility rites that were supposed to ensure abundant crops.

In some games the ball represented the sun and was ceremonially kicked across planted fields. In others, the "ball" was the head of a sacrificed animal, with teams from neighboring villages fighting for its possession so that they could bury it in their own fields. The original contests pitted the men and boys of one village—any number to a team—against those of another in a wild cross-country brawl. The idea was to move the ball—evidently no longer seen as a prized fertility symbol worth capturing—into the opposing village.

Townsfolk saw no reason why the yokels should have all the fun, and by the twelfth century the ball game had invaded the cities. In 1175 a London monk named William Fitzstephen described how teams of students and trades apprentices played a ball game on flat ground just outside the city. Writing in Latin, he describes the game as *ludus pilae*—a game of ball—and his description makes it clear that the event was already a traditional one. Brother Fitzstephen doesn't tell us how the game was played, but he does tell us when: Shrove Tuesday.

A significant day. In the cities, the ball games had lost their ritual meaning, and were now part of the festivities on Shrove Tuesday (Mardi Gras)—the day that was seen as the last chance for enjoyment before the restrictions of Lent.

Of course things got rowdy. Not everyone was as thoughtful as Brother Fitzstephen's players, who sought out a patch of ground away from the city center. The ball game took to the streets and became a major menace to life, limb, and property.

Eventually, the authorities took notice and began to express their alarm at this uncontrolled monster that was threatening the law and order of the kingdom. A celebrated proclamation came down from on high in 1314 when King Edward II warned the citizens of London:

> For as much as there is great noise in the city caused by hustling over large balls . . . from which many evils might arise, which God forbid, we command and forbid on behalf of the King, on pain of imprisonment, such game to be used in the city in the future.

Still no mention of football in this, the first of a long series of attempts to put down the game as a public nuisance.

The attempts were invariably unsuccessful, a series of failures that make up the most convincing evidence of the remarkable grip that the sport had on the people. The proclamations themselves give us, at last, some reliable written evidence about the existence of the sport of football.

George Orwell wrote that he could never read the pompous official pronouncements of heads of state or church or whatever without also hearing in the background a resounding collective raspberry from the world's working men. Which was precisely how Edward II's splendid ban was greeted. Nobody paid much attention to it.

Things were no better in 1349, when an exasperated Edward III, needing all the help he could get in his efforts to annex France, took action. He was greatly put out by the thought of all those men who should have been practicing their archery but instead were playing "skittles, quoits, fives, football or other foolish games which are no use." He threatened to imprison them if they didn't get back to their bows and arrows.

So by 1349 the sport was not only a menace to public order, it was foolish and it was unpatriotic as well. It was also important enough to warrant its own name, and the word *football* entered the English language.

Succeeding rulers, Richard II, Henry IV, Henry VIII, and Elizabeth I among them, all slapped bans on the sport. But football flourished—often in unlikely places. Seeking somewhere other than the streets to play, football players found the space they needed in the local churchyard where, disgraceful to say, they were sometimes welcomed—and even joined by—the clergy. As early as 1364 the Synod of Ely had found it necessary to state that *ludus pilae* was not a sport for clergymen.

The church and the government were probably quite right in viewing football, as it was then played, as a menace. Clearly, it was a dangerous, crude affair that—particularly in the cities—could all too easily turn into a general riot with consequent loss of life and damage to property. There is no reason to imagine that writers of the sixteenth century, such as the diplomat Sir Thomas Elyot, were exaggerating:

Football, wherein is nothing but beastly fury, and extreme violence, whereof procedeth hurt, and consequently rancour and malice do remain with them that be wounded, whereof it is to be put in perpetual silence.

Gory details of football's brutalities were the specialty of the Puritan pamphleteer Phillip Stubbs (though his chief objection seemed to be not so much the dangers of the game but the fact that it was frequently played on Sundays). After defining it as a "bloody and murthering practise," Stubbs wallows in the misfortunes that can befall participants:

So that by this meanes, sometimes their necks are broken, sometimes their backs, sometimes their legs, sometime their armse, sometime one part thrust out of joynt, sometime their eyes start out; and sometimes hurt in one place, sometimes in another. But whosoever scapeth away the best goeth not scotfree, but is either sore wounded, craised [crushed], and bruseed [*sic*], so as he dyeth of it or else scapeth very hardly. And no mervaile! for they have the sleights to meet one betwixt two, to dash him against the hart with their elbowes, to hit him under the short ribbes with their griped fists, and with their knees to catch him upon the hip and pick him on his neck, with a hundered such murthering devices: and hereof groweth envie, malice, rancour, cholar, hatred, displeasure, enmitie, and what not els, and sometimes murther, fighting, brawling, contortion, quarrel kicking, homicide, and great effusion of blood, as experience dayly teacheth. Is this murthering play, now, an exercise for the Sabaoth day?*

An extremist Puritan position that even Oliver Cromwell didn't share—he was to be a keen player of football during his college days at Cambridge** in the early 1600s. But advancing years may have moved him closer to the Stubbs view.

Things were relatively quiet on the football front for the hundred years that followed Cromwell's setting up of the Commonwealth in 1649. Quiet, that is, in the sense of any major progress toward acceptance; things were far from quiet in the streets:

Here oft my course I bend, when lo! from far
I spy the furies of the foot-ball war:
The 'prentice quits his shop, to join the crew
Increasing crowds the flying game pursue.
Thus, as you roll the ball o'er snowy ground,
The gathering globe augments with ev'ry round.
But whither shall I run?

Thus John Gay, writing in 1716 on the dangers likely to beset anyone walking the streets of London.†

Football was still not a game for gentlemen, but forces were at work that would soon make it just that. There had always been, even when football was at its wildest, a few voices of reason that saw something other than wanton violence in the sport. Richard Mulcaster, headmaster of Merchant Taylors School from 1561 to 1586, was one who specu-

---

* "The Anatomie of Abuses," 1583.
** We know very little about that college game, but in all likelihood it was a toned-down version of the street game, with rules notable mainly by their absence. Evidently it had some prestige value. Sir Thomas Overbury, describing college life at Oxford at the end of the sixteenth century, notes that for the student "the excellency of his Colledge (though but for a match at football) is an article of his faith," a sentiment not unknown among contemporary American college students.
† Wherever they could, the authorities banished street football, sending it back to where it had begun: open ground outside the towns. Today a number of these "street" football games are still played (in open country, of course), in a tourist-attraction sort of way, notably in Ashbourne, Derbyshire (where it is known as Royal Shrovetide Football), and at Alnwick Castle, in Northumberland.

lated that football must have something going for it, or it would not be so unquenchably popular.

The trouble, as Mulcaster saw it, was that the sport was abused. If only the numbers playing could be limited, if only somebody were appointed to control each game, then surely there would be an end to "the thronging of a rude multitude, with bursting of shinnes and breaking of legges. . . ." Instead, football played in an orderly manner

. . .strengtheneth and brawneth the whole body, and by provoking superfluities downeward, it dischargeth the head and upper parties, it is good for the bowels, and to drive downe the stone and gravell from both the bladder and the kidnies. It helpeth weak hammes, by much moving, beginning at a mean, and simple shankes by thickening of the fleshe no lesse than riding doth. Yet rash running and too much force oftentime breaketh some ineward conduit, and bringith ruptures.

Even if Mulcaster does make it sound like a patent medicine, his message is clear: Football plus discipline keeps you fit. This was the theme that, nearly 250 years later, brought respectability to football.

At the end of the eighteenth century, the public schools* in England were in a state of great turmoil. In many of them the boys themselves were virtually running things, and the masters found it almost impossible to enforce discipline. When they tried, a student revolt was the usual response, and at Winchester and Rugby the army had to be called in to restore order.

Games were a big problem. The boys were greatly addicted, and the masters greatly opposed. Even the gentlemanly game of cricket was frowned upon by the masters, while football was abhorred—a game, said the headmaster of Shrewsbury School "more fit for farm boys and labourers than for young gentlemen."

Credit for restoring peace to the public school scene belongs largely to the formidable Dr. Thomas Arnold, the headmaster at Rugby School from 1828 to 1842. He did it by allowing the boys to retain a considerable amount of self- government, and by making sports a part of the educational process instead of opposing them.

Football had been played at the public schools for many years

---

* A term that, in England, means exactly the opposite of what it logically should mean (and does mean in the United States). English public schools were and to a great extent still are exclusive private schools catering for the sons (and now the daughters) of the aristocracy and the rich.

before Arnold's arrival at Rugby. Although each school had its own way of playing the sport, a division into two main codes was already discernible. One code allowed players to run while holding the ball—this was the "handling game" that was to develop into the sport of rugby.* The other code allowed the use of the hand for stopping the ball, but insisted that the ball be advanced only with the feet—this was the "dribbling game" that was to become soccer.

Arnold's reforms at Rugby were soon copied by other public schools that played a version of the rugby-style handling game. There remained, however, a hard core of influential older schools that stuck to the dribbling game—Eton, Harrow, and Winchester. For both codes the arrival of respectability was followed by organization, and at long last comprehensive sets of rules were committed to paper. And suddenly the problem was not that there were no sets of rules, but that there were too many. Chaos ruled when students from different schools came together at the universities and tried to form teams.

The first attempt to produce one master game out of the many school versions was made in 1848 by Cambridge University. Those rules have not survived, but we do have a shortened version published in 1862 by J. C. Thring, ten rules for what he called "The Simplest Game." His second rule—hands may be used only to stop the ball and place it on the ground before the feet—makes it clear that Cambridge University wanted to play the dribbling game.

By now there was a deep division between the devotees of rugby and those of the dribbling game. It went beyond the obvious question of handling the ball. Another of Mr. Thring's rules, number three, pinpoints the problem: Kicks must be aimed only at the ball.

This was bound to incense the rugby enthusiasts, who considered kicking an opponent's legs—shinning, or hacking, as it was called—an essential part of the sport. The provocation was increased in 1863 when Cambridge University formulated a new set of rules that confirmed the bans on running with the ball and hacking.

The dispute came to a climax later that same year. The number of football clubs was growing, clubs formed by young men who wanted to

---

* The traditional story of the birth of rugby is that one day in 1823 a student at Rugby School, William Webb Ellis, was playing football when he suddenly picked up the ball and ran with it to his opponent's goal, something that caused great consternation as nobody had ever seen the likes of it before. It is a story that should be taken with an enormous pinch of salt. In its early forms, football had always involved some use of the hands, so that the surprise of the onlookers seems somewhat suspect. The likelihood is that the Ellis story contains about as much truth as the legend that Abner Doubleday invented baseball. Precious little.

continue playing after their college days were finished. A meeting of the leading clubs in the London area was called for October 26, 1863, at the Freemason's Tavern, Great Queen Street, with the idea of forming the Football Association (F.A.), which would regulate the game throughout the country.

One of its first items of business was to lay down an official set of rules, and immediately it was forced to realize that there were now not one, but two, games of football. They tried compromise—the first draft of the new F.A. rules allowed, under rather restricted circumstances, both running with the ball and hacking, but the differences were too fundamental to be papered over.

The final break came over the question of hacking. The majority of the club delegates considered it a barbarous practice and wanted no part of it. Yet a minority considered it vital to the sport—"Hacking is the true football game," said their leader—and, when they were outvoted, withdrew from the association.

If there is a date marking the birthday of soccer, then it is December 8, 1863. The day that the F.A. published its first set of rules—the day that the F.A. banned running with the ball and hacking.

Laws of the London Football Association, 1863

1. The maximum length of the ground shall be 200 yards, the maximum breadth shall be 100 yards, the length and breadth shall be marked off with flags; and the goals shall be defined by two upright posts, eight yards apart, without any tape or bar across them.

2. A toss for goals shall take place, and the game shall be commenced by a place kick from the centre of the ground by the side losing the toss for goals; the other side shall not approach within ten yards of the ball until it is kicked off.

3. After a goal is won, the losing side shall kick off, and the two sides shall change goals after each goal is won.

4. A goal shall be won when the ball passes between the goalposts or over the space between the goalposts (at whatever height), not being thrown, knocked on, or carried.

5. When the ball is in touch, the first player who touches it shall throw it from the point on the boundary line where it left the ground in a direction at right angles with the boundary line, and the ball shall not be in play until it has touched the ground.

6. When a player has kicked the ball, any one of the same side who

is nearer to the opponent's goal line is out of play, and may not touch the ball himself, nor in any way whatever prevent any other player from doing so, until he is in play; but no player is out of play when the ball is kicked from behind the goal line.

7. In case the ball goes behind the goal line, if a player on the side to whom the goal belongs first touches the ball, one of his side shall be entitled to a free kick from the goal line at the point opposite the place where the ball shall be touched. If a player of the opposite side first touches the ball, one of his side shall be entitled to a free kick at the goal where the ball is touched, the opposing side standing within their goal line until he has had his kick.

8. If a player makes a fair catch, he shall be entitled to a free kick, providing he claims it by making a mark with his heel at once; and in order to take such a kick he may go back as far as he pleases, and no player on the opposite side shall advance beyond his mark until he has kicked.

9. No player shall run with the ball.

10. Neither tripping nor hacking shall be allowed, and no player shall use his hands to hold or push his adversary.

11. A player shall not be allowed to throw the ball or pass it to another with his hands.

12. No player shall be allowed to take the ball from the ground with his hands under any pretext whatever while it is in play.

13. A player shall be allowed to throw the ball or pass it to another if he made a fair catch, or catches the ball on the first bounce.

14. No player shall be allowed to wear projecting nails, iron plates or gutta percha on the soles or heels of his boots.

The split was finally official, and from now on the two sports went their own separate ways:

1. The dribbling game was now called Association Football—that is, football played according to the rules of the Football Association, without hacking.

2. The handling game was rugby football—it was to get its own organizing body, the Rugby Union, in 1871.

It was student slang, fond of dropping the end of a word and replacing it with "er" or "ers" (e.g., "brekkers" for breakfast) that coined the two words "rugger" from rugby, and "soccer," evidently based on the abbreviation Assoc.

Most of the Football Association's new rules, which were grandiose-ly called laws, were close to, if not identical with, those for rugger. Just four laws, numbers nine through twelve, were to give soccer its unique nature.

It was inevitable that the two codes would separate, but that the separation should have been caused by the question of hacking rather than by the use of the hands is surprising and is worth studying for a moment.

Reduced to its essentials, the argument was between those who wanted soccer to be a game of skill and those who wanted it to include a hefty dose of sheer brute force. Those in favor of brute force disguised their intentions by talking of "pluck" and accusing their opponents of being rather sissified, and of liking "their pipes and grog or schnapps more than the manly game of football."

But the vote went against the self-styled defendants of manliness. The pioneers who founded the modern game of soccer were determined that it should be a sport in which skill was the foremost factor. It is a point of crucial importance in the development of the game.

Within twenty years, the London-based F.A. had its rules accepted throughout England and Scotland.

What really put the F.A. on the map—and, it could be argued, started the soccer explosion that was soon to envelop the world—was its decision, taken in 1871, to organize a cup tournament. The competition was to be conducted on a knockout basis, and was open to any team caring to enter.

A silver cup was purchased for £20 and inscribed with the words "The Football Association Challenge Cup." A modest enough trophy, but it immediately drew criticism from those who felt that the competition was a bad thing, and would encourage excessive rivalry among clubs. Soccer, it has to be remembered, was, at this stage, very much an amateur game for *gentlemen* amateurs.

The top teams of the day were composed exclusively of ex- public school and university players, all highly educated men who gave their teams names like Wanderers, Old Etonians (alumni of Eton College), and Old Carthusians (alumni of Charterhouse School).

As things turned out, C. W. Alcock, the president of the F.A. and the prime mover in organizing the cup competition, was the first person to receive the silver cup when the team of which he was captain—the Wanderers—beat the Royal Engineers in the final in 1872. (The Engineers was also a highly exclusive team, composed of nine lieutenants and two captains.)

Amateurs and gentlemen continued to rule the roost, both in administration and on the field, for another ten years, while the popularity of the F.A. Cup spread rapidly. In 1872 the competition had attracted fifteen teams, all from the south of England, and its final game had been watched by "nearly 2,000" spectators.

Ten years later the number of teams was seventy-three, and now they came from the midlands and the north of England, too. For the first time, one of the northern teams, Blackburn Rovers, reached the final where, before a record crowd of 7,000, they went down 0–1 to the Old Etonians. That 1882 final was, unknown to all concerned, the swan song of the southern amateur clubs.

The following year another Blackburn team, the Olympic, beat the Old Etonians in the final and for the first time the trophy was taken north where, it is recorded, they thought it looked like a teakettle.

Behind the success of Blackburn lay two factors that were to revolutionize soccer in England: The game was no longer solely the province of the upper classes, and professional players (or "professors," as they were called) were beginning to appear. The Blackburn team was composed mainly of artisans—weavers, iron-foundry workers, plumbers, and a picture framer—plus two "professors." Immediately before the final the entire Blackburn team spent several days at the seaside, the nearest soccer had yet come to organizing a training camp.

Given the growing popularity of soccer, it seems certain that nothing could have prevented the rise of professionalism. It began in the industrial cities of the midlands and the north in a covert way, and many of the earliest "professors" were Scots who had come south in search of work and found that their soccer talents were much in demand. Soon clubs in Blackburn and Preston were deliberately importing such players, providing them with jobs, and paying them secretly after each game—a sort of soccer Santa Claus would go round the locker room while the players were bathing, placing money in their boots.

The very idea of professionalism was anathema to the gentlemen of the F.A. and, predictably enough, they bitterly opposed it. Their power was considerable. Any club that wanted to take part in the prestigious F.A. Cup competition—and what club did not?—had to be a member of the F.A. In 1883 the F.A. expelled Accrington for "offering inducements" to a player, and the following year Preston, a team that was heavily populated with Scots, was banned from the competition.

But professionalism was by now too widespread, too obviously successful, for the F.A. to stop it. When the northern clubs threatened to withdraw en masse to set up their own competition, the F.A. capitulated. At a special meeting in 1885, it accepted the inevitable. The situation was not after all exactly unprecedented, for there had been professionals in cricket since at least the early 1800s. Now there would be soccer professionals, too. They had to be registered annually with the F.A., which was adamant on one point: The professionals would not be allowed to serve on any committees or attend any meetings of the F.A. The gentlemen-amateurs, having given way to professionals on the field, were determined to retain the administrative control of soccer.

Popularity and professionalism brought their own problems, not least the chaotic state into which most clubs' schedules had fallen. Attempts were made to play a regular schedule of games, but they were continually being interrupted by the attractions of the various local and regional cup competitions, not to mention the F.A. Cup itself.

The Athletic News and Cyclists' Journal, a sporting daily published in Manchester, suggested a way out. Why not do what professional baseball had been doing since 1871 across the water in the United States, and form a league of the top professional teams? The suggestion was taken up by William McGregor, chairman of the Aston Villa club in Birmingham, who had been active in the fight to legalize professionalism.* Within six months he had organized the Football League, composed of twelve clubs, all from the north and the midlands. The first games were played in the fall of 1888.

The men who ran the Football League were the same men who ran the clubs, mostly successful middle-class businessmen, a very different set from the aristocrats of the F.A. Yet there was no split between the two. The F.A. remained the overall supervisor of the game, the authority on the rules, and the organizer of international games—something that was to become, if not its most important, then certainly its most glamorous, function.

The first international game was played in 1872 between England and Scotland, the idea being that each country should be represented by its eleven best native-born players. The selection of the English team was made by the F.A. and included players from ten different clubs, only Oxford University being represented by more than one player. This is still the method of selecting a national team, which is, in effect, an all-star team assembled only for international games.

* McGregor was a Scot, an example of the important role that Scots have always played in the development of soccer in England. Ironically, at this time the Scottish F.A. was still strongly opposed to professionalism, and had banned the sixty-eight professionals registered in England from ever playing in Scotland.

The players selected obviously have to have the permission of their clubs to play, but because of the great honor involved, this was never withheld—at least not in the early days of soccer. In England, from 1886 on, the honor was, and still is, marked by the presentation to each player of a velvet cap, complete with long tassel.*

Wales played its first international game in 1876, against Scotland, and in 1882 Ireland joined in and was beaten 0–13 by England. The scope of international soccer at the end of the nineteenth century was not really international at all, for all four "nations" were simply different parts of the same country: Great Britain. It was the World Series of its time, the best not because the whole world took part, but because it represented all there was.**

Things were not to remain that way for very much longer. Soccer, so long an exclusively British obsession, was about to become a truly international sport.

But before we follow soccer's global spread, a look at the state of the game in England at the end of the nineteenth century is in order, for it was the English experience of that period that provided the model for the organization of soccer in other countries.

The most important characteristics of the structure of English soccer in the year 1900 were as follows:

1. The various quarrels over what the rules should say had been settled. In 1882, the Football Associations of the four British "soccer nations" (England, Scotland, Wales, and Ireland) had formed an International Board that was now accepted as the supreme authority on the laws of the game. Among other changes agreed by the Board, the use of the hands (except by the goalkeeper) had been completely banned, the goals themselves were now equipped with a crossbar and with nets, and the system of officiating had been changed from two umpires to one referee aided by two linesmen.

2. The sport was now professional at its top level, with a well-organized national league of thirty-six teams (eighteen in the first division and eighteen in the second division) playing throughout the fall and winter. Within each division, each team played all the others twice, on a home-and-home basis, receiving two points for a win, one

* In England, the phrase "to be capped" means to be chosen for the national team.
** Well, nearly all. Teams representing the United States and Canada played each other twice, in 1885 and 1886. The games are not well documented. The United States Soccer Federation lists these games as the first appearance of the U.S. national team, but there is doubt about the representative nature of the teams.

for a tie, and none for a loss. At the end of each season the bottom two clubs in Division I were relegated to Division II, to be replaced by the top two clubs from Division II.

3. Despite the strength of the professional Football League, the overall control of the game was firmly in the hands of the Football Association, an amateur body. The F.A. had, through the International Board, the last word on rule interpretation; all professional players had to be registered with it; and it was the organizer of the annual F.A. Cup competition.

4. The F.A. Cup competition was conducted simultaneously with the professional season, and was open to all clubs, amateur and professional. The names of all the clubs entered (by 1900 there were 242) were placed in a hat and drawn out in pairs—the two to play each other at the field of the first-drawn. The losers were out, while the winners went forward to another draw, and so on, until just the two finalists were left.

The Cup competition was immensely popular for a number of reasons. It provided an opportunity for small clubs to meet, and perhaps beat, the famous clubs. Each game was played in an exciting winner-take-all atmosphere. Above all, there was the deciding game, the Cup final, a wonderful occasion of pomp and pageantry that was—despite the professional league championship—still viewed by many as the climax of the English soccer season. From the "nearly 2,000" who had watched the first Cup final in 1872, attendance rose to over 110,000 for the 1901 final.

5. The concepts of national teams and of international play were well established; from 1884 the national teams of England, Scotland, Wales, and Ireland competed regularly for the British International Championship.

That is the way it was over ninety years ago, and it is remarkable how little has changed since then. Maybe, just as in baseball, there is nothing new in soccer either. There was, in 1878, a soccer match played under floodlights in Sheffield. And by 1898 the professional players had formed themselves into a players' union.

At the turn of the century, soccer conquered Europe and South America with all the irresistibility of an idea whose time had come. Its spread was not a slow country-by-country crawl, but a sudden explosion. Within a decade, the game had sprung up all over the two continents.

Soccer had gained widespread popularity in England at the very moment when England was at the height of its maritime and commercial strength. English sailors were regular visitors to foreign ports, and English businessmen, engineers, and artisans often spent long periods living in foreign countries. They took their sports with them, and a pattern emerged that was repeated in country after country.

The sailors or the British residents would play cricket or soccer or rugby among themselves; if there weren't enough resident Brits, they would invite some of the locals to join in. Cricket never really made it (it needed a lot of space, a well-tended grass wicket, and a fair amount of equipment, and the games could last up to three days), while rugby caught on only in one or two places like France and Argentina. But soccer—that was a different story.

In no time at all, the clubs that the British had founded for their own amusement were flooded with local residents who liked what they saw, started to play, and eventually took over the running of the sport.

What happened in Italy was typical of events in the rest of Europe. In 1887, Edoardo Bosio, an Italian businessman, returned from a trip to London, bringing with him to Turin a soccer ball and a vibrant enthusiasm for the F.A. Cup games that he had seen in England. His attempts to get other Italians interested in the sport were unsuccessful, until events in nearby Genoa changed the scene dramatically.

There, in 1892, a group of Brits founded a sports club that they called the Genoa Cricket and Football Club, but there was to be very little cricket in its future activities. At first there wasn't too much soccer either, for opponents were difficult to find. But whenever a game was played, crowds of Italians turned out to watch. For the moment, watching was all they could do, for the membership of the club was limited to Brits until 1896 when James Spensley, a ship's doctor who was also a star goalkeeper, proposed that the club accept Italians as members, just fifty of them for a start.

The following year, the citizens of Turin at last took up soccer in a big way, and the most famous of all Italian clubs, the Juventus Football Club, was founded. In Sicily, at the southern tip of the country, another group of Englishmen founded the Palermo Football and Cricket Club, another club that was to produce little cricket and a good deal of soccer. In 1898 came the Federazione Italiana di Football, the Italian equivalent of England's F.A. A championship was organized the same year, and was won by the Genoa Cricket and Football Club with a team that already included seven Italians.

The first decade of the twentieth century saw clubs springing up all over Italy—Lazio (Rome) 1900, Verona 1903, Naples 1904, Inter-Milan 1908, Bologna 1909—and in 1910 an Italian national team took the field for the first time, to score a 6–2 victory over France. Just two more stages—a Cup competition, which was started in 1922, and the arrival of professionalism in 1929—brought Italy level with England, at least in organizational terms.

Professionalism was introduced to Europe in 1924 by the Austrians; the Czechs followed in 1925, the Hungarians in 1926, and the Spaniards in 1929, along with Italy. But in all these countries, exactly as in England, the game was under the control of amateur organizations, the local equivalents of the Football Association.

Soccer found its way to South America almost as quickly as it did to Europe; it was being played in Argentina in 1889 at clubs organized by British employees of the railroads, which were at that time British owned. It was an Englishman, Alexander Hutton, who founded the Argentine F.A. and who is thought of as the father of soccer in Argentina.

The founding of Uruguayan soccer is virtually told in the title of the first club, formed in 1891: Central Uruguay Railway Cricket Club. English railroad workers wanted to play cricket but ended up as soccer players and the prime movers in the formation of the Uruguayan F.A. in 1900. Their club, which changed its name to Peñarol in 1913, is today one of the most famous in the world.

Football, in its original sense of a wild soccer/rugby melee, made its appearance in Brazil sometime in the early nineteenth century, in the streets of São Paulo. The usual riots ensued and the authorities clamped down, apparently with more success than those in England, for the game survived only as the name of a street—Rua da Jogo da Bola (which has also disappeared, renamed for Republican hero Benjamin Constant).

But soccer was brought back to São Paulo by Charles Miller, born in the city in 1874, of English parents. They packed him off to be educated in England, where he took up the sport. He returned to Brazil in 1894 with two soccer balls in his suitcase. These he took along to the São Paulo Athletic Club, a cricket club run by Englishmen. Yet again, soccer killed off the cricket, and by 1902 enough clubs were operating for the formation of a São Paulo League.

The events in São Paulo were being duplicated in Rio de Janeiro, where the first soccer was played in 1897 by the Rio Cricket Club. But the lack of good communications between the two cities made a joint league out of the question, and a separate Rio League was formed in 1906.

There was absolutely nothing democratic about the Brazilian game in those early days. The clubs were for high society, the players were composed of wealthy Europeans or the sons of well-to-do Brazilians. The game was described as a "refined and fashionable spectacle."

A foreign team made up of Englishmen from South Africa arrived in 1906 and beat the São Paulo All-Stars 6–0, showing that the Brazilian game was a little too refined and exclusive. The lesson was driven home four years later by the famous English amateur club Corinthians, which played teams in both Rio de Janeiro and São Paulo, and made a huge impression, winning all of its games comfortably—the Rio All-Stars went down 1–8!

A direct result of this tour by an elite team of ex-university students was, perversely enough, that soccer became a game for the whole Brazilian people. The Corinthians had barely left São Paulo when a new club was formed in the city and named after them—Corinthians Paulista, a club that included lowly clerks and factory workers among its members. Then came a few mulattoes, who were accepted as whites. The mulattoes were to be followed by a tidal wave of brilliant black players. The Brazilian national team played its first game in 1914, traveling to Buenos Aires and losing 0–3 to Argentina, and the cycle of soccer progress was completed in 1933 with the introduction of professionalism.

The widening popularity of soccer found the English only vaguely interested in what was happening. Foreigners could play the game, by all means, but they would never be as good as the English. Regularly, English teams traveled overseas to show the Brazilians or the Austrians or whoever just how the game should be played, and regularly they won all their games with ease. Thus confirmed in the correctness of their judgment the English stuck to their insularity—though arrogance would be a more accurate characterization of their attitude.

When a meeting was held in Paris in 1904 to discuss the founding of an international organization to oversee soccer throughout the world, the English did not bother to attend, though they had been invited to do so. They were actually rather put out by the whole business, as they considered their own International Board (see page 13) all that was needed.

The English no-show was disappointing but hardly unexpected. The representatives of Belgium, Holland, Denmark, Switzerland, Spain, Sweden, and France went ahead anyway, and FIFA was formed. The acronym FIFA comes from the official French title of the organization: Fédération Internationale de Football Association. In English it is the International Federation of Association Football.*

Within two years England was a member of FIFA. One of her conditions for joining was that the British International Board would remain responsible for the rules of the game. By the time World War I broke out in 1914, FIFA had twenty-three members, including four non-European countries—Argentina, Chile, Canada, and the United States.

From the very beginning FIFA was unashamedly democratic in structure. Each country was represented by its football association, which had one vote. Except Great Britain, which was represented by the English, Scottish, Welsh, and Irish F.A.s and thus had four votes, but this was considered a price worth paying for the soccer experience and knowledge that these F.A.s brought with them.

Passing on that experience to developing countries was one of the functions of FIFA. But its main aim was to do on an international scale what the F.A. had done within England: to standardize the rules and to make sure that everyone was playing the same game. By 1913 things were going so well that the British even allowed FIFA two votes on the International Board. Just two votes, compared with Britain's four, but the move represented an enormous change in attitude by the British.

World War I temporarily put an end to the friendly atmosphere within FIFA. When the war was over the British wanted Germany, and her former allies Austria and Hungary, banned from FIFA. It was not a popular stand and the four British F.A.s, unable to gain any support, resigned from FIFA in 1920 and, for good measure, took away FIFA's two votes on the International Board.

In 1924, with the war over for six years, the British position was looking a trifle ridiculous. They backed down, and the four British F.A.'s came trooping back into FIFA. But not for long. In 1928 FIFA—which was now running the Olympic soccer tournament—ruled that "broken time" payments (i.e., money to make up for loss of earnings) were permissible in that tournament. Britain saw this as a breach of the true spirit of amateurism, and once again all four F.A.s

---

* And not, as it frequently appears, the International Federation of Football Associations.

marched out. This time, though, FIFA was allowed to keep its seats on the International Board, and reasonably cordial relations were maintained.

The British did not return to FIFA until after World War II, a period of almost twenty years during which the rest of the world not only caught up with, but surpassed, them in playing standards.

Not that anyone realized at the time what was going on. Throughout the 1930s England was quite sure that it was the best and, strangely, everybody else agreed. At first, there was reason enough. Up to 1929, England had played foreign teams twenty-four times, winning twenty-three of the games and tying one (this did not include games against Scotland, Wales, and Ireland, who were not considered foreigners).

Then, in 1929, Spain beat them 4–3 in Madrid, a result that the English shrugged off as a fluke. The Spaniards were invited to play in England in 1931 and were thrashed 7–1, and that showed just who was who when it came to soccer.

The crucial test came the following year with the arrival in London of the Austrian national team, the so-called *Wunderteam*, at that time the undisputed kings of continental Europe. England won the game 4–3, but there were many who thought the better team had lost. The English, having gained the expected result, paid no attention to the inventiveness of the Austrians' soccer and made no allowance for their nervousness. "What the English could not know," wrote Willy Meisl, an Austrian journalist who later lived in England, "was the incredible inferiority complex under which these early continental sides labored when they stepped onto a British football field. For them it was sacred soil. They were so overawed they hardly dared to put a foot down."

And so the English went on believing they had nothing to learn, and in so doing they missed out on the birth in 1930 of the greatest of all international sports tournaments, the World Cup.

CHAPTER 2

The World Cup, 1930-1954*

One of the first things that FIFA had done at its inaugural meeting in 1904 was to proclaim that it alone had the right to organize a world championship of soccer. There was no talk of actually *starting* such a championship. The English, disdainfully following the proceedings from across the Channel, could dismiss the proclamation as mere words.

The English were wrong about FIFA and had to admit their error within a couple of years. But they had learned nothing, and now they got things wrong again. The idea of a world championship was not to be ridiculed out of existence.

The desire for international competition grew rapidly throughout the early 1900s. The British should certainly have known that, for their club teams, both amateur and professional, had been playing exhibition games in Europe since the turn of the century. In 1904—the very year of FIFA's formation—Nottingham Forest had completed a triumphal tour of Argentina. The idea of national teams was spreading, too. Five countries were represented in the first Olympic soccer tournament in 1908, rising to eleven in 1912, and fourteen in 1920 when, for the first time, a non-European country (Egypt) was represented.

In the 1924 Olympics, the Western Hemisphere joined in with Uruguay (the eventual winner) and the United States, and the number of countries competing had risen to twenty-two. South American

---

* For tabulated scores of all tournament games, see pages 282–91. For tactical analyses of the World Cups, see Chapter 6, page 149.

teams dominated the soccer tournament in 1928, with Uruguay defeating Argentina in the all-Latin final.

On the face of it, there was now a true *world* championship of soccer. It looked as though FIFA's grandiose assertion of twenty years earlier—that it alone had the right to organize such a tournament—had been swept aside by the International Olympic Committee.

Things were not what they seemed. In fact, the moment was tailor-made for FIFA. It now knew that soccer in the Americas had reached, if not surpassed, the European level, and that international games were crowd-pulling attractions. Both points had been conveniently demonstrated in 1924 when 51,000 fans had turned up to watch Uruguay beat Switzerland 3–0 in the Olympic final.

FIFA's trump card was the fact that soccer was now becoming a professional sport. The Olympics, with its strict insistence on amateurism, was forbidden territory for many of the world's best players, particularly those from Britain, Austria, Hungary, and Czechoslovakia, where professionalism had been legalized. The FIFA tournament would have the immense advantage of not having to worry about the impossibly fine distinctions between amateurs and professionals. It would be open to everyone.

Behind FIFA's determination to get its world championship started were two remarkable Frenchmen: Jules Rimet, who had been elected president of FIFA in 1921, and Henri Delaunay, its secretary since 1919. Between them, building on their experience in organizing soccer within France, these two provided exactly the right combination of vision, coaxing, arm-twisting, and ruthlessness necessary to transmute their dream into reality.

Delaunay set his proposal before FIFA's 1928 congress: Preparation for the world championship should start at once. It was passed by twenty-five votes to five. The championship was to be held every four years, between the Olympic years, starting in 1930, a mere two years away.

Logically—because FIFA membership was at this time overwhelmingly European—it should have been one of the European nations that received the honor of being host.

But Uruguay, which had impressed everyone with its Olympic victories, wanted to stage the tournament to coincide with the hundredth anniversary of its independence. The Uruguayans backed up their bid with an astonishing offer: They would pay all the expenses for visiting teams, including travel to and from Europe, and they would construct a new 100,000-capacity stadium in Montevideo to stage the games. This was sweet music to Rimet's ears, for he had been worrying about FIFA's ability to finance the tournament. Bids from Holland, Italy, Spain, and Sweden were turned down. Uruguay it would be.

Uruguay, 1930

The decision to hold the first tournament in Uruguay immediately raised almost as many problems as it solved. The four disappointed European candidates went into a sulk and decided not to participate at all. Their lack of enthusiasm spread throughout Europe. With the British nations ineligible (they had walked out of FIFA in 1928), January 1930 arrived with not one European team committed to making the trip to Uruguay.

One of the problems was that the boat trip to Uruguay took nearly three weeks, so that teams would be away for over two months. Neither the club management of the professional players nor the employers of the amateurs found that to their liking. The situation was particularly embarrassing to Rimet, and he set to work to make sure that France, at least, was represented in Montevideo. The Uruguayans, after all, had made the trip to Paris for the 1924 Olympics.

In Romania, it took the royal intervention of King Carol, who personally selected the team. The European contingent eventually reached the grand total of four when Belgium and Yugoslavia agreed to compete, but not one of the major soccer powers—such as England, Hungary, Austria, or Italy—was represented and the Uruguayans were understandably piqued.

Uruguay, along with Argentina, Bolivia, Brazil, Chile, Mexico, Paraguay, Peru, and the United States, represented the Americas. The teams were divided into three groups of three and one of four, each team playing the others in its group once, and the four group winners advancing to the semifinals.

The United States was grouped with Paraguay and Belgium. The "Americans," who were mostly ex-English and Scottish professionals, received no praise for their soccer, but everyone was impressed with their powerful physique. "Shot putters" the French called them. But the shot-putters beat both Paraguay and Belgium by 3–0 scorelines and found themselves, along with Argentina, Yugoslavia and Uruguay in the semifinals.

The lopsided results of those games—Argentina 6, USA 1; and

Uruguay 6, Yugoslavia 1—confirmed that Argentina and Uruguay were a considerable cut above the other teams. The final would be a repeat of the 1928 Olympic final in which Uruguay and Argentina had drawn 1–1, with Uruguay winning the replay 2–1.

The new stadium, which had not been ready when the tournament started, was in use, but the crowd for the final was limited to 90,000. Thousands of Argentine supporters made the short boat trip across the Rio de la Plata from Buenos Aires, to be met by highly suspicious Uruguayan police who searched them thoroughly for weapons before admitting them to the stadium.

Before play could begin there was the matter of the ball to settle. The Argentines wanted to play with one of theirs, the Uruguayans insisted on one manufactured in Uruguay. Both balls were used, the Argentine in the first half, the Uruguayan in the second.

And perhaps, after all, the ball did make a difference. The Argentines had the better of the first half, scoring twice after Uruguay had taken the lead, while the Uruguayans dominated the second and, with three goals in the last half hour, became the first official FIFA world champions. The absence of the strongest European countries rendered the title slightly suspect, but the Uruguayan celebrations demonstrated that they had no doubts at all.

As Jules Rimet handed over the trophy to José Nasazzi, the Uruguayan captain, the huge crowd sang the national anthem at full voice, then flooded out into the streets of Montevideo for a night of singing, drinking, and dancing. The following day was declared a public holiday, and each of the victorious players was given a house to mark the nation's appreciation.*

The tournament had not been without its dramatic and its farcical episodes, and most of them centered around referees. Before the games started, there had been a meeting of the fifteen referees at which all agreed on the importance of a uniform application of the rules and of dealing harshly with any rough play. Agreements, alas, so much more easily arrived at than put into practice. When Argentina met Mexico, the Bolivian referee clamped down on fouls so furiously that he awarded no fewer than five penalty kicks. At the other end of the scale, John Langenus, the Belgian who refereed the Argentina vs. Chile game, seemed blind to rough play until a general fist-swinging

---

* Meanwhile, back in Buenos Aires, Argentines were bombarding the Uruguayan embassy with stones and rocks.

brawl broke out between the two teams and the police had to be called to the field to calm everyone down.

In yet a third game involving the Argentines, this time against France, the Brazilian referee reduced the game to a joke and the French to tears by whistling for the end of the game at the very moment when a French forward was perfectly placed to score a goal that would have tied the score.

As the triumphant Argentines celebrated on the field and the disconsolate French trudged to the showers, a linesman rushed to the referee to bring him the bad news that he had ended the game six minutes early. Clapping his hand to head, the referee finally admitted that, yes, by golly, he *had* made a mistake. The police cleared the fans off the field, the French were recalled from the locker rooms, and the Argentines were persuaded that the game was not yet over. The missing six minutes were duly played, but the French had had their opportunity stolen from them, and there was no further addition to the score.

Despite the eccentric refereeing—something that remains a problem for international soccer today—the first World Championship of football was a success. Admittedly, the European press had cold-shouldered it, but it had aroused enormous interest in South America. It had produced a vividly exciting final, full of good soccer. It had even made a modest profit.

Italy, 1934

Perhaps the most important achievement of that first tournament was simply to demonstrate that it could be done. Clearly, the tournament was here to stay, and almost immediately it was recognized by the Italian Fascists as a useful means to political ends. By 1932, Mussolini had been in power for ten years, during which time his regime had assiduously cultivated the idea of a return to the glorious days of the Roman Empire.

A rash of grandiose buildings, mostly post offices and town halls, was breaking out all over Italy as a sign of the new Italian greatness. Modern stadiums* were being built, too.

Sport was particularly suitable as a vehicle for the blend of pageantry and pomp and inflated nationalism with which fascism sought to inspire the masses.

---

* Many were of advanced design. They included Pier Luigi Nervi's Stadio Berta in Florence, an elegant example of the use of reinforced concrete.

What better political ploy than to stage and, of course, to win the World Football Championship? The Italians, whose bid to hold the 1930 tournament had been turned down, started lobbying as soon as it was over, and in 1932 FIFA granted them the right to stage the 1934 competition.*

Since 1929, the task of selecting and coaching the Italian national team (the *azzurri*, or "blues," after the color of their shirts) had been in the hands of Vittorio Pozzo, a native of Turin who had become enamored with the sport while studying languages in England. Pozzo had been appointed after a disastrous 0–4 defeat by Austria. Until then the selection and management of the *azzurri* had been the work of an ever-changing succession of committees, but a look at the victorious Austrian team, which was virtually the personal creation of their manager Hugo Meisl, convinced the Italians that they, too, should make their team the responsibility of one man.

Although he had never played the game competitively, Pozzo had a deep understanding of its strategy and tactics, and perhaps equally important, he possessed an uncanny ability to select the right players and to make them play the way he wanted. By 1932 he had already built Italy into one of the strongest teams in Europe.

The strongest, by general consent, were the Austrians of Hugo Meisl. The son of a wealthy banker, Meisl, like Pozzo, had been intended for a career in business, but, again like Pozzo, he developed an unquenchable devotion to soccer. His desk at his father's bank, where he spent as little time as possible, was invariably piled with letters and documents relating to soccer.

As early as 1905, Meisl was organizing tours of British teams in Austria, but it was not until 1927 that he finally extricated himself from the family bank and devoted his attentions full-time to soccer. Hugo Meisl's passion for soccer also infected his younger brother Willy, who was to become one of Europe's most respected soccer journalists.

Although Austria, in 1924, was the first continental European country to recognize professionalism, most of the players on Hugo Meisl's national team had outside jobs and were in effect only semipros. The

* Fascism had, in fact, already applied its Italianization process to soccer, decreeing that the sport was not of English origin, but was derived directly from a medieval Florentine game called *calcio*. The word *calcio* is the Italian word for soccer.

One of the country's most famous clubs had been formed in 1899 by Englishmen and called Milan. The Fascists changed it to the Italian Milano. After the fall of Mussolini it was changed back to Milan.

best known were goalkeeper Rudi Hiden (who, appropriately enough for a Viennese, worked in a bakery) and center forward Matthias Sindelar. Known as *der Papierene* (the paper man) because of his slim build, Sindelar was the living expression of Austrian soccer, an artist who used his brain rather than his muscles, skill rather than force.

The Austrian style was modeled on the classic Scottish short-passing game that had been introduced into Central Europe by an English coach, Jimmy Hogan. Meisl, a great admirer of Hogan's methods, brought him to Vienna in 1912. Between them, they laid the groundwork for the growth of Austrian soccer, which reached its climax in 1931–1932 with a team that beat Scotland 5–0, Germany 6–0, Switzerland 8–1, and—in a personal triumph for Sindelar, who scored three of the goals—routed Hungary 8–2.

The Austrian *Wunderteam,* unbeaten in eighteen games, was certainly one of the best the world had ever known. Even mighty England had struggled to beat them 4–3, in London in 1932. A scoreline that showed there was no longer a yawning chasm between England and the rest.

As far as the 1934 World Cup was concerned, the strength of the England team was of no interest. The British nations were still not members of FIFA, and would not be competing. The reigning champions, Uruguay, were also absent. They had pulled out partly as a snub to Italy, which had refused to go to Uruguay in 1930, and partly out of fear that their team had lost its edge and would not be able to retain the trophy.

Not that there was any shortage of countries wishing to compete; quite the contrary, there were thirty-two, and preliminary games had to be played to reduce the number to the required sixteen.

On the eve of the competition, the Italians got a nasty shock from the Austrians, losing 2–4 to the *Wunderteam* in, of all places, the new Stadio Mussolini in Turin. Pozzo was not perturbed; he had built his team with great care and was confident they could win the championship.

He had made full use of the Fascist theory according to which children born of Italian parents living abroad were Italian citizens. This convenient doctrine enabled him to recruit to his team four Argentines who were playing for Italian clubs.

These foreign-born Italians were known as *oriundi.* One of them—the rugged center half Luisito Monti, around whom the defense was built—had actually played on the Argentine team in the 1930 final. In the forward line was another Argentine, Raimondo Orsi,* the classic winger of the period, speedy, with magnificent ball control and a strong shot.

The star of the *azzurri* was nonetheless a native Italian, the Milan-born Giuseppe Meazza. Originally a center forward, but now converted into an inside forward who became the brains of the team, Meazza was the schemer who excelled in feeding his teammates with defense-splitting passes.

Right up to the last moment, it had not been decided whether Mexico or the United States had qualified for the finals. The two countries should have played each other in an elimination series, but couldn't agree on the travel arrangements between Mexico City and New York. The impasse ended with both teams traveling all the way to Italy. They played each other in Turin, the Americans winning 4–2. Once again, the Americans' soccer skill was considered negligible. The Italian press praised only their competitive spirit.

The Mexicans went home, while the Americans went to Rome for the alleged honor of opening the tournament against the hosts, Italy. The Italians, who had spent the previous six weeks in a secluded camp near Lake Maggiore, romped 7–1, and the *azzurri* were off to a flying start.

The knockout rules of the 1934 tournament meant that a team had only to lose one game and it was out. It was a particularly unhappy arrangement for Brazil and Argentina, both of which lost in the first round and had thus, like Mexico, traveled several thousand miles to play only one game.

Italy's next game, the quarterfinal against Spain, proved to be the tournament's hardest in every sense of the word. This was the Spain of the legendary Ricardo Zamora, the acrobatic and fearless goalkeeper who has remained to this day one of the great heroes of Spanish soccer, indeed of Spanish life. It was Zamora's superb agility that kept the Italians out and very nearly won the day for Spain.

Tied 1–1 after the regulation 90 minutes, the game went into an extra half hour. But after 120 bruising minutes it was still 1–1. There

---

* Orsi had played for Independiente in Buenos Aires. His acquisition by the Turin club Juventus in 1928 greatly upset the Argentines, who did not take kindly to their teams being plundered by the Italians. The Argentine F.A. made him sit out a year, without playing, before he was allowed to leave the country in 1929. The soccer drain to Italy continues today. Over one hundred top Argentine players have moved there since the 1930s, including Diego Maradona, who played for Napoli between 1984 and 1991.

would have to be a replay the very next day, to keep to the tournament's tight schedule. Exhausted and battered, both teams were forced to make changes. The Italians brought in four new players, while the Spaniards had lost no fewer than seven of their team, including Zamora. Even so, it was not easy for the *azzurri*, who eventually scraped through on a lone goal from Meazza.

Next came the semifinal against the Austrians in Milan. The *Wunderteam* was two years past its peak, and Hugo Meisl, who knew that many of his players were not fully fit, was as usual pessimistic before the game. "We have no chance," he said. But most observers felt that these were the two strongest teams and that whoever won would take the trophy.

For the Austrians, little went right. Johann Horvath, one of their key players, was out of the lineup with an injury, and heavy rain had turned the field to mud, the surface least suited to their on-the-ground passing style. In the nineteenth minute of play, the Austrians fell behind on a goal that neutral observers felt should have been disallowed for a foul on the goalkeeper by Meazza; the ball had run loose, and there was Enrico Guaita (another of Pozzo's Argentine *oriundi*) to slam it home.

The lone goal was all the Italians needed, and 40,000 partisan fans, crowding right up to the touchlines, roared their team through to the final where they would meet Czechoslovakia, conquerors of Germany in the other semifinal.

Not among the favorites when the tournament started, the Czechs had impressed everyone with their skillful soccer. They played in the Austrian style, but with considerably more flair and stamina. They had had a comparatively easy passage to the final, but they were clearly a force to be reckoned with. Just before the tournament, they had beaten England 2–1 in Prague.

Rome, capital of the ancient and the new Italian empires, was the scene for the final, which was staged with a curious lack of Fascist ceremony. In their determination to make a profit on the tournament,* the Italians replaced pomp with parsimony and did without bands and parades. A Fascist salute from both teams, a handshake between the two captains, Gianpiero Combi for Italy and Frantisek Planicka for the Czechs (a unique moment in World Cup history, for both were goalkeepers), and the game started under the glowering gaze of Benito Mussolini himself.

---

* They were strikingly successful, to the tune of 1,440,000 lire.

Both teams were nervous, but the Italians seemed to be more affected. The Czechs gradually took control of the game but could not score until twenty-six minutes into the second half, when their left winger Antonin Puc at last drove the ball into the Italian net. Czechoslovakia piled on the pressure and Svoboda crashed the ball past Combi, only to see it hit the post. The Italians were in deep trouble, and it took a moment of incredible luck to get them back in the game. With less than ten minutes to go, Orsi tried a rather hopeful right-footed shot from his left-wing position. Spinning and swerving, the ball escaped Planicka's lunge, and the Italians had tied the score.

Thirty minutes of overtime was something that the Italians—who had played one more game than the Czechs, that grueling replay against Spain—could have done without. But they got a quick goal—after only five minutes, Angelo Schiavio took a pass from Guaita and drove the ball past Planicka. In the test of stamina and will that followed, it was the Italians, sustained by the roar of the crowd, who proved slightly the stronger of two exhausted teams. They held on for a 2–1 victory.

Mussolini, who was never known to show the slightest interest in soccer, changed his glower to a smile, and applauded. Obviously, the Fascist way had triumphed. Jules Rimet, who had been trying unsuccessfully throughout the game to engage Mussolini in conversation, went down to the field and presented the cup to Combi. For the second time, the host nation had won the championship.

France, 1938

Jules Rimet brought the World Football Championship to his homeland France in 1938. A brave move, because soccer was but one of three major sports in France (rugby and cycling were the others). It was not a national passion as it was for the Uruguayans and the Italians.

There was no longer any doubt about the popularity of the championship itself. Thirteen countries had entered in 1930, thirty-two in 1934, and now thirty-six for the 1938 edition. Preliminary games were again required to whittle the number down to the required sixteen.

But there was another force at work reducing the entrants. Fascism, an irritating shadow during the 1934 games, was now a threatening black cloud. Spain, on the rack of civil war, was a nonstarter. Then, two months before the tournament was due to start, the Austrians, who had already qualified for the final sixteen, informed FIFA that their country—and hence their soccer team—no longer existed. *Anschluss* had made them part of Nazi Germany.

The tournament was played with only fifteen countries,* the missing Austrian team an ominous reminder that sport and politics were inextricably mixed. There were, however, four Austrian players present who had been drafted into the German team. What the Italians could do with "their" Argentines, the Germans could do with "their" Austrians, and, for that matter, the French, who included an Algerian, could do with "their" colonials.

Of the Italian team that had won in 1934, only two players remained, Giovanni Ferrari and Meazza, now the captain. Pozzo was still in charge. In the 1936 Berlin Olympic soccer tournament he had led Italy to victory with a team of questionable (to say the least) amateurs, and he now included three of those players in his World Cup team. All the Italian-Argentines had gone, and the only *oriundo* was now center half Michele Andreolo, a Uruguayan. Silvio Piola, the tall and powerfully athletic young center forward from the Rome club Lazio, was a new star.

The championship opened sensationally in Paris when Germany, Austrian stars and all, was held to a draw by little Switzerland. An embarrassing result for the Third Reich, which was quickly made worse when Switzerland won the replay easily, 4–2. The Germans went home in disgrace, but their coach Sepp Herberger (who had opposed the addition of Austrians to his team) survived. We shall meet him again in this story.

Sensation in Paris ... and very nearly in Marseilles, where Italy met Norway. Before the kickoff the *azzurri* lined up to give their Fascist salute and were enthusiastically booed by a large contingent of political exiles from Mussolini's Italy. From then on it was the Norwegians who caused all the trouble. After Italy had scored first, the Norwegians piled on the pressure. They hit the goalposts three times and had a goal disallowed for offside, before tying the game with seven minutes left. Two minutes from the end it needed a near-miraculous save from the Italian goalkeeper Aldo Olivieri to keep them out. In extra time, the wily Piola snatched a goal, and the Italians staggered through to the next round to play France.

It was obvious to all that there was something wrong with the Italian team, but Pozzo knew immediately what that something was. He made

---

* England, still not a member of FIFA, was invited to fill Austria's place, but predictably declined.

three changes in the lineup and suddenly the *azzurri* looked irresistible, sweeping aside the French hosts 3–1 with nonchalant ease.

In the semifinal, the Italians would be up against Brazil, a team that bristled with individual talent but that had made heavy going of its first two games. First Brazil had beaten Poland, but only after extra time, by the extraordinary score of 6–5. Four of the Brazilian goals had come from their brilliant center forward Leonidas, the Black Diamond, famed for his acrobatic bicycle kick. The next game, against Czechoslovakia, quickly degenerated into a brawl; one Czech and two Brazilians were sent off, extra time was played, but the score remained tied at 1–1. The Brazilians won the replay with a team containing nine new players.

But the price was high. Leonidas was exhausted and could not play against Italy. Coach Ademar Pimento then shocked everyone by omitting another star forward—Tim—from his team.

The story that both were being rested for the final was no doubt an exaggeration, but Brazilian confidence was certainly at a high level— as the celebrated incident of the flight reservations demonstrated.

Due to play Italy in Marseilles, the Brazilians booked all the seats on the only subsequent flight available to Paris, where the final would be played. When Pozzo went to see them, suggesting it would be better if the seats were made available to whoever should win the semifinal, the Brazilians professed amazement. Such an arrangement would be quite unnecessary, as they would win. "Then I'm sorry to have troubled you," said Pozzo. Ever looking for psychological advantages, Pozzo used the story to fire up his team.

Piola was singled out by the Brazilians as the Italian danger man. Throughout a scoreless first half he was closely marked by the splendid black defender Domingos da Guia. The second half was a different story. Piola began to wander, to draw Domingos da Guia out of position, and winger Colaussi raced in to score. Four minutes later Domingos da Guia and Piola exchanged kicks inside the Brazilian penalty area. Play was going on downfield, but the referee saw the exasperated Domingos da Guia bring Piola crashing to the ground. He awarded the penalty kick, from which Meazza scored the winning goal. Although they scored a consolation goal late in the game, the Brazilians did not need their plane reservations.

It was the Italians who traveled to Paris for the final against Hungary. A clash of styles: the older, more methodical, more artistic play of the Hungarians against the swifter, more direct Italians, noted for the deadly efficiency of their sudden counterattacks. The final score, 4–2 to Italy, was a fair reflection of the way the Italians had dominated the game. The perfect understanding of the Italian trio of inside-forwards—Meazza, Piola, and Ferrari—was too much for the Hungarians. Piola scored twice, while Meazza had one of the finest games of his career. Fittingly, he was the man to receive the trophy from French President Albert Lebrun.

Pondering on his two World Cup–winning teams, Pozzo later said that the 1938 team could have beaten England if the game were to be played anywhere but in England. The chance to test his boast was never there. In September 1939 Europe went to war, and World Cup soccer disappeared for twelve years.

Brazil, 1950

Devastated by six years of war, Europe in 1950 was busy rebuilding its cities and industries; soccer stadiums were not high on the priority list. Not so in Brazil, where the Fourth World Football Championship was to be staged. An enormous 175,000-seat stadium, Maracaná, was being frantically erected in Rio de Janeiro, to be ready in time for the opening game on June 24.

Despite FIFA's record membership of sixty-five nations, it wasn't easy finding sixteen finalists. The war had left political and economic casualties in its wake. The Soviet Union, which had joined FIFA for the first time in 1946, snubbed the tournament and all the Eastern European countries followed suit, except Yugoslavia.

In a satisfying reversal of the 1938 situation, Germany was suspended by FIFA, while Austria was free to enter; but the Austrians dropped out with the excuse that their team was too inexperienced. When Scotland and Turkey, which had both qualified, decided not to compete, Portugal and France were invited to replace them. The Portuguese said no. The French said yes, until they discovered how much traveling they would have to do within Brazil. Then they, too, declined.

The result of all the jockeying was that the tournament got under way with only thirteen teams. Instead of four groups of four, there were now two groups of four, one of three, and one with only two teams—Uruguay and Bolivia. This last coupling was a concession by the Brazilian organizers to the Uruguayan F.A., which was having financial problems. Uruguay had to play only one, absurdly easy, game in the first round—they beat Bolivia 8–0—a piece of generosity that the Brazilians were later to regret bitterly.

The big story of the 1950 World Cup was not the teams that were absent, but the one that was present: England. Having rejoined FIFA in 1945, the English—*i maestri*, the masters, as the Italians called them—decided at last to test themselves in World Cup competition. Just before the tournament, the team lost key defender Neil Franklin. He joined Independiente-Santa Fe in the Colombian outlaw league,* a move that made him ineligible for international games. But the team was still a powerful one. It included two of the most renowned names in the history of English soccer: Stanley Matthews, dribbler extraordinaire, still, at the age of 35, one of the most dangerous forwards in the game; and Tom Finney, perhaps the most complete all-around player ever to wear an England shirt.

Italy, the Cup holder, was rebuilding its team after the Superga air disaster of 1949,** and the new team had been playing surprisingly well. Coach Pozzo had retired, but because it was playing in a relatively weak group along with Sweden and Paraguay, Italy was expected to go through to the final round without too much trouble.

Brazil was the joint favorite with England, partly because it was playing on its home turf, but mostly because of the impression its immensely talented if somewhat undisciplined players had made in the 1938 World Cup. The 1950 Brazilian team was considered the best ever, with a blend at last of individualism and teamwork.

Upsets were not exactly unknown in World Cup play, but the 1950 competition outdid itself in shock results. In its first game, Italy went down 2–3 to Sweden. When they went on to tie Paraguay, the Swedes, unfancied to say the least, became the group winners and Italy was out of the tournament.

Nobody was paying much attention to the Americans, a team of part-timers, that included an undertaker, a carpenter, a teacher, two mailmen, a machinist, an interior decorator, and a factory worker. In

* See Chapter 5, page 143.
** Between 1945 and 1949, when the Italian national team had a 7-2-1 record, it was composed mainly of members of the Torino club team. It once included ten Torino players, never fewer than five. On May 4, 1949, Torino was returning from a game against Benfica in Lisbon when, in thick fog, its plane crashed into a hill at Superga, on the outskirts of Turin. There were no survivors. The entire team, the manager, trainer, and coach, were killed. The Italian Soccer Federation awarded the 1949 championship to Torino, and the victims were given a state funeral. The memory of the tragedy was still very much alive in 1950, and the Italian team traveled to Brazil by boat.

1930 the Americans had stood out for their massive physique: the shot-putters. In 1934 they had been praised for their competitive spirit. The 1950 team had no distinguishing feature. They were just a nondescript bunch of Americans who had played only two games together before arriving in Brazil. The classic no-hopers.

One thing, though. Where the 1930 squad had relied heavily on foreign-born players, all but three of the 1950 players were born in America. Playing in Belo Horizonte in a group that included Chile, Spain, and England, their chances of scoring a goal, never mind winning a game, could charitably be described as slim.

In their first game the Americans did score a solitary goal in response to Spain's three. Then they went into one of the classic mismatches of all time, against England, which had comfortably beaten Chile, 2–0.

The scoreline that came over the wires on June 29, 1950, was England 0, USA 1. It caused worldwide disbelief, but the score was correct. Mighty England, the masters, had been humbled by the Yankee part-timers.*

The hero of the day, scorer of the historic goal, was the Haitian-born Joe Gaetjens. Nobody seems too clear about what really happened. Right halfback Walter Bahr remembers taking a cross-shot from some 25 yards out, a well-hit shot that the English goalie, Bert Williams, was moving across his goal to cover.

Enter Gaetjens. The English press claimed that the goal was a farcical accident, that Gaetjens was trying to duck out of the way when the ball hit him in the ear and deflected past Williams. All nonsense, said U.S. fullback Harry Keough: "Joe dove headlong for the ball to head it past Williams."

"Those were the sort of goals Gaetjens scored," said Bahr, "If it had been anyone else I'd say it was probably an accident. But not Joe—he always went for the ball."

England now had to beat Spain to remain in the competition, something that proved beyond them. They went down 0–1 and returned home, their first World Cup adventure an ignominious failure.

Yet another shock occurred in São Paulo: pesky little Switzerland, conquerers of Germany in 1938, now held Brazil to a 2–2 tie. Suddenly

* Said the Italian referee: "If I hadn't refereed the game myself, I would not have believed the result, no matter who had told me." When the competition was over, the journalists in Belo Horizonte voted this performance of the English team the most perfect of 1950 . . . except that they omitted to score any goals.

it was panic time. Brazil was now in danger. They would have to beat Yugoslavia in their next game. A loss, or even a tie, would let the Slavs through, and Brazil would be eliminated. Unthinkable.

A "Save Brazil" campaign sprang up, with the whole country being urged to support their team. The stars of the 1938 team, Domingos da Guia and Leonidas, were heard continually on the radio, inciting their colleagues of the 1950 team to supreme effort.

Inevitably, the game was an anticlimax, with Brazil winning 2–0 comfortably enough. It might have been a different story but for an absurd accident to Rajko Mitic, one of the Yugoslavian midfielders, immediately before the game. Leaving the locker room to go out on the field, Mitic walked into a protruding metal beam (Maracaná was still not completed) and cut his forehead open. Heavily bandaged, he ran onto the field four minutes late—just in time to see Brazil score its first goal.

For the first time, the final round of the tournament was not played on a knockout basis. The four surviving teams—Brazil, Uruguay, Spain, and Sweden—would play each other once in a minileague, and whichever topped the table was the champion. There would be no single game that could be called the final. But things didn't work out that way. With one game left to play, the position of the top two teams was:

	Played	Won	Drawn	Lost	Points
Brazil	2	2	—	—	4
Uruguay	2	1	1	—	3

The one remaining game was between Uruguay and Brazil. It would be the World Cup final, the game that would decide the championship. For Brazil a win or even a tie would do it. Uruguay had to win.

Brazil was the overwhelming favorite. It had annihilated the other two teams in the final round: Sweden was beaten 7–1, Spain 6–1. By contrast Uruguay had edged Sweden 3–2, and had been held 2–2 by Spain. Realistically, the Uruguayans hadn't a prayer. One of the top directors of the Uruguayan Soccer Federation told his players: "We'll be lucky if they don't drown us in goals. Do your best, but even if you lose 4–0 it will be a victory of sorts."

For the Brazilians the question was not whether they would win, but how many goals they would put past the hapless Uruguayans. An enormous crowd, estimated at 200,000, packed the barely finished

Maracaná to see the slaughter. On an afternoon of high emotion, the national anthem was sung as it had never been sung before, and the governor of Rio de Janeiro delivered a final, impassioned plea to the team: "Fifty million Brazilians await your victory!" before the referee's whistle started the most important game in Brazil's history.

The Brazilian onslaught began immediately, and the Uruguayan goal was under siege for the entire first half. The brilliant Ademir, who had already scored seven goals in the tournament, supported by the wiles and skills of Zizinho and Jair, worked his magic for forty-five minutes, but the expected avalanche of goals would not come. In the Uruguayan defense, the thirty-three-year-old veteran Obdulio Varela found a tireless partner in Victor Andrade, eleven years his junior. A series of spectacular saves from goalkeeper Roque Maspoli (another thirty-three-year-old) helped to shut out the Brazilians in the first half.

Two minutes after the interval, Maracaná exploded as Brazil at last broke through and Friaça drove the ball past Maspoli. What should have been the beginning of the end for Uruguay turned out to be the signal for their awakening. Varela, absolutely tireless, foresook his defensive duties and moved into the attack, getting the ball more and more to right winger Alcide Ghiggia who, even in the first half, had shown that he could beat the Brazilian defense. After twenty minutes he threaded his way through yet again, drawing defenders away from the middle; his pass found Juan Schiaffino just outside the penalty area. The slender Schiaffino coolly controlled the ball and beat Barbosa in the Brazilian goal with an unstoppable shot: 1–1.

Even with the score tied, Brazil would still be world champion, but the Brazilian players—and the fans—knew that something was awfully wrong. The roar of the crowd was hushed as the nervousness of their team could no longer be ignored. Schiaffino was knocked down in the area, surely a penalty . . . but Brazil survived the moment of suspense as the referee waved play on. The Brazilian defense was once more a shambles as Omar Miguez raced through and hit the post with Barbosa beaten.

Then, the death blow for Brazil. This time their defense was caught with too many men in the middle; the ball was pushed out to the right, where the inevitable Ghiggia ran on to it and slammed the ball between Barbosa and the near post. The goal—the most important of the tournament—was received in stunned silence. "That was when I knew we were going to win," said Schiaffino, "when I heard that silence."

What was to have been an afternoon of national rejoicing was fifteen minutes away from being a total catastrophe. Those minutes slipped away, so impossibly quickly for Brazil, so agonizingly slowly for Uruguay, until there was nothing left to hope for. Uruguay 2, Brazil 1. The 1950 World Cup, so full of upsets, had saved the most astonishing for the final game.

Twenty years after it had won the first-ever tournament, Uruguay was world champion again. In 1930, as Jules Rimet had presented the trophy, the crowd was on its feet, singing and cheering. Now, in 1950, the vast terraces of Maracaná were half deserted as the disillusioned Brazilians filed sadly out, ashamed to watch as Varela and Rimet shook hands on the field.

Said Jules Rimet: "There were no guards of honor, no national anthem, no speeches in front of the microphone, no magnificent victory celebrations." By the time the Uruguayans made their traditional lap of honor, the stadium was virtually a hollow shell.

Brazil, confident of success in 1938, certain in 1950, had failed again.

Switzerland, 1954

An unlikely choice as host, tiny Switzerland got the nod because FIFA—headquartered in Zurich and fifty years old in 1954—wanted to celebrate the anniversary in its own backyard.

It turned into a very wet celebration that will always be remembered as a tournament of rain, of mud . . . and of goals, 140 of them in twenty-six games for an extraordinary average of 5.3 per game.*

Hungary, riding the crest of a twenty-eight-game unbeaten string that stretched back over four years, was a clear favorite. They had beaten all the top teams in Europe. They had humiliated England by a resounding 6–3 score—in Wembley Stadium no less, the first foreign team ever to win there. Three weeks before the World Cup began, England had journeyed to Budapest seeking revenge, but found only further humiliation, losing 7–1.

The victories of the Magic Magyars, as the English press had dubbed them, had further damaged the already tottering reputation of England as a world soccer power. Neither England nor Scotland—in the World Cup for the first time—was rated very highly.

Italy was another of the Hungarians' victims. The Italians had made

* In 1950 it had been 4.0 per game, and in 1958 it was to go back down to 3.6.

the mistake of inviting the Magyars to play them at the ceremonial opening of the Stadio Olimpico in Rome in May 1953. The Hungarians repaid the compliment by trouncing the *azzurri* 3–0 with almost insulting ease. The Italians promptly fired their coach and, for the first time ever, appointed a foreigner: Lajos Czeizler, a Hungarian.

Germany, or at least West Germany, was back, coached by the same man who had suffered defeat at the hands of Switzerland in 1938, the remarkably durable Sepp Herberger. The South American challenge came from the two countries that had played in the 1950 final. Uruguay, the Cup holders, still had five members of their winning team, including Andrade, Schiaffino, and the thirty-six-year-old Varela. Brazil had what was virtually a new team—only Bauer remained from 1950—yet such was the strength of Brazilian soccer that this new team was installed as one of the favorites.

There were also the weak teams that made their way into the final sixteen because of the regional arrangement of the elimination games. In the whole of Asia there was not a national team that was in the same class as even the poorest of those in Europe or South America. But there *was* an Asian qualifying group of Japan, South Korea, and Nationalist China. The Koreans beat Japan, China dropped out, and South Korea, the best of a very weak lot, found itself a finalist. Really a ludicrous state of affairs, considering that countries like Sweden and Spain had been eliminated in the much tougher European qualifying groups.

Sweden's elimination, at the hands of Belgium, was something of a surprise for the team that had finished in third place in 1950. But Sweden's failure in 1954 was a direct result of its success in 1950, when its players had caught the eyes of Italian clubs. No fewer than nine of that 1950 team had been lured to play as professionals in Italy.* Thus Sweden lost most of its best players because the Swedish F.A., a rigorously amateur body, would not allow professionals to represent Sweden.

Television made its World Cup debut on June 16, 1954, with the transmission of the game between Yugoslavia and France. A move that at once brought millions of new fans to the sport and began the move (some would call it the slide) to rampant commercialism that has marked the most recent tournaments.

Not that money had ever been far from the thoughts of the organiz-

---

* Signing Swedish players was a profitable exercise for the Italians. As the players were all amateurs, no payment was necessary to their former Swedish clubs.

ers. Their arrangement of the groupings proved that. There would be the usual four groups of four teams each, but this time each group would contain two seeded teams who would not play each other. The seeded teams—that is, the ones that were expected to attract the fans—played two games each, against the two weaker teams in their group. It was an arrangement that made it almost certain that all the seeded teams would have an easy passage.

It was left to the hapless but seeded Italians to demonstrate that the best-laid plans do, indeed, gang aft a-gley. In their first game they were beaten 1–2 by the hosts Switzerland (robbed, they would ever after maintain, by the biased decisions of the Brazilian referee). A playoff game—also against Switzerland—was necessary, and this time the Italians went down 1–4.

The Germans got involved in a playoff game, but this was the result of a deliberate gamble by their coach Sepp Herberger. Playing in an absurdly unbalanced group, along with the favorites Hungary and the no-hopers Turkey and Korea, Germany was, incredibly, unseeded.

This was because when the groupings had been arranged, it was assumed that Spain would qualify. All it had to do was to beat the minnows Turkey in an elimination game. The result was a forgone conclusion—Spain was one of the strongest teams in Europe. So the seeded place was given to the as yet unknown winner of the Turkey-Spain game. The game was tied and had to be decided by drawing lots; to the embarrassment of all, it was Turkey's name that came out of the hat.

With Turkey seeded, Germany would have to play Hungary in the first round. Looking far ahead, Sepp Herberger reasoned that if Germany were to reach the final its most likely opponent there would be Hungary. And so he decided to hide his first team. By fielding six reserves against the Hungarians, he virtually threw the game away. Hungary 8, Germany 3 was the score. The loss made a playoff game against Turkey necessary, but Herberger was confident that his team, having easily beaten the Turks 4–1, could beat them again in a playoff game, which they did 7–2. Herberger now felt that he knew a lot more about the Hungarian team than they knew about his team.

Scotland's baptism in the World Cup was a dismal affair: beaten 0–1 by Austria, then absolutely outclassed by Uruguay, who scored seven goals without reply.

The goal riot went on in the quarterfinals. Switzerland scored five, but lost to Austria, who scored seven! Uruguay, with a fine display of the open, quick-moving soccer that was making it the most admired team in the tournament, took care of England, whose baggy shorts and heavy shoes seemed to symbolize its outdated style, by a score of 4–2.

Between Germany and Yugoslavia there was little to choose, unless it was the increasingly obvious physical aspects of the Germans' game. Two Yugoslavs were badly injured, so that for much of the game Yugoslavia had to play with only nine men.* The Germans were 2–0 winners.

The remaining quarterfinal, between Brazil and Hungary, was theoretically the most attractive. But, alas for theory, it turned out to be one of the ugliest games in the history of the World Cup, remembered as the Battle of Bern. Two penalty kicks were awarded and three players were sent off, two Brazilians and one Hungarian.** As the game finished, with Hungary 4–2 victors, there was the unedifying spectacle of a general punch-up among players, police, photographers, and others (who were they? some thought they were spectators, some said they were members of the Hungarian and Brazilian parties). The brawl went into overtime outside the locker rooms, long enough for the Hungarian coach Gustav Sebes to be punched in the face, and for the Brazilian captain Pinheiro to collect a three-inch gash in his head.

From the disgraceful to the sublime. Hungary's semifinal against Uruguay is remembered as one of the greatest games of all time. Those who felt that the two teams should have been kept apart in the semifinals viewed their meeting as the "true final" of the 1954 tournament. It was a great game despite both teams being without their number one stars—Ferenc Puskas of Hungary and Obdulio Varela of Uruguay were both injured—and the rain that fell incessantly throughout the match.

Hungary was one up within fifteen minutes, using the sort of rapid, first-time passing movement and brilliant finishing that is so difficult to defend against. A long, probing pass from Nandor Hidegkuti was headed perfectly down by Sandor Kocsis toward the onrushing Zoltán Czibor, a spectacular volley—goal for Hungary. Throughout the first half, the Hungarians dominated without being able to add to their score.

Victor Andrade, captaining Uruguay in place of Varela, was everywhere, an agile muscular obstacle to the inventiveness of the Hungarian attack. Behind him, hardly putting a foot wrong, was the young fair-haired center back José Santamaria.

The second half had barely begun when Hungary scored again—a

---

* Substitution was not allowed in World Cup soccer until the 1970 tournament.
** The Hungarian was their captain Jozsef Bozsik, who also happened to be a deputy in the Hungarian National Assembly.

powerful diving header by Hidegkuti that was in the net before Maspoli had a chance to move. Well on top now, the Hungarians showed signs of overconfidence—or were they lulled into it by the clever Uruguayans? Exactly as they had done in the 1950 final against Brazil, almost as though it were the result of a signal from the touch-line, Uruguay suddenly raised the level of its game.

Schiaffino, always dangerous, became positively deadly; he and inside forward Juan Hohberg, urged on by the indefatigable Andrade, now totally committed to attack, began to systematically maul the Hungarian defense. Twice Schiaffino was just wide with rasping shots. Then, with only fifteen minutes to go, his perfect pass put Hohberg through to score. There were just four minutes remaining when Hohberg scored again. Emotionally and physically exhausted, Hohberg collapsed and had to be dragged off the field for a whiff of smelling salts.

Tied 2–2, the game went into overtime, and almost immediately the revived Hohberg was through again. This time his shot hit the post and Schiaffino pounced on the rebound, only to be thwarted by a prodigious save from Gyula Grosics. An injury to Andrade spelled the end for Uruguay. While he was off the field receiving treatment, Kocsis headed Hungary into the lead. Five minutes later he scored again, and Uruguay was beaten for the first time ever in a World Cup game. As the final whistle blew, the two teams saluted each other with smiles, handshakes, and embraces as the crowd rose to cheer them. After the sordid Battle of Bern, Hungary and Uruguay had provided a magnificent affirmation of the sport.

In the other semifinal Germany made surprisingly short work of Austria, to the tune of six goals to one. The Germans had been helped by a number of banal errors by the Austrian goalkeeper Walter Zeman, but the pace and rhythm of their athletic game had impressed previously skeptical observers.

Hungary vs. Germany in the final—exactly as Sepp Herberger had foreseen three weeks earlier. This time, of course, he would field his full team. But the Hungarians had a problem with Puskas, who had not played since he was kicked—ominously enough—in that first game against Germany. The injury was the result of a bad foul by the German defender Werner Liebrich, a foul that Puskas later claimed was intentional. Italian journalists, looking at film of the incident, said there could be no doubt that the kick was deliberate.

The Hungarian coach Gustav Sebes had some doubts about Puskas's fitness. But Puskas, a major in the army, was a commanding personality. He said he was fit. So Sebes played him. After eight minutes of play the decision looked like the masterstroke. Hungary scored twice (one goal to Puskas himself) and was toying with the Germans almost as easily as if Herberger had again put out his reserve team. Professors Puskas, Hidegkuti, and Bozsik seemed set to give another of their celebrated soccer academies.

It was not, however, to be skill that won the day. It was to be stamina. The Germans had played two comparatively easy games in the quarter- and semifinals. The Hungarians had struggled through the Battle of Bern, and then suffered the tension of the emotionally supercharged overtime victory against Uruguay. As the rain poured down, the heavy going began to tell against Hungarians. On top of that, the longer the game went on the clearer it became that Puskas was not really fit.

Three minutes after Hungary's second goal the Germans scored when Max Morlock jabbed the ball home after a mix-up in the Hungarian penalty area. Seven minutes later Germany was level on a ferocious shot by right winger Helmut Rahn. At the other end, Hidegkuti hit the post, and Anton Turek saved Kocsis's header when it looked almost too late.

Hungary opened the second half with almost frantic energy, hitting the bar, having a shot kicked off the goal line and forcing Turek to make two more fine saves. But nothing came of it, and when the fury died down, Germany took over again, finally going ahead on another goal by Rahn with seven minutes left. Hungary, desperate now, threw everything into attack, and Puskas scored—only to have the goal disallowed for offside. It was a desperately close call and for the Hungarians, certain the goal was legitimate (as were many neutral observers), it was the final blow.

Exactly as in Rio four years earlier, the favorites, the "better" team, had gone down. The Magic Magyars, beaten for the first time in four years, had succumbed to a team out of the classic German mold: high on fitness, discipline, and morale, uncomplicated in tactics.

Standing on a small podium, with an umbrella held over his head against the relentless rain, Jules Rimet presented the trophy to the mud-spattered German captain, Helmut Rahn. It was his last official act before retiring after thirty-three years as president of FIFA.

CHAPTER 3

The World Cup, 1958-1974*

Before 1958, the World Cup had always been won by a nation from the continent where it was played: Uruguay had won both times that the championship was held in South America, while of the three played in Europe, two had been won by Italy and one by Germany. The 1958 competition changed all that when the Brazilians came through in sparkling fashion to win in Sweden. The result satisfied everyone, for, after the upsets of 1950 and 1954, justice was done and the best team had won.

Sweden, 1958

A tournament without a clear favorite: Both 1954 finalists, Hungary and West Germany, were present, but neither was in sparkling form. Politics had played a cruel trick on Hungary. At the time of the 1956 uprising in Hungary, Honved (the army team for which most of the national team members played) was touring in South America. Three key players—Puskas, Czibor, and Kocsis—decided not to return home, and the Hungarians lost the nucleus of their great team. Hidegkuti was still there, but his thirty-six years were beginning to tell. To the sorrow of all, the Hungarians quickly demonstrated that there was very little left of the Magic Magyars.

Immediately after winning the 1954 championship, the Germans had gone downhill with a vengeance. They won only four of their next

---

* For tabulated scores of all tournament games, see pages 282–91. For tactical analyses of the World Cup, see Chapter 6, page 149.

seventeen games, amply confirming the views of those critics who felt their win had been a fluke. But Sepp Herberger—and who was willing to ridicule him anymore?—was supposed to have a four-year plan that would ensure maximum strength when it mattered: to wit, during the 1958 finals.

The captain, Fritz Walter, was still playing, aged 38 but wily as ever. Helmut Rahn, the goal-scoring hero of the 1954 final, had been recalled and had vowed he would get in shape by cutting out his remarkable beer-drinking activities. The new players included a twenty-two-year-old center-forward, Uwe Seeler, destined to become the most popular player in the history of German soccer.

An unknown quantity among the finalists was the Soviet Union, which had at last decided to come out of hiding and put its talents on the line. It had won the 1956 Olympic title, it had a formidable goal-keeper in the giant Lev Yashin, and everyone was raving about the skill of the captain, Igor Netto. But were they ready for the pressures of World Cup play?

For the first and so far only time, all four of the British soccer nations were represented. England was still rebuilding after suffering the same sort of blow that befell the Italians in 1949. On February 6, 1958, a plane carrying England's champion club, Manchester United, had crashed on takeoff at Munich airport. Eight of United's players were killed, including three who were regular members of England's team. A month before the finals, England had been swamped 0–5 by Yugoslavia in Belgrade.

The Welsh were present only because of political problems. Israel, drawn in the same preliminary group as Turkey, Indonesia, Egypt, and the Sudan, found itself, apparently, with a free passage into the finals when all four opponents refused to play it. FIFA was having none of that and decreed that Israel would have to play off against Wales, which had finished second in one of the European qualifying groups. And so Wales, which had already been eliminated by Czecho-slovakia, got another chance and, by beating Israel twice, went to Sweden as one of the final sixteen.

Northern Ireland qualified on merit by eliminating Italy. This was the first time the Italians had failed to qualify for the finals. Their dis-appointment was particularly intense because their team included two brilliant *oriundi*, the Uruguayans Ghiggia and Schiaffino, who were now playing for Italian clubs.

Also playing for Italian clubs were most of the top Swedish players.

George Raynor, the Englishman who was Sweden's coach, recalled five of them to make up the nucleus of his team. Among the returning exiles was the 36-year-old veteran Nils Liedholm, who had played so brilliantly for the great Swedish 1948 Olympic team, before being snapped up by Milan.

The Argentine squad had once again been ravaged by the wealthy Italian clubs. One year earlier Argentina had won the South American championship with what many rated as their best team ever. In six games they had scored twenty-five goals, thanks to their dazzling young forwards Omar Sivori (twenty-two years old), Antonio Angellilo (twenty), and Humberto Maschio (twenty-four)—a sassy, skill-laden trio that had toyed with opposing defenses.

The Angels with Dirty Faces they called them, but within the year the angelic threesome was no more. The angels took wing for Europe, lured away by Italian clubs, and Argentina refused to have anything further to do with them, though all three did later return to international soccer, playing for Italy.

As far as most Europeans were concerned, Brazil had been written off as a serious World Cup threat. The team had shown a frightening lack of discipline in the 1954 Battle of Bern. The same thing had happened during Brazil's 1956 tour of Europe, when players and officials had tried to attack the referee after a game in Vienna.

But 1958 was to be the year in which Brazil redeemed itself. The Brazilian Soccer Federation had produced a secret and brutally honest report on the failings of their players. At last attention would be given to the psychological needs of players—many of them from humble homes—asked to live for long periods thousands of miles from Brazil. The team traveled with its own psychologist.

The new coach was Vicente Feola, a large, easygoing man who hid his sad, slow-moving eyes behind tinted spectacles. He confessed uncertainty about the team he would select, bemused, perhaps, by the wealth of talent at his disposal. In fact, during the 1958 series he never did field the same team twice running. In Brazil's first game, against Austria, only the cool, unflappable Didi and the cultured fullback Nilton Santos remained from the 1954 team. Brazil won the game 3–0, but Feola felt the score should have been higher.

Against England he brought in Vava, a fast-moving aggressive forward, for more scoring punch. The move was not a success and England held the Brazilians to a 0–0 tie. While Feola pondered what further changes to make, a deputation of his players arrived. They wanted the devastating right winger Garrincha—the Little Bird—in the starting lineup. Feola had the good sense to listen. He also brought in two players from the Santos club—halfback Zito and the seventeen-year-old forward . . . Pelé.

It was the Soviets who were unlucky enough to get the first taste of this new Brazil. In the first minute Garrincha hit the post, two minutes later Vava scored on a pass from Didi, and the Soviets spent the rest of the afternoon defending grimly, particularly against the Little Bird's dizzying dribbles. The Brazilians were limited to just one more goal by Vava, but it seemed absurd to measure the margin of their victory in goals. The Brazilian soccer was on a different plane than that of the Soviets.

At long last, here was the team that the whole country of Brazil had been dreaming about. All the natural individual brilliance was there, now allied not with arrogance but with a cool confidence. Brazil swept through to the quarterfinals, joined by France, Yugoslavia, Sweden, Wales, Germany, Northern Ireland, and the Soviet Union, which had beaten England in a playoff game.

Against Wales, Feola left out Vava and brought back Mazzola, a move that didn't work, for the Brazilians struggled to gain a 1–0 victory. The lone goal was scored by Pelé. It was his first in World Cup play, and one he would later rate as one of the most important of his career. Elsewhere, the inevitable Rahn had scored for West Germany to give them a 1–0 win over Yugoslavia, while Sweden, to the delight and somewhat to the surprise of its supporters, had been well worth their 2–0 victory over a stolid Soviet side, in which only goalkeeper Yashin had enhanced his reputation.

The fourth semifinalist was France, 4–0 conquerors of Northern Ireland. The French, never among the world's soccer powers, had caught everyone off guard with their spirited and skillful attacking soccer. They had scored fifteen goals in four games, eight of them coming from Juste Fontaine, the fruits of a wonderful understanding with inside forward Raymond Kopa. They were the tournament's highest scorers, and in the semifinal they would face Brazil, whose defense had not yet conceded a goal.

For the game, Feola brought back Vava to play at center forward, and it was Vava who got Brazil off to a roaring start with a goal in the second minute, only to have Fontaine equalize at the nine-minute mark. The outcome of the game was sealed in the thirty-fifth minute when the French defender Robert Jonquet collided heavily with Vava. Jonquet was carried off with a badly injured right knee, and though he returned later he was merely a passenger. With substitution not permitted, France had to soldier on with only ten fit men.

While Jonquet was off the field, Didi scored one of his rare goals for Brazil, and in the second half Pelé shone with dazzling brilliance, eclipsing even Garrincha, and scored a hat trick against the disorganized French defense. After the game, the French goalkeeper Claude Abbes said, with considerable feeling: "I would rather play against ten Germans than one Brazilian."

At Gothenburg, in the other semifinal, Sweden took on West Germany, and the authorities decided they had to do something to fire up the Swedish fans, still strangely lethargic when it came to rooting for their team. Cheerleaders, familiar enough to college football fans but almost unheard of in soccer, were the answer.

Thus encouraged with cheers, chants, and flags, the Swedes perversely allowed the Germans to score first, but quickly equalized through Lennart Skoglund, an Italian repatriate. Kurt Hamrin, also back from Italy, then set about picking the German defense apart until, after fifteen minutes of the second half, fullback Erich Juskowiak despairingly kicked him, and was ejected from the game. Against ten men, Sweden's Gunnar Gren scored the go-ahead goal, and Hamrin crowned his afternoon by waltzing the ball past three defenders before beating the German keeper with a violent cross-shot.

Before turning to the final, a quick look at the game for third place. What is traditionally an uninspired affair between two disappointed teams turned out to be a festival of goals: final score, France 6, West Germany 3. Fontaine scored four of the French goals, bringing his total for the tournament to thirteen, a record that still stands.

To say that Brazil was the favorite in the final is to state the obvious. Sweden's own coach admitted that his was the oldest and the slowest team in the tournament. Brazil was younger and faster, and infinitely more talented. All that Sweden seemed to have going for it was the fact that it was playing at home and the memory that Brazil, so often in the past, had self-destructed when the big moment arrived. The European coaches still believed that the Brazilian temperament was suspect, that if the team gave away an early goal, the players would not fight back—a theory that was shattered within ten minutes of the start of the final. The Swedes went ahead after only four minutes on a goal by Liedholm. The ball was calmly picked out of the net by Didi almost as though nothing had happened, and the Brazilians set about playing soccer.

It took them six minutes to level the score, and the goal was a beauty. Garrincha took the ball down the right touchline, beat two Swedish defenders with impish ease, raced almost to the goal line, and drove the ball, hard and low, across the middle, where Vava, running in at full speed, darted between two opponents and turned it into the net.

Garrincha was to be a tantalizing thorn in the Swedish left side all afternoon. Twenty minutes later he broke through yet again and created another goal for Vava. As if Garrincha were not enough, Zito and Didi were now controlling midfield at will, while up front Vava and Pelé were throwing the Swedish defense into chaos with their constant interchanging of positions. Every so often Djalma Santos (playing his first game of the tournament—that was Feola's "change of the day") would come racing up from fullback to join in the attack. In the second half Pelé volleyed the ball past goalkeeper Karl Svensson for number three, then Mario Zagalo (in 1970 he would be Brazil's coach) scored the fourth. Sweden got one back through Agne Simonsson, but Pelé had the last word. To make the final score 5–2, he leaped high to head the ball in a perfect arc over Svensson's grasping hands. Sweden, never disgraced, had been outclassed. But could any of the other finalists have done better?

Chile, 1962

FIFA now began a policy of alternating the World Cup sites between Europe and the Americas. The 1958 competition had been in Sweden, so it would be South America in 1962, and the country chosen was Chile. A curious decision, given the disastrous earthquake and drought of 1960 that had all but wrecked the country's economy. But the Chileans were insistent, and they were willing to build new stadiums.

In World Cup history, 1962 will not go down as a vintage year. Where 1954 had featured the Magic Magyars, and 1958 the Brilliant Brazilians, 1962 had very little to excite the imagination.

It was thought the Yugoslavs might spring a surprise, because almost anything seemed possible when their mercurial inside forward Dragan Sekularac was in form. England, of course, would go on being steady and unimaginative—gone was the day when anything exceptional was expected from the English.

The Soviets had made a successful tour of South America at the end of 1961, playing Argentina, Uruguay, and Chile and beating all three. Yashin was now being talked about as the greatest goalkeeper of all time. Based mainly on players from Dukla-Prague (the Czech army team), Czechoslovakia had a well-knit side that would be difficult to beat, but they had lost their young goal-scoring star, Rudi Kucera, to a serious head injury. And West Germany . . . well, the Germans still had Herberger, though this was to be his last World Cup.

Of the European teams, the most talented was surely Spain, which was able to profit from the strength of the Real Madrid team that was dominating European soccer. Real had brought together a galaxy of world stars—Ferenc Puskas (whom we last saw playing for Hungary in the 1954 final), José Santamaria from Uruguay and, perhaps the greatest of them all, Alfredo di Stéfano from Argentina. As naturalized Spaniards, they were now playing for Spain alongside two brilliant native-born Spaniards, inside forward Luis Suarez and winger Francisco Gento.

The favorite had to be Brazil, if only because they had so many of their 1958 team back again. All four years older of course (the fullbacks Djalma and Nilton Santos were thirty-three and thirty-seven), but who could forget how superb the team had been in Sweden? Anyway, there was always Pelé, who was fast becoming a legend, and he was still only twenty-one years old. Ill health had forced Vicente Feola to resign as coach, to be replaced by Aimoré Moreira, brother of Zeze Moreira, who had coached the 1954 team in Switzerland.

The Chileans themselves were an unknown quantity. Never rated as a particularly strong soccer nation, they nevertheless had the psychological advantage of being hosts. National fervor was there to be harnessed—the Swedes had pointed the way with their flag-waving cheerleaders—but no one was ready for what happened when Chile played Italy.

The Italians, always fragile and unpredictable when playing away from home, had nonetheless arrived with high hopes. They had a young team, average age twenty-four, including five members of their 1960 Olympic team, which had been eliminated—on the toss of a coin!—after holding the eventual winners, Yugoslavia, to an overtime tie. The team also included four *oriundi:* the Brazilians José Altafini (who had played for Brazil in the 1958 World Cup under the name Mazzola) and Angelo Sormani, and the Argentines Sivori and Maschio.

The Italian downfall was the result of events that happened off the field—in particular, the bad luck of being drawn in the same group as Chile. Shortly before the competition was due to start, an Italian journalist wrote a series of highly critical articles about the living conditions in Chile. A Chilean living in Italy read them and, scandalized, sent them to the Chilean ambassador in Rome who sped them back to Santiago.

The articles alleged widespread illiteracy, alcoholism, and prostitution and compared Chile unfavorably with underdeveloped nations in Africa and Asia. At once there began a campaign in the Chilean press, radio, and television systematically denigrating the Italian players. They were accused of being Fascists, members of the Mafia, sex maniacs, and, because there had recently been a doping scandal involving the top Italian club Inter-Milan, drug addicts.

By the time the Chile-Italy game came around, the atmosphere in Santiago was so dangerously charged that the Italians selected their team more on the basis of players who would control themselves under provocation than out of any tactical soccer considerations. Before the game, the *azzurri* tried to calm the crowd of 66,000 by waving greetings and throwing roses to them. The Chilean fans replied with insults and threats, and threw the roses back—a suitable start for the carnage that was to follow: kicking, spitting, punching, one Italian with a broken nose, two Italians sent off.

The Italians have never forgiven the English referee Ken Aston, accusing him of at best incompetence, at worst overt hostility. He seemed to see only Italian reaction, and not Chilean provocation, of which there was plenty. Notably the sensational haymaking punch with which the Chilean left winger Leonel Sanchez broke Maschio's nose—unpunished, and apparently unseen, by Aston.

Later, Aston confessed that he had wanted to call the game off at halftime, but was afraid the crowd would riot if he did so. Reduced to nine men, the Italians went down 0–2, and Chile had fought—in the most literal sense—its way to a quarterfinal game against the Soviet Union, 1,000 miles to the north in Arica. A game that to the astonishment of all they won 2–1, mostly because Yashin had a woeful afternoon and let in two simple shots that he should have saved.

From Viña del Mar came the sensational news that Pelé was out of the World Cup, the victim of a badly pulled muscle during Brazil's 0–0 tie with Czechoslovakia. His loss clearly affected Brazil in their next game against Spain, who were without the injured di Stéfano. After many an anxious moment, Brazil won 2–1 on two late goals by Amarildo, Pelé's replacement. From the Spanish camp came the news that di Stéfano was out of the tournament. It meant that one of the world's greatest players was never to play in the World Cup.

In the quarterfinal the Brazilians recovered their poise and beat England 3–1 with consummate ease. Amarildo was now fitting in well, but the victory belonged to Garrincha, who scored two of the goals. On one of them, Garrincha—a mere five feet seven inches—outleaped the towering English defenders to head the ball home.

Chile vs. Brazil in the semifinals: a game guaranteed to bring to boiling point the already simmering Santiago fans, who were beginning to suffer the delusion that their team was good enough to win the championship. The fears of those who foresaw a repetition of the Italy game were eventually confounded—but only just—by the self-discipline of the Brazilians and the infinitely superior quality of their soccer.

Had the game been played anywhere else, the Chileans would certainly have been swamped, but they hung on grimly throughout the game. After two early goals by the irrepressible Garrincha, Chile narrowed the gap when Jorge Toro scored direct from a free kick. Vava, deadly as ever with the half chance, headed a third for Brazil two minutes into the second half. Chile scored again from a penalty, after Zozimo handled in the area, only to have Vava head his second goal.

The score was to remain 4–2 in Brazil's favor, but in the closing minutes of the game the Brazilians' sorely tried patience began to wear thin. Garrincha, who had been kicked methodically throughout the game ("at least fifty times," he later claimed), at last returned the blows and was ejected. As he walked to the locker room, he was hit on the back of the head by a bottle.

The organizers, probably not imagining for one moment that Chile would get that far, had made the mistake of scheduling both semi-finals for the same hour on the same day. While Chileans throughout the country were gathered around television sets watching Chile lose to Brazil, the game between Czechoslovakia and Yugoslavia in Viña del Mar drew a pathetic 5,000 spectators.

Against the run of the play, the Czechs beat the Yugoslavs 3–1, exactly as, in the quarterfinals, they had been outplayed by but had eventually beaten the Hungarians. The difference in both games was the Czech goalkeeper Wilhelm Schroiff, who made save after incredible save.

To universal relief the Chileans won the third-place game against Yugoslavia, giving their fans something to cheer about. Steam was duly let off in the streets of Santiago, leaving Brazil and Czechoslovakia to play the final in the cordial atmosphere of the afterglow.

For Brazil there was the unwelcome possibility that Garrincha might be suspended for the final. FIFA's disciplinary committee was busy deciding whether his ejection in the game against Chile should be followed by a one-game ban. Possibly their deliberations were swayed by the telegram that arrived from Tancredo Neves, the president of Brazil, possibly not. The decision was announced by Sir Stanley Rous, the Englishman who had replaced Jules Rimet as president of FIFA: Garrincha was cautioned, not suspended.

Except for Schroiff and the wing half Josef Masopust, the Czechs had no outstanding players. Their game had a deliberate, almost plodding, air to it, mired in a defensive mentality that seemed to find attacking a tedious but necessary chore.

How surprising, then, when the Czechs opened the final with a series of enterprising attacking moves and went ahead on a well-taken goal by Masopust. Amarildo had the Brazilians level within two minutes, shooting violently from the narrowest of angles and squeezing the ball between the badly positioned Schroiff and his near post. Half an hour into the second half, Amarildo crossed from the left and there was Zito, unchallenged, to head home.

For poor Schroiff, who was not having the happiest of afternoons, there was worse to come. From the touchline, a good 40 yards out, the Brazilian fullback Djalma Santos got his foot under the ball and booted it high into the air. Schroiff, looking into the sun, was dazzled as the ball dropped toward his goal. He lost it, found it again, caught it, then dropped it, right at the feet of Vava, who tapped it in for Brazil's third goal.

Brazil thus joined Uruguay and Italy as two-time winners of the Jules Rimet trophy. With an average age of just over 30, it was the oldest team ever to win the World Cup. But the veterans, without Pelé, and without dazzling as the 1958 team had done, had been clearly the best in an off year for soccer.

England, 1966

One hundred and three years after the London Football Association had drawn up the rules that laid the foundations of the sport, the World Football Championship arrived in England. Back where the game began, where the first professionals had played, and where international competition itself had started with that meeting between England and Scotland in 1872.

The organizers could be certain that there would be no problems with unfinished stadiums. The English had not built a new stadium since Wembley was opened in 1923, and they were not about to start now. What was good enough every Saturday afternoon for the English League clubs was certainly good enough for foreigners, and the games would be played on six club grounds.*

England, as it turned out, would play all its games at Wembley.

No new stadiums then, but for the first time the World Cup would have a mascot: the traditional English lion was turned into a cuddly, boylike creature, complete with soccer shoes, and dubbed World Cup Willie. He would grin out from thousands of posters and advertisements, the first of a line of increasingly commercialized World Cup symbols.**

The World Cup trophy was brought to England and put on display at the National Stamp Exhibition, from which, to the horror of all, it disappeared. The chances of it ever turning up again were evidently not good. The Cup, after all, was solid gold, worth 50,000 francs in 1930. Incredibly, it did turn up. A spotted dog called Pickles, out for a walk with his master in South London, rummaged about in a garbage heap and unearthed . . . the World Cup.

England's embarrassment was relieved, and they could now set about acquiring the trophy in a more orthodox manner. They were the favorites, if only because it was still a rare occurrence for a foreign team to beat England on its home soil. But there were other reasons for believing that the English would do well. In 1963 they had appointed a new manager, Alf Ramsey, who had said confidently and had gone on saying, "We shall win." Ramsey, who had played for England thirty-two times in the early fifties as a fullback,† had built up a solid

---

* There is a story of an American who visited an English first division ground soon after the war—a ground that had emerged unscathed from the blitz—and remarked: "Gee, this must have been quite a place before it was bombed." The story is, no doubt, apocryphal, but it does give a fair idea of the haphazard, ramshackle appearance of most English soccer grounds. It appears the English have something against stadiums; Wembley itself, built for the 1924 Empire Exhibition, narrowly escaped demolition in 1927.

** Another innovation, and a clear sign of the times, was the drug-testing scheme. After each game, urine samples were taken from four randomly selected players (two from each team) and under conditions of great security dispatched to a London laboratory for analysis. In this way, 128 samples were tested—all proved negative.

† He was a member of the English team on both of its blackest days: the 0–1 defeat by the USA in the 1950 World Cup, and the 3–6 drubbing by the Hungarians at Wembley in 1953.

England team that was going to be difficult to beat. In defense there were the supremely safe goalkeeper Gordon Banks and center back Bobby Moore, the captain, cool and solid as a rock. In attack the team could rely upon the balding Bobby Charlton, a survivor of the Munich aircrash of 1958, a world-class forward with a bewildering body swerve and ferocious shot. The quicksilver Jimmy Greaves, the most dangerous goal scorer in the English game, was something of an individualist, and was dropped after the first round. Ramsey's taste was more for hardworking team players.

Looking for its third successive win, Brazil was once again being coached by Vicente Feola. From the 1962 team there were Gilmar, Djalma Santos, Garrincha, and Pelé. Plus, astoundingly, Bellini and Orlando, two players from the 1958 team who had not been selected in 1962.

Portugal was a new name in the World Cup finals, its team built around players from the Lisbon club Benfica, at that time one of the strongest in Europe. Their stars were two black players from Mozambique: Mario Coluna, a strong, intelligent midfield player, and the explosive Eusebio, whose thunderous shooting was to be one of the highlights of the competition.

Sepp Herberger had retired at last. The new coach of West Germany was one of his disciples, Helmut Schoen. The team included Uwe Seeler, playing better than ever at center forward, and two young midfielders, the left-footed Wolfgang Overath and the very right-footed Franz Beckenbauer, only twenty-one years old but already playing with the confidence and poise of a veteran.

Italy, too, had a new coach, Edmondo Fabbri, who had enjoyed great success as a club coach, guiding Mantova from the fourth to the first division in seven years. In Giacinto Facchetti, the tall attacking fullback, Sandro Mazzola, an inside forward of superb quickness and ball control, and the twenty-two-year-old Gianni Rivera, the Golden Boy of Italian soccer, Fabbri had some of the most talented players in Europe. But his lack of experience in international soccer was to be a fatal flaw.

North Korea qualified from the Asian-African group. The Koreans had beaten Australia, and were then to have played the winner of the African group. That never happened because all fourteen African countries withdrew. They were miffed because they felt the winner of their group should go straight through to the finals, and not have to play off against the Asian winner. And so North Korea came to the finals, a country with no soccer tradition, about which almost nothing was known. Had the team dropped from Mars it could hardly have been more mysterious.

England opened the Eighth World Championship at Wembley Stadium with a game against Uruguay, and a pretty dreadful game it was. The Uruguayans packed their defense and made little attempt to score, clearly and cynically playing for a tie. England was made to look pedestrian, without the skill to cut through the Uruguayans' massed defenders. The result, a tedious 0–0 tie, was unhappily a portent of the defensive nature of much of the soccer that was to come.

Brazil got off to a winning start, 2–0 over Bulgaria, but it was a wretched, physical game from the start, with the Bulgarians providing another example of negative, defensive soccer. Pelé was treated mercilessly, kicked repeatedly by his marker Dobromir Zhechev, who was not even cautioned by the German referee.

Then came Hungary vs. Brazil, their first meeting since the infamous Battle of Bern twelve years earlier. So far neither team had looked particularly impressive, but Hungary (beaten 1–3 in its first game by Portugal) and Brazil (without Pelé, who was still recovering from the mauling the Bulgarians had given him) produced the most memorable game of the 1966 tournament. Not that Brazil had much to do with it; the glorious soccer came almost exclusively from Hungary.

In Florian Albert, Hungary had a worthy successor to the great Hidegkuti. Gracefully body-swerving and accelerating his way through the Brazilian defense, passing with accuracy and almost supernatural insight, Albert had the English crowd chanting his name long before the game was over.

Hungary went ahead after two minutes on a goal by Ferenc Bene, another of their dazzling young forwards. Pelé's substitute, Tostão, tied the score, but after the interval Hungary was irresistible, sweeping forward time after time with the superb Albert always the catalyst. It was his powerful run through the middle and pinpoint pass to Bene on the right wing that led to Hungary's second goal. Bene raced on to the ball, took it to the goal line, and centered hard and low. The ball was met by Janos Farkas with a crushing right-foot volley that sent it flashing into the net. It was soccer perfection—for many, the finest goal they had ever seen. The Brazilians' tattered defense held on for another ten minutes of torture until Bene, dancing through for yet another shot, was pulled down in the area. Kalman Meszoly scored from the penalty.

Brazil, beaten 1–3, was now in danger of being eliminated. It would have to beat Portugal in its remaining game. Panic set in, the team was purged, and nine changes were made including the return of the questionably fit Pelé. The result was a disjointed, ineffective team that was no match for the confident Portuguese. Eusebio scored two goals in a clearcut 3–1 win for Portugal. Once again Pelé was liberally kicked and once again the referee (another European, this time from England) did little to protect him. Brazil, the champions, were out. Pelé, bitterly disillusioned by the thuggery and the permissive refereeing, vowed that he would never play in the World Cup again.

The shock of Brazil's elimination was to some extent tempered by the brilliance of Hungary and Portugal, the two teams that had survived. A much larger shock was on its way from Group IV. Italy had won its first game, unconvincingly, over Chile, and had then lost 0–1 to the Soviet Union. To advance, it would have to beat North Korea. Not exactly a tall order. But, just as the Brazilians had done, the Italians panicked.

Fabbri announced his tactical plan to deal with the speedy little Koreans and then proceeded to select players who seemed least capable of putting it into practice. And he persisted with Giacomo Bulgarelli, who had been injured in the game against Chile, and who had a massive question mark hanging over his fitness. Half an hour into the game Fabbri's gamble backfired. Bulgarelli twisted his injured knee, collapsed in agony, and was carried off.

Already finding the Koreans something of a handful, Italy struggled on with ten men. Just before halftime, disaster struck. Gianni Rivera, like most of his teammates having a melancholy afternoon, failed to control a pass. The ball was whipped away from him by Pak Doo Ik, who slammed it into the goal past the vainly diving Enrico Albertosi, the Italian 'keeper. The Italians fought back, created enough chances in the second half to win the game, but seemed fated to miss them all.

The dejected Italians flew home to Genoa airport, where they were greeted by 600 fans who had waited all night to scream abuse at them and pelt them with rotten fruit. It was rumored that Pak Doo Ik, a corporal in the Korean army, had been made a sergeant.

On to the quarterfinals went the extraordinary Koreans, there to meet and scare the life out of the Portuguese. Playing with almost boyish enthusiasm the Koreans scored three times in the first twenty minutes, an avalanche of goals that stunned the Portuguese. The image persists of Portugal's goalkeeper José Pereira, standing on his line, hands on hips after the third goal had gone in, looking blankly about him, trying to make sense of it all.

For a few precious minutes the idea flared that the Koreans had discovered the secret of perfect soccer, and that they were going to beat everybody. Then Eusebio took over to score twice in the first half, adding two more in the second, leading a remarkable Portuguese comeback that saw them safely through, 5–3.

Had the Koreans been more worldly-wise in soccer tactics, they would have known how to protect a 3–0 lead. But had they been that tactically sophisticated, they would almost certainly never have played with the gay abandon that gave them those three goals. They disappeared back to Korea as suddenly and as mysteriously as they had arrived, never to excite the soccer world again.

Another sad note for soccer was the quarterfinal elimination of the artistic Hungarians by the ponderous Soviets. Even the skills of Albert and Bene could not compensate for two dreadful errors by the Hungarian goalkeeper Jozsef Gelei.

The other two quarterfinals caused no end of trouble, both on and off the field. Both were Europe vs. South America matches: England vs. Argentina and West Germany vs. Uruguay, and both were refereed by Europeans. Worse, an Englishman refereed the German game, while a German refereed the English game. It was not a sensible arrangement.

This is what happened. The English referee sent off two Uruguayans, and the Germans won easily, 4–0. The German referee ejected the Argentine captain, and the English won, though not so easily, 1–0. Immediate and passionate protests came from the South American camp. The Brazilians were already complaining, with substantial justification, about the lax European refereeing standards that had allowed Pelé to be so maltreated. Now the Argentines and Uruguayans descried an Anglo-German plot that had maneuvered both South American teams out of the tournament.

The English coach Alf Ramsey did not help matters when he characterized as "animals" the Argentines who had tried to attack the referee after the game. The South Americans threatened to withdraw from FIFA and demanded an apology from Ramsey. They did not get their apology, did not withdraw, and the World Cup continued with four European teams in the semifinals.

England and Portugal delighted a huge crowd at Wembley with a pulsating game of rare soccer and sportsmanship. England won because Bobby Charlton, at his incomparable best, scored twice, while Eusebio, kept comparatively quiet by England's defense, scored only once. England, in the World Cup final for the first time ever, at last looked as though it had a team capable of winning the trophy. Only West Germany, victors over the USSR in the other semifinal, now stood in the way. Since 1936, England had played Germany seven times: The balance sheet read England six wins, the remaining game tied.

Thousands of German supporters made the trip to Wembley, and after only thirteen minutes they were waving their red, gold, and black flags in ecstasy. Pouncing onto a poor clearance by the English defense, Helmut Haller shot. Banks was screened, dived too late, and Germany was one up—the first time in the tournament that England had been behind.

The reaction was swift and devastating. A long free kick by Bobby Moore seemed to be dropping harmlessly ahead of the English forwards when suddenly Geoff Hurst, who had sprinted from the other side of the field, was there to head the ball powerfully past Hans Tilkowski in the German goal.

The game swayed one way, then the other, with both teams playing fast, attacking soccer. Banks saved superbly from Overath and Seeler. Tilkowski was lucky to scramble away another header from Hurst. It was England who appeared to be gaining strength and with twelve minutes to go, when the German defense failed to clear properly, Martin Peters slammed home a loose ball. With the deafening roar of the triumphant English fans ringing in their ears, the Germans pushed everyone up for a final assault, and it was fullback Wolfgang Weber who pushed the ball home for the dramatic last-minute equalizer.

For the first time since 1934, the final would go into extra time. A cruel test for already exhausted limbs, but one that little Alan Ball, the English midfielder, seemed to revel in. Karl-Heinz Schnellinger, whose task was to mark him, was outpaced time and time again. It was from one of Ball's centers that Hurst drove the ball viciously past Tilkowski. The ball smashed against the underside of the crossbar, bounced down to the ground, and back into play. England appealed for a goal, claiming that the ball was over the goal line before it bounced out. Referee Gottfried Dienst, from Switzerland, was not sure. With 95,000 fans holding their breath, biting their fingernails, and watching his every move, Dienst walked over to his Soviet linesman, who confirmed the goal with a sharp nod of his head and an imperious sweep of his flag.

It seemed unlikely that the ball could have been over the goal line*
but the sporting Germans did not press their protests.

They attacked desperately, but England, boosted by the goal, was
clearly the stronger team now. Geoff Hurst scored again right before
the end, making him the first, and so far only, player to score a hat
trick in the final.

England, 4–2 winners, had earned its victory with a solid, workmanlike side that reflected Ramsey's no-frills approach to the game. It
was not a particularly exciting team to watch, but in a tournament
that had revealed a depressingly widespread tilt toward defensive
play it was the most efficient.

Mexico, 1970

Four years later soccer mascotry marched on, and World Cup Willie
gave way to Juanito, a chirpy, chunky little muchacho with a soccer
ball and a sombrero that had "Mexico 70" on its brim. The Mexicans
had worked hard to make the tournament a success, building new stadiums, including the magnificent 105,000-seat Aztec Stadium, but
there were still many who worried about the altitude problem. The
1968 Olympics had shown that there were very real dangers of
exhaustion.

When the organizing committee decided to start some games,
including the final, in the full heat at twelve noon instead of at 4:00
P.M., apprehension about the location increased. European television,
which wanted the noon kickoffs so that it could transmit the games
live during prime evening time back home, was now powerful enough
to get its way.

Rough play was something else to worry about. It had been all too
evident in 1966, as Pelé, among others, had reason to remember. Fortunately for the sport of soccer, Pelé had revoked his decision not to
play in 1970, but if he had been hacked out of the tournament in 1966, it
could happen again. He and all the other skillful, creative players had
to be protected. Strict instructions were given to the thirty referees to
clamp down on foul play. They had a new weapon in the card system.
They would show a player the yellow card for a caution, the red card
for an ejection—a sign language to clear up communication problems
between referees and players who did not speak the same language.

* The rules state that *all* of the ball must have crossed the full width of the line.

Another novelty for referees would be the waving of substitutes onto the field. Long resisted in soccer as either a gimmick or something that was akin to cheating, substitutes had finally arrived in the World Cup. They were limited to two per team.

The tournament had drawn a record entry of seventy-one nations, and elimination games had started in 1968. The vagaries of regional qualification were even more apparent than usual: Yugoslavia, Hungary, and Portugal were all eliminated in tough European qualifying groups. Israel, Morocco, and El Salvador* had made it as winners of much weaker groups.

The most surprising of the qualifiers was Peru, coached by the former Brazilian star Didi, but it clearly was not to be taken lightly as it had eliminated Argentina. To get themselves used to the climate and the altitude, England arrived in Mexico a month before their first game. The party consisted of twenty-two players, one coach, two trainers, and a doctor. Already in Mexico, waiting at the hotel that was to serve as England's headquarters, were tons of frozen and canned English food ("What happens if foreign food gives our boys a bellyache?" read the advertisement of one of the suppliers). The preparation was nothing if not thorough, and the team looked a strong one, stronger than 1966 according to Alf Ramsey, who was now Sir Alf. Queen Elizabeth had knighted him in 1967 for "services to football."

João Saldanha, a controversial ex-journalist, was in charge of Brazil's squad until March, two months before the tournament. Then he committed the two cardinal sins of Brazilian soccer: His team lost to Argentina, and he threatened to drop Pelé. The pressure began to tell. Criticized by the Flamengo coach Iustrich, Saldanha turned up at a Flamengo training session brandishing a revolver.

Saldanha had to go. He was replaced by Mario Zagalo, who had been the left winger on Brazil's 1958 and 1962 championship teams. In its qualifying group Brazil had scored twenty-three goals in six games, nine of them to Tostão and six to Pelé. Tostão, a member of the

---

* In the North and Central American qualifying round, El Salvador had to play Honduras, a neighbor with which she had a long-standing quarrel over alleged discrimination against the 300,000 Salvadoran immigrants living in Honduras. The games were played in an atmosphere of mounting tension, culminating in the flight of some 50,000 Salvadoran refugees back to their homeland. After El Salvador had won the playoff game, which was played in Mexico, full-scale war broke out when 12,000 Salvadoran troops invaded Honduras. El Salvador became journalistically famous as "the nation that went to war over soccer," a facile explanation of a much more complicated series of events.

disappointing 1966 team, had been playing brilliantly until, in late 1968 he was hit in the eye by the ball and suffered a detached retina. He had undergone surgery at an eye clinic in Houston, Texas, but his fitness was very much in doubt.

Just as it had done in 1966, the tournament opened with a dreary 0–0 tie. This time Mexico and the USSR were the culprits. Things were not helped by the martinetish performance of the German referee Kurt Tschenscher, who rushed hither and thither, stopping the game at the slightest suggestion of an infringement. The Soviets, who seemed to be his chief victims, became exasperated, and four of their players, along with one Mexican, received yellow card cautions.

But Tschenscher's meddlesome refereeing was a hidden blessing. He had obeyed his instructions with commendable Teutonic thoroughness and he had made it unmistakably clear to players and coaches alike: The referees *were* going to be stricter than in 1966.

Pelé & Co. opened in commanding style against Czechoslovakia, winning 4–1 with exuberant, almost carefree attacking soccer. Tostão played brilliantly, as he was to play throughout the tournament. Jairzinho and Rivelino were revelations with their powerful dribbling and shooting. Pelé, twenty-nine years old, less athletic but more cerebral, looked better than ever. The defense was supposed to be weak, but with such attacking strength, did it really matter? The English players, who all watched the game, felt that it did, and that they could exploit the weakness.

Drawn in the same group, the two teams met four days later in one of the most fascinating games of the tournament. Brazil, without Gerson, its left-footed midfield playmaker, was slightly more cautious than usual, its attacks more methodical, slower to develop. But when they did come, as at the tenth minute ... a sudden burst down the right wing by Jairzinho, a cross on the run to the far post, and there was Pelé leaping high to head the ball powerfully down, just inside the post. But the ball did not go in. Gordon Banks in England's goal, guarding the near post one second, was across the width of the goal the next, flinging himself full length to somehow scoop the ball off the line, up and over the bar as Pelé raised his arms in disbelief. Banks's save, televised all over the world, was hailed as one of the greatest ever.

England had its moments, particularly an overlapping run on the right by fullback Tommy Wright, whose center found Francis Lee, unmarked in front of the goal. Lee headed powerfully, but straight at goalkeeper Felix, who thankfully grasped the ball. After fifteen minutes of the second half, Tostão dribbled into the English penalty area, turned, and chipped the ball to Pelé, who flicked it on for Jairzinho to beat Banks from 10 yards.

Late in the game, with England pressing, Everaldo miskicked and teed the ball up for the England center forward Jeff Astle, standing almost on the penalty spot. His left-foot shot went wide of the goal, an incredible miss, and Brazil were 1–0 winners, the only time in the championship that they scored fewer than three goals in a game. However, England, by winning against Romania and Czechoslovakia, joined Brazil in the quarterfinals.

Mexico, too, made the quarterfinals, for the first time ever. After their opening tie with the Soviets, the Mexicans went on to beat El Salvador and then Belgium before 112,000 spectators in the cauldron of Aztec Stadium. This last game had revived memories of Chile in 1962: A huge, bitterly hostile crowd had intimidated the Belgians and—more important—the referee, who awarded the Mexicans a ludicrous penalty from which they scored the only goal of the game.

In the quarterfinals they met Italy, who had accomplished the seemingly impossible feat of topping their qualifying group while scoring only one goal, but 0–0 ties with Israel and Uruguay and a 1–0 win over Sweden had seen them through. Against Mexico, they at last opened up, scoring four times, with two of the goals going to Gigi Riva, the sturdy left winger who was the current idol of Italian soccer.

The Peruvians, who had shown themselves to be a spirited and skillful team during the first-round games, were unlucky to run into Brazil in their quarterfinal. They scored twice, but Brazil got four, with Tostão again in devastating form. West Germany avenged its 1966 final defeat, fighting back to beat England 3–2 after being 0–2 down. Its equalizing goal came from the veteran Uwe Seeler, playing in his fourth World Cup, while the man destined to replace him as Germany's ace goal scorer, Gerd Müller, got the winner in extra time. Uruguay (coached by Juan Hohberg, hero of its epic game against Hungary in 1954) completed the four semifinalists by beating the USSR 1–0.

The Italians scored early in their semifinal against West Germany, and promptly and predictably withdrew into their customary defensive shell. For most of the second half the Germans battered away at the well-marshaled Italian defense. Beckenbauer, gliding about the field with the grace, balance, and power of an Olympic ice skater, was a constant menace. Late in the game he was on yet another full-speed run when a brutal foul sent him crashing to the ground. The fall dislocated Beckenbauer's shoulder, but he played on with his right arm strapped across his chest.

The score was still 1–0 to Italy when, in the final minute, Schnellinger equalized for Germany. In extra time the goals came thick and fast. Gerd Müller snatched a typical opportunist goal to put Germany ahead. Italy, goaded at last into attacking play, showed they could do it when they tried, equalizing through fullback Tarcisio Burgnich, then going ahead again on a goal from Riva's mighty left foot. Müller, flinging himself full length at the ball like a torpedo, brought Germany level again, only to have Rivera score the winning goal for Italy straight from the restart.

In Guadalajara the Brazilians met their old nemesis Uruguay, the first time the two nations had played each other in a World Cup game since that fateful final of 1950. Brazil gave away an early goal, equalized with a goal from their gifted young midfielder Clodoaldo, then struggled for the winner. When it did come, late in the game, it was a beauty—Jairzinho dribbling irresistibly down the right, cutting in and scoring with a perfectly placed cross-shot. Rivelino made it 3-1 in the final minute, converting a pass from Pelé, but it had not been easy. Beating Uruguay has never been easy for Brazil.

The final would see the attack-minded Brazilians against the defensive Italians, soccer's version of the Forces of Light against the Forces of Darkness. But there was some hope that the Italians, having scored eight goals in their last two games, might be tempted to adopt a more offensive style.

It was a hope that was dashed almost as soon as the game started. The Italians packed their defense at once, giving Brazil a numerical advantage in midfield, a situation much to the liking of the cunning Gerson, who became a key figure of the game.

First blood fell to Brazil, and Pelé. A throw-in by Tostão was lofted into the goalmouth by Rivelino—it looked innocuous enough, but Pelé turned it into a goal. As the ball dropped, Pelé leaped high over Burgnich, twisted powerfully in midair, and nodded the ball wide of Albertosi. Twenty minutes later Roberto Boninsegna equalized for Italy with a goal that sprung less from Italy's own efforts than from a calamitous mixup in the Brazilian defense.

The halftime score of 1–1 in no way reflected the reality of the game or that, as an attacking force, Italy was nonexistent. The goals, surely, would come from Brazil. And come they did. Gerson, receiving the ball some thirty yards out, brought his devastating left foot into action ("He could stir his tea with it" was the thought of an admiring English player). Two quick, delicate touches got him past an Italian defender, then a scorching twenty-five-yard drive left Albertosi grasping thin air.

Five minutes later Gerson's left foot struck again: His superbly accurate forty-yard pass was headed down by Pelé to Jairzinho, who ran the ball in. The rout was complete with a breathtaking fourth goal by captain Carlos Alberto, who came storming through from his full-back position to joyfully thump home Pelé's exquisitely judged pass.

A wonderful afternoon for positive soccer, and a fitting moment for the retirement of the Jules Rimet trophy. Brazil, having won it for the third time, now took permanent possession. A new trophy would be designed for the 1974 championship. The Brazilians took the old trophy home to a triumphant reception in Brasilia, and a bonus of some $20,000 for each player. The Italians, despite finishing in second place, went home to their by now almost traditional welcome of insults and rotten fruit, this time at Rome's Fiumicino airport.

Germany, 1974

The World Cup flame, were there such a thing, would now pass from Juanito to Tip and Tap, two rather ugly little boys with toothy grins whom the Germans had selected as the official mascots for 1974. And the new trophy, now officially called the FIFA World Cup, made its first appearance. The Italian sculptor Silvio Gazzanigga explained his work: "The lines spring out of the base, rising in spirals, stretching out to receive the world. From the remarkable dynamic tensions of the compact body of the sculpture rise the figures of two athletes at the stirring moment of victory. In a flowing and spontaneous language, the work expresses the force and purity of the spirit of sporting competition." It was announced that the cup was solid eighteen-carat gold, and had cost $20,000.

Mention of its cost was not at all out of place in 1974, for suddenly the World Cup seemed to be more about money than soccer. It was estimated that Brazil had spent $4.5 million preparing to defend their title. The Dutch, having qualified, very nearly did not get their team to Germany because of a squabble over bonuses—eventually settled when the players were guaranteed a payment of $24,000 each plus 70 percent of the profits made from the tournament by the Dutch F.A. The Australians, one of the "weak group" qualifiers (the others were Haiti and Zaire), were said to be on a $4,000 bonus per man if they managed to win a game. Gross income to the German organizing committee would be around $40 million. Tip and Tap were evidently sitting on top of a gold mine; the contribution from companies licensed to use their grinning faces was over $2 million.

Politics, too, made its presence felt. Just before the USSR was due to play Chile in a home-and-home playoff series, the Marxist Chilean government was overthrown on September 11, 1973, by a bloody coup in which the president, Salvador Allende, was killed. The first game, in Moscow, was tied 0–0. When the Chileans announced that the return game would be played in the National Stadium in Santiago, the Russians balked. Not unreasonably, for the stadium was already famous as, at best, a detention center for opponents of the new regime, at worst (as the Soviets claimed) "a concentration camp, place of tortures and executions of Chilean patriots." The Soviets wanted to play in a neutral country; FIFA said no, and so the USSR withdrew.*

Security measures, already substantial with the memory of the 1972 Munich Olympic tragedy strong in everyone's mind, were strengthened for Chile's games in case of demonstrations from German leftists. Trouble was also expected at the other end of the political spectrum from German rightists protesting the presence of the East German team. Scotland, fired by the success of Scottish Nationalist candidates in the recent British election, was casting a jaundiced ear at being introduced with "God Save the Queen" as its national anthem.

England was not present, having been knocked out in the qualifying rounds by Poland, the 1972 Olympic champions. It was the first time they had ever failed to qualify, and the failure was to cost Sir Alf Ramsey his job.

The favorites, in a rather on-and-off sort of way, were the West Germans. Two years earlier they had won the European Nations Cup with a magnificently inventive team, but the departure of midfield star Gunter Netzer, who had gone to seek his fortune with Real Madrid in Spain, seemed to have upset the team's rhythm. Its recent results were not convincing, but it did have the superb Beckenbauer as captain, and the master goal scorer Gerd Müller—*Der Bomber*, as he was now known.

Brazil had lost its chief star. Pelé had retired from the national

---

* Chile went through to the finals after a mock "game" in the National Stadium in which their team, unopposed, kicked off, dribbled the ball downfield, and shot it into the empty goal for an official 1–0 victory. Their poor form in the subsequent tournament led to rumors that it had taken them three tries to score the goal.

team in 1971 and had stuck to his decision despite immense pressures in Brazil. There was even a financial offer from German businessmen who wanted his drawing power in the tournament. For the first time in sixteen years, Brazil would play the World Cup without him. His absence, plus the fact that it was playing in Europe, had dimmed Brazil's chances of retaining the title.

If strength at club level meant anything, then surely the Dutch had a strong chance. Their two leading clubs, Feyenoord and Ajax, had dominated European soccer since 1969, and it was from the players of these two that most of the national team was drawn. One exception was the captain, Johan Cruyff, a former Ajax player whom the Spanish club Barcelona had bought for $2.2 million. It was Cruyff, the new Golden Boy of soccer, who was expected to replace Pelé as the sport's superstar.

The Dutch had arrived explosively on the world soccer scene, and their freewheeling style seemed to reflect the open, liberal nature of Dutch society. They were even allowed to have their wives with them in training camp.*

Because of their strength in defense, the Italians were much fancied. Their goalkeeper, Dino Zoff, had not been beaten in eleven international games. Experience was not a problem—five members of the squad had played in both the 1966 and 1970 World Cups—but advancing age might be.

Breaking with the tradition that the host nation opens the tournament, West Germany gave that honor instead to the holders, Brazil. The Germans had realized that the ceremonial importance of the occasion made for nervousness, and had noted that in 1966 and 1970 the games had been played ultracautiously, both finishing in 0–0 ties.

"The poisoned gift," the Brazilians called it, and, in drenching rain, proceeded to play a cautious, dull game against the equally cautious and dull Yugoslavia: result, yet another boring 0–0 tie.

Despite ducking the opening game, West Germany started disastrously anyway, laboring to a 1–0 win over Chile while the Berlin crowd booed and shouted rude remarks about the number of Munich players in the team. Scotland recorded its first-ever World Cup victory by beating Zaire, but the narrowness of the win (2–0) suggested

---

* An innovation that would have appealed to the Brazilian defender Luis Pereira. Trapped in a month-long, isolated Brazilian camp before the tournament, Pereira complained to a journalist: "This is supposed to make us world champions. World champions of what? Masturbation?"

either that the Zaireans were a lot better than expected, or the Scots were a lot worse. It turned out to be mostly the latter.

Poland was off to a fine start when its team beat Argentina 3–2 in a vastly entertaining game. Gregor Lato and Robert Gadocha, the tricky and admirably direct Polish wingers, did most of the damage, but Kazimierz Deyna stood out as an attacking midfielder of considerable talent. Argentina, which had earned a reputation for callous, rough play during the 1960s, surprised everyone with its sparkling—and clean—soccer.* In Carlos Babington they unveiled one of the most gifted players of the competition.

Once again the first major surprise came at the expense of the Italians. Little Haiti took a 1–0 lead over the *azzurri* when its muscular winger Emmanuel Sanon, with defender Luciano Spinosi tugging desperately at his shirt, powered his way through to score. The Italians recovered quickly to score three times, but Zoff's scoreless record was gone. Worse was to come. Italy were held to a 1–1 tie by the increasingly confident Argentines, and then beaten 1–2 by a rampant Poland, which had by now convinced everyone that its elimination of England was no fluke. The loss to Poland put Italy out of the competition, and as the team bus drew away from the stadium in Stuttgart, it was stoned by angry groups of immigrant Italian workers.

The Haitians, too, were eliminated, though not before one of their team—Ernst Jean-Joseph—had become the first player in World Cup history to record a positive drug test.

Scotland was out, too, but they went home to a hysterical welcome in Glasgow. Their record was two ties (with Brazil and Yugoslavia) and that 2–0 win over lowly Zaire, not good enough to qualify for the second round, but they *were* unbeaten! All three minnows—Australia, Zaire, and Haiti—were eliminated, and the 9–0 thrashing that Yugoslavia administered to Zaire, to say nothing of Haiti's 0–7 loss to Poland, brought renewed criticism of the regional qualifying system that permitted such feeble teams to reach the final sixteen.

The toast of the first round was unquestionably the Netherlands. In their first game the orange-shirted Dutch demoralized Uruguay with a dizzying display of fast-moving soccer, a merry-go-round of constant position switches by the whole team, with, always, at the center of things, the flowing, impudent skills of Johan Cruyff. Held to a 0–0 tie

---

* The reason for the Argentines' good behavior was not hard to discern. They had been selected as hosts for the 1978 World Cup and were determined not to do anything that would cause FIFA to think again.

by Sweden in their next game, the Dutch came back with another masterful display to thrash Bulgaria 4–1.

The East Germans, as expected, proved to be the most disciplined team in the competition, making up in fitness what they lacked in originality. Their 1–0 victory over West Germany, while a considerable boost to their political pride, really meant very little, as West Germany had already made sure of its own place in the second round.

The form of the second round was a new one. Instead of the eight teams playing a single quarterfinal each, followed by semifinals, they were grouped into two groups of four teams: Brazil, Netherlands, East Germany, and Argentina in one, West Germany, Poland, Sweden, and Yugoslavia in the other. The winners of each group would meet in the final. It meant, of course, more games—twelve instead of six—which meant, naturally, more gate money.

The Dutch had little difficulty in the first group, beating all three opponents, though their game against Brazil was one of the roughest of the tournament. This was by no means the Brazil of 1970. The defense was certainly one of the strongest and toughest in the competition, but with Pelé and Tostão gone and Jairzinho painfully out of form, nothing could hide the poverty of Brazil's attack. The star of their side was, appropriately enough, a fullback with a flair for attack, the blond Francisco Marinho. Netherlands beat them 2–0, with Cruyff setting up the first goal and scoring the second himself with a gloriously controlled volley on the run.

West Germany struggled against Sweden, eventually beating them 4–2, but not before the Swedes had shown, yet again, what a formidable team they are in World Cup competition. Next, the Germans faced the Poles in Frankfurt. Whichever team won would play in the final against Holland. Sad then, that such a crucial game should have been played under conditions that made good soccer impossible.

A torrential downpour flooded the field and delayed the kickoff for half an hour. The Frankfurt fire brigade arrived with a monster squeegee roller that they trundled up and down the field. Their valiant efforts made little impression. Parts of the field were virtually under water when play did start.*

Bad news for the Poles, who found one of their major weapons, the speed of Lato and Gadocha, severely blunted by the clinging mud. Even so, they were by far the better team in the first half, and only a

---

* The German organizers had fed sixty years of German weather into a computer to pinpoint the driest three weeks of summer for the tournament. The result was a dismal failure, for it rained almost as much as it did during the sodden 1954 finals.

number of excellent saves by Sepp Maier in the German goal kept them out. Seven minutes after the interval, Jan Tomaszewski, the giant Polish goalkeeper, excelled himself by saving a penalty kick.

The save should have inspired the Poles. Instead it seemed to bring the Germans more into the game. With fifteen minutes left, Gerd Müller, inexplicably allowed to lurk unmarked on the edge of the area, snapped up a pass from Rainer Bonhof and beat Tomaszewski with a low shot into the corner for the only goal of the game. A desperately unlucky loss for Poland, the one team in the tournament that was always ready to attack wholeheartedly. By beating the indecisive Brazilians 1–0, Poland claimed third place in the tournament, but few would have begrudged them a place in the final.

After an enormous 1,500-member choir had sung "Tulips from Amsterdam" (for the Dutch) and a jazzed-up version of the Schiller/Beethoven "Ode to Joy" (for the Germans), after Henry Kissinger had taken his seat, after the playing of the national anthems, and after the referee had noticed that the punctilious German organizers had forgotten to put up the corner flags, the tenth World Cup final got under way.

The Dutch kicked off, and passed the ball methodically among themselves while the Germans held off; Cruyff, bored by such dithering, came back to collect the ball, surged into the German penalty area, and was blatantly tripped up by Vogts. Penalty kick to the Netherlands, a mere eighty seconds after the start. The Dutch had made sixteen passes, and not one German had as much as gotten a foot on the ball. Johan Neeskens scored from the penalty (the first ever to be awarded in a World Cup final), and the Dutch were ahead.

The advantage turned out to be another poisoned gift. Two things were now against the Dutch: tradition (in six previous finals the team scoring first had ended up as the loser) and the well-established fact that the Germans were at their best when fighting back.

Throughout the first half the early goal hung like a lead weight around the Dutch players. They failed to press home their advantage. Indeed, they started to play conservatively, protecting their one-goal lead. An approach totally at odds with their normal swashbuckling style. Inevitably, the Germans forced their way back into the game. After half an hour of hard physical play and mounting German pressure, the equalizer arrived through another penalty kick, though this one of much less obvious validity: Bernd Holzenbein, running the ball into the Dutch penalty area, appeared to drag his foot into Wim Jansen's admittedly late tackle. Paul Breitner scored to tie the game.

The Germans stepped up their attacks. Berti Vogts broke through, shot hard and true, to be thwarted by a lightning-quick one-handed reaction from Dutch goalkeeper Jan Jongbloed. Six minutes later, after Jongbloed had punched an insidious Beckenbauer free kick over the bar, it was the Netherlands that should have scored. Catching the Germans upfield, Cruyff and Johnny Rep broke free. Cruyff drew Beckenbauer and pushed the ball through to Rep with only goalkeeper Maier to beat. Rep hurried his shot and banged the ball against the desperately lunging Maier.

Three minutes before halftime Bonhof raced away on the right, the Dutch defenders were slow to cover, and his center reached Müller in the area. Müller seemed, for a moment, to overrun the ball, then turned quickly to shoot right-footed along the ground past Jongbloed to make the score 2–1. A typical Müller goal, not struck particularly hard, but perfectly timed and placed.

Try as they might—and they swarmed around the German goal for most of the second half—the Dutch could not score again. They came close, but Maier was equal to everything. When he did make a mistake, Breitner was there to head the ball off the line. As time ran out, the Dutch attacks became frenetic and anxious, and Cruyff, strangely, seemed content to hang back in midfield. The second-half statistics, which showed Germany with just one shot at the Dutch goal, bore out Cruyff's bitter lament: "Germany didn't win the World Cup. We lost it." But the Germans had survived everything that the Dutch could throw at them, and they were the new world champions.

CHAPTER 4

The World Cup, 1978-1990*

The 1974 World Cup had marked the end of Sir Stanley Rous's thirteen-year reign as FIFA president. FIFA's full membership had to vote twice, but on the second ballot he was beaten 66–52 by the Brazilian millionaire João Havelange.

For Havelange, this was the reward for a two-year campaign in which he had assiduously courted the votes of the growing number of African and Asian countries. For the European powers it was a shock to realize how easily they could be outvoted, to know that the vote of Lesotho or Nepal was now equal to that of England or West Germany.

For the first time, a non-European was in charge of FIFA, elected by non-European votes—and the Europeans were not sure that they liked it. There was talk of Europe seceding from FIFA to set up their own international body.

Havelange's promise to the Third World countries had been that he would increase the number of places available to them in future World Cups. This meant increasing the number of finalists—it was supposed to go up to twenty in 1978, then on to twenty-four in 1982.

Where Rous had been a soccer referee and an administrator, Havelange had played Olympic water polo, and came from a business background. He was to bring some very different attitudes to FIFA.

---

* For tabulated scores of all tournament games, see pages 282–91. For tactical analyses of World Cups, see Chapter 6, page 149.

Argentina, 1978

In 1978 it was back to Latin America for the World Cup road show, but not quite as intended. The tournament had been awarded to Argentina in 1966. The Peronists had assumed power in 1973 and taken over the organization of the World Cup, believing—just as Mussolini and the Italian Fascists had believed in 1934—that it would bolster their popularity.

The theory was never put to the test—at least not by the Peronists. In 1976 the roof fell in on their government. The country was approaching anarchy. Left-wing guerrillas, the Montoneros, were operating openly, carrying out daring raids and kidnappings in the streets. The armed forces seized power, and "the generals" took over the country.

A brutal war against the guerrillas followed. Many people—particularly in Europe—felt that the World Cup should be taken away from Argentina, that it should not be staged under a repressive military regime. FIFA turned a blind eye, and the new government was quick to announce that the tournament, Mundial-78, would go on. For the generals, the World Cup filled the same bread-and-circuses role that it would have done for the banished Peronists.

General Omar Actis was appointed to head the preparations. Driving to his first press conference, he was assassinated in a Buenos Aires street by the Montoneros. But within a year, the generals had gained the upper hand.

It was not pretty. In the Plaza de Mayo, a growing group of brave middle-aged mothers started to gather regularly to protest the disappearance of their sons and daughters—the *desaparecidos*, taken away by the government's secret police, most of them never to be seen again.

But the Montoneros were reeling. They issued a famous statement, vowing that they had never intended to disrupt the World Cup, because *estamos hombres y mujeres del pueblo*, we are men and women of the people.

A captain from the navy, Carlos Alberto Lacoste took over the running of the World Cup, complaining that between 1973 and 1976 "the Peronists talked but did nothing. We are replacing their paper with real things, with buildings and stadiums. Under the Peronists you had 3 days of work and 362 days of strikes. Today there are no strikes. We have banned them."

Havelange's vow to increase the number of finalists was not acted on. It remained at sixteen. Three new stadiums were built, three others were renovated. It was claimed that some $200 million was being spent on permanent improvements to roads, railroads, airports, and communications systems. Color television was introduced for the first time in Argentina, but only in the press centers for the 4,500 journalists covering the event.

Beyond the control of the generals were the qualifying round results. Uruguay was ousted by Peru. A big financial blow. The hordes of Uruguayans who had been expected to make the short ferry trip across the Rio de la Plata in search of tickets would not now be coming. England didn't make it either, but the other former World Cup winners did: Italy, West Germany, and Brazil.

World Cup tradition showed that when a major world soccer power staged the tournament, it won: Uruguay in 1930, Italy in 1934, England in 1966, West Germany in 1974. Only Brazil in 1950 had failed. So if Argentina was a world soccer power, as everyone surely believed, then it should win.

But could it? For all the great players it had produced, Argentina had always flopped in the World Cup. Skepticism among Argentine fans was widespread. It increased when the tournament draw—usually so kind to the host team—placed Argentina into an ominously strong first-round group along with Hungary, France, and Italy.

The man appointed to lead Argentina to glory was César Luis Menotti, coach of the national team. Tall, thin, long-haired, a constant smoker, Menotti had been at work since 1973. Immediately, he had to confront the perennial problem: So many of Argentina's best players were with European clubs. Menotti knew he could not build a team on such players, who were rarely available to him. He declared that his team would consist mainly of home-based players.

It was a decision that, incredibly, led to his toughest battle: to convince the administrators of Argentine soccer to take its own national team seriously. This meant getting full cooperation from club teams in releasing players for training camps and games—cooperation that had never been willingly given in the past.

Menotti, a determined man who knew exactly what he wanted, got his way. But he had to fight off continual attacks on the style of his team. He wanted players with exceptional ball skills—the traditional Argentine skills, as he saw them. His critics insisted that a more vigorous, more physical approach was needed for the World Cup, and mocked his style as *fulbito*, little football.

The start of Mundial-78 was not promising. West Germany and Poland, first- and third-place finishers in 1974, produced what was (and hopefully will remain) the worst opening game ever. Two teams unwilling to take the slightest risk, content to play for a massively boring tactical tie.

Much more was expected from Germany, despite the loss of two key players from its 1974 side: goal scorer Gerd Müller, and captain Franz Beckenbauer. In 1977, at the peak of his game—he had just been voted the 1976 European player of the year—Beckenbauer had stunned the soccer world by signing for the New York Cosmos, and then announcing that he would not play in Mundial-78. But coach Helmut Schoen had a new crop of promising youngsters, including the smoothly skilled twenty-two-year-old midfielder, Karl Heinz Rummenigge.

Poland had the look of a spent force, a bland team with only the lively young Zbigniew Boniek promising anything out of the ordinary.

The Scots arrived bursting with totally misplaced confidence. Despite losing their last warm-up game to England, they were given a rousing send-off from Glasgow by delirious crowds lining the route to the airport. Evidently convinced of his team's superiority, coach Ally MacLeod didn't bother to scout his first opponent, Peru. So the Peruvians ran them ragged and beat them 3–1.

MacLeod said he was surprised at the speed of the Peruvians. He got another shock the following day when winger Willy Johnston became the second player in World Cup history to fail a drug test. He was banned and sent home in disgrace, guilty of taking the pep pill fencamfamin before the 3–1 loss to Peru ("the sort of performance that gives pep pills a bad name" remarked a Scottish fan).

The Scots were even worse in their next game. Their goal in a 1–1 tie with a weak Iran team came when Iranian defender Andranik Eskandarian (soon to join Beckenbauer at the New York Cosmos) put through his own goal. But the tie kept Scotland's hopes of a place in the next round alive. Just. It would need to beat the Netherlands— one of the tournament favorites—by a margin of three goals. Could the Scots score three times against the Netherlands? Jan Jongbloed, now the reserve goalkeeper for the Dutch, pondered the matter and replied "Yes . . . but not in one game."

With all the perverseness that has characterized Scotland's fruitless World Cup adventures over the years, the three goals were duly scored. One of them, a corkscrew dribble and rasping shot from little

Archie Gemmill, was rated one of the best goals of the tournament. But the Netherlands scored twice, so Scotland's famous 3–2 victory was to no avail.

The Dutch went on the second round. They, like the Germans, were without their inspirational figure from 1974: Johan Cruyff, like Beckenbauer, had opted not to play. Without Cruyff, the Dutch total soccer was a less intelligent style, relying more on sheer athletic ability than soccer artistry. The typical player was now Johan Neeskens, the combative, nonstop midfielder. Neeskens certainly had his share of soccer skills, but he was a totally different type of player than the subtle, inventive Cruyff. Coach Rinus Michels had been replaced by the Austrian Ernst Happel, who liked to pack his midfield with five or even six players.

Brazil had changed its coach, too. New man Claudio Coutinho came from a physical education background. Cultured, multilingual, Coutinho brought an excess of theory to the largely instinctive Brazilian game. When he stressed the need for "polyvalent" players, some of his team members had no idea what he was talking about. More damaging was Coutinho's continuance of a trend that had been seen in 1974: the swing toward a more physical, more "European" approach. A policy that meant only sporadic playing time for two of his more skilled players, Zico and Rivelino.

Playing in the seaside town of Mar del Plata, Brazil cut a sorry figure in the first round. It tied Sweden 1–1 in a game that it might have won but for a moment of absurdly fastidious refereeing from Welshman Clive Thomas. In the game's final seconds, Brazil took a corner kick and Zico leaped to head what looked like the winning goal. No, said Thomas, no goal, the game is over. He had blown the final whistle while the ball was in the air, just before it reached Zico.

If luck was against Brazil in that game, it favored them abundantly against Spain. With the score still tied at 0–0 late in the second half, the Brazilian goalkeeper Leao came out of his goal to intercept a cross. He missed the ball, which went through to the Spanish forward Julio Cardenosa, unmarked, some 8 yards in front of the now empty goal. As the crowd roared Goal! for this simplest of scoring chances, Cardenosa froze. He delayed his shot for what seemed an eternity, as the Brazilian defenders scrambled back to cover. Cardenosa's shot, when it did finally come, was weak. Defender Amaral cleared the ball off the goal line, and Brazil escaped with another tie.

An unconvincing 1–0 win over Austria was enough to get Brazil into the second round. But the Brazilian fans were not happy with a team that had scored only two goals in three games. They burned an effigy of coach Coutinho in the streets of Mar del Plata.

Brazil's second-round group would include Poland and the other two remaining Latin American teams, Peru and Argentina. It had been tough going for Argentina. A 2–1 win over the skilled but violent Hungarians was followed by a questionable win over France. The French had played delightful soccer in their first game before losing 2–1 to Italy. They were to play equally well against Argentina, particularly their new playmaker Michel Platini and their sweeper Marius Tresor.

Argentina struggled until, right on halftime, they got a break from the Swiss referee. The sort of break, said the cynics, that the host nation will always get. Leopoldo Luque, Argentina's big, direct center forward got behind the French defense. As he tried to left-foot the ball low across the area, Tresor slid desperately in. The ball struck Tresor's hand as he was falling. Penalty to Argentina, said the referee.

That Tresor had handled the ball as he fell was not in doubt, nor was the fact that this had stopped the ball going through to Argentina's René Houseman, waiting in front of goal. But the rules say the offense has to be *intentional*. That was very doubtful.

Captain Daniel Passarella scored from the kick. Platini tied the game for France fifteen minutes into the second half, before Luque's screaming twenty-five-yard volley won it for Argentina. The win assured Argentina's passage to the second round. Which was just as well, for the Argentines lost their next game 1–0 to the increasingly confident Italians.

Coach Enzo Bearzot's team looked excitingly capable of accomplishing his aim: a more positive look for Italian soccer, an end to the defensive negativity of the *catenaccio* system* that had dominated Italian soccer since the early 1960s. Italy had fought back to win after the French had scored the quickest goal of the tournament in just thirty-eight seconds. It had outclassed the Hungarians by a 3–1 score. Now the Argentines were dispatched with comparative ease.

Paolo Rossi—Pablito the Argentines called him, a nickname that stuck with Rossi for the rest of his career—may have been lightly built for a center forward, but his quickness and touch were a delight to watch. And he had scored two goals.

* See Chapter 6, page 175.

Then just as the praise was piling up, the Italians lost their way. In the second round the familiar caution returned. A 0–0 tie with Germany, and a 1–0 win over Austria (goal by Rossi) were followed by a 2–1 loss to the Netherlands. Good enough only to get them to the third-place game. It was the Dutch, winners of the group, who went on to the final.

Deservedly so. Without the brilliance of the team that had been dubbed the Clockwork Orange in 1974, the Dutch were nevertheless playing exhilarating soccer. After annihilating Austria 5–1, they moved on to play the Germans and to seek revenge for defeat in the 1974 final. They had to be satisfied with a 2–2 tie. The Germans were then beaten 3–2 by Austria in coach Schoen's last World Cup game. Schoen went home an embittered man, claiming he felt let down by his younger players.

The Dutch marched on to victory over Italy in Buenos Aires—an eventful afternoon for the young Dutch fullback Erny Brandts. After eighteen minutes, attempting to clear an Italian attack, he visited a double disaster on his own team. He collided violently with goalkeeper Peter Schrijvers and, at the same moment, rocketed the ball into his own net to give the Italians a 1–0 lead. Schrijvers was stretchered off and Jongbloed, veteran of the 1974 team, came on.

All was forgiven four minutes into the second half when Brandts, from twenty-five yards out, thumped an unstoppable drive past Dino Zoff in the Italian goal. The game was decided twenty-five minutes later when Arie Haan ripped another long-range drive past Zoff—this one from thirty yards.

That same evening Argentina crushed Peru 6–0 in Rosario, thus edging out Brazil on goal difference for the right to oppose the Dutch in the final. Brazil and Argentina had both beaten Poland, and had then played each other to a bad-tempered 0–0 stand-off. But Brazil's 3–0 win over Peru put the pressure on Argentina. They had to beat the Peruvians by a margin of four goals.

A tricky situation because Peru, with two losses, was already out of contention. Was it to be expected that they would offer much resistance? The rumors flew in the Argentine press: Brazilian "representatives" had been seen at the Peruvians' hotel with suitcases full of dollars; Brazilian businessmen were offering the Peruvian players plots of land to hold off the Argentines.

The Brazilians certainly did point out that Ramon Quiroga, the Peruvians' erratic goalkeeper, had been born in Argentina. In

Rosario, in fact. Would *he* want to go down as the man who kept Argentina out of the final?

As Argentina piled up its 6–0 win, the crowd in Rosario chanted *Llora Brasil, llora!*—weep Brazil, weep! If they didn't weep, the Brazilians certainly raised a howl of protest, accusing the Peruvians of, at best, not trying. Said Coutinho, "This game will go down in soccer history as the Game of Shame."

Brazil partially redeemed itself with a 2–1 win over Italy in the game for third place. Poor Zoff—yet again he was beaten by a long-range shot, but this one bordered on the incredible. Brazilian fullback Nelinho, some forty yards out on the right flank, started to dribble the ball in toward the goalmouth, then let fly with the outside of his right foot. The ball, hit very hard, appeared to be going harmlessly wide of the left goal post . . . but as Zoff moved across, the ball seemed to take a sudden vicious curve, hooking past his right shoulder and into the goal, just inside the post. Brazil thus went home unbeaten, with Coutinho claiming that it was the "moral champion," a phrase that didn't interest the Brazilian fans. They wanted to be champion, period. Coutinho lost his job.

By now, the atmosphere throughout Argentina was electric. The progress of Menotti's team to the final had been followed first with disbelief, now with almost feverish passion. Each Argentine victory had brought the crowds pouring onto the streets of Buenos Aires, celebrating long into the night as though they feared this would be the last chance to make merry. But the victories went on and the crowds got larger and larger.

Each time Argentina took the field, the stadium exploded into a cauldron of noise, a sea of waving blue-and-white Argentine flags, a shower of streamers, and a whirling blizzard of *papelitos*, the confetti that every fan brought with him.

The spectacle was awesome, and Menotti's players responded with nonstop attacking soccer. They seemed to be driven forward by the crowd, a risk-taking team that played with three genuine forwards— Luque, Oscar Ortiz, and Daniel Bertoni—a team that was always looking for goals. Only Luis Galvan played a determinedly defensive role; the other three fullbacks—Alberto Tarantini, Jorge Olguin, and captain Daniel Passarella—were ever eager to join in attacking moves.

In midfield the neat, tireless, little Ossie Ardiles kept the ball moving forward with a string of intelligent passes. Alongside him was the left-footed Mario Kempes, the only foreign-based player on the team.

Part midfielder, part forward, Kempes had been scoreless in the early games, but exploded for four goals in the second round, and was emerging as the tournament's outstanding player.

The final at Buenos Aires' River Plate Stadium got off to a sour start. Blatant gamesmanship by Argentina. The Dutch were on the field at 2:50. Alone. They had to wait four minutes before the storm of *papelitos* signaled the arrival of the Argentines, who promptly objected to a plaster cast worn on his arm by the Dutchman René Van der Kerkhof. A further delay of nine minutes while Van der Kerkhof left the field to have the cast wrapped in a bandage.

If the Argentine idea was to unsettle the Dutch, then—rather surprisingly—it worked. In the first minute of play Jan Poortvliet viciously tripped Bertoni from behind, and seconds later Haan clobbered Ardiles. Referee Sergio Gonella from Italy gave the free kicks, but no yellow cards. Gonella's leniency was duly noted by both teams, and a foul-ridden game inevitably followed.

But if there were too many fouls, there was also plenty of pulsating excitement. How could it be otherwise, with two attacking teams, each likely to leave alarming gaps in its defense? At both ends, the goalkeepers found themselves forced to make heroic saves. For Argentina Ubaldo Fillol saved brilliantly from Johnny Rep then, just before the break, instinctively used his feet to keep out a shot from Robby Rensenbrink.

Jongbloed had to save twice from Passarella, whose forward incursions were a serious menace. But it was Kempes who drew first blood with two telling left-foot touches, darting between two defenders to collect Luque's pass at the edge of the box, and slipping the ball under Jongbloed as he came out.

The 1–0 scoreline stood up for most of the second half, though it was a nail-biting time for the Argentine fans as the Dutch fought desperately for the equalizing goal. It came with only eight minutes left. The Argentine offside trap broke down, René Van der Kerkhof had space and time for a precise cross, and Dirk Nanninga headed home. With only seconds left, the Dutch had their moment. A long ball from Ruud Krol put Rensenbrink through; his shot beat Fillol, but hit the post.

At 1–1, the game went to overtime, and the Argentines took over. After fourteen minutes it was Kempes again, with that uncanny ability to spot an opening in the Dutch defense. This time it took four left-foot touches, as the ball bounced off Jongbloed, but Kempes got to the rebound first to put Argentina 2–1 up.

With four minutes left, the rampant Kempes again bamboozled the

Dutch defenders with a powerful dribble into the penalty area to set up Bertoni for the final goal.

The host country had won again. The Menotti miracle was complete. The generals, led by President Jorge Videla, were at the game to see Argentina triumph. Of course, they—like the Peronists—had been right. Soccer had brought the country joy. The incredible scenes in Buenos Aires that night proved the point. Streets jammed solid with hundreds of thousands of men, women, children, singing and cheering, dancing if they could find space, as wave after wave of *papelitos* drifted down from the windows of apartment buildings.

A moment of release for an entire people. After decades of frustration—years that had seen their neighbors and rivals Brazil and Uruguay carry off five World Cups between them—Argentina's long-awaited ascent to soccer supremacy had arrived. For a short while, soccer was more important than anything. But the shadow of the Plaza mothers, with their simple, anxious faces, was not something that could be forgotten. The full horrors of the *desaparecidos* and the dirty war waged by the junta would emerge later.

Spain, 1982

España-82 was touted as the biggest and best World Cup ever. The biggest it certainly was, with twenty-four teams in the final tournament instead of sixteen. This was what FIFA president João Havelange had promised during his election campaign in 1974 in return for votes from Third World countries.

Africa now got two slots, instead of one, as did Asia/Oceania and CONCACAF (the North and Central America and Caribbean region that includes the United States). South America went up from three to four teams. European opposition to the plan had died down—after all, Europe, with four more places, was the biggest gainer.

The additional slot for CONCACAF countries was enticing news for the United States. The region had always been dominated by Mexico, which had repeatedly won the single slot available in the finals. It had been so in 1954, 1958, 1962, 1966, and 1970. Haiti had pulled an upset in 1974, but Mexico was back in 1978.

But the United States failed at the first hurdle, and was quickly eliminated after finishing last in a three-team preliminary group with Canada and Mexico. By the time the qualifiers were over, Mexico was out, too. To the amazement of all, it was Honduras and El Salvador that went to Spain.

The biggest shock was the elimination of the Netherlands, runners-up in the last two tournaments.

Elsewhere, the regional qualifying system operated as erratically and unfairly as ever. Chile booked its place in Spain by playing just four games, while New Zealand had to play fifteen games. Altogether, between March 1980 and December 1981, 319 games were played, involving 106 countries.

From the start, España-82 was an ill-defined tournament. Spread throughout the length and breadth of Spain—its fifty-two games were played in fourteen different cities—it lacked an obvious center of attention. It was also a tournament without a clear favorite. Spain found itself rated among the top teams, but this had more to do with its position as host nation than any obvious playing strengths. Coached by former Real Madrid star José Santamaria (a naturalized Uruguayan), Spain had a solid goalkeeper in Luis Arconada, and a powerful defender in José Camacho. But its offense depended too heavily on the occasionally brilliant but invariably inconsistent midfielder, Zamora.

France looked a more likely champion. The team was now built around Platini, who had matured into Europe's top player. As midfield partners he had Alain Giresse and Jean Tigana, both small but immensely skilled players. Presiding majestically over the defense from his sweeper position was Marius Tresor from the tiny Caribbean island of Guadeloupe—a French *département*.

The French had acquired a nickname—the Brazilians of Europe—a tribute to their skillful, artistic style. Weighing against them was a long tradition of failure. No French team, national or club, had ever won a major title.

The West Germans, as always, had to be taken seriously. Under new coach Jupp Derwall, they had won the European title in 1980. But a knee injury had ruled out the star of that team, Bernd Schuster. Paul Breitner, whose penalty kick goal had helped Germany to win the 1974 World Cup was back, Rummenigge had just been voted European Player of the Year, and there was an exciting twenty-one-year-old winger, Pierre Littbarski. But it was the huge, surprisingly mobile defender Hans-Peter Briegel who personified the German threat: strength and stamina. For good measure, they were said to be using a new drink called MS-61, based on ginseng and "biocatalysts," that was marvelous for fighting off tiredness.

Defensively, the Italians looked as good as ever. Sweeper Scirea was the best in his position; Fulvio Collovati and Antonio Cabrini were talented, intelligent defenders in the best Italian tradition. Giancarlo Antognoni ran the midfield in his elegant, rangy style, but there were problems up front.

Goals were hard to come by. In its final qualifying game, Italy had managed to score only one goal against the feeble Luxembourg! Coach Bearzot recalled Paolo Rossi—a daring and risky move. Things had not gone well for Rossi since he starred as Pablito in Argentina four years earlier. He had not played competitive soccer for nearly two years because of a suspension for his part in a game-fixing scandal. The suspension ended on April 29, less than two months before the start of España-82. Could that possibly be enough time for him to return to match fitness?

Brazil's team had undergone a revolution since Coutinho's "moral champions" of 1978. The new coach, Tele Santana, had a philosophy far removed from Coutinho's theories and tactics. For Tele, the players came first. He gathered in the stars of Brazilian soccer and, as one Brazilian newspaper put it, happiness returned to the game. Key players were Zico, who had proved such a problem for Coutinho, and Falcao, whom Coutinho had not even chosen. Add to them two scrawny midfielders—lanky Socrates, a medical doctor, and the elusive Toninho Cerezo. Plus the powerful Junior with his violently swerving free kicks. Less convincing was the forward line, normally the Brazilians' greatest strength.

Argentina-82 looked very much like Argentina-78. Menotti was still in charge. Only Luque and Ortiz were missing from the championship team, but the average age of the nine returning players, 29, suggested that this was a team in decline.

Among all those veterans there was the precocious, youthful talent of Argentina's new star, the twenty-one-year-old Diego Maradona. A member of Menotti's original 1978 squad, he had been the last player to be cut. "He is strong, he has talent . . . his time will come," Menotti had said. Maradona had left the training camp in tears, a bitterly disappointed seventeen-year-old boy.

His time had arrived. The powerful, stocky little left-footer was being hailed as the new world superstar—evidently an opinion endorsed by the Spanish club Barcelona, which paid a world record $8.8 million to sign him just before the tournament. Despite the record total of twenty-four teams, it seemed almost certain that the new winner would be one of the previous champions: Italy, West Germany, Brazil, or Argentina. England, another ex-winner, was not given a chance. Always difficult to beat at Wembley, England had proved time and again that it did not do well on foreign soil.

There was one other team to be considered, one that nobody paid much attention to at the time. The referees. The Men in Black. Forty-one referees from as many different countries, from Hong Kong to Libya, from Australia to Bolivia. They were to have a determining role in España-82.

A new regulation was on the books. If either semifinal was still tied after overtime, the winner would be decided by a penalty-kick shoot-out.*

The Spanish organizers displayed the worst and the best of taste. For a mascot they chose an orange, gave it arms and legs and an idiot grin and called it *Naranjito*. Laughable kitsch, happily balanced by the superb official poster, a boisterous riot of color and excitement, painted by an 82-year-old soccer fan, artist Joan Miró.

The good taste extended to the opening ceremony in Barcelona, where hundreds of white-clad athletes crouched on the rich green grass of the Nou Camp stadium to form a huge, shimmering Picasso dove of peace. A young boy, dressed in the red and blue of Spain's team, walked to the center of the field and released a real dove. The bird opted for safety rather than freedom. It flew into the stands, and perched under the roof, indignantly straightening its feathers.

Nothing even remotely as beautiful as the Picasso dove was seen in the opening game that followed: Argentina vs. Belgium. The Belgians packed their defense and tackled heavily and dangerously. Maradona was hacked down from behind and muscled off the ball, and referee Vojtech Christov smiled benignly on everything. An advance warning. Worse was on its way.

Argentina had no answer to Belgium's cynical tactics. But at least the opening game, for the first time since 1962, featured a goal. Just one. Belgium got it, in the second half. Not a happy World Cup debut for Maradona in the stadium that would be his new home after the tournament.

Six four-team groups was the new format. Down in Sevilla the Brazilians fired things up. They beat the USSR 2–1, and the word

---

* In which five players from each team alternate in taking one-on-one shots from the twelve-yard penalty spot against the opposing goalkeeper. If the shoot-out score is still tied after the ten shots, then the shoot-out goes into its sudden-death phase, in which the kicks are taken in pairs. All eleven players from each team who were on the field at the end of the game must take kicks in rotation.

went around that the *real* Brazil, the joyful attacking Brazil, was back. The Soviets kept quiet for a couple of days, then bitterly criticized the Spanish referee Augusto Lamo Castillo for denying them two penalty kicks. They had a point.

But the Brazilians were rolling. Poor Scotland was taken apart, out-classed, by a 4–1 score, goals from Zico, Falcao, Eder, and defender Oscar. Zico got two more, along with one each from Falcao and Serginho, in a 4–0 rout of New Zealand, and Brazil had established themselves as the favorites.

Spain started dismally. Little Honduras gave the Spaniards the fright of their lives, leading by 1–0 for much of the game, until Spain leveled matters—on a penalty kick.* The tremendous pressure from their fans and from the press was clearly unsettling the Spanish play-ers. Against Yugoslavia, they again gave up an early goal. They were rescued from further trouble when the Danish referee awarded them a penalty kick, though it was clear (as was amply confirmed by televi-sion replays) that the Yugoslav foul had been committed outside the penalty area.

Even so, the Spanish needed more help. Roberto Lopez Ufarte smashed his penalty kick wide of the goal. Retake, said the referee, indicating that the Yugoslav goalkeeper had moved. This time Lopez Ufarte made no mistake. A late goal from Saura gave Spain its only win of the tournament.

In the last of its first-round games, Spain lost 1–0 to unfancied Northern Ireland in Valencia. In their lineup, the Irish included Nor-man Whiteside—at 17 years and 41 days the youngest player ever to appear in the World Cup finals (Pelé had played in the 1958 tourna-ment at 17 years and 235 days).

Spain had done enough to squeak into the next round, but it was glar-ingly obvious that not much more could be expected from this team.

All in all, the so-called weak teams did quite well. El Salvador was the only one that played like a weak team, going down 10–1 to Hun-gary and setting a new World Cup record for goals-against in one game. Cameroon tied all three of its first-round games and delighted the Spanish fans with its fast-moving, athletic style. Algeria provided a major shock, with a 2–1 victory over the Germans.

The Kuwaitis arrived with an unusually large mascot: a real live camel. It was said they had somehow wangled a press accreditation

---

* Playing at center forward for Honduras, and playing extremely well, was Armando Betancourt, former Indiana University star, who had won the 1981 Hermann Trophy for college player of the year.

for it—a story that was good for many cynical remarks about the profession of journalism but which turned out not to be true.

In its first game, Kuwait, coached by the Brazilian Carlos Alberto Parreira, very nearly beat the Czechs, but had to settle for a 1–1 tie. The Kuwait-France game in Valladolid will long stick in the memory for the extraordinary goings-on in the second half.

The French were totally in command, already leading by 3–0, when Giresse ran through the Kuwaiti defense to score a fourth. Not so fast, there. The Kuwaitis protested vigorously to the Russian referee Miroslav Stupar that they had heard him blow his whistle for offside. He denied it. The Kuwaitis persisted. They had heard a whistle from *somewhere*, so they had stopped playing.

Confusion reigned. The Kuwaitis kept looking up to the stands, where the president of the Kuwaiti Soccer Federation, Sheik Fahed was sitting. Not sitting for very long, though. He rose to his feet and headed down to the field, his robes billowing majestically behind him.

Even the formidably unbending Spanish police quailed before the withering royal gaze, and the prince was allowed to sweep sternly onto the field to confront the referee. Incredibly, Stupar gave way, and the goal was annulled.*

The French then protested, to no avail. The field was cleared, the game restarted, and the French scored a fourth goal anyway.

From dark humor in Valladolid, to just plain disgraceful darkness in Gijon. In the final game of their group, which also included the surprising Algerians, West Germany met Austria. Both teams were well aware of the situation. A 1–0 win for Germany would allow the Germans and the Austrians to go to the second round, at the expense of Algeria. A bigger win for Germany, a tie, or a win for Austria would let Algeria in.

The Germans went ahead 1–0 after ten minutes, and then the farce began. Neither team made any further serious attempt to score, or even to play. As the crowd of over 40,000 whistled and chanted Algeria! Algeria!, Germans and Austrians, cozy Teutonic brothers for an afternoon, disgraced the sport of soccer for eighty minutes.

It was a contemptible performance. Algeria protested, requesting that both Germany and Austria be thrown out for violating the spirit of the tournament. Regrettably, FIFA rejected the protest. It was Algeria that was out.

The new second-round format had the twelve remaining teams

* In August 1990, Sheik Fahed—by then a vice president of FIFA—was one of the first people to be killed during the Iraqi invasion of Kuwait.

divided into four groups of three teams. The group winners would go
to the semifinals. West Germany disposed of England and Spain without much trouble. The Germans would meet the French, who were
looking better and better. Now, the talk was of a "dream final"
between France and Brazil. It looked increasingly likely.

Poland won its group, beating Belgium 3–0, and tying the USSR
0–0. Banners supporting the banned Polish union Solidarity appeared
in the crowd during the Poland vs. USSR game, but they were
removed by the police. Eliminating the USSR seemed to give the
Poles more satisfaction than advancing to the semifinal.

Barcelona got the cream of the second-round action with a group
containing Italy, Brazil, and Argentina. The teams were loaded with
talent, but the refereeing, alas, was to be quite horrendous.

Italy had scraped into the second round on the strength of three
ties with Poland, Cameroon, and Peru. It had scored but two goals.
The players, incensed at the vitriolic criticism in the Italian press,
were refusing to talk to journalists. They would chat about the weather, or politics, perhaps, but not about soccer. "Speak to the captain,"
they said. A joke, for captain Dino Zoff was known as the most taci-
turn of men.

The Italians beat Argentina 2–1, but it was a distorted game.
Defender Claudio Gentile's task was to mark Maradona. This he did
with sustained ferocity: ninety minutes of holding, tripping, obstructing, shirt-pulling, elbowing, and kicking. Referee Nicolae Rainea from
Romania saw nothing wrong. After one particularly brutal foul,
Rainea did at last get out the yellow card—but it was Maradona who
got it, for protesting! Gentile got a yellow later, but went on fouling
anyway. With six minutes left in the game, Rainea finally discovered
his red card. It want to Americo Gallego, of Argentina.

After the game, a stony-faced Menotti sardonically asked the press:
"I believe there is a rule that a player who fouls repeatedly must be
ejected, no?" A rule that Rainea blatantly ignored. There had been
ample reason to expel Gentile even before halftime.

Barcelona seemed to be taken over by Brazilian fans, singing and
dancing their sambas in the streets, unfurling their vast banners
and flags in the stadiums. Their team was playing brilliant soccer, and
Argentina was simply swept aside 3–1. Maradona, unable to make any
impression on the game, finally gave vent to his frustration and
viciously kicked Batista. He was ordered off, rightly so. But it was a
sad moment to watch such a talented young player take his leave of

the 1982 World Cup in a slow, solo walk to the bench, his head down, his eyes seeing nothing.

The final game in the group, Brazil vs. Italy, would decide who went through to the semifinal. For Brazil, a tie would be good enough. Italy had to win. Had Gentile been red-carded, as he so thoroughly deserved to be, against Argentina, he would have been under suspension, unable to play. But Gentile would play, and everyone knew that he would mark Zico. The full effects of Rainea's disastrous refereeing were still to be felt.

For Bearzot the problem was this: He had gone with Rossi in every game so far, but Pablito was not playing well and had yet to score a goal. After much agonizing, Bearzot decided to give him one more chance.

The referee was Abraham Klein of Israel who, for all his officious strutting about, was only marginally better than Rainea had been. Gentile was yellow-carded and then allowed to take up against Zico where he had left off against Maradona. At one point, Zico ran up to Klein to show him the huge hole in his shirt, which Gentile had just nearly ripped off his back. Klein was not interested.

Suddenly, miraculously, Rossi regained his scoring touch. His three beautifully taken goals steered Italy to a 3–2 win. The Italians had found their center forward. The Brazilians never did find theirs. With Reinaldo, Roberto, and Careca all ruled out by injury, Serginho was their fourth choice. He had a nightmare game against Italy, squandering three golden chances to see Brazil safely through.

Now the Italian press was full of praise, delighted at a rare win over Brazil. "We are the real Brazilians!" screamed a headline over a story claiming that Italy had outdone Brazil at its own game of skillful soccer.

The Italians played well, no doubt about that. But, more than anything, they could thank the referees Rainea and Klein for their success. Complacent refereeing had destroyed half of the dream final. Down in Seville, in the France vs. West Germany semifinal, refereeing of almost unimaginable ineptitude finished off the other half.

A game of immense drama. The Germans were playing without their star and captain, Rummenigge—still, apparently, suffering from a mysterious muscle pull that had plagued him since the start of the tournament. Even so, they took an early lead through the dynamic little winger Littbarski. The French began to organize their swift-passing game as Platini took impressive charge of midfield. Within twenty minutes they were level. Rocheteau was brought down in the penalty area by Bernd Forster, and Platini hit the equalizer from the penalty spot.

In a pulsating, wide-open game both sides created numerous scoring opportunities, but neither could get the decisive goal. Jean-Luc Ettori, in the French goal, made a series of brave saves. But it was Toni Schumacher, Germany's arrogantly confident 'keeper, who struck the key blow. Ten minutes into the second half, the German defense was ripped open by a through ball that put Patrick Battiston in the clear. Schumacher came roaring out of his goal, made no attempt to play the ball, and simply wiped Battiston out—flattened him, with a massive body block and a forearm in the face.

Battiston, concussed and minus two teeth, stayed down. After three minutes he was stretchered off and taken to the hospital. As brutal a foul as one could imagine. Schumacher should have been ejected and France should have had a penalty kick, which would likely have settled the game. Yet referee Charles Corver, from the Netherlands, found everything okay. No foul, no penalty kick to France, no red card to Schumacher. Nothing.

The game went to overtime and France went ahead 3–1, which seemed to mean the end for Germany. But Corver had not yet finished. Rummenigge was now on the field and scored Germany's vital second goal after Corver had ignored not one, but two, German fouls in the buildup. Klaus Fischer tied it up at 3–3.

For the first time ever, a World Cup game would be decided on penalty kicks. The Germans won the shoot-out because of two saves by Schumacher, a player who should not have been on the field.

Germany were through to their fourth World Cup final. They would face Italy, who disposed of the Poles without any great exertion, by a 2–0 score, both goals coming from the reborn Rossi. Gentile sat this one out, but his absence was more than balanced by Poland having to play without their star and goal scorer, Boniek, also suspended.

Italy was the overwhelming favorite in the final. The Germans, after the contrived tie with Austria, after Schumacher's hideous foul, had few friends. THESE CHEATS MUST NOT WIN IT! was the day's headline in the London *Sun*.

Plus, there were solid soccer reasons for fancying Italy. It had played an easy semifinal, while the Germans had labored into overtime in the heat of Seville. Rummenigge was still in doubt—at the very moment that he was telling German television he was fit, coach Derwall was declaring that he would not start.

If that was a battle of wills, it was won by Rummenigge. He did start. But there was a key player missing from the Italian lineup. Antognoni, who had injured a foot against Poland. More trouble for the Italians after only seven minutes, when Wolfgang Dremmler's clattering tackle sent Francesco Graziani crashing to the ground. Off went Graziani, his collar bone dislocated, on came the lanky Alessandro Altobelli.

A moment of triumph for Italy came in the twenty-fifth minute with the award of a penalty kick after Briegel had pulled down Bruno Conti. But Cabrini made an awful mess of the kick, putting his shot wide of the goal. Yet, through all these setbacks, the Italians kept playing their steady, defensive game, with Scirea the cool, calculating mastermind.

The Germans did most of the attacking, but it was sterile stuff, and Zoff had little to trouble him in the Italian goal. No score at halftime, but it was clear that the German gamble of starting the unfit Rummenigge had failed. They had hoped for an early lead, and they hadn't got it.

Now, that draining semifinal began to take its toll. Rummenigge was substituted, and as the Germans tired, the Italians pushed forward. Rossi—who else?—opened the scoring, heading in a Gentile cross from close range. At the sixty-eighth minute the magnificent Scirea came forward, skillfully held the ball in the German penalty area as though he were a born attacker, then set up Marco Tardelli for goal number two. Altobelli added the third before Breitner scored for the Germans (and in so doing kept alive the tradition that no team has ever been shut out in the World Cup final).

The Italians were worthy winners. They had played with more spirit and more skill than the Germans, and they had joined Brazil as the only nation to win the trophy three times. But it was a poor, bleak final, full of fouls, short on artistry. As such, it reflected far too much of the soccer that had preceded it in the tournament. Mediocrity reigned. The little that had been outstandingly good had been sabotaged by scandalously bad refereeing.

Mexico, 1986

In line with its plan of alternating Europe and Latin America as World Cup sites, FIFA had, in 1974, designated Colombia as host country for the 1986 tournament. It seemed a precarious decision. The World Cup was becoming ever more expensive to stage, an event that required not only top class stadiums, hotels, and airports but also highly sophisticated communications systems.

Possibly Colombia could have handled a sixteen-team World Cup, as the original agreement had envisaged. But FIFA itself undermined that when, in 1982, it increased the number of finalists to twenty-four. The Colombians held out until January of 1983, when they reluctantly admitted that they couldn't handle it.

With just three and a half years to go before the 1986 tournament, FIFA needed a new host country—quickly. It solicited bids, and Brazil, Mexico, Canada, and the United States spoke up. The United States took its bid very seriously, even to the point of flying Pelé, Beckenbauer, and Henry Kissinger to Sweden to address the decisive FIFA meeting in May.

FIFA made out that it was offended by all this pressure. It gave the tournament to Mexico. The Americans were convinced that FIFA had already struck a deal with the Mexicans, and that the bid process was a charade. There was talk of suing FIFA. Nothing came of it.

FIFA did have a deal. Not with the Mexican Soccer Federation or the Mexican government, but with the private television company Televisa, and its immensely rich owner Emilio Azcarraga. One of Azcarraga's top executives was Guillermo Cañedo, who also happened to be a FIFA vice president, and chairman of its World Cup Organizing Committee.

Azcarraga, through Televisa, was able to give FIFA—quickly—the financial guarantees that it had to have. So Mexico, hosts in 1970, became the first country to stage two World Cups. That earlier experience was of immense value, and Mexico already had eleven modern stadiums. It needed to build only one new one, at Queretaro.

Fear of the debilitating effects of heat and altitude was now much less than it had been in 1970. Advances in sports medicine had proved that these could be handled. Then, suddenly and wantonly, another more deadly natural phenomenon struck.

At 7:18 on the morning of September 19, 1985, one of the most powerful earthquakes in recent history (Richter 8.1) devastated large areas of downtown Mexico City. The death toll was over 7,000 with up to 30,000 made homeless.

Could the World Cup continue? Yes, said the Mexicans, in the best show-must-go-on spirit. None of the twelve stadiums had been damaged, and the tournament was now needed more than ever as a morale booster. They would succeed, just as the Chileans, battered by an earthquake in 1960, had persevered to stage the 1962 tournament.

The Mexican team had been under intensive preparation since 1983. Bora Milutinovic, a former Yugoslavian player who had moved to Mexico in 1972, was the coach. Mexico, a soccer-mad country of 82 million people, had always had ambitions far beyond its strength. It had qualified for eight of the twelve World Cup tournaments, but had achieved little beyond that. Usually it was knocked out in the first round. Only in 1970, when it hosted the event, had it advanced to the quarterfinals. Milutinovic was expected to at least repeat that feat.

In 1984 he took his team to Rome for an exhibition game against the world champions, Italy. Before the game, the players had an audience with the pope. "He gave us his blessing," said Milutinovic. "He held up one hand. Five fingers. The next day the Italians scored five goals against us. We were just happy he didn't bless us with both hands."

The heavy defeat, nevertheless, was a blessing. It proved that it was time for the Mexican Soccer Federation to get serious with its clubs, to make them release the players Milutinovic wanted. In 1985, the Mexican clubs were forced to play their championship without national team players; they were all in the permanent camp that Milutinovic had set up. The only major absentee was center forward Hugo Sanchez, Mexico's one world-class player, who was playing in Spain for Real Madrid. For him, Milutinovic was willing to wait, until the end of the Spanish season in the spring of 1986.

Mexico, host nation or not, was simply not strong enough to be ranked among the favorites. That honor was shared by Brazil, Argentina, and France—an interesting, and at first glance, puzzling trio. Three teams that played a game built around artistry and ball skill. Why should they be favored over teams that practiced the athletic, power game that was becoming increasingly prevalent, particularly in Europe?

Call it the positive effect of heat and altitude. It had already been noticed in 1970 that the conditions had slowed down the pace of the game. Teams that relied on a vigorous all-running, all-action, ninety-mph game simply couldn't keep it up. Brazil, the supreme artists, had triumphed.

A repeat performance by the Brazilians was definitely on the cards. The creative nucleus of the team that had been so dazzling in Spain four years earlier was still there: Zico, Junior, Socrates, Falcao. After an interlude in Saudi Arabia, Tele was back as coach. And in the twenty-six-year-old Careca, Brazil had what it had so fatally lacked in Spain: a goal-scoring center forward.

Argentina had a new coach. Carlos Bilardo was now in charge, a man with a philosophy very different from that of Menotti. Bilardo was a more cautious man. Not for him the adventurous extravagance of Menotti's 1978 team, with its three forwards and two attacking midfielders. He favored all-round players and packed his team with midfielders who were expected to do a little of everything.

Qualifying had been a struggle. In the final game, against Peru, Argentina had been staring down the barrel of elimination: 2–1 down with only ten minutes remaining in the game. A typically gritty run from Passarella led to the tying goal and ensured qualification. But the team was anything but convincing.

Criticism rained down on Bilardo. His team was overly cautious, it was dull, it lacked an attacking mentality. Certainly, the team lacked the explosiveness of Menotti's 1978 crew—but then, Bilardo had Diego Maradona.

We last saw Maradona in 1982, plodding dejectedly off the field in Barcelona, red-carded for kicking a Brazilian opponent. Since then his career had taken him from Barcelona to the boiling cauldron of soccer fanaticism that is Naples. By now, few doubted that he deserved his title of the world's best player. With his powerful, twisting dribbles, his superbly clever and accurate passing, his formidable left-foot shooting, Maradona was a match-winning player. Could he also be a tournament-winning player?

If there was one player who could challenge Maradona's supremacy, then it was France's Michel Platini. Now thirty-one years old, Platini knew that this was likely to be his last chance for World Cup glory. Two years earlier France had at long last won a major title, when Platini led it to the 1984 European championship. The team, it was asserted, was more mature and more worldly than it had been in Spain. A lesson had been learned from the harsh elimination in 1982. The artists Tigana, Giresse, and Platini were still there in midfield, but alongside them now was the bulky, uncompromising Luis Fernandez.

West Germany, beaten finalists in 1982, was now coached by its former captain, Franz Beckenbauer. Rummenigge had much in common with Platini: a thirty-one-year-old facing his last big chance. His heir was already on the scene, Lothar Matthäus. Schumacher, the villain of 1982, was still in goal, and a new crop of robust defenders suggested that Germany, at the very least, would be hard to beat.

England posed a rather special sort of threat. Nothing to do with its soccer strength, which was not rated too highly. The menace came from its wild supporters, now internationally famous for their acts of violence and vandalism. When soccer people talked about security, they were worried less about terrorism than about the presence of the English hooligans.

For years these so-called fans had followed English teams as they played in Europe. Their presence always meant drunkenness, wrecked bars and stores, assaults on innocent bystanders, and pitched street battles with local fans or with the police.*

Making its first-ever appearance in the tournament was Denmark. The Danes, rather like the Dutch in the 1970s, had seemingly undergone an overnight transformation. Always viewed as a second-rate soccer country, they had suddenly produced a lively, skillful team that was a serious contender for the world title.

What made the achievement even more astounding was that there was no professional soccer in Denmark. The coach was a German, Sepp Piontek. Of his eleven starters, ten were with foreign clubs, in England, Italy, Germany, the Netherlands, Belgium, and France. The stars were two Italian-based players, Michael Laudrup of Juventus and Preben Elkjaer of Verona.

The Italians themselves had shown indifferent form since the 1982 triumph. Of the twenty-nine games played by Bearzot's team since, thirteen had been won, nine lost, and seven tied. They had performed abysmally in the 1984 European championship, failing to qualify for the final tournament. Hardly championship form.

The Dutch again failed to qualify, so, too—for the ninth consecutive time since 1950—did the United States. For the Americans this was a major disappointment. Their team was now made up of young American-born players, with plenty of professional experience gained when playing alongside foreign veterans in the North American Soccer League. The failure was made even more galling when neighbor Canada won the qualifying tournament.

Black African soccer, so excitingly represented by Cameroon in 1982, was in eclipse. All four semifinal spots in the African region qualifiers were claimed by countries from Arab north Africa, with Algeria and Morocco the winners.

FIFA, not happy with the way things had gone in España-82, had introduced two format changes. In the first round, the final two games in each group would be played on the same day at the same time—this to avoid another West Germany vs. Austria fiasco. The arrangement

* See Chapter 7, page 202.

of four three-team groups in the second round was scrapped. Looking for more drama, FIFA ruled that direct elimination would apply after the first round. Sixteen teams would advance—the first and second in each first-round group, plus the four best third-place finishers.

The ill luck of the draw had predetermined that the opening game, in the magnificent 114,000-capacity Estadio Azteca, should be between Italy, the holders, and Bulgaria. Everyone knew this would be yet another in the long line of inaugural clinkers.

The Italians would be cautious and as meticulously defensive as only they could be. The Bulgarians were as utterly characterless as only the duller Eastern European sides could be. The most interesting discovery about them was that all twenty-two of their players had names that ended with the letter *v*. Bulgaria had already played twelve times in four previous World Cup tournaments, and had yet to win a game.

After a lively festival of Mexican dances and mariachi music, and after President Miguel de la Madrid's speech had been loudly jeered and whistled (many Mexicans were dissatisfied with his government's efforts to help the earthquake victims), the Italians and the Bulgarians did their best to put everyone to sleep.

In fact the Italians themselves, having taken a 1–0 lead in the first half, nodded off and allowed the Bulgarians, in one of their pitifully few attacks, to tie the game five minutes before the end.

A game to forget, but fortunately much better was to follow. The following day Spain and Brazil played a splendid game in Guadalajara's Group D. Socrates got the winner for Brazil, but the Spanish had reason to feel hard done by, because five minutes earlier they appeared to have scored. From a slashing drive by Michel, the ball beat the Brazilian goalkeeper Carlos, hit the underside of the bar, bounced to the ground and out of the goal. Had the ball gone over the goal line or not? Déjà vu for those who remembered the 1966 World Cup final. Then, the English rejoiced as the goal was confirmed. This time the Spanish were in despair as the goal was not given.

In the end, both Brazil and Spain would advance to the next round. Brazil climaxed its first round with a resounding 3–0 win over Northern Ireland. They had unveiled a new star in the dynamic Josimar. The twenty-four-year-old fullback was a late addition to the team, and even the Brazilian journalists confessed that they didn't know much about him. His goal against the Irish, a screaming thirty-yard drive, made everyone take notice.

One who noticed, but couldn't do much about it, was the veteran Pat Jennings, playing his final game in the Irish goal. It was Jennings's 119th appearance for his country, a world record at the time.

In Group B, Mexico sent its supporters into a frenzy with a 2–1 win over Belgium in the Azteca. Defender Fernando Quirarte, who came forward on a free kick to head the first goal, admitted after the game that he now had a problem: explaining the goal to his mother, who had told him to stick with his defensive duties and not to go forward.

The Mexican fans celebrated all night in Mexico city, to such an extent that the police ordered the boarding up of monuments and the closing of streets.

Argentina topped Group A, with Italy in second place. The Argentines had not been seriously tested, but one thing was very clear. Maradona was in tremendous form, both as a player and as a team leader.

The woeful Bulgarians tied Italy and South Korea, and then lost 2–0 to Argentina. During the postgame press conference coach Yvan Vutzov was in subdued, apologetic mood as he admitted that Bulgaria had played badly and dismissed the remote chance that his team could be still alive.

Wrong. When all the first-round results were in, it turned out that Bulgaria—with one loss, two ties, and with a 2–4 goals for-and-against record—had scraped into the second round!

The Uruguayans made it out of Group E with an even worse record of a loss, two ties and a 2–7 goals record. But then, they had known life wasn't going to be easy when the draw gave them Denmark, West Germany, and Scotland as opponents. The Group of Death, they called it.

The group was dominated by the Danes, who scored nine goals (four of them to Elkjaer) in a triumphant path that included a 6–1 dismantling of Uruguay, and a first-ever win over West Germany.

A 1–1 tie with West Germany was not a bad start for Uruguay. But the behavior of the Uruguayan bench during the game, and of the players during the subsequent dope-control tests prompted FIFA to issue a stern warning. The Uruguayans chose to ignore it; one red and two yellow cards in the 6–1 rout by Denmark didn't improve their image.

When Uruguay met Scotland in its final game, a second-round place was at stake. FIFA had primed the French referee, Joel Quiniou, to stand no nonsense. Advice that he took so energetically to heart that he set a new World Cup record by sending off Uruguay's José Batista in the very first minute of the game.

Playing virtually the entire game with only ten men, the Uruguay-ans still held out for the 0–0 tie that they needed. After the game, coach Omar Borras commented: "The Group of Death? Yes, there was a murderer on the field today. The referee."

So the Scots made their customary early exit, while Uruguay advanced to meet Argentina. Without its coach. FIFA banned Borras from the bench for calling Quiniou a murderer.

In Group C it was France and the USSR that qualified. The Canadi-ans had lost all three of their games. They never looked like winning any of them, and were content to make life difficult for their opponents.

That lesser teams need not be so unambitious was sharply demon-strated in Monterrey, where Morocco topped Group F after ties against England and Poland, and victory over Portugal. It thus became the first African team to reach the second round.

Money was very much on the minds of the Portuguese players. In a dispute over bonuses with their federation, they threatened not to take the field for their first game against England. The Portuguese requested permission from FIFA to fly in a twenty-two-man reserve squad. The dispute was resolved, Portugal beat England 1–0 . . . but lost its other two games and finished at the bottom of the group.

After losing to Portugal and barely surviving a 0–0 tie with Moroc-co, England was on the brink of elimination. Then Gary Lineker, just as Paolo Rossi had done for Italy in 1982, suddenly found his touch. His hat trick against Poland saw England through.

On the whole, the Mexicans were praised for an excellently orga-nized first round. Except for one thing. Amazingly, in a World Cup that was basically being run by a television company, Televisa, it was the television transmissions that came badly unstuck. The early broadcasts were a nightmare. The Dutch received a picture, but no sound. The Brazilians got the Italian commentary, the Colombians got the Portuguese. The French got neither picture nor sound. Many countries had to use the regular telephone system to get their com-mentators on the air.

The European Broadcasting Union was furious and went public with its complaints, calling the shambles "the biggest disaster in the history of sports broadcasting." It accused the Mexicans of incompe-tence, even of sabotage. Pointing out that its member countries had paid some $30 million for the broadcast rights, it handed FIFA an ulti-matum: Get it fixed, *now*, or we sue for return of our rights fees. The problems were corrected very quickly.

The Mexicans opened the second round with a 2–0 win over Bulgaria. An uneventful game that featured one moment of sheer magic, when Manuel Negrete put Mexico ahead with a spectacular flying scissor-kick volley. It was hailed as the goal of the tournament, but Maradona would have the last word on that topic. This time Bulgaria was definitely out, its World Cup record was now sixteen games without a win.

A huge shock in Queretaro, where the Danes' inexperience, to say nothing of their hubris, let them down badly. All along, the Spanish had been saying that they had the Danes' number. So it proved. The Danes, insanely overconfident, quickly went ahead through a Jesper Olsen penalty kick. Spain then picked Denmark apart, most of the damage being done by center forward Emilio Butragueño, who scored four times in a 5–1 romp.

The holders Italy went tamely out to France, which controlled the game from the start and ran out 2–1 winners. West Germany sweated and strained unimaginatively against Morocco. Three minutes from the end, the Moroccans negligently set up a defensive wall that didn't cover the goal. Matthäus saw the gap, and scored the only goal of the game with his free kick.

Goals galore in Leon. Belanov got three for the USSR, but it was not enough. Belgium—a third-place finisher—got four in a 4–3 overtime win. Brazil rolled over Poland by 4–0, with two of the goals coming from defenders—Edinho, and the unstoppable Josimar, who picked his way merrily though the Polish defense before unleashing a cannonball shot from an acute angle.

A chastened Uruguay, without coach Borras, played defensively against Argentina. The game finished 1–0 to the Argentines, but they had dominated throughout. More significantly, Maradona had dominated. Even the experienced and canny Uruguayan defenders had no answer to his wiles.

With its 3–0 win over Paraguay, England set up a quarterfinal against Argentina—a politically sensitive game that FIFA and the Mexican authorities would have preferred to avoid. It was the first meeting between the two countries since the 1982 Malvinas/Falklands war, and both teams had sizable contingents of boisterous fans with them.

A massive army presence, complete with tanks, was on duty in and around the Azteca stadium for the clash. Some minor scuffles between the opposing fans did develop during the second half, but most of the fireworks came on the field. From Maradona.

After a scoreless first half, Maradona took over. His surging dribble into the penalty area had the England defenders in trouble. When Steve Hodge tried to lob the ball back to goalkeeper Peter Shilton, Maradona darted in and leaped high to head the ball away from Shilton's lunging hands and into the net.

Or did he head the ball? England protested that Maradona had used his hand. But the Tunisian referee said the goal was legitimate. Nobody was really certain—even the television replays needed careful study before it was clear that Maradona had blatantly cheated, *had* punched the ball into the net.

Three minutes later, Maradona struck again—this time with ten seconds of pure, unimaginable soccer skill, to score one of the greatest goals in the history of the World Cup. Starting inside his own half, he corkscrewed his way past three defenders as he dribbled down the right flank. At the edge of the penalty area, he swerved past Terry Fenwick, and then, while holding off a challenge from Terry Butcher, pulled the ball past Shilton and shot into the empty net as he fell.

Late in the game, England fought back. Lineker headed a goal with nine minutes left, then almost tied it up with another header. Only some remarkable goal-line acrobatics by José Cuciuffo, who somehow scooped the ball off the line with the back of his head, prevented the goal. So Argentina marched on, and Maradona evaded questions about his first goal. If there was a handball, he said, it was the Hand of God that had scored for Argentina.

Another classic unfolded in Guadalajara, where Brazil met France. After an early goal by Careca was canceled out by Platini's equalizer, Brazil had its chance in the second half. Zico, coming on as a substitute, sliced open the French defense with a pass to Branco. As Branco raced to the ball, he was brought down by goalkeeper Joel Bats. Penalty to Brazil. But Zico's kick was weak, Bats saved, and the game finished 1–1 after overtime.

It was settled in France's favor by a penalty-kick shoot-out, a patently unfair way to decide any game, made even more farcical when Bruno Bellone's kick came back off the post, hit the Brazilian goalkeeper Carlos in the back of the head, and rebounded into the goal. The referee allowed the controversial goal, but many felt it was illegal. FIFA was quick to support the referee's decision, but the regulations that it cited were anything but clear on the point. A year later, FIFA changed the wording of the regulation.

Mexico's success so far had its fans believing that the miracle was possible. If West Germany could be beaten ... It might have happened, had not Mexico lost its chief playmaker, Thomas Boy, after thirty-two minutes, victim of a clumsy challenge by Andreas Brehme. In a dull game, played in the intense heat of Monterrey, neither side could muster much of an attack. This one also went to penalty kicks. No contest. Klaus Allofs, Brehme, Matthäus, and Littbarski scored for Germany, but only Negrete found the net for Mexico, and the host country's dreams of World Cup glory vanished.

Penalties were also needed to decide the fourth quarterfinal between the evenly matched Belgium and Spain. Victory in the shoot-out put the Belgians into a semifinal against Argentina. This was Maradona's chance of revenge for the mauling that the Belgians had given him in 1982 in his first World Cup game. And how he made them pay.

Two more breathtaking individual goals scuttled the Belgians, and Argentina had reached the final for the first time since 1978. Their opponents would be West Germany. The French had succumbed again at the semifinal stage, again to the Germans. This time it was poor goalkeeping that let them down. Brehme's free kick in the eighth minute was far from unstoppable, but Bats moved late and allowed the ball to slip underneath him.

The French—all-out attack now their only choice—battered away at the disciplined German defense. A frantic final five minutes saw them camped in the German goalmouth. Chances were created, but each the time the Germans got the ball away. Soccer's perversity had the last word when, with less than a minute to go, Rudi Voeller scored a late breakaway goal to give the Germans a 2–0 win.

Bilardo's Argentine team was now brimming with midfielders. It contained only one genuine forward, Jorge Valdano, and he was an example of Bilardo's "ideal" player: an inexhaustible runner who spent a good deal of energy falling back on defense. Arguably, another midfielder.

The lack of front players was not hurting Argentina, for it had scored eleven goals, nearly two per game. The secret, of course, was Maradona. So commanding was his form, so overwhelming his influence on his team, that it seemed natural to think of the final as West Germany vs. Maradona.

German tactics were discussed in terms of one issue: Whom would they put on Maradona? Almost every German defender and midfielder was mentioned, but none of them seemed up to the job. So the job was shared, Matthaus trying to subdue Maradona when he played deep, Karl-Heinz Forster taking over when Maradona went on attack.

Obsessed with the Maradona threat, the Germans played a tentative, disjointed first half. It was that obsession that led to the first goal. Matthäus, quite unnecessarily, fouled Maradona. Jorge Burruchaga curled the free kick into the area, Schumacher came out to grab the ball but never got to it as it swerved away from him, and there was sweeper José Brown to head home.

Strangely, there was no German reaction. The team went on playing its pedestrian game, rarely threatening the Argentine goal. Ten minutes after halftime, the deep-lying Maradona slid the ball to Hector Enrique, who dribbled forward and then pushed a perfect pass out to Valdano on the left wing. No German defender was near him as Valdano cut into the penalty area and stroked the ball past Schumacher.

At 2–0, Argentina, inevitably, relaxed. The Germans began to apply pressure, but it was a disordered sort of pressure, and in the twenty-third minute it needed a terrible call from the linesman to save them from more trouble. Burruchaga's pass to Enrique was right on the money, sending him sprinting yards clear of the German defense—only to be called back for a nonexistent offside.

The German attacks continued, formless but with growing insistence. Only determination, the famed German ability to fight back, could save matters now. And it very nearly did. The Argentine defense caved in twice within eight minutes, both times to close-range shots. First Rummenigge prodded the ball home from 5 yards out, then Voeller made it 2–2 with a header from 3 yards.

Bilardo had boasted of his team that it could "press the accelerator" and move up a gear any time it chose. Evidently, it was no idle boast. Three minutes after Voeller's morale-wrecking equalizer, Argentina was back in the lead, thanks to the genius of Maradona. His pass, through the middle of the German defense, was perfect. Burruchaga raced on to it, outpaced the lumbering Briegel, and calmly rolled the ball past the onrushing Schumacher.

A 3–2 win for Argentina, and vindication for Bilardo, whose style and tactics had been heavily criticized in Argentina. A large banner displayed by Argentine fans at the final read: FORGIVE US, BILARDO!

Above all else, Argentina's victory was a personal triumph for Maradona. No player in the history of the World Cup had ever dominated a tournament in the way that Maradona ruled over Mexico-86.

Italy, 1990

By losing all three of its games in Mexico-86 and failing to score even one goal, Canada ended up as the least successful team. A big flop for the Canadians, right? Not exactly. Their three defeats earned them a check for $966,000.

When the Mexicans had done all the accounting mathematics, they announced a profit of nearly $48 million. FIFA regulations allowed them to keep 30 percent. The other 70 percent ($33.5 million) was distributed among the twenty-four nations that played in the finals on a per game basis. Each of the fifty-two games was thus worth $644,000, or $322,000 per team. Teams knocked out after the three first-round games took home $966,000. The finalists, Argentina and West Germany, played seven games, worth $2.25 million—clear profit, because FIFA paid each team's travel and living expenses during the championship.

Income for Mexico-86 amounted to $96 million, equally divided among three sources: the sale of tickets, television rights, and advertising. Also of vital importance to the running of the show were sponsors. There were twelve of them for Mexico-86, including Coca-Cola, Fuji Film, Gillette, Seiko, Budweiser, Canon, and Opel cars.

There was also Camel cigarettes, which offended many people. When asked whether he felt it advisable for soccer to promote tobacco smoking, FIFA president Dr. João Havelange replied that he had been looking at cigarette ads all his life, and *he* had never smoked. It was hardly the sort of response to encourage sponsors who had each paid several million dollars for rights that ranged from using the official logos and mascot, to exclusive promotion of their products and commercials on the game telecasts.

At its birth sixty years earlier, the World Cup had been primarily about soccer. By 1990, as it moved to Italy for its fourteenth edition, it was very much about money, and marketing, and advertising, and sponsorship.

That message came over loud and clear in November 1986, at the first press conference for Italia-90. A gathering of top soccer people, of coaches, and perhaps players? Not at all. Francesco Cossiga, the president of Italy was there, along with a host of top political, business, and even church figures.

The talk was of marketing contracts and of sponsors, suppliers, products and services, collaborators, and licensees. The official emblem of Italia-90 was introduced. So was Ciao, the official mascot, an imaginative stick figure with a soccer ball for a head.

Almost as an afterthought came the list of twelve cities where the games of Italia-90 would be staged. The money theme was taken up by the Italian government in a big way, which announced the incredible sum of $5 billion in aid to those cities, to allow them to upgrade stadiums, roads, public transport, airport facilities, and the like.

The amount was progressively scaled down, but the message remained: Italia-90 was an event of great national importance. Just as it had been in Mussolini's Italy in 1934. One monument from that earlier World Cup still stood: Nervi's beautiful stadium in Florence. It would be used in 1990, renovated and modernized along with nine other existing stadiums. New stadiums would be built in Bari, and in Turin, where the architecturally futuristic structure dubbed the Spaceship would cost $128 million.

More millions of dollars would have to be spent on security, which was a major concern. Both the Netherlands and West Germany had by now spawned bands of thuggish fans, while the Italians had their home-grown *ultras*. But the English hooligans were still the biggest threat to law and order.

They would follow England to Italy, that was not in doubt. What could be done with them? The thought of drunken hooligans trashing downtown Rome or Turin was too ghastly to contemplate. The answer was to isolate England. The Italian government was consulted, and England was assigned, by a seeding arrangement, to the island of Sardinia. That would keep the hooligans reasonably contained, at least for the first round. It was a cynical arrangement that said a lot about Italian attitudes toward Sardinia.

Police work—or detective work—of a rather different sort was required from FIFA during the qualifying rounds. A spectacular scandal erupted in South America, where Brazil and Chile were fighting it out for a place in the final twenty-four. The first leg, in Santiago, had been a violent 1–1 tie in which the Chilean coach, Orlando Aravena, had been ejected. Sebastião Lazaroni, the Brazilian coach, had carried on alarmingly on the sidelines, and had been manhandled by a large contingent of steel-helmeted Chilean police. He had called Aravena "an imbecile," and accused him of inciting the Chileans to play violently.

Accusations and counteraccusations flew to and fro during the three weeks leading up to the second leg. The Chileans said they were afraid of the hostile atmosphere in Brazil. "At the first sign of trouble, we're coming off the field," said Roberto Rojas, their goalkeeper and captain.

Trouble arrived with twenty minutes left in the game, Brazil leading 1–0. From somewhere in the 140,000 crowd packing the Maracana stadium in Rio de Janeiro, a flare took flight. It dropped softly to earth in front of the Chilean goal. In the drifting smoke, Rojas could be seen flat on his back, holding his head. His teammates carried him off the field, his shirt apparently bathed in blood. Twenty minutes later, with the Chileans refusing to take the field again, the game was called off.

A week later, FIFA acted. The game—and therefore qualification for Italia-90—was awarded to Brazil. Rojas was banned from international games for life. FIFA pressed its investigation, convinced the whole incident had been contrived with the aim of getting Brazil banned or, at the least, a replay of the game at a neutral site. "It is hard to believe," said FIFA, "that the imprudent goalkeeper hatched and enacted that stratagem unaided and unabetted."

Eventually, Rojas admitted that he had not been struck by the flare, and that he had faked his injuries. He was banned from *all* soccer for life, as was the president of the Chilean Soccer Federation. Aravena got a life ban from international soccer, and the Chilean federation was fined $60,000. Chile was banned from taking part in the 1994 World Cup for "the most ignoble incident of attempted fraud in the history of FIFA."

Another fraud had been attempted by the Mexicans, who fielded overage players during the qualifying round for the 1989 World Youth Championship. The players used false passports, but the scheme was undone by the Mexican federation's own yearbook, which included the correct birth dates of the players.

The wrath of FIFA descended on Mexico, which was banned from the 1990 World Cup, thus giving the United States its best chance ever of qualifying. Coach Bob Gansler's cautious, unimaginative team made hard work of it against Guatemala, El Salvador, Trinidad and Tobago, and Costa Rica, managing to score only six goals in eight games. It all came down to the final game, in which Paul Caligiuri's goal gave the Americans a memorable 1–0 win in Trinidad to ensure a place in Italy.

In Europe there were no frauds, but there were a couple of mild shocks when both France and Denmark narrowly failed to qualify, beaten out by Scotland and Romania.

Italy, of course, was the favorite to win its own tournament, just as it had done in 1934. But there were plenty of people around who felt that the pressure to win was precisely what would undo coach Azeglio Vicini's team. If not Italy, then the Netherlands. Defeated finalists in 1974 and 1978, the Dutch had recently struck scintillating form. Led by their tall, elegant, dreadlocked midfielder Ruud Gullit, they had won their first major tournament, the 1988 European championship. And, of course, the Germans. No one would count them out. Brazil or Argentina? Probably not, given how difficult it always was for South American teams to win in Europe.

Italia-90 opened in Milan with the now obligatory pregame extravaganza. Forty minutes of screaming rock music, dancing, fashion models, even a taped segment of grand opera. Argentina against Cameroon followed. In the 1982 opening game in Barcelona, Menotti's Argentina had been roughed up by Belgium, and lost 1–0. The script in Milan was the same. Bilardo's Argentina lost 1–0; this time it was Cameroon dishing it out.

The game highlighted a worrying problem. Michel Vautrot, the French referee, did his best to cope with the violence, giving out three yellow cards to the Cameroons, and sending two players off. Yet they still won the game. Perhaps there was just no way to compensate for the abysmal performance by the Argentines. Their ineptitude was capped in the sixty-fifth minute, when Omam Biyik outjumped the leaden-footed Argentine defense to head the ball straight at goalkeeper Nery Pumpido. It should have been a routine save, but Pumpido fumbled the ball and it rolled into the net.

Only four of Argentina's 1986 team were present, including Maradona. Admittedly, he had taken a beating, but on those occasions when his magic shone, his teammates had not responded. Up front, Aldo Balbo was a one-man nonevent. Claudio Caniggia, coming on in the second half, caused some problems with his speed (both Cameroon ejections came when defenders brought him down as he sped away). The irony was that in Ramón Diaz, Argentina had a center forward who would have walked onto any other team. He was not even on Bilardo's squad because, it was said, Maradona didn't like him. On this form, Argentina would be lucky to survive the first round.

Argentina's next game, against the USSR, started badly. Bilardo had made five changes to the team, and soon was forced to make another. After only ten minutes the misfortunes of goalkeeper Pumpido, whose gaffe had cost Argentina the opening game, took a tragic turn. He was stretchered off with a broken leg after colliding heavily with his own defender Julio Olarticoechea. Sergio Goycochea came on, and was to prove a splendid deputy.

One minute later, the Hand of God struck again. Oleg Kuznetsov's header was speeding goalward when Maradona popped up, almost on his own goal line. Like a striking snake, his right hand flashed out and knocked the ball down to his feet. Swedish referee Erik Fredricksson, standing no more than five yards from Maradona, staring straight at him, saw nothing.

Argentina won the game 2–0. The Brazilian coach Sebastião Lazaroni remarked: "What a versatile player Maradona is. He can score goals with his left hand, and save them with his right."

A 1–1 tie with Romania followed and Argentina did, just, creep into the next round, as the third-place team.

Topping the group were the Cameroons, who had shown that they were capable of some very good-looking soccer. They had also unveiled their secret weapon, the thirty-eight-year-old Roger Milla, who had come on against Romania to score twice within ten minutes. The big question mark against Cameroon was its tackling, some of which was disgraceful. It had already saddled the team with seven yellow and two red cards.

Yugoslavia was supposed to be a good long-shot bet, but the Germans blew them out, 4–1, in their first game. Lothar Matthäus got two of the goals, and the Germans really did look as though they were enjoying things, as though there were plenty more goals to come. After all, with players like Rudi Voeller, Jurgen Klinsmann, Thomas Haessler, and Pierre Littbarski in the squad, everything was in place for an attacking festival.

There was, as it happened, a demonstration of German offensive power that same night. It came from hordes of German fans, who went on a rampage in downtown Milan, fighting police and damaging property. Twenty-three injuries were reported. All this despite a day-of-game ban on alcohol sales in Milan.

The hope of a free-scoring Germany seemed to be confirmed by a 5–1 romp over the United Arab Emirates. But the goal flow dried up after a shaky 1–1 tie with Colombia, a game that the Germans were lucky not to lose. After that, they never managed more than two goals in a game.

Even though it was the Germans, and not the expected English, to set the hooligan ball rolling, there was no doubt about which was the big match, as far as fan violence was concerned. England vs. the

Netherlands, in Cagliari. Over 1,500 police and *carabinieri* on duty at the stadium, 4,000 more in the town.

Of course, there were ugly scenes. About a thousand English fans chose to march, en masse, to the stadium. Mayhem followed. The fans threw rocks and bottles, police in riot gear replied with nightsticks and tear gas. The injuries were many, the arrests few—only five. The English issued their now customary statement about "a minority of troublemakers bringing disgrace to English soccer."

On the field, England had slightly the better of the Dutch, but the game ended 0–0. There was a change, almost a revolution, in English tactical thinking. Coach Bobby Robson used Mark Wright as a sweeper; every other country in Europe used a sweeper, had been doing so for two decades. The English had found it difficult to change from their dual-center back system. Wright had a good game against the Dutch, but the innovation was not repeated against Egypt, which was beaten by the minimum 1–0 score.

England topped the group. Next came the Netherlands and Ireland, with identical records: three ties, two goals for and two against. A special draw was necessary to decide which team had finished second, which third. The Irish "won" that, the only thing they were to win in Italy. They were assigned second place, and would play Romania in the next round. The Dutch would have to face West Germany.

The Irish team was a monument to soccer's tangled eligibility requirements. Very few of the players had actually been born in Ireland. Most qualified because they had an Irish parent, or maybe a grandparent. Or, like forward John Aldridge, a great grandmother. The coach was an Englishman, Jack Charlton, who had been a center back on England's World Cup–winning team in 1966.

Charlton's idea of soccer was to hit the ball long, to get it forward as quickly as possible. The direct approach. His players were workhorses who made life difficult for opponents, and the game boring for spectators.

Spain, Belgium, and Uruguay qualified from the uninspiring Group E. All would fall at the next hurdle.

The United States bombed calamitously in its first game. Czechoslovakia missed a penalty kick, but it hardly mattered as they slammed in five goals anyway. Bob Gansler's team of college players was not ready, had not been properly prepared, for this level of soccer. Against Italy they regrouped, packed their defense, and held the Italians to just one goal, though they were lucky when Gianlucca Vialli hit the post with a penalty kick in the first half.

Late in the game the Italian goalkeeper Walter Zenga misplayed a stinging free kick from Bruce Murray, the ball ran loose and fullback Ricardo Ferri had to kick Peter Vermes's shot off the goal line. It was the Americans' only chance of the game, but it became the basis of a legend that the United States had given as good as it got and had "nearly tied" Italy. Hardly. The Americans had their backs to the wall for virtually the whole game. But the fact that the young players did not panic in the fever-heat atmosphere of Rome's packed Olympic Stadium was certainly to their credit.

For Italy, that was its second 1–0 win. Against Austria it had played some of the best soccer of the first round—fast-paced, inventive, attacking soccer—but the goals would not come. The score was still 0–0 when, with fifteen minutes left, coach Vicini brought on Salvatore "Toto" Schillaci. A short, bustling center forward, Schillaci was that rarity in Italian professional soccer, a Sicilian. Three minutes was all he needed. Gianluca Vialli crossed the ball, and Schillaci emphatically headed it in, to detonate the stadium into an explosion of joy—and relief.

Vicini again used Schillaci as a substitute against the Americans. But the scrappy little Toto had quickly become an immensely popular hero, the symbol of Italy's hope for the world title. From then on he would start every game. Against Austria he scored again, and Italy marched into the next round with three wins out of three.

Meanwhile, remarkable things were happening in Group C. Costa Rica, probably the least fancied team in the whole tournament, had beaten Scotland and Sweden. Sandwiched between was a 1–0 loss to Brazil. The Costa Ricans could boast just one outstanding player—goalkeeper Gabelo Conejo. For the rest, this was a modest team, coached by Bora Milutinovic to play a modest game. Defensive yes, but always looking for a goal-scoring opening. Their modest skills got the Costa Ricans into the second round

Brazil made it, too. It managed to win all three of its games and at the same time infuriate its fans. What caused the rumpus was coach Sebastião Lazaroni's insistence on adopting a European approach. For the first time Brazil would play with a sweeper. That meant reducing the number of forwards from three to two. Pelé, among many others, was aghast: "That is not Brazil. Brazil always plays with three forwards."

Nine of Lazaroni's starting team played for European clubs. They had become used to Europe and European soccer, something that opened up a huge rift between them and the Brazilian press. The journalists, living and working in Brazil, regarded the players almost as foreigners who had forgotten what it was like to be Brazilian, who didn't understand that the Brazilian people would not accept a Europeanized game.

That Brazil should only beat little Costa Rica by 1–0 was an insult to the Brazilian press, which gave Lazaroni a torrid time. They wanted to see goals, they wanted to see the traditional *jogo bonito* (beautiful game) style of Brazil. Instead, here was midfielder Dunga boasting "No more *jogo bonito*, this is the Brazil of sweat and sacrifice."

But the critics, headed by Pelé, turned out to be right: "As soon as we play a good team, we'll lose," he said. The second round brought the old enemy—Argentina. This time Brazil failed to score, and it went down 1–0. A wickedly unfair result, because the Brazilians had dominated the game, had created chance after chance, had hit the goalposts three times. But the old scoring fluency was not there.

It was Maradona who sunk them. He had a quiet game, but just one moment of razzle-dazzle was enough. Ironically, it was the defense, supposedly the strong point of the new-look Brazil that fouled up. A penetrating Maradona dribble unnerved the defenders. Their soccer instincts, their tactical discipline, vanished as Maradona dominated their vision. Four of them converged on him, leaving Caniggia free.

As the defenders rushed in, Maradona somehow spirited the ball away, through the forest of legs, to the lurking Caniggia. The defenders barely had time to spin around and watch helplessly as Caniggia rounded goalkeeper Claudio Taffarel and scored the game-winning goal. To add insult to injury, Maradona had made the pass with his rarely used right foot.

For the first time in four attempts, Argentina had beaten Brazil in a World Cup game. "We must try to work out the reasons for this incredible and undeserved defeat," said Lazaroni, but the press didn't want to hear. They already knew the reason: Lazaroni's betrayal of *jogo bonito*.

Brazil went home, and the saddest thing was that no one really cared. When the Brazilians were eliminated in 1982 and 1986, it was as though the heart had been wrenched out of the tournaments. This time, Brazil had been just another team. Said a banner at the Argentina game: IF LAZARONI IS A COACH, I'M THE POPE.

Costa Rica bowed out, heavily beaten 4–1 by Czechoslovakia, though it would surely have been closer had Conejo not been out with an injury. Ireland and Romania, predictably, produced the worst game, a 0–0 tie that had to be resolved by penalty kicks. Ireland took the shoot-out, which put them into the quarterfinals without having won a game. Charlton, dubbed Saint Jack by the Irish press, mused: "We could end up winning the whole tournament without winning a game."

Yugoslavia disposed of Spain 2–1 in overtime, and England also needed the extra thirty minutes before getting past Belgium 1–0. Two of England's younger players teamed up on the only goal of the game. David Platt volleyed a spectacular winner after receiving an inch-perfect free kick from Paul "Gazza" Gascoigne. The twenty-three-year-old Gascoigne was emerging as a new talent, extravagantly gifted, but a player of unpredictable moods who coach Bobby Robson had once described as "daft as a brush."

Colombia and Cameroon put on a vastly entertaining game in Naples. Attacking soccer, attractively and intelligently played, flowed from both teams. Carlos Valderrama, Colombia's flamboyant midfielder caught the eye—partly for the explosion of orange-gold hair that enveloped his head, partly for his superb passing and dribbling.

Joining in the fun was Colombia's extrovert and adventurous goalkeeper René Higuita, known for his dribbling forays upfield. Colombia had the better of the first half, and was unlucky when Freddy Rincon's pile-driving free kick smashed against a goal post.

Old Man Milla came on for Cameroon in the second half and again proved to be the game winner. In overtime, he blasted a left-footer past Higuita, and then three minutes later showed that he could still move as quickly as anyone. Higuita, yet again, had come out of his area, the ball at his feet. Milla pounced, stole the ball, and scored. That was the vital goal, for Colombia scored to make it 2–1.

Higuita showed up at the postgame press conference to admit his error: "I have asked my teammates to forgive me. It has never happened to me before, but it was a mistake that a lot of people were waiting for. Well, you all saw it, it was as big as a house."

As always, the Dutch and the Germans threw everything they had into their clash. A little too much, at first. Frank Rijkaard and Rudi Voeller got involved in a series of nasty incidents, with Rijkaard clearly seen to spit on Voeller. The referee red-carded both of them after twenty minutes. It seemed much too harsh on Voeller.

Klinsmann put the Germans ahead in the first half, and Andy Brehme added a second late in the game. With under a minute left, the Netherlands pulled a goal back from a Ron Koeman penalty kick.

The Germans had been the better side, and were now solidly established as the second favorites, right behind Italy.

Rome's Olympic Stadium was packed yet again to see the Italians take on Uruguay. Defensive play dominated until the sixty-seventh minute when Toto Schillaci had the Italian fans roaring again with a left-footed rocket from the edge of the penalty area that screamed past goalkeeper Fernando Alvez. Aldo Serena made it 2–0 Italy.

Italy was now the clear favorite to take the trophy. With the home crowds providing frenetic support, the early nervousness had gone, the team was playing well, and had yet to concede a goal.

The Irish came to Rome, duly played their uncompromising, unimaginative game, and were duly beaten, 1–0. Goal by Schillaci. Roberto Donadoni's shot was too strong for goalkeeper Pat Bonner, who could only fend it off. Toto got to the loose ball first and rapped it home.

The Irish, said Vicini, showed "athletic power and strength," but some of their tackling was too vigorous for his liking. He suggested that the Italians needed more protection from the referees. Jack Charlton had little to say about the game: "To tell the truth, I've had it with these press conferences. We're going home. I'll probably be fishing on Monday."

The expected Italy-West Germany final moved a step closer when the Germans also advanced, beating Czechoslovakia 1–0 on Lothar Matthäus's penalty kick.

Argentina played another poor game, and again they came away with a win. This time, Yugoslavia was the victim. The 0–0 overtime tie went to penalty kicks. There had been very little excitement, and no moments of Maradona magic. In fact Maradona, to the crowd's delight, muffed his penalty kick. It didn't matter because Goycochea came up with two saves and Argentina, the same Argentina that had looked so awful in the opening game, was in the semifinal.

Just two goals in the first three quarterfinals. England and Cameroon offset that by coming up with five in their game in Naples. Although England went ahead on a Platt goal, Cameroon came back to take a 2–1 lead in the second half, played some of the best soccer of the tournament, and looked as though they might overrun the English defense.

England was saved by Cameroon's old failing: wild tackling. Twice Lineker was brought crashing down, twice he scrambled up to convert the resulting penalty kicks. A 3–2 overtime win for England, but Cameroon had only itself to blame for not reaching the semifinals.

England, so wobbly against Cameroon, traveled up to Turin to play its best game of the tournament, against West Germany. After dominating the first half, England fell behind on the hour. Brehme's free kick hit Paul Parker's foot, and spun up into the air, heading for the English goal. Veteran goalkeeper Peter Shilton was slow to react, and his last-second backward lunge was too late to stop the ball curling in just under the crossbar. A fluke—but a goal, nonetheless.

Lineker tied it up, and yet another World Cup game had to go to the penalty kick lottery. But not before a touching incident in overtime. Gascoigne fouled Thomas Berthold and was given a yellow, his second of the tournament. It meant a one-game suspension. If England made it to the final, Gascoigne would not play. Television caught it beautifully, Gascoigne staring at the yellow card, realizing what it meant, tears beginning to roll down his cheeks. Gazza's Tears became part of English soccer lore.

But England did not make it. Stuart Pearce, England's top penalty kicker, hit his shot straight at goalkeeper Bodo Ilgner, and on the next kick, Chris Waddle missed the goal completely. Germany was through to a record sixth World Cup final.

In the other semifinal, Italy tangled with Maradona's Argentina. The twist was that, for the first time, Italy had to play outside of Rome. In Naples—the city where Maradona played his club soccer, where he was regarded almost as a saint. The street-smart Maradona hinted that the Neapolitans should support Argentina. After all, everyone knew that there was a great deal of prejudice against southerners in the rest of Italy: "Italy wants your support now, but the other 364 days of the year it doesn't even consider you Italians," was Maradona's message.

Whatever, Naples was not Rome, where the stadium had always been jammed, the noise intimidating. In Naples, there were 10,000 empty seats and an appreciably lower decibel level.

Vicini baffled everyone with his lineup. He dropped Roberto Baggio, who had struck up a smooth partnership with Schillaci, and brought back Vialli, so unsuccessful in the early games. The move looked good after only seventeen minutes when a rasping Vialli shot was parried by Goycochea and there was the irrepressible Toto on hand to slam home the rebound from 6 yards out. The Italians, already assured of a $120,000 bonus per man for reaching the semifinal, looked set to collect the extra $40,000 for a win. For the Argentines, who had been running on empty for so long, the end was surely in sight.

Not yet. The Argentines proceeded to play their best game of the tournament. Slowly they took command. The flow, the pace, even the enthusiasm, seemed to hemorrhage from the Italian game. The defense was a bundle of nerves as Caniggia, Burruchaga, and Maradona piled on the pressure. In the fiftieth minute goalkeeper Walter Zenga had set a new World Cup record, 500 minutes without conceding a goal. But he looked far from comfortable on this day, stretching to make last-second saves, badly bobbling a corner kick.

His record lasted another eighteen minutes, until Caniggia beat him to Olarticoechea's cross, and flicked the ball neatly into the goal. Overtime came and went, though it took much longer than it should have done when referee Michel Vautrot inexplicably allowed the first fifteen-minute period to run for twenty-three minutes. The Italians, spent and dispirited, were beaten on penalty kicks. Goycochea saved splendidly from Donadoni and Serena, and it was Maradona who hit the winning penalty.

Argentina, incredibly, absurdly, was in the final. Italy was in mourning. City streets, so riotously jammed after each Italian victory, were silent and sullen. Third place was all that remained, and the Italians settled that by beating England 2–1. Toto Schillaci got another goal, his sixth, which made him the tournament's top scorer.

But what a price Argentina had paid in beating Italy. Ricardo Giusti had been red-carded, Caniggia, Olarticoechea, and Sergio Batista had received second yellows. All four were suspended, out of the final. Maradona was showing the effects of a badly swollen ankle that he had been nursing for the whole tournament.

If the Italians had a hero in Toto, they now had a villain in Maradona, who was painted as the man who had eliminated Italy. His house in Naples was stoned, and it was clear that—probably for the first time in soccer history—most Italians wanted a German victory.

Before the final in Rome, the Italian fans whistled and jeered all through the Argentine national anthem, just as they did every time Maradona touched the ball. The raucous catcalls provided a fitting background for a truly awful, totally forgettable final.

Any hope that Argentina would play as openly as it had against Italy was ruled out by the suspension of so many key players. In particular, two things demanded defensive tactics: The absence of Caniggia, its one dangerous forward, and the threat (or the hope) of the penalty kick tiebreaker. Argentina knew that if it could defend its way to that stage, it stood a good chance of winning the shoot-out. It had already won two of them on the strength of Goycochea's catlike reflexes.

So the Argentines defended, methodically, dourly—and effectively. The Germans could not find a way through. They attacked constantly, but with little in the way of imagination or cunning. Even after Argentina was reduced to ten men when Carlos Monzon distinguished himself by becoming the first player ever ejected from the final, it held on. Until, with only five minutes remaining, a highly questionable call from Mexican referee Edgar Codesal gave Germany a penalty kick. The Argentines surrounded Codesal, protesting, menacing.

When that was over, Brehme hit the penalty perfectly—hard, low, just inside the post. It had to be perfect, for the diving Goycochea got within inches of saving it. The game was over soon afterward.

Argentina had become the first team to be shut out in a World Cup final. Germany, after failing in the finals in 1982 and 1986, was world champion. Beckenbauer, like Brazil's Zagalo, had now gained a winner's medal both as a player and as a coach.

The Argentines again besieged Codesal. Maradona was in tears. When his stricken face appeared on the huge television screen, the fans screamed in delight. Ugliness, ugliness.

Maradona refused to shake the hand of FIFA president João Havelange when he received his loser's medal. For Maradona, it was all a plot by FIFA. Argentina was being punished for dumping Italy, which was the team that FIFA—for unspecified reasons—wanted as winners. "There is a Mafia in the soccer world," accused Maradona. "That penalty did not exist, It was awarded to let the Germans win."

As in 1986, Maradona had left an indelible image on the tournament, but a very different one this time.*

Italia-90 had been a sour tournament, lacking in colorful players, lacking in adventurous, entertaining play. Above all, lacking in goals. The average per game sank to an all-time low of 2.2.

But soccer has always survived its dark moments, has always been confident of a bright future, always certain that if today's game was a disappointment, well, tomorrow's, or next week's, or next month's would be sublime. In Rome, even as the curtain came down on that awful final, there was a feeling of exhilaration in the stadium: The fire-

---

* The career of Maradona, one of soccer's all-time greats, turned tragically to ashes after the 1990 tournament. Playing for Napoli in 1991, he failed a routine blood test when traces of cocaine were found in his blood. FIFA banned him from soccer for fifteen months. An attempted comeback with the Spanish club Sevilla in 1992 lasted only one season; the club accused him of being more interested in nightlife than in training.

works soared noisily into the night, the stadium was bathed in a warm, friendly glow of hundreds of red flares, and the scoreboard flashed

CIAO ITALIA-90—HELLO

USA-94.

Soccer was on the move, heading for unconquered territory. The Americans, with all their economic power, their inventiveness, their optimism, were about to discover the World Cup—surely a reason for excitement.

CHAPTER 5

Soccer in the Nineties

The traveling circus of the World Cup—now in Brazil, now in Germany, now in the United States—is built on fast, economical airline flights. As long as the only way to get around Europe was by endless train journeys, and a two- to three-week boat voyage was needed to get from Europe to South America, competitive international soccer was going to be a rare occurrence. The 1930 World Cup highlighted the problem: Only four of the weaker European teams were willing to make the trip to Uruguay, and that only after a good deal of arm-twisting.

The coming of air travel, and particularly the jet era that began in the late 1950s, changed all that. Oceans and continents could now be crossed in a matter of hours. In 1962, every European country entered the World Cup qualifying rounds, and all ten survivors made the trip to Chile.

But the World Cup, the competition for national teams held once every four years, accounts for only a small part of the global comings and goings of soccer teams. The lion's share of the traveling is done by *club* teams involved in one or another of the international competitions for clubs that are played every year and, it begins to seem, all year round.

The earliest of these tournaments dates back to 1927, when that pioneer of European soccer, Hugo Meisl, started a cup for the champion clubs and runners-up from Austria, Hungary, Czechoslovakia, Yugoslavia, and Italy. The winner, the first club to capture an international trophy, was Sparta of Prague. The Mitropa Cup (a contraction of *Mitteleuropa*, central Europe) is still played, but it has dwindled to a relatively minor affair, deserted by the champion clubs.

For them a new competition was born in 1955, the brainchild of a Frenchman, Gabriel Hanot, soccer editor of the renowned sports newspaper *L'Equipe*.

In April 1955, *L'Equipe* made its own prediction of which clubs would end up as 1955 champions in eighteen European countries. It sent a letter to each, inviting it to enter the new competition, starting in the fall of that year. Prague and Dynamo-Moscow declined to participate, but the other sixteen clubs were enthusiastic.

So quickly and smoothly did things go that FIFA announced it would recognize the tournament, and the Union of European Football Associations (UEFA, a sort of mini-FIFA, formed in 1954, to deal only with matters in Europe) agreed to be the organizer. The official title was the European Champion Clubs Cup—now known simply as the European Cup.

The games were to be played on a home-and-home basis, and to avoid conflicts with each country's own league games (which are mostly played at weekends), they would take place in midweek under floodlights.

On the whole, *L'Equipe*'s crystal ball worked remarkably well; of the sixteen clubs that went into the draw for the first round, eight were national champions. Among them was Chelsea, which for the first, and so far the only, time in its history had won the English league—a feat that was greeted with universal amazement, for Chelsea was the butt of a thousand jokes about its ineptitude and inability to win anything.

What Chelsea did next was anything but a joke. Under pressure from the English Football League, which feared that its own competition would suffer if clubs started to get involved in Europe, Chelsea withdrew from the European Cup, and was replaced by a Polish club. The English, insular as ever, had once again chosen to miss the international boat.

Unaffected by yet another of Albion's perfidies, the 1956 European Cup forged ahead through a schedule of twenty-nine games to a magnificent final in Paris, where Spain's Real Madrid beat France's Stade de Reims by four goals to three. Real's blond Argentine, Alfredo di Stéfano, stamped his authority on the game, causing journalists to roll out all their superlatives. He was a revelation in his inexhaustible ability to be everywhere on the field, scoring a goal one minute, making a crucial defensive play the next, always at the heart of the game.

Twenty-two clubs entered the following year, including the new English champions, Manchester United, who disdainfully ignored the Football League's warnings, but it was Real Madrid, inspired by di Stefano, that triumphed.

These were very much Real's years, for they won the first five editions of the Cup with one of the greatest club teams ever assembled, and assembled is surely the word for a process that brought together di Stéfano from Argentina, Raymond Kopa from France, José Santamaria from Uruguay, Didi from Brazil, and Ferenc Puskas from Hungary. On the backs of these stars the European Cup rode to success, for the whole of Europe wanted to see Real Madrid. The 1960 final, in which Real Madrid annihilated Eintracht-Frankfurt 7–3, was watched by 127,600 fans in Glasgow's Hampden Park stadium. The average attendance for all fifty-two games of the competition that year was 53,000.

UEFA was not slow to cash in, and by 1961 it was running two more interclub competitions: the Cup Winners' Cup, for each country's cup winner (Czechoslovakia, which didn't have a national cup competition, started one so that it could participate); and the Fairs Cup, which began as an invitational tournament between cities that staged Trade Fairs, but was soon expanded to include most of Europe's top teams other than the champions and the cup winners. This one is now called the UEFA Cup. By 1993 the three competitions involved 136 clubs from thirty-six countries.

European competition, which once meant nothing more than a train journey between London and Glasgow, is now a complicated web of scores of jet flights between Moscow and Dublin, Athens and Reykjavík, Madrid and Helsinki. On September 16, 1992, the opening night of the thirty-eighth edition of the European Cup, the schedule of games looked like this:

First Round European Cup Games, September 16, 1992

APOEL (Cyprus) vs. AEK Athens (Greece)
Besiktas (Turkey) vs. IFK Gothenburg (Sweden)
Brugge (Belgium) vs. Maccabi Tel Aviv (Israel)
CSKA Moscow (Russia) vs. Vikingur Reykjavík (Iceland)
CSKA Sofia (Bulgaria) vs. FK Austria (Austria)
Dinamo Bucharest (Romania) vs. Kuusysi Lahti (Finland)
Ferencvaros (Hungary) vs. Slovan Bratislava (Czechoslovakia)

Leeds United (England) vs. Stuttgart (Germany)
Lyngby (Denmark) vs. Glasgow Rangers (Scotland)
Marseille (France) vs. Glentoran (Northern Ireland)
Olimpija Ljubljana (Slovenia) vs. Milan (Italy)
Porto (Portugal) vs. US Luxembourg (Luxembourg)
Skonto Riga (Latvia) vs. Lech Poznan (Poland)
Tavria Simferopol (Ukraine) vs. Sion (Switzerland)
Viking Stavanger (Norway) vs. Barcelona (Spain)
Zhalgiris Vilnius (Lithuania) vs. PSV Eindhoven (Netherlands)

On the same night there were sixteen similar games in the Cup Winners' Cup, and thirty-two more in the UEFA Cup. And that is just the beginning. Because the other continents now all stage similar club competitions.

The most famous is the South American Copa Libertadores, which features the two top clubs from each of the continent's ten countries. Add in the African Champions Cup, the Asian Cup Winners' Cup, the Champions Cup of North and Central America, (each with thirty-eight clubs)—to say nothing of the legion of youth teams that now go on tour in the summer months—and you begin to understand just why American Airlines has become a major soccer sponsor.

In Europe and South America, the vast majority of the clubs involved are professional. The top players are well paid—some of them extravagantly well paid. Just like their football, baseball, and basketball counterparts in America, they are national heroes—their names, their faces, their playing careers and their private lives familiar to everyone. Except that, with the *really* top soccer players, it goes further. They are known throughout the world. Television sees to that, with its huge global audiences; witness the 1.06 *billion* who tuned in to the 1990 World Cup final.

How much does a professional soccer player earn? Not an easy question to answer, because the rates of pay differ enormously from country to country. Published figures are often not reliable, suspected of distortion by the "three contract" factor: one set of figures for the press, one for the tax man, and the real total somewhere in between.

Salaries depend heavily on the number of games played and a system of bonuses that varies according to the importance of the games. For example, a club in the twenty-two-team English Premier League will play forty-two league games. It will be involved in at least two Cup competitions in England. Assuming it is knocked out of the Cups in the first round and is not involved in any of the European competitions, it will play forty-five games. If, in addition, the club is not in contention for the league championship, there will be no vital games calling for large bonuses.

Compare this with a club that plays in one of the European competitions, that wins its way through to the English Cup final, and is in the race for the league championship. The number of games played will be forty-two in the league, six in the Cup (more if replays are necessary), plus anything from two to twelve games in the European competition—say a total of fifty-eight games. For players on this club there will not only be thirteen more bonuses, but they will be increasingly large the nearer the club gets to winning one of the cups or the league.

Keeping these variables in mind, let us take a look at the wage structure of the English Premier League. For the average player, the basic wage would be between $50,000 and $75,000 a year. Bonuses are normally $750 for a win, $375 for a tie, perhaps adding $20,000 a year. If his club wins the league or one of the cups, a player may get another $45,000 for that—for a total of between $115,000 and $140,000 a year. Should his team win two major competitions in the same season his income might reach $185,000, but this is not so easy to attain. Only three English clubs in this century have accomplished "the double" of winning the league and the Cup in the same season. The top players in England can earn up to $750,000 a year, plus bonuses.

Which is about the same as a top player in Germany, though there the average wages are higher: between $195,000 and $260,000 a year, plus bonuses ($2,000 for a win, $1,000 for a tie), for *Bundesliga* (i.e., first division) players.

In Spain, the basic wage is around $100,000 a year, but the two main clubs—Real Madrid and Barcelona—have a history of paying huge amounts to their stars. Robert Prosinecki, bought by Real Madrid from Belgrade's Red Star club, earns a reported $2.5 million a year.

Top players have additional sources of income from personal publicity contracts with sponsors and from national team games. Bonuses for a win with the national team are usually around $1,000. For World Cup games the bonuses are considerably higher. The English players who won the World Cup in 1966, for instance, received $5,000 each, which was thought to be a staggering figure at the time. Eight years later it was made to look utterly puny when each West German player got $25,000 for winning the 1974 trophy. And so on to 1990, when the winning players—West Germans again—got $75,000 each. That was the bonus from the German Soccer Federation. Add in their share of money from team sponsorship deals, and it is believed that the players probably cleared twice that amount.

Affluence has come comparatively recently to soccer. For years the Football League in England enforced a maximum-wage limit that stood at $2,800 a year in 1958, the same year that Ferenc Puskas was signing for Real Madrid for $11,500 a year. A number of top British players left to play for Italian clubs, but it was not until the players threatened to strike that the maximum wage was abolished in 1961.

Neither England nor Germany can claim to be the El Dorado for soccer players. Italy is where the soccer fields are paved with gold, nowhere more so than in the northern city of Milan. There, in 1992, the average annual income of the first-team players of AC Milan was $1.79 million. The figure includes the substantial signing-on fee that each player pockets when signing a contract (it varies according to the contract), and the whopping $365,000 bonus paid to each player for winning the 1992 Italian league.

Marco Van Basten, Milan's Dutch striker, has a contract that guarantees him $2.66 million net a year. Milan is known as the highest-spending club in the world, but things look pretty good in nearby Turin, too. There the Juventus players average $1.28 million each in 1992.

Figures like these explain why Western Europe has become a magnet for top players from all over the world. Very few South American players, for instance, can hope to make that sort of money if they stay at home. In Brazil, the average player gets between $36,000 and $60,000 (plus bonuses at $150 for a win, $75 for a tie), with a handful of top players earning between $100,000 and $240,000.

There are now Africans from Ghana, Nigeria, Senegal, Gabon, and Togo, playing in Germany, Belgium, and France. Russians and other Eastern Europeans—formerly barred from joining foreign clubs—are arriving, too. They are an attractive proposition for Western clubs, because they cost less to buy and accept lower salaries than South Americans. Hardly surprising: A top player in Russia could expect only $400 a month, plus apartment and car.

But things are changing rapidly. After a 1992 win against mighty Barcelona, CSKA Moscow players were given a bonus of $25,000 each—"an obscene example of capitalist soccer," said a Russian newspaper, pointing out that it would take the average laborer, earning $20 a month, 100 years to make that amount.

Once big money came to professional soccer, the player's agent was not far behind, although his wings are slightly clipped by a FIFA regulation that forbids the employment of agents to negotiate the transfer of players from one club to another.* In England the rule is sometimes observed to the point of farce. The player negotiates with the club, but the proceedings suffer frequent interruptions as he leaves to consult his agent, who is hovering in the adjoining room.

The focus of all this money making and money spending is the soccer player himself. He may be Dutch or Brazilian or English or Italian or Mexican or, indeed, from almost anywhere in the world. To try to paint the picture of a "typical" professional soccer player is like chasing a will-o'-the-wisp, because the game is played by too many cultures and races in too many countries for a meaningful average to be arrived at.

Not too long ago, there were two characteristics likely to hold good for any randomly selected player: He would be from a working-class background, and he would have finished his formal education in his midteens.

The working-class background should not surprise anyone who has read this far, for one of soccer's greatest strengths has always been that it is everywhere a game of the people. As to the brief period of schooling, it should be remembered that the United States is the only country in the world that uses its colleges as farm teams for professional sports. Everywhere else, professional sport is seen as a trade that needs no academic qualification, a way of making a living that one starts as soon as one is able.

But that traditional pattern is changing, along with a changing society. As the dividing line between working class and middle class becomes increasingly blurred, so the stigma that once attached to soccer is disappearing. Soccer is no longer looked down on as a coarse, unworthy profession. There is now plenty of money to be made, and the idea of a middle-class boy leaving school to pursue a career as a professional player is no longer unthinkable.

This is not to say that soccer is suddenly being flooded with intellectuals. You will not find many university graduates among pro soccer players. During the late fifties and early sixties Phil Woosnam—a B.A. from the University of North Wales—played professionally in the English first division. Such was the novelty of a university graduate on the soccer field that in the press Woosnam's name was invari-

* FIFA is preparing a scheme under which it would approve agents who have passed a licensing examination.

ably followed by some such reference as "the footballing B.A." (Woosnam later came to the United States and was a leading figure in the
establishment of the North American Soccer League; see Chapter 8.)

Today, more attention is being paid to the whole question of education for young soccer players. There has been a general acceptance of
the need for professional clubs to provide alternative training for their
youth players. Such training is frequently pretty rudimentary—a day,
or a couple of evenings, a week featuring instruction on sports
management, for instance. But it does represent a massive change of
attitude on the part of the clubs, an admission that they should help
prepare boys for an alternative life in case something goes wrong with
their soccer careers.*

And those careers stand a pretty high chance of going wrong. In
England, it is estimated that three out of every four boys who join pro
clubs as youngsters are out of the pro game by the age of twenty-one.
Throughout the soccer world it is the same story, because nobody has
yet discovered an infallible, or even a reliable, way of developing
young players, of detecting which boy will make it and which will not.

A look at three young soccer players from Italy, England, and
Argentina, will give an idea of how top clubs go about nurturing talent,
and what is involved in becoming a pro soccer player.

Italy

You take the highway heading northeast out of Milan, heading for
Lake Maggiore. About forty kilometers along you get off the
autostrada, and the narrow roads twist and turn until you reach the
little town of Carnago. More twists, more turns, then just when it
looks like the road is running out, you see the buildings on your right.
A small, red-roofed complex nestling behind a substantial metal gate,
it has the quiet, well-ordered air of a prosperous convalescent home.

The gate slides quietly open, you ease your car onto the crunchy
gravel of the driveway as the gate slides back into place behind you.

---

* Before and immediately after World War II soccer was, by and large, a poorly paid
occupation of the working classes. But it had immense glamour, and most of those who
made it as professionals gave little thought to what they would do once they stopped
playing. The results were seen in many countries—men who were once idols working at
menial jobs and living in obscurity, even poverty. A poignant reminder came in 1993.
Eighty-year-old Raich Carter, who had partnered the great Stanley Matthews on England teams in the 1930s and 1940s, announced that he was selling all his soccer medals
and trophies to pay his medical bills.

This is Milanello, built in 1963 as a training area for AC Milan soccer club. It has everything—fields, both grass and artificial turf, gymnasiums bulging with modern training equipment, medical clinic, lecture rooms, recreation areas, and dining facilities. And, as you would expect of Italy's richest club, AC Milan, everything is first class.

There are dormitories, too, where twenty-two young hopefuls live while training to become the Milan stars of the future. Boys from the *primavera* team (ages 18–20), and the juniors (ages 16–18). Boys from all over Italy, from Tuscany, Sardinia, Calabria, Liguria, Puglia.

Among them is Alessandro Ercolani, born in 1976 in the small central Italian town of Sassocorvara, east of Florence. Soccer life began early for Alessandro, playing with older boys in the local park and—not always happily—in his schoolyard: "There was this time when I was running backward, watching the ball, and I jumped up to head it . . . but I didn't know there was a tree there, a pine, with a low branch. I hit my head so hard, it knocked me out, right out. . . . I was all right, though, just a big bump. . . . I don't think there was any blood!"

He has vague memories of Italy winning the 1982 World Cup. "We all watched on television, but after Italy's three ties in the first round, there didn't seem much hope. Then, with Paolo Rossi's goals and a bit of luck, we began to think we could win. After the final, we all went out into the street with flags and banners."

As a boy, Alessandro didn't care much for Milan. He was a Juventus fan. The Milan adventure began in May 1989. A trial game was organized in nearby Montecchio, by Milan, to showcase all the best local boys. Alessandro was invited to play—hardly a surprise, as he had already been contacted by several top clubs, including Torino and his favorite Juventus: "The game was on a Wednesday, after school. I was very nervous all day, right up to the moment when I arrived at the stadium. But once I got on the field, I was all right, and I played like it was a normal game."

Evidently, things went well. Three days after the game, the Milan club telephoned to say they wanted to see more of Alessandro. In June 1989 the fourteen-year-old Alessandro, along with his mother and father, traveled up to Milan, where they stayed in a hotel for three days, at Milan's expense: "It was a special tournament that Milan had arranged. I really felt exhausted in the end—it was so hot, and I had to play in two games in three days."

Milan was impressed and invited Alessandro to join them. He entered Milanello in August 1990. It seems right to talk of "entering" Milanello, for there is something monastic about the setup. It is

known, jokingly, as the Golden Cage, or—perhaps not quite so jokingly—as the Golden Prison.

The typical day for Alessandro and his teammates starts with
breakfast at 7:00, then a special bus takes them to the local high school
in Cargano. Says Milanello director Antore Peloso: "The education is
very important, our president insists on it . . . but there are some clubs
that don't."

The boys will attend the school until they leave Milanello at age 18.
They take the regular classes, but Alessandro found that "at first, the
local boys didn't look on us too well, they didn't like us missing classes
when we had to be away playing in tournaments. But slowly, we made
some friends."

At 1:00 P.M. the boys take the bus back to Milanello, where the
metal gate closes them in for the rest of the day. A light lunch is followed by training from 3:00 P.M. until 5:00 P.M.. Dinner is at 7:30. The
time between 8:00 P.M. and 11:00 P.M. is for recreation—television, bil-
liards, chess, darts, or studies. Tutors come in the evenings to help
boys who have fallen behind because of absence from school.

There is school on Saturday mornings, too, but the afternoon is
spent relaxing, getting ready for Sunday morning, when the boys play
their games in a regional league. In the afternoon they go into Milan,
to attend the Milan first team games, or—every other Sunday—those
of the city's other pro team, Inter-Milan.

The boys are paid a monthly allowance of between $100 and $135,
but spending opportunities are very limited. An unnatural life for
fifteen-year-olds, this Golden Cage? Alessandro demurs: "I've always
wanted to play soccer at the highest level, to become famous. I want to
make the most of this opportunity. And here, I think we mature a little
earlier. At home there would just be school. Here, we have two
schools.

"If there are no girls, well, that's a sacrifice we have to make. We
are at work all the time, there are so many things to do. Girls would be
a distraction—there's time for that during the summer vacation, we
get one and a half months at home then."

Taking young boys away from their homes does sometimes cause
problems, as Peloso admits: "We've had cases of homesickness, but we
always explain to the boys and the parents that this is part of growing
up. We pay for journeys home for the boys, once a year, and, of course,
in case of need, illness in the family."

The anxious time for the boys comes each year, in June, when the
one-year contracts expire and they find out whether they have been

"confirmed" (whether they will be invited back for the following year). Says Peloso: "We have meetings here among the staff, discussions to decide who should be confirmed and who not. We send a letter to the parents telling them, though in most cases we will have telephoned. Probably most of the boys know before they leave here—about 50 percent are not confirmed."

For Alessandro, confirmed every year since his arrival, the big moment arrives with his eighteenth birthday, when he can be signed as a full professional—if Milan offers him a contract. He would then leave Milanello and probably be sent on loan to a club in the third division of the Italian league.

He expects to make it, expects to become a top first division player. "That is my dream. But you don't live in dreams, now is what counts. I must work hard now." And Alessandro Ercolani, 5'10" left-footed midfielder, assesses his play: "I'm not so fast—sometimes when I go up, I can't get back in time, so I have to compensate with my brain, anticipating the play. I've got a strong left foot. . . . I'm not a goal scorer, I'm the one who makes the last pass—the assist" (Alessandro uses the English word, which has become part of the Italian soccer vocabulary). "I'm good at taking free kicks, pretty good with my head. But no one is born the perfect player, you can always learn something.

"If something goes wrong with my soccer career, well, I'm a good student, I would go to university to get a degree. My favorite subjects are math, electronics, computers, but I don't know what I would study, it's too early to say."

England

Goal scoring was something that came naturally to young Adrian Clarke. When he was nine years old, he once scored 9 in a single game for his team, Haverhill Echo. The following year, 1985, he scored 121 goals in the season, averaging around 4 a game.

That summer, he was playing in a five-a-side tournament, lots of short games, lots of waiting between games. During one of those pauses: "This tall man came up to me and asked where my dad was. I pointed him out—my dad was the coach of my team. When I was playing the next game, I could see them talking. I thought he was a coach, too, and they were arranging a game. My dad didn't say anything, but at the end, when we were in the car driving home, he showed me the man's card."

The card read "Steve Rowley. Assistant Youth Development Offi-

cer. Arsenal FC." Adrian was being scouted by one of most famous
clubs in England. "My dad gave him our fixture list, and he came to
four or five games next season. I remember he drove a Volvo. My dad
never told me when he'd be there, so I suppose I just played naturally,
but I could always spot him, in his long trench coat. After the games,
he wouldn't say much, just ask me how I was."

Until one day, Rowley popped the question: Would Adrian like to
join the Arsenal Centre of Excellence? All the pro clubs in England
run these training centers for young players, who could join when
they are eleven years old, which Adrian now was. (The admission age
has since been lowered to nine.)

By now, other clubs were looking at Adrian. He, in turn, looked at
the training facilities at Arsenal, at Southampton, and at Colchester—
and chose Arsenal. Attendance at the Arsenal Centre of Excellence in
Grays (about one hour's drive from his home), started Adrian thinking
seriously about becoming a pro player.

Soccer had always been a part of his life. He was born in Haverhill,
a small town some fifteen miles east of the university city of Cambridge. His father Harry, a chemical analyst, had been a keen player
in his youth with the London club Leyton Orient, had encouraged
Adrian to play, and coached his son's team.

The usual escapades for Adrian: "They tell me—I don't remember
it—that when I was a little kid, in the living room, it must have been a
party or something, I tried to head a balloon, and I head-butted the
sideboard instead. They had to take me to hospital to put stitches in
the cut."

And the trips with Dad to Ipswich, the nearest first division pro
club: "The first game I ever saw was Ipswich against Wolves, I was
maybe seven. I was an Ipswich fan, a Junior Blue, that's what they
called the kids. I remember that day, because it snowed the whole
game, it was settling on the pitch [field]. And Ipswich won 3–1."

In 1982 there was the World Cup in Spain, but Adrian doesn't
remember much about that, only that the England captain Brian Robson scored the fastest goal, in twenty-seven seconds, against France.
Adrian's own goal-scoring exploits were continuing, and the invitation
from Arsenal followed.

On his fourteenth birthday in 1988, Adrian signed for Arsenal as an
Associated Schoolboy. He had to do some thinking about that, for
there were now about a dozen clubs interested in him, including other
big names like Chelsea, Manchester United, Southampton, Ipswich,

and West Ham United. "I narrowed it down to three in the end—
Ipswich, West Ham, and Arsenal. I was still an Ipswich fan, but I was
beginning to switch to Arsenal—well, Ipswich were in the second division now. I was the one who made the decision. I'd been coming to
Arsenal for two years, I'd got to know everyone. They've got a good
youth record and good facilities. But in case Arsenal didn't want me, I
visited all the others."

Adrian was now linked contractually to Arsenal. In addition to his
training session every week, he played games for Arsenal's under-
fifteen team every Sunday.

In 1989 came another invitation, this one from the English Football
Association. An offer of a scholarship at Lilleshall. This was the F.A.'s
residential School of Excellence to which, each year, the sixteen best
fourteen-year-olds in England were admitted.

Clearly, there was a lot of prestige attached to this one, and it was
something that Adrian and his family thought about deeply. In the
end, Adrian decided it wasn't for him: "I was happy at my school, and
anyway I didn't think I needed Lilleshall to improve my football. And
wanting to live at home was part of it."

National recognition came to Adrian even without Lilleshall, for he
was chosen seven times to play for England Schoolboys during the
1988–1989 season, including games in Wembley Stadium against
France and the Netherlands.

Another decision day arrived in March 1991 when Arsenal—more
than happy with his progress—offered to sign Adrian as a full-time
trainee. To stay on at school, or to leave (which, being sixteen, he
could now legally do) and start as a trainee with Arsenal in July? "I
was a good student, I suppose, I'd taken all ten "O" levels, and got
seven A's and three B's, but it wasn't a difficult decision. I had no
doubts; I wanted to be a professional player."

Adrian's decision to quit school and sign as a trainee meant that
now he had to leave home. English clubs do not put their young players in dormitories, preferring to place them with families who can provide a cozy "Mum-and-Dad" home-away-from-home atmosphere.
Adrian moved into lodgings in North London, where he and another
trainee stayed with a family.

Arsenal would pay for that. And Adrian received a weekly wage of
$56, paid not by Arsenal, but by the government. He was now part of
the Youth Training Scheme, a job-training program that the British
government introduced in 1984. He could make a little more from the

youth games he played each week for Arsenal, bonuses of $6 for a win, $3 for a tie.

Four days a week, Adrian got up at 7:30 and took a bus to Palmers Green, where he was picked up by a special Arsenal bus taking the trainees to London Colney, Arsenal's training facility at the northern edges of the city.

Once there, he and the other trainees (there were sixteen of them) spent around twenty minutes performing some very menial tasks— pumping up balls, setting out cones, cleaning boots for the first-team players, who arrived for their training around 10:00.

While the first team practiced, the trainees went through their own two-hour session under the Arsenal youth coach. At 12:30, the trainees would clean up after the first team, change and shower, and eat lunch in the canteen. Then it was back home on the team bus.

Wednesdays were different. No training, this was school day, part of the YTS program that requires trainees to study on one day a week. The trainees would come into the Arsenal stadium at Highbury from 9:30 until 4:00 P.M. to study for a certificate in recreation and leisure. A two-year course that included field trips to leisure centers to study their management and to swimming pools, where lifesaving could be learned, plus courses on social skills—visiting restaurants, learning how to communicate with the media.

Adrian had a slightly different program, returning home to Haver-hill every Tuesday night and spending Wednesdays at his old high school, studying A-level math. He also studied for the recreation cer-tificate, but in his own time.

Saturdays there were games at 11:00 A.M. In the afternoon, if the Arsenal first team was at home, the trainees would attend that game at Highbury. Sundays were a day off.

The life of a seventeen-year-old learning to become a pro soccer player feels good to Adrian: "I enjoy the life. I can't think of a better way to make a living. It's a very competitive situation here, but that makes you more mentally tough. All the shouting, from the coach and from the other players, it's tough. But after three months, once you get over that, it's much easier."

Adrian Clarke, 5'10", 158 pounds, left-footed forward: "I'm left-footed, but I play left or right wing, sometimes in midfield. I don't really like it right up front; I don't like playing with my back to goal. I quite fancy midfield—I like dribbling, running at people. Those are my strengths, running at defenders, dribbling, getting in shots and crosses. I score goals—they tend to be longer-range goals, from the edge of box—not close-range tap-ins. My favorite players? Pelé and Platini. Nowadays, Chris Waddle and John Barnes, when he's on form."

Adrian Clarke, waiting, along with the other fifteen trainees, for the big day that comes soon after their eighteenth birthday. The day they learn whether Arsenal is going to offer them the chance of a pro career.

Argentina

Rafael Sanchez was born in December 1974 in the small Argentine town of Zapala, an undistinguished place of some 30,000 inhabitants in the foothills of the Andes, just seventy-five miles from the Chilean border.

Buenos Aires, the center of Argentina's soccer activity, lies over 700 miles away to the northeast. There were no top pro games for Rafael to watch as he grew up. He recalls some games on television, which he watched without any great interest. His father, Alberto, originally from Buenos Aires and a passionate Boca Juniors fan, tried to stir Rafael's interest in the sport, but it wasn't easy. Alberto worked long hours as a civil servant for the Neuquen state government and never had the time to devote to playing soccer with his son.

Enter Uncle Florentino. Rafael recalls: "It's funny how that happened, because my uncle was never a serious player, and he wasn't all that interested in the sport. But when I was about six, we used to play in the street every evening, just the two of us. Just fooling about, you can see that it wasn't really serious, because we never bothered with a ball—we played with those cardboard soft-drink cartons that we used to ball up. We would get through two or three of those every evening. But he knew enough about the sport to teach me how to kick and volley, you know, which part of the foot to use, because I really didn't know anything. It took maybe six months, and then I started to get interested in the sport."

The 1982 World Cup passed by without leaving much impression on Rafael. He watched some of Argentina's games on television but—pressed for a memory—can recall only Daniel Passarella's free-kick goal in Argentina's 1–2 loss to Italy.

By the age of ten, Rafael was a confirmed fan of Boca Juniors. His idol was Diego Maradona, who had once been a Boca player. He joined his first team, Don Bosco, and the coach gave him the #8 shirt. In Argentina, that corresponds to the position of offensive midfielder. His father Alberto now made the time to come and watch Don Bosco's games and was impressed with his son's play. He promised Rafael that if he wanted to become a professional player, he would take him to Buenos Aires where the big clubs could get a look at him.

Around the time of Rafael's fifteenth birthday, Alberto went to the telephone directory and looked up the number of the Boca Juniors training camp in the suburbs of Buenos Aires—La Candela, as it is called. He gave them a call to sing the praises of his son.

One of hundreds of such calls that Boca Juniors get every year. The man in charge of the youth division, Silvio Marzolini—once a world-class defender with Boca who had played for Argentina in the 1966 World Cup—gave his standard response. Bring the boy along to La Candela, and we'll take a look at him. No promises—and no expenses. Rafael's father would have to pay for everything, the journey and the accommodation in Buenos Aires.

Rafael has no trouble remembering the date: "The trial was to start Monday, February 18, 1990. So we left Zapala, me and my father, at six in the evening on Saturday. We got to Buenos Aires around midday on Sunday." An eighteen-hour bus journey, but the fifteen-year-old Rafael found he was too interested in all the new sights to be nervous.

The plan was for Rafael and his father to stay for a week in a hotel near La Candela, which is in the Buenos Aires suburb of San Justo. One Monday and Wednesday Rafael would go to La Candela for training with some twenty-five other young hopefuls from all over Argentina. On Friday the boys would play a regular ninety-minute game.

Things didn't start well. On Wednesday Marzolini spoke with Alberto and told him that Rafael's chances were slight. Rafael admits: "Physically, I wasn't up to it. I couldn't keep up the pace that they wanted." But the coach of the fifteen-year-olds had seen something that he liked in Rafael's play, and said he wanted to see Rafael in Friday's game.

The Friday session decided matters. Boca invited Rafael to stay on at La Candela. Alberto went back to Zapala, and Rafael, at age fifteen, remained to take up the life of a trainee professional.

At La Candela he joined seventeen other boys ranging in age from fifteen to twenty-one. They lived in a dormitory, two to a room, with all their meals provided. Boca paid for two trips home each year. That was it. There was no cash payment from the club. Pocket money for the boys had to come from their families.

A typical day consisted of an 8:30 breakfast, followed by training from 9:30 until 11:30 or midday. Each day the boys living at La Candela were joined by around a hundred boys who traveled in from their homes in the Buenos Aires area for the training sessions. Lunch was taken at 1:00 P.M., followed by an afternoon of relaxation, or studying, or maybe some TV watching—each of the boys' rooms had a television set.

At 6:15 the boys boarded a bus for a short ride to the neighboring suburb of Moron, where they attended regular secondary school classes from 6:30 until 10:30. After that, it was back to La Candela, a meal, and lights out around 11:30.

Saturday afternoons, from April through December, was when the boys played their league games. At age eighteen they played in what is, in effect, the country's fourth division, featuring the youth squads from all the big-name teams like River Plate, Newell's Old Boys, Independiente, and so forth.

During his three years at La Candela, Rafael was also called up to play for the Argentine under-seventeen national team. He helped the team to qualify for the under-seventeen World Cup in Italy in 1991, but injury kept him off the team in the final tournament.

He continued to play his original position, to wear the #8 shirt of the offensive midfielder, and still felt that he needed to be physically stronger: "I need to work on my stamina. And my heading, I should be better at that, for defensive play. But I prefer attacking, that's where my strengths are. I'm not a dribbler or a goal scorer, but I have good vision of the game, I can find the open man with a pass."

His boyhood idol, Maradona, was replaced by a couple of favorite players: defender Oscar Ruggeri of Velez Sarsfield, and Gerardo Martino, the #8 for that Argentine club with the very English name, Newell's Old Boys.

At age eighteen—not before—the young players can be offered a professional contract. That is what Rafael Sanchez and the other boys at La Candela dream of—the opportunity to make the jump from living on the pocket money provided by their parents to earning around $25,000 a year plus bonuses, to move from La Candela into an apartment in Buenos Aires.

Despite the geographical and cultural distances that separate them, Adrian, Alessandro, and Rafael have quite a lot in common. All three lead a soccer-centered existence, characterized by an early attachment to a professional club and a meager income. They continue at school until the legal leaving age—sixteen in England and Argentina, eighteen in Italy. The chances of them going on to college are slim, not because they lack the qualifications, but simply because a college education is not, and never has been, a part of the soccer scene.

Which means that in the traditional soccer countries college soccer teams are rarely of any great caliber—all the best players are already with pro clubs. In Italy and Argentina, as in most European and South American countries, high school soccer barely exists. Rafael did not play soccer at all in high school. Alessandro did, but dismisses it as "not serious." He and Rafael learned to play with their club teams.

The situation is considerably different in England, where the English Schools' Football Association has been in existence since 1904, and schoolboy soccer is a well-organized national sport. Adrian's appearances for the England Schoolboys team at Wembley were organized by the ESFA.

These different frameworks for youth soccer are reflected in the varying methods used for recruiting young players.

In Brazil, for instance, all of the big clubs used to hold regular *dias de peneira* (sieve days) for boys ages twelve and up. Any boy who fancied his chances could come along to the stadium for a trial—and they would come by the score, sometimes as many as one hundred to a session, raw talent, many of them without even a pair of soccer shoes to their name. A haphazard procedure, but it worked because there seemed, in the fifties and sixties and on into the seventies, to be an endless supply of gifted kids.

Social factors have undermined that system. The breeding grounds that spawned all those kids have been eaten up. The massive migration of people to the cities has meant much less space for kids to play on. Heavy traffic has dealt a mortal wound to street soccer, and even on the famous Rio beaches space and time are now restricted as everything gets more organized. Rising standards of living have meant that soccer is no longer the only career option for poor boys.

The search for young stars can no longer be left to chance. Sieve days are held much less often now. Instead, the top Brazilian clubs now operate like the Italians. They employ coaches to scout young players, to cooperate with small second and third division clubs to organize trial games featuring all the local hopefuls, exactly the sort of game that Alessandro Ercolani played in when he was fourteen. The coaches are modestly paid, but get bonuses for the players they discover.

Sieve days are regarded as a waste of time in England. "Yes, I was once with a club where we had invitational trials every Sunday," said the manager of a first division club, "and in one and a half years we must have seen sixty boys a month, and never one that amounted to anything. What would you expect? School soccer is so well organized, anyone who's any good will already have been spotted and grabbed by a professional club."

The earliest age at which an English professional club can "grab" a schoolboy is nine, when the boy—or rather his parents—can sign a contract under which he attends the club's Centre of Excellence. The contract lasts for one year, and at the end of that term the boy is free to renew or to sign another one-year contract with a different club.

At age fourteen, the boy can sign for a club as an "associated school-boy." Each pro club is allowed to sign thirty of these associated schoolboys. This is a different form of contract, one that gives the club much more control over the boy's future. He cannot now switch to another team without his club's permission; if the move is agreed, the club is entitled to receive a fee from the new team. If the boy continues to impress, a trainee contract will follow at age sixteen, followed by a pro contract at age eighteen.

As there is no such thing as a draft system in England (or anywhere else in soccer), outstanding schoolboy players are likely to find themselves getting a lot of attention from professional club scouts. Inducements or bonuses—either in cash or in kind—are illegal, say the Football League regulations, but plenty are offered, invariably to the boy's parents. Cash up to $100,000 has been paid to secure a schoolboy player, while in other cases the father has been given a bogus job as a club scout, complete with car and liberal mileage allowance.

As we have seen, waste from the ranks of the junior players is considerable. Only one boy in four can expect to make it to the professional level, and three out of four of those survivors will probably have to be satisfied with something less than regular first-team play in the Premier League.

For a boy who does make it all the way to the top, the glamour part consists of million-dollar contracts, fast cars, and national fame. For that he will be expected to play soccer virtually year-round, for the old two-month summer break has all but evaporated, taken over by longer seasons, overseas tours, and summer tournaments.

We are talking here of the player in England, but the situation is little different elsewhere. Just as with the junior players, the lives of pro soccer players are remarkable for their similarity throughout the world.

The English season starts in late August, but approximately five weeks before this, say the middle of July, the players report to their club for preseason training, always the toughest part of the schedule. This involves two sessions a day, Monday through Friday, plus a half day on Saturday. The mornings, from 10:30 to 12:00, are devoted to basic fitness and stamina—sprints, jogging, interval running, work with weights, calisthenics. After a light lunch, the afternoon session (ninety minutes to two hours) begins at 2:00 and centers on ball skills, usually ending with a series of five- or six-a-side games.

The second and possibly the third week of preseason training still occupies five and a half days, but the emphasis now turns away from fitness to individual performance and skills and the development of team tactics, though there will almost certainly be a couple of sessions during the week at the running track, with timed sprints. The remaining two or three weeks will be taken up with a schedule of games against not-too-difficult opponents; many English clubs now spend this period overseas, in Sweden or Holland, for instance, playing against local opposition.

Once the season proper has begun, the players train four days a week, in the mornings only, for two to two and a half hours each session. There is no training on game days, or on the day after. In England and Germany, game day is Saturday, with Sunday off. Other European countries, for example, Italy and Spain, play on Sundays, taking Monday off.

A typical week's timetable might look like this:

Typical Weekly Training Schedule
for a Player in the English Premier League

All sessions last from 10:30 until 12:30 or 1:00 and all begin with a light workout: jogging, sprints, calisthenics, etc.

MONDAY Individual skills—ball control, dribbling, tackling, heading, etc.; six- or five-a-side games. Detailed discussion of previous Saturday's game.

TUESDAY Hard day. Either a full-scale game, dealing with specific points (usually weaknesses) of team play, or a morning at the track, including running of timed sprints.

WEDNESDAY Day off (during most of the season, there is a league or cup game on Wednesday evening).

THURSDAY Thorough rundown of the opposing team in the coming Saturday's game. Practice of specific game situations linked to this.

FRIDAY Sharpening up team play, with emphasis on "set-piece" plays such as throw-ins, corner kicks, free kicks.

SATURDAY Game in the afternoon.

SUNDAY Day off.

Typical Weekly Training Schedule
for a Player in the German Bundesliga

Morning practices begin at 10:00, afternoon practices at 3:00. Players do their own stretching, then warm up playing five v. two games. On most days this will be followed by a spell of jogging and sprinting.

MONDAY Morning: three-mile run, forty-five minutes of six-a-side games.

TUESDAY Morning: three-mile run. Afternoon: ten minutes of five v. two games, forty-five minutes of six-a-side games.

WEDNESDAY Afternoon: ten minutes of five v. two, sixty minutes of eight-a-side or nine-a-side (or as close as numbers will allow to a full 11 v. 11 game).

THURSDAY Afternoon: ten minutes of five v. two, thirty minutes of eight- or nine-a-side, thirty minutes of "fun play"—e.g., keep-away, using hands and feet.

FRIDAY ten minutes of five v. two, fifteen minutes shooting and crossing drills, twenty minutes of eight- or nine-a-side, fifteen minutes of set plays.

SATURDAY Game day.

SUNDAY Day off.

This is an attempt to picture "typical" weeks, if there be any such thing. Some coaches may place their emphasis on different aspects of the game, some may want to include a session of weight training, some may insist on additional afternoon sessions if their team has struck a bad patch. In hot climates training will probably be held in the early morning or late afternoon, while in some countries, Italy and Brazil for example, it is the custom for a team to retire to the quiet of the countryside or the mountains for a day or two before a big game.

The man in charge of all this preparation is, of course, the coach.

He will be an ex-player, though not necessarily a star. Many of the most brilliant soccer players have been a complete washout as coaches, while many of the best coaches were no more than average players. The chances are high that he will have been a defender in his playing days.*

The modern preference is for "track-suit" coaches, those who are young enough and fit enough—and skilled enough—to get out there with the boys and show them how it should be done. Most of today's coaches have attended training courses organized by their national F.A. and possess a coaching certificate or license.

As for the money, in Germany, where all *Bundesliga* coaches *must* have attended a six-month, full-time course to attain the German Federation's coaching license, the average salary is around $300,000 per year. The English do not require any formal qualification for their coaches; the Premier League average is $175,000 a year (plus bonuses), with the top figure being around $375,000. At the bottom end of the English pro game, in the third division, the average salary is $43,000.

Brazilians tend to give a monthly figure when talking of coaching salaries—a reflection of the chronic economic instability of the sport in the country. Coaches are hired for a season. If they don't win anything, and obviously most of them do not, they are likely to be looking for another job within a year. Coaches with top clubs like Flamengo and Palmeiras can earn $12,000 a month ($144,000 a year), but the average is closer to $50,000 yearly.

Not that job insecurity is limited to Brazilian coaches. If a highly paid coach doesn't produce a winning team, he is likely to be shown the door, pronto. In early 1993, Gigi Radice had his Fiorentina team purring along nicely in second place in the Italian league. Then it lost a home game to Atalanta. There was a violent locker room confrontation between Radice and one of the Fiorentina owners, and that night Radice found himself out of a job. An extreme case, but one that forcefully makes the point: Big-time soccer is no laughing matter.

The impetuous owner of Fiorentina was Vittorio Cecchi Gori, son of Mario Cecchi Gori, rich and famous as a film producer. The two of them, both keen soccer fans, own Fiorentina. The powerful business-tycoon-owner has come late to soccer, but he is making his mark in Italy.

For most of soccer's history, there was no place for that very visible power group, so familiar in American sports: the owners—rich, power-

* See Chapter 7, page 201.

ful men running their clubs as profit-making businesses. The reason is to be found in soccer's history, in the insistence with which the English F.A. first spelled out in 1885 that the game be controlled by amateurs.

That sentiment was written into FIFA's regulations (with which all national F.A.s have to comply), which stated that a soccer club "shall not be used as a source of profit to its directors or shareholders."

The English F.A. regulations flatly prohibited a director from receiving any remuneration at all, while the shareholders' dividends were limited to 7.5 percent, a figure that was certainly not going to make anyone very rich. Which was exactly the idea: to keep the profiteers, the smart operators and the hucksters out of soccer, to ensure that the men who ran soccer clubs had the interests of the sport at heart.

But who would want to be a shareholder or even a director under those conditions? Well, plenty of people did. People who wanted to get close to the game, who wanted to be part of its excitement, who wanted a say, however slight, in its control. These were people who felt the soccer image was good for their business, but all were fans of the game.

The typical owner or director was—and at most levels of soccer still is—a local businessman, with little or no playing experience and certainly none at the professional level. Far from making any money out of soccer, if his club falls upon bad times he will be expected to come up with an interest-free loan. When the club does make a profit, the money goes "back into the game"—higher salaries for the players possibly, or better facilities, but not into the director's pocket.

That the idea works cannot be denied, but it is a double-edged sword. The get-rich-quick boys were kept out, but so, too, were the wealthy backers that the sport needs. Far too many soccer clubs suffered from a marked lack of skill in administration and personnel management—a lack of professionalism.

Club control by small businessmen is common throughout Europe, at all levels of the game. But the situation has changed dramatically in the past decade. The English F.A. has removed the restrictions on profit making from its regulations. FIFA has modified its ban, and is pressing for soccer clubs to become limited-liability companies.

In Italy, where the game is at its richest and most commercialized, the situation now resembles the American experience. Wealthy individuals or families control most of the big clubs. Italy's most popular club, Juventus of Turin, is owned by the immensely rich Agnelli family, also the owners of the Fiat automobile company.

Wealthiest of all is unquestionably Silvio Berlusconi, the billionaire owner of AC Milan. He is the head of a holding company that grosses

$18 billion a year and has 34,000 employees. It includes the fourth largest private television network in the world, along with publishing houses, department stores, property, construction companies, and 290 cinemas. Berlusconi has poured money in to AC Milan, turning it into the most famous soccer club in the world. In 1992 he paid over $90 million to buy six top foreign players.

Spending at that level is rarely seen elsewhere. Jack Walker, owner of the Blackburn Rovers, caused a sensation in England with his 1992 player purchases, by paying out $9 million.

The Spanish club Real Madrid has a totally different way of running its affairs, a way that is also popular in South America. At Real Madrid they do much more than just play soccer. There are facilities for swimming, athletics, tennis, and gymnastics, and the club has one of the strongest basketball teams in Europe. The financial core of Real Madrid is the money paid by the 62,000 members of the club: an annual fee of $200. Participation in any of the sports activities means further payments, the amount depending on the sport.

So successful has Real's formula been that their original buildings, grouped around the 115,000-seat stadium near the heart of Madrid, have long since proved too small. Since 1960 the club has developed a Sports City on a forty-acre site two miles from the city center, a complex of tennis courts, four swimming pools, basketball arena, gymnasia, track and field stadium, skating rink, five soccer fields, and two restaurants.

Madrileños who want to join the Real Madrid club face a two-year wait before they can even put their names on the waiting list. The club has had so many cases of fraudulent applications by people trying to jump the queue that it has a special committee to investigate them.

The 62,000 members elect the president, who in turn appoints a fourteen-member board of directors to run the club which, in 1992–1993, had an operating budget of $55.3 million.

Social aspects are even more pronounced in the major Brazilian clubs, particularly those in Rio de Janeiro—like the Fluminense club, which runs a rather exclusive operation including, in addition to soccer and many other sports, dinners, dances, theater and movie shows, picnics, and parades. In São Paulo, Corinthians have built Corinthians City in the eastern suburb of Penha. It has a thousand-seat cinema and a hundred-room hotel, in addition to the usual swimming pools, gymnasia, stadiums, restaurants, and the like.

But whatever its structure, a soccer club lives or dies according to the number of spectators who pass through its turnstiles. The table below gives an idea of crowd sizes and admission prices in some of the major soccer countries throughout the world.

Average Crowds and Admission Prices in First Division Soccer, 1993

Country	Average Crowd	Admission Prices
Argentina	20,000	$5–$50
England	22,000	$7–$35
Italy	33,000	$20–$145
Spain	30,000	$15–$100
Germany	25,000	$8–$45

Other important sources of income to soccer clubs are sponsors, advertisements displayed at their stadiums, sale of game programs (though these are rare outside England), and radio and television.

Sponsors include banks, and manufacturers of electronic goods, food, gasoline, and soft drinks. In Italy and Germany, a club may receive from $325,000 to $3.5 million a year from its sponsor. For the sponsor, the most obvious advantage is to have its name prominently displayed on the front of the team's playing shirts.

Soccer has tended to treat television with a great deal of suspicion. Live coverage of regular league games, for instance, is comparatively rare. The fear throughout soccer has always been that fans will desert minor league games en masse if they know they can stay at home and see first division games on the box.

Television coverage was also held back by the fact that most of the major television networks were state-run monopolies that did not carry commercials, which meant a lack of interest from sponsors. The networks were loath to telecast from stadiums where there were visible advertising signs. Teams that carried a sponsor's name on their shirts had to change to plain shirts for a televised game.

The conservative approach received solid backing from the state networks. They were quite content to pay small rights fees for broadcasting tape-delayed games and highlight shows.

As late as 1974, the money being paid by English television to the Football League was derisory by American standards. That year television offered a three-year contract at $4.7 million, or $1.57 million a year. When that was divided equally among the ninety-two clubs of the Football League's four divisions, it worked out at around $17,000 each. (That same year, National Football League clubs were getting over $1.5 million a year each from network television.)

Deregulation of television in the 1980s and the arrival of cable and satellite broadcasting shattered the old order forever. Competition and open sponsorship arrived, advertising boards proliferated all around the soccer fields, and the fees paid for game rights skyrocketed.

Such was the lure of the millions on offer that the structure of English soccer, unchanged for over one hundred years, was at last altered. The top English first division clubs had long been fretting that they were held back in making commercial deals by their association with the three lower divisions of the Football League. When it came to television, the top clubs were the attraction; why should they share the money with second, third, and fourth division clubs?

In 1992, the top clubs quit the Football League and formed the Premier League, under the nominal control of the Football Association. The new league's first move—indeed, the very thing that made it possible—was to sign a five-year, $600-million deal with the BBC and the satellite broadcasting company, BSkyB Television. In Germany, each *Bundesliga* club receives $2.7 million a year from a league deal with state television. In Spain, television rights for top games command fees of up to $400,000.

FIFA entered into a long-term contract with a World Consortium of broadcasting unions, selling the rights to the 1990, 1994, and 1998 World Cups for a total of $228 million. But while FIFA pocketed TV money with one hand, the other hand was waving frantically, trying to ward off the flood of televised games being made available around the world.

The old problem—that televised top-class soccer would kill off live soccer of lesser caliber—had taken on an international aspect. Now Brazilian and German and English and Italian and Spanish championship games were available anywhere in the world, via satellite. Highlight packages from the leagues were being aggressively marketed—to say nothing of the ever-growing list of international games between clubs or national teams.

International soccer, which had started its life in leisurely fashion aboard steam trains and transatlantic liners had now moved on through jumbo jets into the electronic age of instant travel. "The tide must be stemmed," said FIFA, but control of the airwaves, in the face of powerful TV-oriented entrepreneurs like Milan's Berlusconi and the growing army of viewers equipped with satellite dishes, was not going to be easy.

While American sports have always raised their hands in horror at the very thought of gambling, soccer made peace with it many years ago and takes substantial sums of money from legal betting on its games. The weekly "flutter on the pools" is as much a part of English life as the pot of tea, engaged in by over 12 million English men and women, many of whom have not the slightest knowledge of, or interest in, soccer. Each pools coupon contains a list of the week's games and the idea is to forecast a certain number of results—simply as a home win, an away win, or a tie.

There is no equivalent of point-spread betting in England. The winnings, tax-free, can be enormous: In June 1992 a man from Bournemouth (who did not want to be named) won over $3.3 million for a stake of 80 cents, the sixth time that season that someone had won over $3 million. The pools are based on the Football League's game schedules, and for the rights to use these schedules the pools promoters pay the English soccer authorities over $13 million a year.*

In Italy, the pools—*il totocalcio*—are run by the National Olympic Committee, and 35 percent of the money wagered is used to develop all amateur sports (not just soccer) throughout the country.

One of the biggest items in any soccer club's budget, one that figures under both income and expenses is "transfer fees," the money spent or received for players who are traded. Very few of these deals involve the swapping of players. Usually, they are straight cash deals, which gives everyone the satisfaction of putting a price on a player's head, of knowing exactly how much he is worth.

In 1973 the soccer world was astonished at the sum that Barcelona paid to buy the Dutch superstar Johan Cruyff, who became the first player to be valued at $2 million.

Twenty years on, nobody bats an eyelid at $2 million, you get an ordinary player for that. Now the almighty lira rules. Italian clubs dominate the transfer scene, and the prices have soared. Currently, the most expensive player is the Italian Gianluigi Lentini, bought by Milan from Torino in 1992 for 30 billion lire—$20 million. Right

---

* The only problem with the Football League's schedules is that the season does not last long enough. The insatiable English bettors spend the summer forecasting the results of soccer games played in Australia featuring teams they have never heard of and whose names they cannot pronounce.

behind him is another Italian, Gianlucca Vialli, who moved from Sampdoria to Juventus for a fee of $19 million.*

The rest of the world is left way behind. The record transfer fee for an English club is the $5.5 million that the Blackburn Rovers paid to buy Alan Shearer from Southampton in 1992. In France it is $7.5 million (the Liberian forward, George Weah, from Monaco to Paris St. Germain, 1992), in Argentina $2 million (Alberto Acosta, San Lorenzo to Boca Juniors, 1992).

Paying high transfer fees carries tremendous risks. The player may turn out to be not nearly as good as imagined, or the mere fact of knowing that he is so highly valued may upset him. On the other hand, some clubs have paid out small fees and picked up bargains, none greater than Real Madrid's signing of Alfredo di Stéfano—arguably the greatest player in the history of the game—for whom they paid $70,000 in 1953.

Pelé, another "greatest ever" candidate, never had a price placed on him in this way, for he played all his career for Santos and did not figure in a transfer deal. What we do know is that when, during the 1960s, there were rumors that the Italian club Juventus wanted to buy him, the Brazilian government stepped in to declare him a "national resource" and therefore nonexportable.

The explosive escalation of transfer fees draws regular and bitter complaints from the top soccer clubs on how ridiculous and potentially ruinous it all is. But no sooner has the latest broadside been delivered than one of their number forks out a new record sum for another star player.

Menacing as they may seem to the clubs that have to pay them, large transfer fees can be the salvation of the smaller clubs that are lucky enough to receive them. Such clubs frequently live a precarious financial existence, and their continual hope is to discover and develop a young player whose sale will wipe out their overdraft.

Behind the whole system of transfer fees is what, in American sports, is called the reserve clause: the clause in a player's contract that binds him to his club. In soccer, it used to be an unbreakable bond. Well, unbreakable as far as the player was concerned; the Italians called it the *vincolo a vita*—the bond for life. Once a player had signed for a professional club, he remained the property of that club unless

---

* Being the most expensive player evidently does not mean being the best. When FIFA organized a vote among the world's coaches to come up with the World Player of the Year, 1992, Lentini and Vialli came in equal thirty-third, with only two points each. The winner, Milan's Marco Van Basten, polled 161 points.

and until they agreed to release him or transfer him to another club.

The arrangement allowed the player very little say in his own career. He could not, when his contract expired, go shopping around, dealing with any club he chose, to see where he could get the best deal. He *had* to deal only with his current club; it would decide if he was to be traded and to which club.

Today, the reserve clause has been considerably weakened. Most countries now have tribunals that settle disputes between players and clubs and set reasonable fees for player transfers. In some countries, for example, Brazil, players over thirty are permitted to own their contracts.

A player who is in dispute with his club cannot jump his contract and leave the country to play for a foreign team. Soccer's restrictions take in the whole world, and they work like this. All professional players are registered not only with the league that they play in but also with their national F.A. Whenever they change clubs, the transfer has to be registered with the F.A.; indeed, the player cannot play for his new club until that registration has been made.

If a player moves from one country to another, he must present a certificate of transfer, duly signed by his old F.A., stating in effect that he is a player in good standing and not in violation of any contracts with previous clubs.

A copy of this certificate has to be sent to FIFA because one of the functions of FIFA is to see that its members respect each other's regulations and disciplinary measures: A player under suspension in one country, for example, is automatically under suspension in every other FIFA country. If a dispute arises between two national F.A.s that they are unable to settle among themselves, then FIFA will investigate and decide where the guilt lies. FIFA's power to enforce its decisions is considerable, as it can effectively ostracize a player, or a club, or a league, or even an F.A. from worldwide soccer.

If a player defaults on a contract, his national F.A. suspends him and informs FIFA, which then alerts all its members. The player becomes a pariah, shunned worldwide by any club he may approach. Dealing with single players is easy enough for FIFA, but even whole leagues do not fare much better, as the celebrated Colombia episode demonstrated.

In 1950 a group of wealthy businessmen decided to introduce professional soccer into Colombia. Unable to come up with enough top-class Colombian players to make a go of it, they started to look around for foreign stars. What they didn't particularly like about that arrangement was that it would mean paying hefty transfer fees to the foreign clubs.

Or would it? It occurred to the new league that if it ignored FIFA regulations and broke away from the Colombian F.A., it would then be free to approach directly any player it wanted and sign him without having to pay a cent to his club. Large salaries and signing-on bonuses were offered to top South American players.

The Colombian promoters were greatly helped by the fact that Argentine soccer was going through one of its recurrent crises, with players striking for more money. Eventually a group of top Argentine players (they included Alfredo di Stéfano) joined the Colombian pirate league, despite dire warnings from FIFA that any player doing so faced certain worldwide suspension and fines should he ever want to play again outside the league.

The "millionaires' league," totally cut off from international competition and unable to attract more than a handful of top stars, was brought to its knees and collapsed in 1952.* The Colombian F.A. resumed control of the sport in Colombia, and the clubs of the league were granted two years to return the players they had poached to their former clubs (one who did not go back was di Stéfano—he joined Real Madrid instead).

FIFA brings together the national governing bodies of soccer—the F.A.s—from throughout the world, and constitutes an international network that is often referred to as "organized soccer." It has almost as many members as the United Nations; at latest count the score was 180–178 in favor of the UN.

A meeting of the full FIFA Congress is not unlike a UN General Assembly meeting: 178 countries, each identified with printed cards and represented by up to three delegates, many of them using headphones to listen to proceedings in simultaneous translation. The congress meets once every two years, each time in a different city. The detailed running of FIFA is done by the Executive Committee (the members are elected by the congress for a four-year term) and by the full-time secretary and a staff of forty-two at FIFA's headquarters in Zurich, Switzerland. In addition, there are fourteen standing committees, plus a disciplinary and an appeals committee.

The Continental Confederations (see Diagram on page 145) are a way of decentralizing some of FIFA's activities, and allowing a degree

---

* A similar situation involving a pirate league arose in the United States in 1967; see Chapter 8, page 217.

Structure of the Fédération Internationale de Football Association

FIFA CONGRESS

The legislative body and supreme authority • Meets every two years
Composition:
Voting: each of FIFA's 178 national associations has one vote and may be represented by up to three delegates
Nonvoting: members of the FIFA Executive Committee

FIFA EXECUTIVE COMMITTEE

The executive body • Meets twice a year
Composition:
President (elected by Congress)
8 vice-presidents (appointed by the Continental Confederations)
12 members (appointed by the Continental Confederations)

GENERAL SECRETARIAT

The administrative body
Full-time Secretary-General, plus supporting staff, working out of FIFA's headquarters in Zurich, Switzerland

STANDING COMMITTEES

Emergency • Finance • World Cup Organizing • Olympic Tournament Organizing • Youth Competitions • Five-a-Side (Indoor) Soccer • Women's Soccer • Referees • Technical • Sports Medical • Players' Status • Legal Matters • Security Matters and Fair Play • Media • Protocol •
Plus two judicial committees:
Disciplinary • Appeal

CONTINENTAL CONFEDERATIONS*

Africa
Confédération Africaine de Football (CAF)
North and Central America and the Caribbean
Confederación Norte-Centroamericana y del Caribe del Fútbol (CONCACAF)
South America
Confederación Sudamericana de Fútbol (CSF or CONMEBOL)
Asia
Asian Football Confederation (AFC)
Europe
Union of European Football Associations (UEFA)
Oceania
Oceania Football Confederation (OFC)

INTERNATIONAL FOOTBALL ASSOCIATION BOARD

Responsible for the Rules of Soccer
8 members
4 of the members are appointed by FIFA (they normally include the FIFA president, the secretary-general, and the chairman of the Referees' Committee)
The other 4 members are one representative each from the English, Scottish, Welsh, and Northern Irish Football Associations
Any proposed change in the Rules must have at least six votes in favor to pass

* For full list of all the member nations of each confederation, see Appendix C, pages 279–81.

of home rule. UEFA runs the various European club competitions and the European Championship for national teams, the South American Federation (CSF) organizes the Copa Libertadores and the Copa America—but in both cases the competitions have to be conducted according to FIFA regulations.

A glance at the statistics issued by the Players' Status Committee underlines the inescapable fact that in terms of the *number* of players organized soccer is an overwhelmingly amateur sport. FIFA recognizes two classes of registered players: amateur and nonamateur. Grouped according to Continental Confederations, the relative numbers in these two classes are shown in the table on page 147.

FIFA estimates that there are some 150 million registered players in organized soccer. Of these, only 32,000 are professionals, which means that over 99 percent of the world's soccer is played by amateurs. Appropriately, their games are officiated by amateur referees.

Not so appropriate is the use of amateur referees in professional games. It has to be that way, because there are no pro referees in soccer. Top referees will have taken courses run by their own country's F.A., they will have passed certification tests, they will undoubtedly be devoted men. But they are part-timers.

The fees paid to referees vary from modest ($250 per game in the English Premier League) to pretty good ($1,500 in the *Bundesliga*). In Brazil, referees are paid .005 percent of the gate money from their games; a $50,000 take will give them a $250 fee. In Italy the per game fee is $600; expenses are liberal, and referees can receive up to $30,000 a year in compensation for time lost from their jobs.

At best, the leading referees can be classified as semiprofessionals. But in one key respect they remain out-and-out amateurs, because the vast majority of them have never played professional soccer.

This is a disadvantage at the pro level right from the start, for it undermines their authority and induces a defensive (or an overly assertive) frame of mind. Sad but true, the prevailing attitude of pro players to referees ranges from mild scorn to utter contempt. Not that too much should be read into that, for by the very nature of their work referees are hardly likely to find themselves showered with praise from players.

Nobody, not even the most critical of players, suggests that the soccer referee's life is an easy one. He is in sole command of a fast-moving, physical game on a field that is about sixteen times the size of a basketball court. For ninety minutes he has to be everywhere, see

Soccer Players Registered Throughout the World

Continental Confederation*	Pro	Amateur & Youth	Over 35	Women	Indoor	Totals
Africa	1,436	944,896	160,881	30,475	21,084	1,158,772
Asia	1,211	46,122,761	5,562,755	949,430	713,960	53,350,117
CONCACAF**	5,005	4,663,854	146,956	2,174,188	270,980	7,260,983
Europe	20,610	21,310,868	285,567	679,075	264,271	22,560,391
Oceania		609,591	33,032	17,864	18,000	678,487
South America	4,406	2,090,272	871,960	95,500	21,771	3,083,909
TOTALS	32,668	75,742,242	7,061,151	3,946,532	1,310,066	88,092,659

These figures represent the number of players in so-called organized soccer, i.e., players who are registered with their national associations. The overall total of soccer players throughout the world is considerably larger than the 88.1 million total shown in the table, for there are large numbers of all ages who play casually. Estimates go as high as a total of 120 million players. Based on figures supplied by FIFA.

* For full list of all the member nations of each confederation see Appendix C, pages 279–81.
** North and Central America and the Caribbean.

everything, and make a constant string of snap judgments—and they had better be the right ones.

But what is undeniable is that under the present system of part-timers, there is a huge variation in the performance of referees, and even in the way in which they interpret the rules. Increasingly, the part-time referee looks like an anachronism in the supercharged, highly commercialized world of pro soccer.

"While football has changed dramatically in terms of pace, competitiveness and anxiety for reward, it is still controlled on the field, where it matters most, from the ranks of the clerks, and shopkeepers and foremen. . . ." That was how an English writer saw things in 1968.*

The clerks and the shopkeepers and the foremen are still in charge, even though the changes in the game have accelerated rapidly.

* Arthur Hopcraft, *The Football Man* (London: Collins, 1968).

CHAPTER 6

Tactics

Hop into your time capsule and whoosh yourself back to England in the year 1873. They've been playing soccer under the London Football Association's 1863 rules for ten years now. Head for the nearest soccer field, and ask the players what tactics they employ (don't bother looking for the coach, there won't be one). Note the way the players look at you. They have no idea what you are talking about. Before they start giving each other sidelong glances, before they send for the men in the white suits, retire quickly to your capsule and head back to the present.

There were no tactics in 1873, and even the word itself was unknown in a soccer context. Coaches were not in vogue. For soccer, one of the consequences of being born in England was that nobody really thought about it in depth. It was, after all, only a sport, and all of its early exponents were amateurs who played it simply for enjoyment.

The English have always had a suspicion of analyses and intellectual explanations (something best left to foreigners, the French perhaps), and certainly sport was the very last thing to start getting intellectual about. Soccer was fun, it was healthy, it was manly—why complicate it with thought?

So there is little evidence in soccer's early days of any methodical, thought-out approach to the game. Soccer was, on the whole, a game that was improvised by the players on the field. Things happened during play, perhaps by chance, and if they worked they could be adopted and tried again.

The inspiration of the improvisations, the very lifeblood of those early games, was the skill of dribbling. The sport was often called "the dribbling game." The reason for all this dribbling was built into those 1863 rules, which totally banned the forward pass. Any attacking player who ran ahead of the dribbler was automatically "out of play" as it was then termed, offside as it is now called. Only lateral or backward passes could be used, and evidently they were not considered as much fun as dribbling. Even when the rule was changed, in 1866, to permit an advanced player to receive a pass—providing he had at least *three* opponents between him and the goal line—it made little difference to the way the game was played.

Heads-down dribbling continued to rule. You got the ball, and you dribbled past as many opponents as you could. If you lost the ball, there would hopefully be one of your teammates nearby to reclaim it and start his own individual dribbling odyssey.

Indeed, the mere fact of a teammate *being* nearby might be considered a tactical triumph in the 1870s, when C. W. Alcock, an early soccer pundit, was writing of "the grand and essential principle of backing up. By 'backing up' of course I shall be understood to mean the following closely on a fellow-player to assist him, if required, or to take on the ball in case of his being attacked, or otherwise prevented from continuing his onward course." There is no suggestion here that the player with the ball should actually *pass* it to the backer-up.

With this tremendous emphasis on individuality, soccer was not yet a team game and there was no place, indeed no need, for team tactics. The idea of the game was simple enough—to score goals. To this end the early teams swamped their offenses with eight or nine forwards, left two or three defenders to cope as best they could, and got on with the business of dribbling the ball through enemy lines. The goalkeeper, as a specific player who could handle the ball, did not enter the picture until the 1870s.

At about the same time, the Scots—those incorrigible rogues from the north who have never since lost the art of upsetting the staid ways of English soccer—fomented soccer's first revolution. Simply by doing what today seems so utterly obvious: They invented the pass. At last the potential for the forward pass, opened up by the 1866 rule change, began to be realized.

Teamwork based on passing entered the game. The Scots exhibited their talents during that first 1872 international against England in Glasgow. The English went home suitably impressed with the new "combination play," as they also were with the Scottish system of using two fullbacks rather than one. Both teams were still using seven or eight forwards, and for those who think that such extravagance in attack ought to have produced a deluge of goals, it didn't. The result was a 0–0 tie.

The new Scottish style was based on short passes made along the ground. It radically altered the nature of soccer and the mentality, to say nothing of the skills, of the players. From being a game of individuals in which one skill, dribbling, was paramount and in which players tended to cluster around the ball, it opened out into a team game.

Now, instead of opportunistic backers-up trailing the dribbler like carrion crows in the hope of picking up a loose ball, players had to start thinking about their positional play. They had to take up positions where they could receive the ball. The dribbler was now obliged to get his head up to see what was going on, to decide when to continue dribbling, when to pass, and where to pass. And he had to master the new skill of passing the ball accurately.

Soccer soon found another weapon to add to dribbling and short passing—the long pass. In the light of the subsequent development of the English game, it is entirely appropriate that the English themselves thought up this new development. It was the "secret weapon" of Blackburn Olympic, that team from the north of England that broke the eleven-year stranglehold that southern teams had maintained on the famous F.A. Cup. In the 1883 cup final, Blackburn used the long pass to repeatedly bamboozle the Old Etonians with wing-to-wing passing.

More new skills were needed—not only the ability to hit a long ball accurately, but the techniques necessary to receive, or intercept, or clear long passes. As the ball was more frequently in the air, heading, chest-trapping, receiving on the run, and volleying were now much more important parts of the game.

Suddenly soccer was no longer a game where the action was centered around the ball and a few nearby players. Now play might suddenly switch seventy yards from one touchline to the other. The field was getting smaller, no player could now feel that he wasn't involved, wherever the ball might be.

Players had to cover a lot more ground, they needed to be fitter than in the past. Then, in 1885 the English F.A. gave up its losing battle and legalized professionalism. The game was getting serious, turning into something more than a pastime for amateurs.

With the old individualism being replaced by team play, with professional players now entering the picture, tactics became inevitable.

Thus began the slow evolution of the sport, a sort of numbers game that reflects attempts to arrive at formations that ensure an ever-more effective distribution of the eleven players on the field.

Depictions of soccer formations always start with the defense, and always include only ten players. It is not considered necessary to include the goalkeeper, as his is the one position in soccer that has remained unchanged over the years.

The fullbacks come first. The formation of those early, offense-laden teams with two fullbacks and eight forwards would thus be 2-8. This was gradually modified to create a balance between defense and offense. First one forward dropped back to become a halfback (2-1-7), then two (2-2-6). By 1900 there were three halfbacks, giving a 2-3-5 formation.

Which is a good moment to pause for some general comments on soccer terminology. As the sport spread throughout the world, it took English words with it, words that were soon "adapted" into foreign languages. The very word *football* became, phonetically, *fútbol* in Spanish, *futebol* in Portuguese, and for the French *le football* (or simply *le foot*). The cry of "Goal!" was heard all over South America, though they spelled the word *gol*. The Brazilians called the backs *os beques*, the Italians called them *i bec* and shouted *enz!* for "hands" when a player touched the ball. It wasn't long before each country began to invent its own terms, and scores of soccer vocabularies, in scores of languages, were born.

But not in the United States, where the English soccer vocabulary came into use. Not only was it authoritative, but it was conveniently in the same language (or one near enough to pass as the same language) as well. The use of English terms has persisted. This is not a particularly satisfactory arrangement. English terminology has failed to move with the times.

Once a simple and acceptable soccer formation had been worked out (the 2-3-5), and the player positions had been given names, the stubborn English resistance to change took over. The game *did* alter on the field, but the English, in their terminology, did not acknowledge the changes. They went on using (and to some extent still do use) the original but now highly misleading terms for player positions.

Not all the eccentricities of soccer's technical language can be laid at the door of the English. Soccer is the least static of games, in which twenty of the twenty-two players are in almost constant movement, making the concept of "positional play" an extremely elastic one. Play-

Diagram 1 · The 2-3-5 Pyramid Formation

"Wing half" was a term applied to either the right or the left half. The right wing and the left wing are known alternatively as the outside right and the outside left, or as the right winger and left winger.

ing roles that are so easy to define on paper, or to illustrate in diagrams, tend to become alarmingly vague on the field.

The 2-3-5, for instance. With the team lined up in its own half of the field, waiting to kick off, the 2-3-5 can be represented as in Diagram 1.

Neat, but deceiving. Anyone watching a 2-3-5 team in action and hoping to see a line of five forwards moving smoothly up and down the field, with a line of three halfbacks always just the right distance behind it and the two fullbacks correctly positioned farther back, would watch in vain. There is altogether too much fluidity about soccer for it to be a game of rigid positional play.

The names given to each player position are shown in the diagram and need no further explanation. The numbers next to each position need a great deal of explaining. First, we are jumping the gun by about fifty years, for numbering was not introduced in soccer until the 1930s. Second, when it did come, it came more as a means of identifying positions than players. No. 2 was always the right back, No. 3 was always the left back. If right back Joe Smith was switched to left back for a game, then he would swap his No. 2 shirt for the No. 3 shirt. A pattern was set—and it still exists today—of describing a player by use of his number. "He's a good No. 9" means he's a good center forward. There was never any question of a player being assigned a number that was always his, to wear whatever position he played. That is still the general rule in soccer throughout the world. Only in certain major tournaments, like the World Cup, are players required to always wear the same number.

Because it was the first widely applied team formation and remained the standard for nearly fifty years, the 2-3-5 is often called the classic formation. And for obvious reasons it is also known as the pyramid.

That was the shape of things in the early 1900s. Rudimentary tactics there undoubtedly were, team play, too, but the English still did not use either term. In *Association Football and the Men Who Made It*, a four-volume, 850-page encyclopedia of the sport published in London in 1907, you will search in vain for any mention of tactics. Team play is referred to as combination play and is seen as something desirable that—even at this comparatively late date—is being resisted by the hardy individualists.

Clearly, with five forwards, the 2-3-5 stressed attacking soccer. Only three players, the goalkeeper and the two fullbacks, were out-and-out defenders. The job of the fullbacks was to protect the vital central area in front of the goal. The three halfbacks were expected to be both attackers and defenders. The two outside halfbacks (the wing halves) had, as their defensive duties, the job of keeping the opposing wingers quiet.

But it was the center half who was the focal point of the team. Primarily an attacking player, he was the brain of the team, the instigator of attacking moves. From his key position at the center of things, he was the team leader. He could decide whether to pass left or right, long or short, whether to dribble, or whether to surge forward into the opposing penalty area looking for a scoring chance.

Like some brilliantly plumaged bird he strode around the field, glittering in all directions, the multiskilled all-rounder of his day, the glory of the 2-3-5 game. And like many another gaudy-feathered creature, he is now long dead and gone.

What killed him off was a change in the rules in 1925. The complaint in that year (the very same one that was to recur sixty-five years later) was that not enough goals were being scored. Worse yet, attacking moves were being stifled before they got anywhere near the goal by defenses that had become masters of the "offside trap."

At that time a player was offside unless he had *three* opponents between himself and the goal line when the ball was passed to him. The complaint was that this made life too easy for the fullbacks. What was continually happening was that at the first sign of an opponent's attack, one of the two fullbacks, instead of falling back to cover, would move quickly upfield, away from his goal, leaving only two defenders (the other fullback and the goalkeeper) deep, and invariably trapping the opposing forwards in offside positions. For the spectators—and soccer was now a well-established professional sport—the repeated interruptions of the game as the referee whistled for offside were sheer frustration.

Something had to be done, and the solution was sought in a way that is familiar enough in American sports, but which is rare in soccer: The rules were changed. The offside rule was amended, and from 1925 on, an attacker needed only *two* opponents between himself and the goal. This made the offside trap a much riskier proposition. Under the old rule if things went wrong, there was still one fullback in a position to challenge. Now *both* fullbacks would have to move up, and the goalkeeper would be left on his own if they mistimed their move.

Justification for the rule change came immediately. The number of goals in the English first division shot up by over 40 percent, from 1,192 in 1925 to 1,703 in 1926. Now it was the defenders' turn to worry.

Reaction was swift, effective—and tactical. Defenses had to be strengthened, and it was Herbert Chapman who worked out how to do it. Chapman, an example of an average player who turned into a first-class coach, took over the London club Arsenal in 1925, the same year the offside rule was altered. He was then fifty-two years old, and his first step was to sign a veteran player, the 34-year-old Charlie Buchan as his captain.

Arsenal made a poor start under this new regime, and after a disastrous 0–7 defeat by Newcastle, Buchan and Chapman put their heads together to work out a tactical plan to counter the newfound freedom with which forwards were scoring. The player who was doing most of the damage, scoring most of the goals, was the center forward. They decided to put a crimp in his activities by deploying a third fullback, stationed between the other two, whose primary task would be to closely mark the center forward. So was born the first example of the modern-style man-to-man marker. He was soon nicknamed "the stopper," or "the policeman," fair assessments of his negative role.

The change set off a ripple of other changes through the 2-3-5 system. The attacking center half vanished from the English game. His position no longer existed. But the English stubbornly and illogically continued to refer to the center half, only now they meant the third fullback. A term that had once (accurately) described an attacking halfback with a glorious repertoire of creative skills, was now applied (inaccurately) to a fullback, who needed to be physically robust, good at heading and tackling, and who never, but never, moved up on attack. (To this day, the English persist in their perversity, even describing the twin centerbacks of the modern game as twin center halves.)

The gaping hole left at the center of the team by the killing-off of the old center half was filled by pulling the two inside forwards back to join the two remaining halfbacks. This gave a four-man midfield and a 3-4-3 configuration, though the formation is usually referred to as the W-M. A look at Diagram 2 will explain why.

Defensive responsibilities were now changed around, with the two outside fullbacks responsible for marking the opposing wingers, and the wing halves the opposing inside forwards.

The diagram, as always, not only simplifies but also falsifies. In the defensive W, Arsenal would have been horrified to see their three fullbacks playing in a straight line across the field (playing "square," as the English call it). Horrified, because with such positioning a fullback who is beaten has no teammate behind him to provide what has become known as defensive cover. To provide this cover, the Arsenal W was always a lopsided one, with the fullback farthest away from the ball retreating to a deep position, and the stopper slightly less deep. Responding to an attack by the opposing left winger, for instance, the Arsenal right back would move up to challenge, while the stopper, the left back and the left half fell back as shown in Diagram 3.

Ultimately any system of play stands or falls with the men who put it into practice. Arsenal's W-M prevailed because of the genius of Herbert Chapman in finding just the right players to fill the roles he had

Diagram 2 · The W-M Formation

The numbers are inserted to show the relationship between this formation and the 2-3-5. Thus the center half of the 2-3-5 system, No. 5, has been withdrawn to become a third fullback. His correct title is center back, but the English continued to call him the center half.

worked out. The ideal stopper was Herbie Roberts, not a greatly skilled player, but strong enough and tall enough to beat opponents on the ground and in the air, and with the placid temperament necessary for the unadventurous job he had to do. Roberts became the prototype of all stoppers, the tall, heavy backs who were to dominate defenses in English soccer for so long.

Arsenal's new tactics, though based on reinforcing the defense, were anything but negative in practice. In attack they employed two fast wingers with the ability to cut inside and score goals, while in the middle there was always a burly and brave center forward like Ted Drake, who could score with his head or with either foot.

The key to the success of the Arsenal W-M, though, lay in the func-

Diagram 3 · Lopsided Shape of the Defensive W

● – defending players   X – attacking players

As X₁ attacks down the left wing, 2 moves forward to meet his challenge, as 5 and 3 drop deeper so that they are in a position to cover 2 should he be beaten.

tion of one of the withdrawn inside forwards. This man now replaced the old attacking center half as the orchestrator of the team, receiving the ball from his own defense and deciding quickly what to do with it—whether to hit it short or long, to the wing or down the middle, or whether to dribble through on his own. The position called not only for a player who had the soccer skills to do all these things but also for one with the coolness and judgment to read situations quickly and decide which was the correct move to make. That was Charlie Buchan's role until his retirement in 1928. Chapman then brought in Alex James, the wee Scot with the baggy shorts, one of the great geniuses of soccer who was to steer Arsenal to triumph after triumph.

Chapman died in 1934, but between 1927 and 1938 the team that he built won the league championship five times, the F.A. Cup twice, and became known throughout the world as the elite of soccer. Such success did not go unnoticed, and by the late 1930s the W-M, complete with stopper, was the standard formation of every English club.

The defensive tilt was beginning to settle on soccer, for where Chapman had been a true originator, his disciples were content to copy mechanically as far as they could what he had done. And it was much, much easier to copy the third-back defensive alignment than it was to copy the attacking system. After all, finding a big stolid fullback to do Herbie Roberts's job was easy enough, but who could copy Alex James?

The old-style attacking center half may have been banished from the English game, but the breed was by no means extinct. It flourished outside Britain, particularly in Hungary, Austria, and South America, where they still favored the 2-3-5.

In the first World Cup in 1930, both finalists—Argentina and Uruguay—used the 2-3-5 formation. Artistry was the essence of South American soccer, and it was by and large individual talent that decided games. Tactics, evidently, were at a minimum. Asked years later about the role of coaching in those days, the Uruguayan left back Ernesto Mascheroni replied: "What are the coaches for? Only the player can solve problems on the field. What does a player do when he meets another who makes a fool of him? Ask the coach?" Argentina's Carlos Peucelle recalled, "We didn't talk about tactics, we just went out and played, and each of us knew what it was that we had to do."

Maybe, but there are strong suggestions that the Uruguayans were a better organized team than the Argentines. After the defeat, the Argentine press complained that whereas the Uruguayan halfbacks advanced the ball with passing movements up to their forwards, the Argentine defense was forever kicking long balls that were picked off by the Uruguayans.

The game finished on a note that, over sixty years later, has a familiar ring to it: Argentina, trailing by three goals to two, was doing all the attacking, but it was Uruguay who scored on a breakaway.

In Italy the national team was coached by Vittorio Pozzo, an implacable authoritarian noted for his astute psychological handling of his players. Pozzo had never been much of a player, but he was greatly interested in tactics. For his 1934 World Cup team he devised a scheme based on the classic 2-3-5, as played by the Austrians, Czechs, and Hungarians, the so-called Danubian school of soccer.

Which is where the ubiquitous Scots enter the picture again. For the Danubian school had developed from the Scottish short-passing game, brought to Central Europe by a remarkable Englishman named Jimmy Hogan.

Hogan, like Chapman and Pozzo, had never excelled as a player. But while with the London club Fulham he developed an interest in the theory of the sport. He played alongside and studied and listened to the Scottish professionals on the team. From them he formed his philosophy of the game, one that was never to change: that soccer was a game where the ball belonged on the ground, where it was to be moved around by short, quick passes, to players who moved intelligently into space. "Keep it on the carpet!" was a phrase much used by Hogan.

Arguably the first true coach of any stature in soccer, Hogan was a prophet without honor in his own country. The English weren't interested in his ideas, and his first coaching job came in Holland, in 1910. In 1912, Hogan moved to Austria, where he formed a lifelong friendship with another student of the game, Hugo Meisl. Wherever he went—and he was to coach in Austria, Hungary, and Germany on and off for the next twenty-four years—Hogan preached his "Keep it on the carpet!" gospel.

The Danubian style, based on the 2-3-5, was faithful to Hogan's concept—a neat, thoughtful, almost artistic approach to the game. By 1934 the Austrians had raised the style to its pinnacle. Hugo Meisl was the now the national coach, and Austria was considered the strongest team in continental Europe, dubbed the *Wunderteam.*

The Italians at this time had little soccer contact with England (they played each other for the first time in 1933), so it was natural that Pozzo should look to neighboring Austria for inspiration.

Pozzo felt that he could not simply copy the Danubian model because he did not have a player to fill the vital, playmaking center half role. The player he had in mind for the position was Luis Monti, an *oriundo* who had played for Argentina in the 1930 World Cup final.

Monti, now 33 years old, had never been known as a great runner. Pozzo abandoned all thought of using him as an attacking center half, and gave him a more defensive midfield role, where his emphatic tackling and excellent long-passing could be exploited to the fullest.

The role of midfield general and playmaker, formerly filled by the center half, was taken over by two players, the inside forwards Giuseppe Meazza and Giovanni Ferrari, who were withdrawn into midfield.

Diagram 4 · The Italian Metodo

A combination of the 2-fullback, 3-halfback formation of the 2-3-5, plus the attacking M of the W-M. In the Italian *metodo* the center half (CH) was still primarily an attacking player.

Thus Pozzo's *metodo*, as it was called, retained elements of the 2-3-5 (particularly the marking assignments under which the fullbacks guarded the penalty area and the wing halves marked the opposing wingers), but used the M formation for the forward line—a 2-3-M (see Diagram 4).

Monti's role at center half was more defensive than in the classic 2-3-5, but he was far from being the relatively static stopper center back that had become the defensive mainstay of the W-M formation.

The *metodo* proved ideally suited to the Italian player. It stressed methodical defense: As one Italian journalist put it, "The other team does all the attacking, but Italy wins the game." This was the birth of the lightning counterattack, which was to be the basis of the Italian game for so long.

In the 1934 World Cup final, the *metodo* triumphed over the Danubian 2-3-5 of the Czechs. Or did it? The general feeling was that strength and stamina, coupled with more than a hint of ruthlessness, had played a large role in the Italians' 2–1 win.

In the 1938 World Cup final, it was virtually the same match-up: Italian *metodo* against Danubian 2-3-5, this time represented by the Hungarians. An easy 4–2 win for the Italians. The *metodo* had proved itself capable of development, of accommodating a new, faster, more athletic type of game. The 2-3-5 was stagnating, its defensive system no longer adequate. The Hungarians looked slow and just plain old-fashioned.

For the first time in a World Cup final, basic tactics, represented by team formations and the Italians' more intelligent disposition on the field, were clearly a factor. After a reign of some fifty years, the 2-3-5 was on the way out. It would not be seen again in a World Cup final.

In the years before World War II, then, three main systems of play were in use:

1. The W-M—the standard formation in England.
2. The Italian *metodo*—part W-M, part 2-3-5.
3. The 2-3-5—the pyramid, still favored in South America and Czechoslovakia, Hungary, and Austria.

Within the various systems, soccer had become a game for specialist players, each with certain rather limited functions. Wingers, for instance, invariably stayed wide, waiting out on the touchline for the ball to come to them. It was not their job to retreat into their own half in search of the ball, nor were they often to be seen tackling opponents. Similarly, the center forward stayed upfield as the spearhead of the attack. The stopper had the most limited role of all, rarely if ever getting into his opponents' half of the field. The two wing halfbacks came closest to being all-round players.

There was one system that flew in the face of this trend toward specialization, a system that did not receive at the time the study that it deserved. Partly this was because it was developed in Switzerland, not exactly a mecca for soccer experts, and partly because it was a difficult theory to put into practice.

The *verrou*, or Swiss bolt, system was concocted by Karl Rappan, a former Austrian international player who from 1931 was the coach of Servette-Geneva, and later of Grasshoppers-Zurich. The aim of the bolt system was to create a team that would outnumber opponents in

Diagram 5 · <u>Verrou</u>: Attacking Formation

(The *verrou* is also called the Swiss bolt formation.)
A 3-3-4 formation, with the center half (CH) playing an attacking role.

both attack and defense, something that was possible only with players capable of switching rapidly from attacking to defensive roles and vice versa. On attack, the bolt had a 3-3-4 shape, complete with an attacking center half, and with all the players, including the three-man fullback line moving well upfield (see Diagram 5).

When possession of the ball was lost, all ten players retreated. The function of the four forwards was to harass their opponents, to slow down their attack, while the other six players raced back deep into their own half to take up the formation shown in Diagram 6.

The attacking center half now became the center back, while the former center back retreated to an ultradeep position behind everyone else. From here he could move laterally across the field, covering

Diagram 6 · <u>Verrou</u>: Defensive Formation

All eleven players are now deep in their own half. The center back of the attacking formation has retreated deepest of all, to the position marked DCB. The center half of the attacking formation (CH) becomes the center back (CB) of the defensive formation.

the other three backs and functioning as the sliding "bolt" to lock out opposing forwards.

The bolt system needed highly fit players who could cope with a good deal of high-speed running, who had the skill to operate both as attackers and defenders, and who possessed a highly developed sense of positional play. Small wonder, then, that it was not a system that caught on widely. It did, however, contain two features—the retreating defense and the lone fullback playing deep—that we shall meet up with again.

In South America the game was changing, too, but the demise of the attacking center half was strongly resisted. After World War II, the

Uruguayans settled for the *metodo*, which allowed them to keep their center half in midfield. This was the system they took to Brazil, to play in the first of the post–World War II World Cups.

For the Brazilians themselves the overriding consideration at that time was to find a system that allowed as free a rein as possible to their exquisitely skilled forwards. They produced an attack-oriented version of the W-M that they called the diagonal system. With only two full-time defenders, who covered the center and the right flank, the system seemed potentially vulnerable on its left side, where the defensive duties were the responsibility of a withdrawn left halfback who was also expected to move upfield to join in attacking moves. This was also a system that relied on an attacking center half and on two withdrawn inside forwards with the skill to dribble their way forward into the opposing penalty area.

In the 1950 tournament, the formation worked beautifully against Mexico, who were seen off by a 4–0 score, but misfired disastrously against Switzerland, who used their bolt system to hold the Brazilians to a 2–2 tie.

Something near to panic took over in the Brazilian camp, and coach Flavio Costa made six changes for the next game, against Yugoslavia. Brazil switched to a new formation—or at least one that was new to them—an orthodox W-M, with halfbacks Bauer and Danilo and inside forwards Zizinho and Jair forming the "magic square" in midfield.

Desperate measures, but they worked. Brazil dispatched Yugoslavia by a 2–0 score. As the tournament progressed the Brazilian W-M proved ever more successful. In the final round, Sweden and Spain were buried by 7–1 and 6–1 scorelines respectively. The final obstacle to Brazil's first-ever World Cup title was Uruguay, which had been struggling along with its hybrid, and seemingly outmoded, *metodo*.

Except that, when it came to the final, the Uruguayans made all sorts of modifications. The danger to them, of course, came from Brazil's quicksilver forwards and the facility with which they were scoring goals. But the Uruguayans had done their homework. They had seen how the Swiss bolt had contained the danger, and, in particular, they had noted the effectiveness of the deep-lying, covering fullback.

"Don't let them shoot from inside the area" was the advice of the Uruguayan goalkeeper Roque Maspoli, and coach Juan Lopez worked out a scheme to accomplish just that end.

Fullback Matias Gonzalez became the deep back—he was not, under any circumstances, to allow himself to be drawn out of the penalty area. Halfbacks Schubert Gambetta and Victor Andrade (who, under the *metodo*, marked the Brazilian wingers Chico and Friaca) were told to mark tightly and not allow the wingers to get in crosses. Should a cross come in from the opposite flank, they were to leave their man to help cover the center of the penalty area.

Even the center half Obdulio Varela, who was normally the play-making sparkplug of the team, was given a primarily defensive role (though "there was no need to give him instructions," said Lopez, "he was the captain"), as was inside forward Julio Perez.

The Uruguayan offense was based on the swift counterattack. Setting off these strikes was the function of the wily Juan Schiaffino, patrolling midfield to pick up balls played out by his defenders. He would then pass long to winger Alcide Ghiggia, who, it was thought, could turn what was considered the suspect left side of the Brazilian defense.

Playing according to this scheme, Uruguay bore little resemblance to a *metodo* team. With the deep-lying halfbacks Gambetta and Andrade operating, to all intents and purposes, as extra fullbacks, the Uruguayan formation was much closer to the 4-3-3 that the Brazilians themselves would use so successfully twelve years later in Chile.

For almost the entire first half, intense Brazilian pressure kept the Uruguayans on the defensive. But the Brazilians were held to one goal. In the second half, the Uruguayan counterattacks exposed the fragility of the Brazilian defense with right winger Ghiggia racing away to provide the pass for the first goal, then breaking through on his own to score the winner.

Uruguay's 2–1 victory over Brazil in the 1950 final is still the most astonishing upset in World Cup history. Tactics played a large part in that win, and in the words of Juan Lopez, "intelligence, skill, and improvisation did the rest." There was also a suspicion that Brazil, late converts to the W-M, had not really mastered its intricacies.

The 1950 final was, in fact, a tactical mishmash. One undisputed strength of the W-M was the clarity and rigidity of its defensive man-to-man marking assignments. Yet the Brazilians, sweeping headily forward on the attack, failed to assign anyone to mark the lethal Schiaffino. Even more disastrously, they failed either to switch, or provide support for, fullback Bigode, even though it was apparent early in the game that Ghiggia was too quick for him.

On the other hand, tight marking was not supposed to be a feature of the *metodo*, yet here were the Uruguayans, marking tenaciously all over the field. The Uruguayans, said an Italian journalist, had proved themselves the world champions at marking.

By the time of the 1954 World Cup, the attacking center half was on his last legs. The Brazilians had abandoned him along with the diagonal and were now experimenting with a third back. Even the Austrians, who in Ernst Ocwirk possessed one of the greatest attacking center halves of all time, deployed him as a third back. Only the Uruguayans persisted.

It was not the center half that occupied soccer's attention in the early 1950s, however, but rather the center forward, and in particular what the Hungarians had done to him. This was the era of the all-conquering Magic Magyars, and one of the reasons for their success was their use of the so-called withdrawn center forward.

To understand just what was happening, we must go back to 1925 and Herbert Chapman. His invention of the third back not only killed off the attacking center half but it also meant the end of the old-style center forward. Until then, the center forward had been an all-rounder who needed all the attacking skills—dribbling, shooting, heading, speed. But to cope with the close marking of the rugged third back, a new type of center forward was required. A strong, powerful, battering-ram of a player, typified by Arsenal's fearless Ted Drake. A crucial feature of games involving two W-M teams was always the man-to-man struggle between stopper and center forward.

Brawny center forwards were Hungary's dilemma in the 1950s because . . . they didn't have any. Marton Bukovi, coach of the Budapest club Voros Loboga, got around the problem this way. At "center forward" he put a player, Peter Palotas, who in ball skills and physique was similar to the pre-1925–type center forward. To keep him away from the smothering attentions of the opposing stopper, Bukovi required Palotas to play in midfield, well behind the usual advanced center forward position. This was fine with Palotas, for it meant that he could virtually continue to play in the style of an attacking wing half—his former position.

He was not, in fact, a center forward at all. From his deep position he would be a prompter of attacks, a distributor of passes, rather than a goal scorer. That role now passed to the two inside forwards, who were moved up front into the area vacated by the center forward. The final touch to the reorganization of the forward line was to pull the two wingers back, so that the attacking M had been turned upside down into a W, as Diagram 7 shows.

Diagram 7 · Hungarian W Attack

In effect, the old attacking M turned upside down. The wingers (RW and LW) were pulled back, as was the center forward—now playing as a so-called deep center forward (DCF). In his place the two former inside forwards moved up, both playing the role of center forward (CF).

These changes were the basis for the great Hungarian national team that coach Gustav Sebes formed in the 1950s.

The formation that he developed is shown in Diagram 8, along with the names of the players and the numbers they wore.

Unlike American football, soccer is not a game in which a team's offense and defense operate as two discrete units. The two are inseparable, and the radical change represented by the offensive W meant altered roles for the defenders playing behind it.

Midfield was occupied by Nandor Hidegkuti, by Jozsef Bozsik, whose duties were primarily offensive, and by Jozsef Zakarias, who concentrated on defense.

While it is probably true to say that any team that contained four

Diagram 8 · The Hungarian National Team, 1953

With this basic formation, the Hungarians went undefeated for over four years, from May 1950 until July 1954. They were Olympic champions in 1952. Defeat finally came in the most important game of all, the 1954 World Cup final, when they were beaten 2–3 by West Germany.

such brilliant players as Hidegkuti, Bozsik, Ferenc Puskas, and Sandor Kocsis would have been successful, it is also true that Sebes's new formation was perfectly tailored to make the maximum use of their talents. The novelty of the style also helped to bemuse opponents, never more so than when Hungary crushed England at Wembley in 1953.

What the English got from the Hungarians was a lesson in the dangers of tactical stagnation. The English took the field with a standard W-M. They had been playing their W-M games for nearly twenty-five years. Week in, week out, in club games all over the country, the stoppers, wearing No. 5, would do battle with the opposing center forwards, who always wore No. 9. The right back No. 2 would mark the left winger No. 11, and the left back No. 3 would mark the right winger No. 7. It seemed as though that was the way God had ordained the game should be played.

If that was the way God wanted it, then the Hungarians were the most dangerous of heretics. The Hungarian attacking W threw the English defenders into total confusion. Incredibly, almost laughably, it seems that the English paid more attention to the numbers on the Hungarian shirts than they did to what the players wearing them were actually doing.

Thus Harry Johnston, the English stopper center half, was quickly confronted with a dilemma. He was accustomed to marking a lone center forward wearing the No. 9 shirt, but he found that the Hungarian No. 9, Hidegkuti, spent most of the time playing behind Puskas and Kocsis, whose numbers, No. 10 and No. 8, suggested that they should have been inside forwards.

If Johnston allowed himself to be lured forward by Hidegkuti, he left vital, central space unguarded. If he protected the space, then he left Hidegkuti unmarked. The English fullbacks, confronted—or rather *not* confronted—by the withdrawn Hungarian wingers, faced the same problem. To go or to stay?

There is no need to labor the point: England simply did not know what was going on; they were beaten 3–6 and the score, if anything, flattered them. In retrospect it seems incredible that the basically simple Hungarian idea of reversing the attacking formation could not have been rather quickly countered by altering the defensive alignment. But perhaps that was asking too much of the English, who still retained something of the early amateur attitude that soccer was something to play, not to think about. Tactics were still viewed with at best suspicion, at worst contempt.

The English, so insistent that anyone wearing No. 9 *must* be a center forward, described Hidegkuti as a "withdrawn center forward." An absurd term, as Hidegkuti was not a center forward at all.

Hungary's dazzling forward play naturally overshadowed everything else about the team, but there was much that was interesting about their defense, too. Diagram 9 shows the Hungarians on the attack, with their forwards deep into enemy territory.

The significant thing about the defense is the extent to which the three fullbacks moved upfield in support of the attack. This left a considerable amount of unguarded space behind them, but the danger of opponents exploiting this by pushing the ball through for their forwards to chase was to some extent mitigated by the adventurous play

Diagram 9 · Hungarian Attacking Formation

All players have moved well upfield. Zakarias is virtually functioning as a fourth full-back. The diagram clearly shows the relationship between this formation and the 4-2-4 that the Brazilians were to develop in 1958.

of the Hungarian goalkeeper Gyula Grosics, who often came out of his area to kick—or even head—the ball away.

The advanced position of the fullbacks also reduced the midfield area (i.e., the space between the forwards and the backs), a desirable effect as the Hungarians had only two players, Hidegkuti and Bozsik, operating there full-time. The other "halfback," Zakarias, was functioning primarily as a fourth fullback.

Way back in the 1860s the English had started playing soccer with one fullback; in 1872 the Scots made it two; in 1925 Arsenal had introduced the third back; and now here were the Hungarians with approximately three-and-a-half fullbacks.

The figure was rounded off to four by, rather surprisingly, the attack-minded Brazilians with the 4-2-4 formation that won them the 1958 World Cup. This is when the numbers game really begins in soccer's vocabulary. The 2-3-5 and 3-4-3 formations that we have been discussing were not talked of in that numerical way at the time; they were the pyramid and the W-M.

But in 1958 all the talk was of the 4-2-4. Methodical coaching was on the rise, and identifying formations with numbers gave them a more modern, a more *scientific* sound.

The seeds of the 4-2-4 had been sown back in 1950, when the Uruguayans had in effect used four defenders in the final. Certainly the club team Real Madrid—built around the greatest all-round player of them all, the Argentine Alfredo di Stéfano—also used a 4-2-4 during the 1950s. But it was the Brazilians who brought it to maturity.

The 4-2-4 is a satisfyingly symmetrical formation (see Diagram 10), but once again the simplicity of the diagram belies the sophistication of the reality.

Despite the four fullbacks, the 4-2-4 as played by the 1958 Brazilians was a far from defensive scheme. An exhilarating feature was the attacking role of the two outside backs. This had not been much to coach Vicente Feola's liking in the beginning. Indeed, when Nilton Santos had raced upfield with the ball in the opening game against Austria, Feola had jumped up and yelled at him to pass and go back to his proper position. But Santos raced on, drew the Austrian goalkeeper out, and flicked the ball past him.

Feola was quick to applaud the goal, and from then on the overlapping fullback was a regular part of Brazilian play. On attack, the formation became 2-4-4, enabling Brazil to commit as many as eight players to the offense.

The new role called for a new type of fullback, quick moving, with a fair share of the forward's talents, the ability to exchange short passes and to shoot accurately. A far cry from the days of the old W-M fullbacks whose main functions were to stay deep, win the ball by hard tackling, then kick it deep downfield.

Up front for Brazil were Vava and Pelé, absolutely devastating as twin spearheads with their delicate passing, constant position-switching, and thunderous shooting, while on the right wing lurked the bandy-legged Garrincha.

More than Pelé, more than any other single player, it was Garrincha who inspired the Brazilians to their 1958 victory. A fact that is worth underlining, for Garrincha was an uncoached, almost uncoachable player.

Diagram 10 · The 4-2-4 Formation

Used by the Brazilians in the 1958 World Cup. The right and left backs were expected to play an adventurous role, even to the extent of joining in attacking moves. The left wing was frequently pulled back to operate as a third midfield player.

In a sense, Garrincha had little connection with the 4-2-4. He was just a brilliant ball player doing his thing out on the right wing, and his success stands—or should stand—as a warning to those who believe that carefully worked out tactics and alignment diagrams are what soccer is all about.*

As Brazil spent most of its time on attack, its defensive adjustment excited little comment at the time. When their opponents had the ball, Brazil's left winger, Mario Zagalo, quickly withdrew into midfield to

* One month before the World Cup, during an exhibition game in Italy, Garrincha had dribbled through the entire Fiorentina defense, right to the goal line. There, instead of cutting in and shooting, or crossing the ball, he waited for another defender to challenge, beat him, and then scored the goal. The Italian crowd loved it, but coach Feola was furious: "Garrincha is undisciplined—there's no place for showing off like that in the World Cup." He dropped Garrincha, only restoring him when the other players demanded his return.

Diagram 11 · The 4-3-3 Formation

The formation incorporates only one winger — the diagram shows him positioned on the right, but he can equally well be on the left.

make a 4-3-3 alignment. If the other team's pressure was sustained, he would fall even farther back, into his own penalty area. During the final he was at one point positioned on his own goal line to head away a Swedish shot that had beaten goalkeeper Gylmar.

The 4-2-4 succeeded in 1958 because their extravagant attacking talents allowed the Brazilians to maintain relentless pressure on their opponents. But it contained a serious weakness. When forced into a defensive mode, the 4-2-4 was dangerously underpopulated in midfield.

Whether the Brazilians really needed to worry about this weakness four years later in Chile seemed questionable. But the times were moving against enterprising soccer. Tactics was fast becoming the science of forging cast-iron defenses. Sadly, the Brazilians mirrored this trend by opting for a 4-3-3 formation (see Diagram 11). Zagalo—who, in Sweden, had been a winger who dropped back to help out in mid-field—now became a midfielder who occasionally ranged forward to help the offense.

Pelé was injured early in the tournament and played no significant part in Brazil's 1962 triumph. The individual star was unquestionably Garrincha, who was, by and large, left alone by coach Aimoré Moreira to use his abundant, unpredictable talent as he wished. It was Garrincha who inspired Brazil's 3–1 quarterfinal win over England and the 4–2 win over hosts Chile in the semifinal.

But, for all his game-winning brilliance, Garrincha was not a representative figure of the soccer of the time. He was an individualist, a freelancer, whose soccer instincts told him where to be and what to do during a game. By the tactical requirements of modern coaching, he was exactly what Feola had called him—undisciplined. Such players, once the game's pride and joy, were becoming problem players.

It was yet another sign of the times, another portent of the defensive clouds that were gathering over the game. Proof of the trend, if proof were needed, could be found in the goal-scoring statistics from the World Cup tournaments. The high point had been reached in 1954, with an average of 5.38 goals per game. In Sweden, in 1958, the average dropped to 3.60 per game. In Chile it sank to its lowest ever, 2.78.

World Cup	Goals	Games	Average per Game
1954	140	26	5.38
1958	126	35	3.60
1962	89	32	2.78

It was Italy that provided the most fertile soil for the growth of defensive tactics. The Italians had perfected a system that used the deep-lying fullback seen in Switzerland's 1950 *verrou* formation. *Catenaccio,* literally meaning a great big chain, was the name the Italians gave to their system.

A chain of defenders, that is, designed to strangle the opposing offense. Three of the fullbacks were given strict man-to-man marking duties. Behind them was the deep fullback—the Italians called him the *libero,* or free man, because he had no specific opponent to mark. His job was to patrol the entire center of the defense and to quickly close any gaps that might be opened by other defenders' errors.

The history of *catenaccio* tells much about the development of soccer tactics. There was absolutely nothing positive about its origin. It was not designed to win games, but rather to avoid losing them, or to avoid losing by heavy scores.

The Italian Serie A (first division) had long been an unbalanced league, with a few rich clubs regularly carrying off all the honors. In 1947, coach Nereo Rocco took over at Triestina, a small club that was barely surviving in Serie A. It was Rocco who loosed *catenaccio* on the soccer world, finding in it the means by which his small club could be competitive. He had immediate and dramatic success: In 1948, Triestina climbed to second place in the league. Other clubs began to copy.

The trend accelerated in the early 1950s when, as we have seen, the rich Italian clubs started to spend large sums of money signing up players from Argentina and Uruguay (the amateur Swedes and Danes could be gotten without having to pay big transfer fees, but only the rich clubs could offer them attractive salaries). Almost without exception these imports were brilliant-attacking players, and to counter them the smaller clubs sank further and further into the grips of *catenaccio*. Soon it was being played at home games, as well as away, then the defense was even further padded by having the *libero* play behind a line of four fullbacks, rather than three, leaving only two forwards to cope as best they could up front.

There was no denying the success, in terms of results, that *catenaccio* brought. It *did* make it very difficult for the opponents to score, and there was always the possibility that the defending team, breaking away suddenly, might snatch a goal. It happened far too many times for it to be accidental.

Eventually *catenaccio* became more than a style of play. It became a mentality that dragged Italian soccer down through boring negativity to almost total sterility. For, inevitably, the big clubs joined in. They did so with considerably more flair than the small clubs, but it was still *catenaccio*.

Helenio Herrera perfected the system with Inter-Milan, who won the European Cup twice using their brand of *catenaccio*. And it must be admitted that Herrera's version was by no means a wholly defensive affair, for Inter featured several fine attacking players such as Jair (from Brazil), Luis Suarez (from Spain), and Sandro Mazzola, while at left back there was the tall and rangy Giacinto Facchetti, who had perfected the role of the "overlapping" fullback, ever ready to race upfield and join in the attack.

When Inter did attack they were an exciting team to see, but it happened too rarely, an occasional firework of brilliance shooting out

Diagram 12 · Catenaccio

In its ultradefensive forms, *catenaccio* features a *libero* playing behind a line of four fullbacks (with an extra center back), three midfielders, and only two strikers up front—or even four midfielders, with only one striker.

from the gloomy darkness of the *catenaccio* defense. Watching them was a frustrating experience, for there was always the feeling that the players were under constraint, that their considerable talents were being shackled by the system.

That was Inter, the cream of the *catenaccio* crop. When two so-so teams met and both employed *catenaccio*, both packing their penalty areas and hoping to snatch a sudden goal at the other end, then the game degenerated into a colossal bore.

But *catenaccio* had a special appeal for the Italians because it relied on the sudden counterattack to score goals. The quick breakaway, the rapid switch from defense to attack, had long been a feature of the Italian game. Now it had been given an almost scientific basis.

The English, ever averse to foreign influence, were not greatly interested in the development of *catenaccio*. They acknowledged the coming of the *libero,* but coined their own term for the position. They called him the sweeper, the man who moved about at the back of the defense, cleaning up the errors of his teammates.

Having named the position, the English proceeded largely to ignore it. In the 1966 World Cup, their two center backs were Jack Charlton—the tall, rocklike personification of the stopper—and the captain Bobby Moore. Moore's role certainly allowed him more freedom than Charlton's, but he was not in any sense a deep-lying fullback. To complete the confusion, the English stuck to their traditional nomenclature, and referred to the two center backs as "twin center halves."

Looking at soccer, for the moment, in geometric shapes, *catenaccio* had turned the old pyramid formation upside down. Now, instead of a team having just two fullbacks and fanning out to a profusion of five forwards, it started off with a phalanx of five fullbacks and withered away to two or even just one forward. In this whittling away of the forward line, the main victim was the old-fashioned winger. The 2-3-5 and the W-M, two systems that between them ruled soccer for nearly seventy-five years, both featured two wingers. To those who remember the "good old days" of soccer, the very word *winger* will always have a magic ring to it. When wingers got the ball, beautiful things used to happen. No matter if it was the electrifying dashes and deadly shooting of a Cliff Bastin on the left, or if it was the subtler, exquisite trickery of a Stanley Matthews on the right. Whichever, it was soccer at its best.

Now, those lovely skills were not seen nearly so often. The blame could, perhaps, be laid on the Brazilians, whose 4-2-4 had required a left winger who could also play midfield, leading to the 4-3-3, which required a midfielder who might occasionally play on the left wing. But the Hungarians had really done the same thing in 1953 when two of the players they alternated on the wing—Laszlo Budai and Jozsef Toth—were more midfield players than true wingers. Brazil, of course, had Garrincha on the right wing, more than enough to compensate for the lack of a left wing, but by the time of the 1962 World Cup he was, at the age of twenty-nine, one of precious few wingers on view.

Wingers were an endangered species and what looked like their burial took place in 1966 when England won the World Cup using a formation that included no wingers at all. It was dubbed the "penguin" formation. Wingless.

Just as the 4-2-4 formation had lost a forward to midfield and become the 4-3-3, the process of denuding the offense went on, and the 4-3-3 became England's 4-4-2. Or more accurately, a 4-1-3-2 (Diagram 13), because the new four-man midfield included a novelty.

Diagram 13 · England 1966

A team without wingers, but with Ball and R. Charlton playing mainly attacking roles. The novelty was the use of Stiles as a sweeper playing in front of the fullback line.

This lay in the use of the tiny but combative Nobby Stiles as a sort of sweeper playing *in front of* the back four. Either he was given a specific marking assignment (as against Portugal, in the semifinal, when he neutralized Eusebio) or he was free to roam, sensing danger and snuffing it out with his ferocious, but usually effective, tackling.

Ramsey's scheme put a premium on what was now, voguishly, called "work-rate." Geoff Hurst and Roger Hunt, the two forwards, had acres of ground to cover. They were expected to be in almost constant movement, not necessarily in expectation of getting the ball, but trying to pull defenders out of position to create gaps that the midfielders—in particular Alan Ball and Bobby Charlton—and even the outside fullbacks, could move into.

Hurst and Hunt were hailed as the epitome of "unselfish" players, prime exponents of the newly discovered arts of "decoy running" and "off-the-ball" movement. Hunt was now a "targetman," the tall strong forward at whom his teammates aimed long passes from the back. His job was to win the ball, usually in the air, and either flick it on, or to hold it while his teammates moved up in support. Along with the new role, came the newly discovered skill of "playing with your back to goal."

It was a time for tactical terms and buzzwords. The Italians, who were the most deeply involved, called the trend *tatticomania*. But the English, who had for so long derided the science of coaching, were now taking it up with a vengeance and had produced a generation of coaches trained and duly licensed by the F.A. They had introduced a serious methodical approach to the game, which was presumably a good thing, but as they all came from the same "school" they brought with them a new orthodoxy which was not so welcome.

Ramsey wanted players with a high work-rate, players prepared for ninety minutes of constant action (there was, remember, still no substitution permitted in World Cup games), players who would attack and defend, players who, to use another term from the new jargon, were willing to indulge in "positive running."

This was definitely not the sort of job for wingers, traditionally rather temperamental players who waited to be brought into the game by their colleagues' passes, who rarely went looking for the ball, and who never came back to help out on defense.

It was only fitting that England's victory in the final was largely due to the inspired and tireless play of Alan Ball, another player whose appetite for running far outstripped his skill. England's "wingless wonders" took the World Cup because they were the best of a rather substandard crop, a solid no-nonsense team that kept errors down to a minimum.

The nationalistic passion that gripped England during the tournament obscured the fact that, by any objective standards, this was not a very attractive team to watch. *Workmanlike* was the word that seemed to best describe it, a group of highly trained men doing a job of work, rather than enjoying a game. From George Raynor, the Englishman who had coached Sweden to the 1958 World Cup final, came a cutting comment: "There is, in football, no substitute for skill, but the manager's job is usually to try to find one. Ramsey obviously found one."

During the 1966 World Cup only the tactically unrestrained North Koreans and the irrepressible Eusebio seemed to remember how to smile . . . but it was the North Koreans' lack of tactical know-how that cost them a place in the semifinals, and after Portugal had been beaten by England in the semifinals, Eusebio left the field with his wonderfully boyish, open face wet with tears.

The 1966 World Cup, despite the advent of so much scientific talk and preparation (for the first time, FIFA appointed a group of coaches to write a technical study of the games), was not technically distinguished. Before the tournament, the participating coaches—the very people who would control the type of soccer played—predicted to the FIFA study group that the 1966 World Cup would show a trend toward defensive soccer and aggressive tackling. Hardly surprisingly, that is exactly what happened.

However it is viewed, 1966 can not be seen as a high point in the development of soccer. The game had become unmistakably harder; much of the enjoyment seemed to have drained away. Replacing it was a mean-spirited atmosphere in which grim-faced players had discovered new "tactical" skills: They argued with the referee, they faked injuries, they snarled at opponents. And they committed cynical fouls which—in keeping with the permissive attitude—were even given an air of justification by being called "tactical" fouls.

The forecasts for the 1970 World Cup in Mexico were, inevitably, gloomy. Attendances were static or falling throughout the world. There had been several disgraceful clashes in the World Club Championship, notably in 1967 when Racing Club of Argentina and Celtic of Scotland indulged in a brawl that saw four Celtic and two Racing players sent off the field, and in 1969 when Milan were so outrageously mauled by Estudiantes de la Plata that three of the Argentine players were slapped with lengthy suspensions—on the insistence of the president of Argentina!

The sport appeared to be going through a dangerously negative period. Soccer badly needed a shot in the arm to restore its tarnished image, and in Mexico fortune smiled radiantly in the form of a wonderful Brazilian team that won all its games by joyously putting the accent on attacking play.

Ostensibly the Brazilians were a 4-4-2 team, with only Tostão and Jairzinho up front. But behind them, in midfield, were Pelé, Gerson, and Rivelino. A total of five magnificent attacking players, three of them (Tostão, Gerson, and Rivelino) superbly, menacingly left-footed, a factor that couldn't be assessed in tactical terms, but one that surely posed massive hidden problems for opposing defenders.

The Brazilian defense, it was said, was weak. Felix was held to be a second-rate goalkeeper ("Weak on crosses," said the English, as they

always do of any non-English keeper), center back Brito's temperament was questioned, Carlos Alberto was too attack-minded, and so on.

In particular, the critics derided the Brazilian midfield as being, in
defensive terms, hopelessly inadequate. There was something in that.
Only the inexperienced 21-year-old Clodoaldo had a defensive role,
doing the sort of thing that Stiles had done for England in 1966. Gerson would play deep, but his role was primarily that of all-seeing brain
for the attack. His effectiveness as a defender, like that of Pelé and
Rivelino, was hardly the toast of Brazil.

Yet it all worked with unmatchable brilliance. None of the criticism
mattered at all. Only once in the tournament—during a tight 1–0 victory over England—did the Brazilians score fewer than three goals in
a game. Otherwise, such was the irresistible surge of their attacking
play that their defenders were rarely put under the sort of pressure
that might have exposed the alleged weaknesses.

It was not formations that carried Brazil to the heights, but the sur-
passing skills of players like Pelé, Tostão, Rivelino, Gerson, Clodoaldo, and Carlos Alberto. The dashing right winger (yes, a winger!)
Jairzinho scored in every game, racing away across the field after
each goal had gone in, leaping and twisting and laughing as he went,
pursued by a stream of yelling and grinning teammates.

Nothing was more appropriate than that this happy band of men
should win the final by swamping the Italians, still enmeshed in the
slough of *catenaccio*.

A sparkling beginning, then, for the 1970s. The attacking message
of the Brazilians was taken up in Europe, notably by the West Germans, who won the 1972 European championship with a team that
attacked, if not with the brio of the Brazilians, then certainly with a
flair that exploded the myth of Teutonic stodginess.

The Dutch seemed to arrive out of nowhere. A small country with a
long but unremarkable soccer record, suddenly produced a most
extraordinary generation of free-spirited young soccer players who
made Feyenoord (Rotterdam) and Ajax (Amsterdam) the strongest
club teams in Europe.

What the Germans and the Dutch were doing was what the FIFA
technical study group had described in its report on the 1970 World
Cup: "The best teams in Europe have freed themselves from rigid
patterns of play. Players are capable of varying their functions
between defense and attack. . . ."

A new phrase, "total soccer," entered soccer's ever-expanding
vocabulary. It was seen as the ultimate marriage of the three Bs of

soccer: brawn, brain, and ball skills. The new breed of total soccer players was fit enough and skilled enough to play any position on the field, and intelligent enough to know exactly when to switch roles.

The style reached its zenith with the Dutch national team in the 1974 World Cup under coach Rinus Michels. Made up mostly of players from Ajax and Feyenoord, the Dutch team was, in terms of time spent together, one of the least well-prepared teams in the tournament. Yet such was the ability and the mutual understanding of the players that it was not necessary to work out complicated systems of play.

The Dutch seemed always able to defend en bloc, to attack en masse, to flood midfield whenever they wished, all their players in constant kaleidoscopic motion, their goalkeeper ever ready to leave his area to clear the ball.

The speed with which the Dutch surrounded the ball with as many as five or six—or was it ten?—players, on both offense and defense, was dizzying. The sudden surge of the whole team on offense left many an opposing forward stranded yards offside.

Off-the-ball movement was constant, all done purposefully. "It's not difficult to get players to move about," Rinus Michels would say, "but to get them to do it intelligently, that is the difference."

Remarkably, the essence of the Dutch style had been foreseen nearly twenty years earlier by journalist Willy Meisl, who wrote in his 1955 book *Soccer Revolution*:

> In my opinion the future belongs to *The Whirl*. It must rotate on *individuality* rooted in *all-round* capacity. . . . A full-back seeing an opening in front must seize his chance without hesitation. A wing-half or winger will fall back, if necessary, and being an all-rounder, will not feel uncomfortable or out of place. The consciousness that he also is a capable forward will give the back's thrust weight and impetus. The knowledge that whoever has taken over from him (behind his back) will make a good job of it should the occasion arise, will enable him to carry on with his action (raid) without undue hurry or nervousness. He must and will be perfectly sure that he has left no exposed flank behind himself.

Thus Willy Meisl's "whirl." It describes exactly what the Dutch looked like to their opponents, a menacing whirl of orange shirts, with the ubiquitous Johan Cruyff orchestrating everything. The Dutch whirl is too fluid to be given any meaningful expression in diagrams or numerical formations. It was 4-3-3, 4-2-4, 2-3-5, 4-4-2, and all their variations rolled into one. It was all of them, but it was none of them.

In the final, Dutch total soccer, led by the brilliant Johan Cruyff was opposed—and beaten 2-1—by the German variety, led by the equally brilliant Franz Beckenbauer.

Single-handed, Beckenbauer had revolutionalized the role of the *libero* in soccer. In his early career as a midfielder, Beckenbauer had always liked to go forward, to score goals. When he switched to *libero* for his club team Bayern Munich, he reshaped the position so that he could still use his attacking talents.

His inspiration came from the Italian club Inter. As *catenaccio* had become more widespread in Italy, most teams had cut back to only two forwards. This left one of the three fullbacks without any compelling man-to-man marking duties. Inter's left back Giacinto Facchetti took advantage of this freedom, by making attacking runs into the opposing penalty area, where he became a potent scoring threat. In an eighteen-year career with Inter, defender Facchetti scored sixty goals.

What Facchetti could do from the fullback position, Beckenbauer decided could be done from the *libero* position. Beckenbauer's sudden forays into enemy territory caused huge problems for defenders already preoccupied with their own man-to-man assignments.

Beckenbauer and Johan Cruyff were, quite clearly, the outstanding players of the age. Soccer geniuses. Their brilliance raised the questions: How much did total soccer owe to their individual skills? And would it work without them?

The feeling that total soccer was, to some extent, an optical illusion, received support four years later during the 1978 World Cup in Argentina. Both the Netherlands and West Germany were present, both apparently still playing total soccer. But each country now lacked its inspiration, Cruyff and Beckenbauer having announced in advance that they would not play in the tournament.

Without Beckenbauer, the Germans were a mundane team that won only one of the six games it played. The Cruyff-less Dutch had a new coach, the Austrian Ernst Happel, a cautious man who, in the qualifying games, had experimented with a five-man midfield. The team was certainly going through the motions of total soccer—the attacking and defending en masse, the quick passing of the ball to a player in motion—but Cruyff's artistry was sorely missed.

Without it, the less acceptable face of total soccer was now more clearly visible. The light, springy quality that Cruyff had given to the team was gone. Now the Dutch players looked heavier and slower ("rugby players" was an Argentine journalist's scornful dismissal of the powerful van der Kerkhof brothers), and their often brutal tackling was there for all to see. And now the offside trap was being deliberately used as a defensive tactic, rather than as an incidental result of fast, mass-attacking play.

Total soccer, it seemed, had owed more to its key individual players than to its tactics. Beckenbauer was later to say: "It owed more to the element of surprise than to any magic formula. I think the Dutch got away with it for so long because the opposition could not work out what tactics they were facing. It never dawned on them, certainly not until it was much too late, that there were no tactics at all . . . just brilliant players with a ball."

Nevertheless, in 1978 enough remained of the total soccer that had so baffled and enchanted four years earlier for the Dutch to reach the final, just as they had done in 1974.

The Argentines, the other finalists, had at last managed to harness the immense individual skill of their players into a functioning team. Coach César Menotti had said from the start that he wanted players who were team players, but that his team would be built around the traditional skills of the Argentine player: "I will always select skill over fitness. You can, with work, take a skillful player and make him fit. But if the player has only fitness, no amount of training will make him skillful."

To allow an Argentine player to use his natural skills is to allow him to attack, and that is what Menotti's team did in every game. Tactically speaking, there was nothing new here. Very much the opposite. Argentina's play was a throwback to earlier times, basically a 4-3-3. Defensively, it was aligned in the way that all Argentine club teams played, with a line of four fullbacks, marking zonally.

But with the tendency of so many players to move forward, the formation was usually closer to a 4-2-4, and there were times when it almost seemed that soccer had returned to the days of the 2-3-5.

The announcement of the death of wingers had evidently been much exaggerated. Menotti used two wingers, Daniel Bertoni and Oscar Ortiz, plus a "big-man," Leopoldo Luque, at center forward—a real forward line, one that any player from the 1930s would have recognized at once. Constantly attacking from midfield was Osvaldo Ardiles, while Mario Kempes varied his role from game to game—

Diagram 14 · Argentina 1978

FILLOL

GALVAN   PASSARELLA

OLGUIN   TARANTINI

GALLEGO

ARDILES

KEMPES

BERTONI   LUQUE   ORTIZ

sometimes striker, sometimes more midfielder—but he was always Argentina's goal-scoring threat.

How strange, then, that the Dutch, who employed man-to-man markers in front of a sweeper, should fail to do anything about him in the final. Kempes was repeatedly allowed to race forward from midfield into the penalty area, scoring two goals and assisting on the third in Argentina's 3–1 victory.

If Happel failed tactically by not paying attention to Kempes, he had a short-lived success when he brought on his first substitute, Dirk Nanninga, in the fifty-ninth minute. For the first time in a World Cup final, a substitution was made with a clear, tactical aim.

The entry of the tall Nanninga, an excellent header of the ball, signaled a switch to an aerial game as the Dutch, losing 0–1, tried to overcome the effectiveness of the Argentine central defense. The move paid off at the eighty-second minute when it was Nanninga's powerful header that tied the score at 1–1.

In the final analysis, the thing that counted in the 1978 final was—

once again—not so much tactics as mentality. The Argentines were a team with an attacking mentality, a team that seemed incapable of slowing things down, of protecting a lead. This was nicely demonstrated at the seventy-fifth minute of the game. With his team holding on to a precarious 1–0 lead, and with Holland beginning to dominate the game, Menotti prepared a substitution. The obvious move, the logical and safe one, was to take off an attacker and send on a defender. Menotti did take off an attacking player—winger Ortiz—but he replaced him with René Houseman, another totally offense-minded player.

When Holland tied the game, the move appeared to have misfired. But the feverish support of the fans, never allowing the team to pause, urged Argentina forward to an overtime victory in which Houseman played a significant part.

The negativity that had been predicted for 1978 was certainly there. Most teams seemed to have as their number one priority the nullifying of their opponents' game. There was almost universal acceptance of the defensive tactic of getting seven or eight men behind the ball as soon as it was lost. The consequently packed defenses led to much sterile lateral and back passing.

Bucking this trend were, surprisingly, the Italians. Under new coach Enzo Bearzot they seemed at last to have cast off the shackles of *catenaccio,* and were one of the more adventurous teams of the tournament. The change in mentality was personified by defender Gaetano Scirea. A sweeper, but not the traditionally Italian defensive sweeper. The immaculately skilled Scirea frequently came forward, in the adventurous Beckenbauer manner, to join in attacks.

In 1978 there was, ultimately, encouragement to be found in that it was Holland and Argentina—the two teams most committed to attacking soccer, most willing to take risks—that reached the final.

But there still seemed to be plenty of coaches and teams around willing to give "attacking soccer" a very different interpretation, one that had been predicted in that 1966 FIFA report that talked of aggressive tackling.

In 1970 the referees had been given clear instructions to penalize rough play by defenders. The result was a clean tournament in which the ball-artists of the game were able to demonstrate their skills and to produce open, attacking soccer.

But by the time of the 1982 World Cup in Spain, all was forgotten. The instructions given out to referees must have been of a totally dif-

ferent order. The opening game, Argentina against Belgium, turned
out to be a bleak warning of what was to come. The Czech referee
Vojtech Christov consistently turned a blind eye to heavy, clumsy,
and dangerous tackling, especially from the overtly physical Belgian
midfield.

The recipient of most of this treatment was, inevitably, the man who
was being talked of as the "new Pelé," Argentina's Diego Maradona.
Repeatedly knocked down, tripped, obstructed, and tackled from
behind, and receiving no protection from the referee, Maradona
dropped farther and farther back into midfield as the game progressed. And, of course, he lost his effectiveness for Argentina.

No doubt this was what the Belgians wanted. It was, for want of a
better word, a tactic. But it was based on repeated fouling, and only
hopelessly lax refereeing allowed it to succeed. It was precisely the
sort of play that has given tactics a bad name. The Belgians won the
game, and the message came over loud and clear: Physical play is okay.

The results were catastrophic, for—very directly—they led to the
elimination from the tournament of its two best teams: France and
Brazil. The French were manhandled out of the competition by West
Germany, while Brazil suffered the same fate at the hands of Italy. In
both cases, hopelessly permissive refereeing was at fault.

"No spectacular systems were created in 1982," said the official
FIFA technical report on the tournament. True enough. France and
Brazil were similar teams, both blessed with intelligent players in
almost every position, and playing magnificent, quick-moving, attacking soccer with an exciting artistic flair.

But they presented nothing new tactically. France used a sweeper
behind three fullbacks (two of them man-to-man markers), Brazil
played a back four, marking zonally, with the outside backs spending
most of their time in midfield. Both teams bristled with midfield talent, both had finishing problems up front.

Italy, the eventual winner, was still a team that defended tightly
and based its game on quick counterattacks, but the overly negative
caution of *catenaccio* had gone. Now there was a much more dynamic
midfield, and four of the five defenders, including the masterful
Scirea, were ready to join in offensive moves.

Total soccer, the talk of the tournament just eight years earlier,
barely got a look. The Dutch, its chief architects, had failed to qualify,
while the Germans had sunk back into their well-known, well-
organized, overly physical mode.

Why the lack of innovation? The FIFA technical report—no doubt

Diagram 15 · France 1982

unintentionally—offered an important clue. The coaches who authored it seemed always to see the sport through defensive spectacles. Analyzing Brazil's failure, the report criticized the four-defender zonal approach, saying that it lacked depth and cover.

Not mentioned, though it was surely more to the point, was that Brazil had ample opportunity to win or tie the crucial game against Italy, and was thwarted only by center forward Serginho's pathetic inability to put away the simplest of chances. It was left to coach Tele Santana to point out what the report omitted to say: that Italy had scored the winning goal after a corner kick—at a time when virtually the whole Brazilian team was pulled back on defense.

As to the relative benefits of man-to-man or zonal coverage, the Italians, and Gentile in particular, had made a rather twisted contribution to that debate. Who could argue now? If the referees were going to allow Gentile's style, which was really more man-to-man

Diagram 16 · Brazil 1982

mugging, then who would bother with the intricacies of a zonal defense?

More ominously, if skilled ball players like Maradona and Zico could be kicked with impunity, for how long could we expect to see such players gracing the game?

That was not something with which the FIFA coaches concerned themselves. In their report was a fine photograph of Maradona surrounded by four Belgian defenders, being knocked down by one of them. The caption read: "Individual actions getting caught in the funnel formation." Only the defensive tactics, the way that midfielders funneled back to close down space, the way that pressure was immediately applied in midfield, were of any interest to the coaches. The constant fouling had apparently become something not worth commenting on.

But the growing trend toward packing the midfield did call for comment. The report had this to say: "Based on the growing consideration

Diagram 17 · Italy 1982

of the players' specific mentality as well as their individual and collective spiritual mobility, a creative dynamism evolved in midfield which made play more positive, diversified, and impenetrable."

Impenetrable seemed exactly the right word to describe such verbiage, which was typical of the high-flown, pseudoscientific parlance that coaching had adopted. Even if its language could be fathomed, even if huge allowance were made for the pro-defense slant of its analyses, how could one take seriously a technical report that contained no reference at all to the crucial effect of referees' decisions during the tournament?

The stark truth was that defenders were brazenly flouting soccer's rules, that they were getting away with it, and that nobody seemed inclined to do anything about it. The view of FIFA, and of coaches in general—as reflected in the FIFA technical report—was that everything was fine.

When the 1986 World Cup rolled around, fitness was very much on everyone's mind. Mexico again—Mexico, with its heat and its altitude. Conditions that demanded fitter and better prepared players, a theme that was constantly stressed by Argentina's new coach, Carlos Bilardo, a medical doctor. Whenever he was asked about the future of the game, Bilardo talked about fitness and speed. Tomorrow's soccer wouldn't be about new tactics, he said, so much as a quickening of the game. Players would have to be more skilled, fitter, and faster.

There was no doubt that modern soccer demanded much more physically from its players than it had done in the past. Total soccer had left its mark. Attacking players now *had* to come back and help the defense, while defenders were expected to get upfield and join in the attacks. (The use of outside fullbacks as attacking players produced a bizarre situation in the 1986 final, when two such players—Julio Olarticoechea for Argentina and Thomas Berthold for West Germany—found that, rather than marking opposing forwards, they were marking each other.)

The theory behind all-purpose players was fine, but in practice it was yet another system that was heavily skewed toward the defensive part of the game—because there was never, on any team, a shortage of defenders, but there was frequently a massive lack of attacking players. Not a lack of players who attacked—a lack of attacking players.

Forwards, real specialist forwards, were hard to find. Argentina, the eventual winners in 1986, exemplified the trend. In the first game, Bilardo fielded only one out-and-out forward, Pablo Pasculli. By the time of the final, Pasculli was on the bench, and the Argentine side was crowded with midfield players.

A state of affairs that led to an anomaly. This was a tournament where attacking soccer was felt to be making a comeback. That was the impression, yet it was contradicted by the statistics, which showed this to be the worst World Cup yet in terms of goal scoring—just 2.54 per game.

Plenty of attacking then, but poor finishing? Possibly. Scoring chances that, in years gone by, would have been snapped up by a specialist goal scorer, were now likely to fall to a much less expert finisher—a midfielder or a fullback.

The six-man midfield had arrived. Argentina had Diego Maradona, Jorge Burruchaga, Jorge Valdano, Sergio Batista, Ricardo Giusti, and Hector Enrique. One of them, usually Valdano, sometimes Maradona or Burruchaga, might be pushed forward to occupy a forward position. Batista was primarily defensive.

Argentina was never an explosively attacking team. Its play was defensively sound, and it would have been an unspectacular team but for the presence of Diego Maradona. It was the totally unpredictable individual skills of Maradona that made Argentina such a dangerous attacking force.

Ever since the arrival of total soccer, soccer had been blurring the differences between defenders, midfielders, and attackers. Very few people tried now to define a team's formation with a numerical formula. How to describe Argentina, for instance? As a 1-2-6-1, perhaps, or a 1-2-5-2, or sometimes a 1-3-5-1, or maybe a . . . ? There was simply too much movement, too much interchanging of roles, for such descriptions to be meaningful. They had always been approximate, anyway. Now they were almost irrelevant.

The ongoing argument over man-to-man or zonal marking swung decisively toward those of the zonal persuasion. Most teams employed one or two defenders as markers, but the rigidities of the system would not work in the new crowded but fluid midfield. The FIFA technical study group, which again refrained from any comment on the refereeing (it had been much better than in 1982) reported that, in the 1986 World Cup, as in 1982, "no truly new tactics were seen."

It was a verdict that gave rise to the thought that perhaps there simply wasn't anything new to come, that we had seen it all before in one form or another. Certainly, the 1982 report, when it talked of "attacking moves starting with a midfield player who switched over to the offensive immediately after getting the ball" brought back memories of the little Scottish genius Alex James and his role for Arsenal back in the 1930s.

But the 1986 technical study group (as usual, it was overwhelmingly European in composition) seemed to come up with a conclusion that would make a comeback for the James-type player unlikely. Playmakers, said its report, are dying out.

The reason? "Today's soccer, with the overpopulated midfield, limits the room of activity of this zone to a large extent. Little time is left for the control of the ball and the vision of the game. The player who awaits the ball standing or in slow run, is attacked immediately and put under pressure. The midfield stars have the tendency, however, to wait for the ball."

Yes, but . . . what about the decisive influence of Maradona, surely a midfielder, surely a playmaker extraordinaire, and surely the outstanding player of the tournament? The FIFA group got neatly around that anomaly by classifying Maradona as a forward.

Which he certainly was, on frequent occasions. Just as he very definitely was a midfielder on others. A point that merely emphasized the decline of the specialist, and the rise of the all-rounder.

Yet, given soccer's long history of anomalous, almost perverse, behavior, it seemed quite absurdly unlikely that the playmakers had gone forever. The betting was that the ghost of wee Alex James would continue to hover over the soccer fields of the world.

By 1988, Bilardo was saying that he had been proved right: "Everyone has copied Argentina." By which he meant that the bloated midfield was the order of the day. He had a point. But the question was, did it matter?

Tactics were beginning to look irrelevant. What mattered was that soccer was losing its attractiveness. Virtually every tactical innovation in the history of soccer has been designed to strengthen defenses. By the time the 1990 World Cup arrived, many teams were playing with just one forward. Goal scoring was down, soccer as a spectacle was suffering.

The great Argentine player Alfredo di Stéfano had said: "A soccer game without goals is like an afternoon without sunshine." Just how bleak the lack of goals could make things was revealed in 1989 when Argentina played Italy to an appallingly tedious 0–0 tie. It was an exhibition game with nothing at stake, yet both teams played defensively. Said the Italian coach, Azeglio Vicini: "This is the sort of soccer that we are going to see in the 1990 World Cup. It will be difficult to find spectacular games."

Vicini got it just about right. The 1990 World Cup, by general agreement, rated poor on the entertainment scale. The World Cup of fear: fear of taking risks, fear of attacking, fear of opponents.

No team illustrated the craven attitude more clearly than Brazil. Brazil, the masters of attacking soccer! Heavily criticized because his team scored only twice against Sweden in its first game, coach Sebastião Lazaroni told the press that they could expect more scoring against the next opponent, the minnows Costa Rica. That same night, Lazaroni went to scout Costa Rica, and saw it beat Scotland 1–0.

A scoreline that scared Lazaroni. The following day there was no more talk of scoring a lot of goals. Lazaroni said he'd be satisfied if Brazil won by an own-goal* in the ninety-third minute. And mighty Brazil duly did beat tiny Costa Rica 1–0, on an own-goal.

Echoing its thoughts in 1982 and 1986, the FIFA technical study group declared that the 1990 tournament "did not produce anything

---

* See Glossary, page 243.

startlingly new." Their report admitted that "at present, the defense
is dominant," and felt obliged to offer a defense of defenders: "Correct
behavior in a defensive role can be an attractive task. There are players who have even turned it into an art."

This, of course, was coaches speaking, and it was not encouraging.
In fact it got worse. Not only were defenders praised, but forwards
were scorned: "It is not at all decisive just how many forwards a coach
includes in his lineup, what is decisive is just how many players can
join in the attack. . . ."

Soccer tactics had evidently switched from a numbers game to a
words game. But what spoke most loudly and most insistently was the
game as seen on the field. Not good enough. Italia-90 produced the
worst final in the history of the World Cup—"A disaster," commented
Rinus Michels. And it touched a new record low on the scoring chart,
with 2.21 goals per game.

We have followed soccer tactics for over one hundred years, from
the primitive days of the backer-up, to the pyramid and the numbers
game, and on to the present where player movement is so fluid that
diagrams and numbers can no longer explain what is going on.

Perhaps they never did. Certainly, they can never be accurate
guides to everything that happens on the soccer field. Rather, they
are a first step to understanding the action. They should provide the
mind with a loose basic structure against which the significance of
player movements can be intelligently assessed. They should *never* be
seen as rigid frameworks into which players and action *have* to fit.

The difficulty of analyzing something as unpredictable as soccer is
already substantial, and it has not been helped by the problem mentioned at the beginning of this chapter, namely, the disorganized state
of the sport's vocabulary, particularly that part of it that deals with
player positions.

Terminology has struggled to keep up with changes on the field,
with the result that old terms are used for new positions, and no
longer describe the function. As the game has become more fluid, the
terms have tended to become more general.

Where once there were center forwards or left or right wingers
there are now, simply, strikers or forwards. Fullbacks have become
defenders, shedding the implication that they stay at the back.
Indeed, the outside backs are now often called wingbacks to emphasize that they do go forward into the areas that used to be occupied by
wingers.

Function is now more important than *position*. A back is described

Diagram 18 · Barcelona 1993

as a marking back, or simply as a man-marker. Halfbacks have become midfielders, and they, too, are not about to be positionally tied down by strict definition as left or right midfielder. They are described as right-sided or left-sided players.

Johan Cruyff, the star of Dutch total soccer in the 1970s, was a key figure in this breaking down of the rigidity of soccer positions. When he turned to coaching at Barcelona, he created a team in the modern image, one of rapid movement and position switching, which he found difficult to describe: "When journalists ask me how Barcelona plays, I give them a 3-1-2-2-1-1 formation, so that they have an approximate idea. But that's just for the journalists." All modern formation diagrams bristle with arrows, the nearest they can get to conveying the bustling movement. Diagram 18 is an attempt to capture the player movement on Cruyff's Barcelona.

If the naming of player positions has caused problems, the numbering has added to the confusion. The original idea that each number would represent a position had some merit in days when there was only one team formation, and when there was no substitution. Today it is patently absurd. Positionally, the numbers mean nothing anymore. The sooner that the American system of assigning a number to a player—his to wear whatever the position he plays—is adopted the better it will be for soccer.*

Before finishing this survey of soccer's tactical history, two important themes that have run through this chapter should be revisited.

First, the relationship between *systems* and *individual players*. Many coaches are fond of saying that players must never be forced into a system, but that the system must always be adapted to the players. An engaging theory, but at best only a half-truth. For the superstars, yes, the system will more likely than not be adapted. But a merely good player who cannot or will not play the role his coach desires will almost certainly be replaced by a player who will. There is no shortage of good players. What *is* true is that the more skillful the players, the more flexible and therefore the better a system will be.

Second, the attitude of the players and, above all, of the coach. The growing defensiveness of soccer has been discussed at length. Yet it should be clear that the decisive factor in this negative trend is not so much the positioning of the players, as their state of mind. A team that *wants* to attack, *will* attack, regardless of its formation.

The opposite, of course, is equally true. A team that is unwilling—read frightened—to attack will not attack, or will do so without conviction. It was that caution, that fear of taking risks, that lay at the root of soccer's problems at the beginning of the 1990s. The orthodox view—and statistical support for it was not lacking—was that coaches who concentrated on building strong defenses were the ones who won titles, and the ones who kept their jobs.

The challenge for the sport's leaders is to devise measures that would change that mentality—that would ensure that risk-taking, entertaining soccer could also be winning soccer.

* Those purists who object to this have already been undermined by the World Cup in which each team is required to number its twenty-two-player roster 1 through 22, and each player must wear only the number assigned.

CHAPTER 7

The Changing Game

Once upon a time, soccer had been a freewheeling, positive game in which the primary aim was to score goals. But as the sport entered the 1990s, negativity ruled, and what mattered most was to prevent the other side from scoring. What had gotten into soccer to so distort its original nature?

In a word, money. Those bewhiskered Victorian English gentlemen who had so stoutly resisted the rise of professionalism in the nineteenth century would have tut-tutted many an "I told you so." The sport moved from recreational activity, on through spreading professionalism, until during the 1970s and 1980s, it became a worldwide industry generating an annual turnover of some $200 billion.

Along the way, it lost its innocence and a great deal of its freedom. Millions of dollars could now be at stake on a single result. At the top, soccer was no longer a game to be played, it was a business venture to be calculated, to be financed—and to be organized.

Organized not only on the business side, but on the field as well. Gone were the days when a team "just went out and played" as Carlos Peucelle's Argentina had done in 1930. No more of that. Organization, which meant tactics, was now required. Enter the coach as the high priest of the modern game.

Suddenly, it was not the players who won games. That was the coach's job. Or was it? Taking the field determined to win at all costs, to play attacking soccer, was considered a rash way of going about things. After all, every game started with the score tied—if you didn't give up any goals, you couldn't lose, right?

Rather than Thou Shalt Win, the first commandment of coaching became Thou Shalt Not Lose. And the way not to lose was to concentrate on defense. Well-organized defenses, often manned by average or even mediocre players, were the representative feature of soccer teams in the 1980s.

This was not exactly new: The Italian *catenaccio* system of the 1960s had been built around a strong defense. But *catenaccio* had always had a place for the skilled attacking players who could operate its sudden counterattacks.

The new defensive mentality of the seventies and eighties paid little attention to the attack. Now, the priority was to destroy the opponent's game—"stop them playing" became a much-valued phrase—and hope to steal a goal that would settle the game. "In the past," said the former French star Michel Platini, "a team made sure that it built up its own game before destroying that of its opponents. Nowadays, the primary objective is to destroy and only afterward, if at all, to build up."

Packed defenses and tight, overtly physical marking became commonplace. The emphasis placed on defense meant that *everyone* was expected to defend, including the forwards, though there was often only one of these. Everyone was expected to cover an enormous amount of territory. Work-rate became another hallowed term. The sad thing for soccer was that it worked. Heavily populated, hard-tackling defenses could make it almost impossible for the opponents to score.

The pendulum started to swing heavily against the skilled players, the ball-artists, the dribblers. Soccer was becoming a game for athletes and for runners; stamina was more important than skill. Irishman George Best, the most talented British player of his generation, had this to say in 1975: "Stamina's all right, you've got to be able to run, but you've also got to be able to do the main thing and the main thing at soccer is to know what to do with the ball. At its simplest level that's what is wrong with British football today. Too many people who can run all day but can't kick a bloody football."

The reliance on physical power was only half the story. As the marking got tighter, the fouling got worse and worse. Defenders seemed to have been given carte blanche to rough up forwards, barrelling into them from behind, tripping and holding them. Nothing was done about it. The kicking went on; the game deteriorated. George Best quit soccer in 1972 at the ridiculously early age of twenty-six because he was tired of being close-marked and kicked, because he no longer enjoyed playing the game.

Claudio Gentile, the Italian defender whose roughhouse play had helped Italy to win the 1982 World Cup, shrugged off criticism with, "Soccer is not a sport for ballerinas." This was the voice of machismo echoing down the ages, the very same voice that, in 1863, had wanted to make soccer a "manly" game in which hacking, or kicking opponents' legs, was okay. The champions of brute force had lost out then, but they had never really gone away. One hundred and twenty years later they were back, threatening to dominate the sport.

The easy answer to those who complained about the trend was that the referees were to blame for not enforcing the rules. But this was much too simplistic. The fact was that flagrant fouling had become accepted by most players and coaches, who excused even the worst transgressors with a cynical "What else could he do?" plea.

Even when a referee did feel inclined to clamp down, the rules did not really offer punishment harsh enough to discourage offenders. Things got to the point where a defender was *expected* to trip a forward who was heading for goal, and would probably be castigated by his coach if he didn't. The resultant free kick and maybe a yellow card for the defender were worth it to prevent a shot on goal.

That was the so-called professional foul, also known as the tactical foul. The new coach-dominated version of the game was never at a loss for words and terms that would hide the ugliness of what was going on.

As the coach became more important, the discipline of coaching started to dress itself up in academic garb. Suddenly, there was the coaching industry. Coaching courses, licenses, and diplomas proliferated all over the world. Coaching seminars, coaching symposia, coaching workshops, and coaching clinics were all the rage. Learned treatises and books on coaching were published at an alarming rate. A pseudo-scientific coaching jargon spread across the sport. What J. C. Thring had called *The Simplest Game* in 1862 was in danger of becoming *The Most Complicated Sport.*

This sport, which had once been improvised by the players on the field, now seemed to be more about charts and diagrams and X's and O's than about people. There was not much room anymore for the freelance, inventive type of player. The coach had his plans and his tactics, and the players had to fit in, had to play their roles, and not wander off into flights of creative fantasy.

The artists were a problem for the coaches, who recognized their brilliance but didn't know what to do with them, didn't trust them to do what they were told. The coaches were right, of course. The artists couldn't be trusted to play according to instructions. The essence of their game was the sudden burst of unpredictable skill, the genius of the unexpected.

Treated with suspicion by coaches, mercilessly fouled by opponents, the artists began to disappear from the game. Pelé, one of the greatest of them, looked at the game of the 1980s: "It used to be, in the 1960s, even into the 1970s, that every national team had two or three world-class players. Now, it is difficult to find five or six in the whole world."

Soccer's slide into defensive negativity was greatly helped by the curious fact that so many of the modern coaches had been defenders in their playing days. Maybe not so curious. The creative players were the instinctive players, the ones who never had to do much thinking about their game, who were not interested in elaborate theories of how to play. Players like England's Jimmy Greaves, a prolific goal scorer in the 1960s, who said of one coach: "The way he talks about football sometimes, I think it must be easier to split the atom than score a goal."

Greaves was never interested in becoming a coach, nor was Pelé or Maradona. Johan Cruyff, the Dutch creative genius of the 1970s, did become a coach and nurtured a wonderfully lively attacking team at Barcelona.

The defenders were often no more than average players who had spent a good deal of time thinking about the game in an effort to improve their own performances. They were the perfect raw material for the age of academic coaching.

Functional. That is the kindest word to describe the type of soccer that dominated in the 1970s and 1980s. A no-frills game that eschewed risk taking and that squeezed the inventive ball players out of the game. Along with those players went the very lifeblood of the sport: goals. In the English first division, the average was 2.5 per game in the 1980s, the first time it had ever sunk below 3.00. In low-scoring Italy, it went from 2.2 in the 1970s, to 2.0 in the 1980s.

And of course, the game suffered as a spectacle. The stars who produced the oohs and the aahs from the fans were lacking. Players were now complimented—by the coaches—for their commitment rather than their skill; teams were praised for being well organized, or hard to beat. The fans voted with their feet, and during the 1980s attendances were at best static, more often they were falling.

The eighties were an unhappy decade for soccer, not only because so much of the soccer was barren, but because no one felt the urge to do anything about it. This laissez-faire attitude produced its most damaging results off the field.

Throughout the 1970s the menace of crowd violence was growing, particularly in England. Games became the excuse for a weekly orgy of bloodletting between rival gangs of fans. Pitched battles on the terraces, field invasions, and skirmishes with the police outside the stadiums became a Saturday afternoon ritual. Excursion trains were wrecked, stores looted, innocent bystanders were often injured.

The problem was exported to Europe. Whenever England, or an English club team, played on the continent they were bound to be accompanied by an army of mindless thugs, intent on getting drunk and causing mayhem. They seemed to have little interest in soccer, and were constantly described as "a small group of troublemakers who aren't even soccer fans."

Maybe so. But they were a frightening menace wherever they went, and if they were a small group, then there always seemed to be far too many others willing to join in once the violence had started.

English soccer stadiums, once the scene of good-natured fraternization among opposing fans, began to resemble concentration camps, as huge metal fences were erected to separate—and cage—the two groups, and hundreds of uniformed police were on duty.

The countermeasures were expensive, and not particularly effective. Arrests and prosecutions were rare. And very little was done to prevent the hooligans—as England's fans were now widely known—from traveling to Europe.

By the 1980s, other countries were producing their own groups of violent fans, frequently—as in England—professing extreme right-wing and racist views. There was talk of an international fraternity of hooligans. Could anyone doubt that a major disaster was on its way?

Just as no one wanted to do anything about soccer's on-the-field problems, so no one wanted to think about hooligan problems. The awful climax duly arrived, on May 29, 1985, at the Heysel Stadium, in Brussels. The day of the European Cup final, the climax to the club season, between Liverpool of England and Juventus of Italy.

Crammed into the ancient stadium were tens of thousands of fans from both teams. A dangerous situation, made lethal because at one end of the field they were separated only by a flimsy wire fence. That was where, before the game, the Liverpool supporters began taunting the Italians. Insults flew, then missiles, then the English charged, and broke through the fence. The Italians, tried to flee, but there was no escape. Thirty-eight people—mostly Juventus fans—were either suffocated or crushed to death.

This carnage had been produced by a "small group of troublemakers"? The lie to that convenient myth was given when the Belgian authorities decided to go ahead and play the game anyway. It started ninety minutes late, while bodies were still being removed from the stadium. The game had to be played because the organizers were afraid that worse trouble would follow if they canceled it!

At long last some action was taken. UEFA banned English clubs from playing in Europe, though the England national team, always followed by some of the worst of the hooligans, was absurdly exempted. The Belgian authorities were roundly criticized for not adequately separating the opposing fans. But the real culprits were those soccer authorities, particularly in England, who had dozed for so long while the problem grew.

Was there any connection between the violence that was now so common on the soccer field, and the violence of the fans? That was one for the sociologists to fathom. Superficially, it did seem appropriate that the grim-faced, cynical soccer of the seventies and eighties, a sport in which kicking opponents was the done thing, should be followed by louts looking for trouble.

It was also appropriate that the Juventus-Liverpool game that was allowed to overlap the killing, was a dull, tedious 1–0 affair that was decided in Juventus's favor when the referee awarded the Italians a penalty kick for a Liverpool offense committed well outside the penalty area.

Heysel had rammed home the message that the gloves had to come off if hooliganism was to be halted. But an unmistakable call for action to clean up the game on the field had yet to be heard. Alarm bells were ringing throughout the eighties, the tide of violence on the field was rising, but FIFA replied only with exhortation.

Before the 1982 World Cup in Spain, FIFA asked all the participating countries to sign a pledge that read: "Violence distorts and disgraces sport.... We are aware of our responsibilities and undertake to play with respect for the rules, the referees, and our opponents." It was during that tournament that Toni Schumacher brutally assaulted Patrick Battiston, and Claudio Gentile fouled his way to a World Cup winner's medal.

A FIFA Fair Play Campaign had been started in 1987, because, said FIFA, "The idea of fair play has been neglected for so long that certain unfortunate excesses have brought discredit to sports." But exhortation was not enough. The "unfortunate excesses" continued, along with all the little defensive tactics that had been developed to stop opponents playing, or to waste time: defenders refusing to retreat 10 yards on free kicks, players feigning injury, goalkeepers freezing the action by holding on to the ball. Players had become so expert at time-wasting that there were games during the 1986 World Cup in which the actual playing time was only forty-three minutes.

Before Italia-90, FIFA general secretary Sepp Blatter had said: "What FIFA wants the sport to do at the beginning of the new decade, is to 'Go for Goal,' so that soccer shall be an enjoyable, attacking game. Scoring goals is the most enjoyable activity on the field."

Italia-90 made a mockery of Blatter's words, by recording the lowest goals-per-game average ever: 2.21. The shortcomings of the soccer played during the tournament could not be ignored. The sport was clearly having problems.

The winds of change began to blow through the hitherto inflexible minds of the FIFA bosses, including the president, João Havelange. FIFA was now looking for ways to make soccer a goal-scoring game, to return it to its attacking roots, if you like. A task force was set up, Football 2000, to evaluate the situation and suggest what needed to be done, including possible rule changes, to "safeguard the game's attraction (motto: more goals)."

This was a spectacular U-turn for FIFA, a body that had always cast a withering eye on anyone brave enough to suggest that the rules be altered. Sepp Blatter, the driving force behind the upheaval, said: "You have to appreciate the change that has occurred in FIFA. Dr. Havelange was for a long time a very conservative man, but now he is very open."

The classic example of FIFA's orthodoxy had come in 1982 when the English—yes, the conservative English—decided that something had to be done to stop the "professional fouls." They ruled that in England such fouls would be punished with a red card.

It was a sensible, long overdue attempt to reverse the "anything goes" attitude that prevailed in the sport. FIFA stepped in and told the English they couldn't do it, they were not entitled to change the rules of the game.

That was FIFA in 1982. But in 1990, FIFA itself introduced precisely the same rule change. By then, it was clear that there *had* to be rule changes if soccer was to escape from the defensive mire that it had fallen into. The idea that the required change in mentality would come about through the development of new tactics was no longer credible.

Even then, the road to reform was anything but smooth. Rule changes had to be approved by FIFA's own Referees Committee, and then by the rigidly conservative International Board. As if those two obstacles weren't enough, it was soon clear that there was a third barrier—the officials (referees and linesmen)—themselves.

One of FIFA's changes was to the offside rule: An attacker in line with the last defender was now onside, rather than offside, a move that would help attacking play and would make the use of the much-disliked offside trap more risky. The benefits were slow to appear because linesmen could not, or would not, change their habits. It was almost as though the officials were intent on sabotaging the change. Jack McCabe, chairman of the United States Soccer Federation's Referees Committee spelled out the attitude: "I think the new rule isn't going to change things very much. Linesmen are still going to call offside pretty much the same. . . ."

That was the view from the United States, but it was an accurate reflection of the worldwide situation. Ironical really, for the world's referees to agree on a question of interpretation. Historically, this had always been the great problem area.

One of the duties of FIFA's Referees' Committee had for years been spelled out as "to establish as far as possible uniformity in methods of refereeing." The very wording—"as far as possible"—reveals a pessimistic view of the possibilities of success.

A more positive note was struck in 1990. The Referees' Committee was to "establish uniformity." Period. No more pussyfooting around with "as far as possible." The referees had obviously been targeted for a shake-up by the increasingly active Sepp Blatter.

Nobody was happy with the referees' performances during the World Cup in Italy. In fact, Blatter was disgruntled ten weeks before the tournament even started, when over 50 percent of the selected referees failed the preliminary fitness test. Blatter openly criticized referee performance during the tournament and announced that, for future World Cups, the maximum age for referees would be reduced from 50 to 45, hinting that he thought it should probably be even lower. For good measure, international referees would also need a basic knowledge of English, and a new class of specialist international linesmen was created.

None of this came easily. "It has taken me five years to get the Referees' Committee to accept the idea of specialist linesmen," said Blatter. "For that we don't even need to change the rules. But they don't want to try anything, they just say no. We have to convince them that they should be part of the spectacle of soccer. They are not messengers sent by God to control the show." The somber image of the referees, dressed in their traditional all-black uniforms, was not much to Blatter's liking. He thought they should be wearing bright-colored shirts.

When he said that "improving the performance of referees and linesmen will be one of FIFA's primary considerations in the next few years," what Blatter had in mind was the introduction of professional referees: "Before the end of the century, the referees in most national leagues will be full-time paid officials."

The future was being shaped in Italy; the plan is to introduce fully professional referees for the 1993–1994 season.

Despite its newly progressive attitude, FIFA remained curiously blind on the matter of tiebreakers. The word itself was comparatively new to the sport. But it cropped up constantly during the eighties as defensive play and coaching caution led to an inexorable increase in the number of tied games. Not *genuine* ties, where both teams had tried their darndest to win but things had finished in a standoff anyway. These were engineered ties, in which one team, or even both teams, had played deliberately for a draw. The scoreless tie was now a common feature of the game.

FIFA intervened, not because 0–0 ties were boring but because tied games messed up the schedules in tournaments. A winner had to pass on to the next round, and there was no time for replays. So the penalty kick tiebreaker was introduced, a move that will not go down as one of FIFA's more thoughtful contributions to the game.

The penalty kick tiebreaker is a gimmick tacked on to the end of a game that has absolutely nothing to do with what has gone before and that is very likely to reward defensively oriented teams. If a team feels that it cannot beat its opponents by playing soccer during the regular game, the alternative is to play defensively for 120 minutes, get the tie, then trust to the 50-50 toss-up of the tiebreaker.

Anyone who doubted that scenario had his eyes opened by Red Star of Belgrade and its performance in the 1991 European Cup final. Its opponent was Olympique-Marseille. It was a game that many had been savoring, as it brought together two attacking, goal-scoring teams. The morning of the game, the London *Times* rejoiced: "The match has all the ingredients for a marvelous final, especially with such a profusion of skill in midfield ... both teams are riding a crest, both attack persistently."

A reasonable forecast, but one that was destroyed by Red Star's tactics. Said coach Ljupko Petrovic: "We realized that we could not beat Marseille unless they made a mistake, so I told my players to hold out for penalties."

Hold out they did. Defending with sullen tenacity, making no use at all of their attacking talent (just three shots in the whole game, all off target), Red Star turned the game into a monstrous bore, and a deplorable farce. But they got what they wanted, a 0–0 tie after 120 minutes, and went on to win the penalty kick tiebreaker.

"We did not invent the present rules, which include penalty kicks and invite the use of tactics to reach the penalty kick shoot-out stage," said Petrovic. In other words, the tiebreaker had encouraged Red Star to play for a tie!

But FIFA did not take the hint, and persisted with penalty kicks, even when its own Football 2000 task force reported that 80 percent of the letters it had received were hostile to the use of the penalty kick tiebreaker.

A much more plausible tiebreaker—the counting of corner kicks during a game—remained unexplored. The advantage of corner kicks was that it was something that worked throughout the regular game. To get corner kicks, a team had to attack, it had to get down the other end of the field. If it played defensively, camped in its own half, it would inevitably give up corners and not gain any. The chances were high that with the game opened up, more goals would be scored and it would not be necessary to use the tiebreaker.

In 1987 the under-seventeen World Championship was won by the USSR—on penalty kicks. An absurd result, for the USSR had been comprehensively outplayed during the game by Nigeria, which did everything but put the ball in the net.

Sooner or later, it seemed likely that the World Cup itself would be decided on penalty kicks, for FIFA had in 1986 altered the regulations. Until then, if the final was tied after extra time—something that had never happened—it was to be replayed a couple of days later. Now it would go to penalty kicks instead, and a storm of protest would no doubt follow.

Much less controversial was FIFA's new "back-pass" rule. The sight of a defender playing the ball backward, into the safe hands of his own goalkeeper—who then took anything up to twenty seconds to release it—could almost stand as a symbol of negative play. FIFA put a stop to that by banning the goalkeeper from using his hands on such a pass. That was a worldwide, permanent rule change, approved by the International Board.

But there were other changes that applied only for the duration of certain FIFA tournaments. Published in memoranda issued to referees and coaches before the tournaments, these were often substantial changes that contradicted the rules of the game. The memorandum put out before Italia-90, for instance, stated: "Coaching of players during a game is permitted only from the team's bench." Yet the rules stated clearly that a referee "shall *not* allow coaching from the boundary lines."

It was a straw in the wind. Three years later FIFA bowed to the fact that it was impossible to stop coaches shouting at their players during a game. The rules were altered to allow the coaches to "convey tactical instructions" provided they stayed within a yard of the bench.

For the World Youth Championship in 1993, the memorandum stated: "The tackle from behind is prohibited." This was another step toward protecting the skillful players, the dribblers, who were always being clobbered from behind. Such tackles invariably resulted in the dribbler being brought down, and quite often injured. The tackler would plead innocence of any foul, claiming, "But I got the ball, ref!" But rarely, if ever, did he get the ball without also getting the man.

To see the tackle from behind banned—even if only for the length of a tournament—was a major step forward for attacking soccer. But it was also a rule change that had been sneaked in by the back door, because the rules themselves contain no mention of such tackles.

Of one thing there could be no doubt: The aim of FIFA's rule changing was to make life more difficult for defenders, to make them clean up their act. A determined effort was under way to counter the situation pictured by the Football 2000 task force members at its first meeting: "Present-day soccer is not very attractive to watch."

Not attractive to watch, maybe, but clearly still very attractive to play. The number of players throughout the world registered with FIFA rose from 18 million in 1976 to 88 million in 1993. Much of the huge increase came from China, which had not been a FIFA member until 1979, and from Africa, where improved organization allowed the counting of previously unregistered players.

Much of the growth was at the youth level. Now there were world championships for players in the under-seventeen and the under-twenty age brackets. In 1989 came the first indoor, or five-a-side, world championship.

Women's soccer was on the rise, too, suggesting that another massive increase in playing numbers was yet to come. Three of FIFA's new realms came together in November 1991 when the first ever Women's World Cup was staged in China . . . and won by the United States.

The growth of the game in the United States was something that had not gone unnoticed by FIFA. The anomaly that this huge country, with its immense resources and its fanatic interest in sports, was not a part of the worldwide soccer family seemed to be coming to an end.

In 1988 the Americans signaled that they were ready to join the big time, and submitted an official bid to act as hosts for the 1994 World Cup. In accepting the bid, FIFA emphasized that this was the opportunity to help the sport conquer the last frontier.

Others saw only a commercial ploy to get American dollars into the sport. A more genuine criticism came from soccer purists, who did not like the idea of giving the sport's crown jewel to a country with no soccer history.

No soccer history? A comment that is worth a closer look . . .

CHAPTER 8

Soccer Comes to the United States

Not even the most chauvinistic American could claim that the United States has had any influence on the development of soccer. In this survey of that development, the United States has cropped up only once or twice for relatively modest achievements—reaching the semifinals of the first World Cup in 1930, beating England in 1950—that were remarkable precisely *because* the United States was regarded as a lightweight in world soccer competition.

The lack of impact on the international scene was a faithful reflection of the sport's minor league status within the United States. But it does not mean that there was no soccer activity at all. There was plenty.

Football, in its primitive rugby-soccer form, had crossed the Atlantic hard on the heels of the first New England settlers, and was soon giving the doughty Puritans the same sort of problems that it had caused in the home country. The Boston town authorities struck a familiar note in 1657:

Forasmuch as sundry complaints are made that several persons have received hurt by boyes and young men playing at foot-ball in the streets . . .

and went on to impose a fine of twenty shillings on anyone who should be caught practicing the sport. It was not the first such ban, nor was it to be the last, but it was, like all the others, a waste of words.

Football found its way into schools and colleges, and by the early 1800s games were being played at several Ivy League universities, notably Harvard, Princeton, and Yale. Just as in England, rules were conspicuously absent, and it didn't take the university authorities long to decide that these tumultuous affrays between freshmen and sophomores were a blot on their academic escutcheon. By 1860 both Harvard and the local townsfolk had had enough of Bloody Monday—as the football day was called—and the sport suffered yet another banishment.

By this time "the dribbling game" had also arrived from England and had found a home in two New Jersey colleges, Princeton and Rutgers. When these two played each other for the first time, on November 6, 1869, the rules they used were a modification of those published in 1863 by the London Football Association.* In other words, the great Princeton-Rutgers game that is alleged to mark the beginnings of intercollegiate football was really a soccer game. Not soccer as we know it today, but soccer as it was then played, which included the use of the hands to catch or stop the ball.

Three years later Columbia and Yale had joined in, and it seemed that soccer was on its way as the fall sport of American colleges. Things did not work out that way because Harvard preferred its own version of football, in which players could pick up the ball (a round ball, let it be noted) and run with it. When other American colleges refused to play Harvard under such rules, the college turned to Canada and in 1874 scheduled two games with McGill University of Montreal.

The second of these was played with an egg-shaped ball under rugby-football rules, and proved greatly pleasing to the Harvard players. They adopted rugby, and induced Yale to follow suit. A game between the two in 1875 was watched by two Princeton players who returned to their own campus singing the praises of rugby and called a meeting to propose that Princeton's brand of football should henceforth be rugby, not soccer. By a narrow margin the students voted in favor of rugby, and as far as the colleges were concerned, soccer had to take a backseat.

To speculate a little, one has the feeling that even if the vote had gone in favor of soccer, the sport would not have lasted very long in the colleges. This was a time when America, beginning to assert its own nationality, was anxious to demonstrate that it was not a country built on other people's traditions.

The English, in particular, were a constant irritant, forever going

* See Chapter 1, page 8.

on about the crudities of American life and declaiming that the only good things about it were those that had been imported from England. If there was one thing that American sportsmen wanted to avoid, it was the accusation that their sports, too, were crude imitations of the English originals. Cricket, that most English of games, had been, up until 1850, the most popular sport in the United States, but it was now condemned as effete and slow, and had given way to baseball, which, it was claimed, was of 100 percent American origin.*

In the colleges, rugby was soon swallowed up by the Americanization process. Within ten years a stream of rule changes had produced a new sport—football—that bore only the slightest likeness to rugby. Soccer, surely, would have suffered the same fate, producing heaven knows what kind of hybrid sports monster. Perhaps it is just as well for those who like soccer more or less the way it is that the sport escaped the clutches of the colleges in the 1870s.

By 1900, despite the college setback, amateur soccer was widely played throughout the eastern seaboard area, particularly around New York, New Jersey, and Philadelphia. The *New York Times* of the period covered many more soccer than football games, featuring teams such as Brooklyn Celtics, Anglo-Saxons F.C., Clan McKenzie F.C., Spanish-American F.C., and Over-Seas F.C.

The team names tell the story—teams composed largely of immigrants, jealously guarding the honor of the old country. What might be called the "ethnic factor" established itself very early in American soccer and has been a considerable nuisance ever since.

Actually, to say that soccer flourished "despite" the college setback is probably a non sequitur, for there is no evidence that the goings-on at Harvard and Princeton held any interest whatever for the organizers of amateur soccer. To them, the word *football* meant soccer, and when they got together in 1884 to form a league, they called themselves the American Football Association.

This was a notable first for the Americans: the first Football Association to be formed outside Britain. But within five years it was in trouble, plagued by internal squabbling, an activity that has since become almost the trademark of soccer in the United States.

---

* When the English, quite rightly, pointed out that baseball was a form of rounders (an English game, of course), the Americans responded by concocting the rather silly tale that Abner Doubleday had invented baseball, all on his own, in 1839. It was not a very convincing story, but such was the desire of Americans to Americanize their sports that it was accepted uncritically.

The New York clubs complained that the league schedule put them at a disadvantage, and threatened to withdraw. Eventually, they did so, to form their own league, the American Amateur Football Association, thus distinguishing it from the AFA, which by the early 1900s had become a semiprofessional league.

In 1912 both the AFA and the AAFA turned up at the FIFA congress in Stockholm, each requesting recognition as the controlling body of American soccer. FIFA, unaccustomed to such bickering among its members, sent them both packing with instructions to get together and form one national body. Within a year the AAFA had rounded up support from almost every other soccer group that it could find and formed yet another organization, the United States Football Association. In 1913 this group, USFA, returned to FIFA representing just about everyone except the semipro clubs of the AFA, but they, too, joined when FIFA announced recognition of the new organization.

Although its membership did include soccer leagues in Chicago, Pittsburgh, and St Louis, the USFA was primarily an East Coast affair. In the soccer tradition it was run by amateurs, most of whom were not Americans. Men like Randolph Manning, the English-born, German-educated doctor who was elected the association's first president and promptly declared that "the USFA aims to make soccer the national pastime of the winter in this country."

American soccer now had its governing body, but it was not headed for the glory foreseen by Dr. Manning. The birth pains of USFA had exposed some irritating faults in the American soccer community. Faults that, unfortunately, were to recur repeatedly throughout the following fifty years. The USFA was to undergo a series of name changes, but it could never move beyond what it had always been: an amateur organization, controlled in the main by immigrants and hyphenated-Americans. Its attempts to promote soccer as a major-league sport, were constantly undermined by its own internal bickering and lack of vision.

Not that there is anything wrong with either immigrants or amateurs. The problem was that over the years the USFA tended to become a gathering place for immigrants whose devotion to soccer was a pretty good measure of their reluctance to become Americans, and for people who were amateurs mainly in the pejorative sense of the word. The very idea of such a group moving soccer into the American major league sports scene is almost hilarious.

There is no need to dwell on USFA's adventures for the next fifty years, for so very little was accomplished. Certainly, the organization slowly expanded its membership throughout the country, but at the same time it was withdrawing farther and farther into an ethnic shell. The colleges and high schools were completely ignored, while attempts to upgrade the professional side of the sport invariably ended in failure.

The most determined push for a pro league came in 1921 with the birth of the American Soccer League, an East Coast loop that included teams backed by major companies such as Bethlehem Steel Mills. A number of top international players, mostly from Scotland, joined the league, and it flourished until the end of the decade. Most of the players on the U.S. team that reached the semifinals of the first World Cup in 1930 were from the ASL.

But the league was greatly weakened—not by competition with baseball or football, but by an ongoing struggle with USFA over whether ASL teams could be forced to play in USFA's Cup competition. For a while, the ASL operated as a pirate league, unsanctioned by the USFA. By the time the dispute was settled, on October 9, 1929, the Wall Street crash was only weeks away. The depression, with its soaring unemployment and factory closings killed off the ASL in 1930.

For fifty years soccer remained an immigrant sport outside the mainstream of American sporting life. Americans had good reason to think of soccer as a foreign sport because, even within the United States, it was practiced mainly by foreigners who seemed to rejoice in giving their leagues and teams foreign titles and names.

Another turn-off was the possibility of trouble at the games. No doubt this was the exception rather than the rule, but it was still far too common. Discipline, exercised ultimately by USFA in the form of club or player suspensions, was simply not enforced, and the newspapers had a field day with stories like these:

From *The New York Times*, April 20, 1927:

FOUR HURT IN RIOT AT SOCCER CONTEST
2 Women & 2 Men Injured
During Fight in Uruguay-Boston Game
at Malden, Mass.

SOUTH AMERICANS RESCUED
Members of Team Rushed from Scene
by Police When Crowd Threatens

TWO PLAYERS UNCONSCIOUS
Boston Athletes Carried Off as
2000 Persons Swarm on Field—
Referee's Decision Starts Melee

From *The New York Times*, February 13, 1928:

POLICE IN BATTLE WITH SOCCER FANS
Reserves Called Out When
the Spectators at Bayonne Join
Fight Among Players

NIGHTSTICKS SWING FREELY
Melee Starts After Hispano Eleven
Beats Rovers for Northern New Jersey Title

And so on, and so on. American soccer, through its own slackness, was building up an image of riots and referee-bashing rather similar to that which had surrounded baseball at the turn of the century. Baseball, in the person of Ban Johnson, quickly solved its problem by taking firm steps to enforce the rules and protect the umpires. Soccer did nothing, and the image of rampaging fans is one that continues, to this day, to damage soccer's standing in the United States.

But even an institution as insular as American soccer had become could not forever remain untouched by what was going on around it. In 1945 USFA showed that it had, at last, realized that the word *football* did not mean soccer in the United States and changed its name to the United States Soccer Football Association (USSFA).

It was the slenderest of straws in the slightest of winds, but it was certainly drifting in the right direction. Then the increased efficiency of air travel resulted in more visits from top foreign teams. Liverpool of England made two highly successful tours in 1946 and 1948. The climax of the second tour was a game against the Swedish team Djurgaardens, played in the old Brooklyn Dodgers stadium at Ebbets Field. Billed as the first meeting on American soil of two major foreign teams, the game drew over 18,000 spectators.

A point had been made. Top teams, playing in major league stadiums, could draw big crowds. Throughout the 1950s an average of six foreign teams a year came to the United States, including some of the really big names: Real Madrid, Manchester United, Vasco da Gama, Celtic, Rapid-Vienna.

They played exhibition games only, and it occurred to one promoter that the games might be better if there were something at stake. That individual was Bill Cox. Significantly, he was an American, and a baseball rather than a soccer man. At least, he had once been a baseball man, owner of the Philadelphia Phillies. Caught betting on his own team, he was banished from baseball by Commissioner Judge Landis.

In 1960 Cox organized the International Soccer League in New York, composed of eleven foreign teams, plus the American All-Stars, playing for a championship. They were by no means top teams (though, looking back, one has to admire Cox's talent for selecting young teams—like West Ham United of London and Dukla-Prague—that were on the verge of success), and the organization of the tournament, played at the Polo Grounds, left much to be desired. But it was still incomparably better than anything the local ethnic leagues had to offer.

The International Soccer League broke no box-office records, but its better games consistently drew five-figure crowds. At a time when the major league sports of football, basketball, baseball, and hockey were falling over themselves to expand or start new leagues, it began to occur to franchise-seekers that pro soccer might have some potential. Better yet, because it would be starting virtually from the ground level, it might have the greatest potential of all.

Suddenly, in the fall of 1965, soccer had what it had never had before: wealthy American businessmen and promoters falling over themselves to invest in it. In fact, it had rather too many of them. Three distinct groups now wanted to start up nationwide pro soccer leagues, groups that included men like Lamar Hunt, Jack Kent Cooke, Judge Roy Hofheinz, and major corporations such as Madison Square Garden and R.K.O.-General.

The scene was set for the showdown that would drag American soccer into the twentieth century. The catch for all the new soccer investors was this: If they wanted to operate within the structure of FIFA-controlled worldwide soccer, which they assuredly did, they would have to have the approval of the USSFA. Most of them were aware of this, but regarded it as a trifling formality, a bit of meaningless form-filling. All three groups duly sent off letters to USSFA requesting sanction for their proposed leagues.

What happened next could have come straight out of a quaint English comedy movie. On one side big businessmen, wealthy, influential boardroom people, with assistants and secretaries and chauffeured limousines at their beck and call. On the other, USSFA, an organization made up of part-timers, mostly foreign-born, housed in an incredibly dingy and untidy office in midtown Manhattan. Presiding over the office, with his sleeves rolled up and his suspenders in full view, a sharp-tongued Irish-American, Joe Barriskill.*

For soccer, there was to be more tragedy than comedy in the confrontation. Suspicion and mistrust were mutual. USSFA appointed a committee—composed of a Romanian-American, a Scottish-American, and a German-American—to deal with the proposals. The committee was, not without reason, dubious about the motives of the new soccer fanatics: Were they genuinely interested in the sport, or did they simply want to exploit it, to make money out of it?

For the new owners, the situation was downright incredible. In any other American sport, if you wanted to start up a league, you just got the capital together and went ahead and did it, yet here they were, asking for permission from an organization run by amateurs.

Poor USSFA. After dozing for decades, it was suddenly confronted with an insoluble problem, not of its own making. It knew that three competing leagues would rapidly kill each other off and urged the groups to get together to form one league. Two of them did combine, but that was as far as anyone would go. USSFA would now have to pick one of the leagues or recognize both.

It chose to sanction the group headed by Jack Kent Cooke, which gave itself the name United Soccer Association—USA, you see. This meant that the other league, the National Professional Soccer League, had either to fold its tents and slink away or to operate as a pirate league, outside organized soccer.

Still bursting with optimism about the future of soccer (at least, as an investment), the NPSL chose the pirate route. At the same time, it made frequent approaches direct to the FIFA headquarters in Zurich, pleading for recognition. FIFA's advice—shades of 1912!—was that it should return to the United States and make peace with USSFA.

One thing that both leagues realized very quickly was that they would not be able to stock their leagues with American players. They just weren't good enough. Foreigners it would have to be. The NPSL was quickly off the mark, sending its scouts around the world to sign up players for a 1967 kickoff.

The scouts ran smack into the problems that came with the NPSL's

---

* Soccer's image was not greatly helped by the fact that Barriskill used to spend his summer evenings working as a ticket usher at New York Yankee baseball games.

outlaw status. USSFA had informed FIFA that this was an unsanctioned league, FIFA had informed all the other national F.A.s, and they in turn had informed all their players that to join such a league was to court suspension from playing anywhere else. The worldwide soccer monopoly was at work.

Despite the barriers, the NPSL managed to sign enough players to stock its ten teams, though they were mostly players from second and third division clubs. This all came as a nasty surprise to the USA, which had not believed that the NPSL would get off the ground, and had been planning to begin its own operations in 1968. Even more alarming, the NPSL had pulled off a two-year game-of-the-week television deal with CBS.

Obviously, the NPSL could not be allowed to have 1967 all to itself. The USA rushed onto the scene by importing whole teams from Europe and South America, one for each of its twelve franchised cities. Again, these were not really top teams.

When 1967 was over, all twenty-two clubs in both leagues had lost money, and the NPSL announced an $18 million restraint-of-trade lawsuit against USSFA, the USA, and FIFA. The suit was settled out of court when USSFA agreed to recognize the NPSL. The two leagues then merged to form the seventeen-club North American Soccer League, and everyone sailed forth to make 1968 the gala year of American soccer.

It was, if anything, even more disastrous than 1967 had been. Everyone lost money again, CBS bowed out, and suddenly there was a rush for the exits. When the 1969 season began, the NASL was down to just five clubs.

Yet another soccer debacle, but one for which the USSFA was only partly to blame. Most of the responsibility lay with the ignorance and the arrogance of the new franchise holders, who blithely assumed that soccer was simply another commodity that could be successfully marketed by public relations puffery. They talked repeatedly of "being in this thing for the long haul," but the moment it became clear that they were not going to be drowned in quick profits, they bolted. USSFA's suspicions had been correct—these men cared not a fig for the good of soccer.

The fiasco had its constructive side. The NASL had taken soccer to parts of America where it had never been seen before—Atlanta, Dallas, Kansas City—and where it had been surprisingly well received, so well that all three cities were among the five survivors in 1969.

By the skin of its teeth, the NASL survived and slowly rebuilt its strength. It is taking nothing away from the enthusiasm and nonstop industry of the league's commissioner Phil Woosnam to say that the key figure in the NASL's survival was Lamar Hunt, owner of the league's Dallas Tornado. As long as he was there, nobody could afford to write off the NASL.

It was not a question of the fabled Hunt millions being poured into soccer—nothing of the sort happened. It was a question of confidence and image. If Lamar Hunt thought that pro soccer had a future, there would always be plenty of other investors willing to lend an ear to what he had to say.

Plenty did. By 1978, the NASL was up to twenty-four clubs; it included the major TV markets and even took in the Canadian cities of Vancouver and Toronto.

The master move came in 1975 when the New York Cosmos—a member of the league since 1971—signed Pelé. But this was something that began back in the dark days of 1969.

Clive Toye and Phil Woosnam, the NASL's only executives, were desperately trying to keep the five-team league alive. For them, a useful exercise for warding off the fear that the league might not last out the week was to leapfrog over the bleak present and to imagine the glittering future.

Soccer would be suffering, both agreed, as long as it did not have its own superstars. Even just one superstar would do. Obviously he could not be American; no American player was good enough or likely to be good enough in the foreseeable future. Whichever way they looked at it, there was really only one man who could fill the role: Pelé.

His popularity had been proved many times when his club Santos toured the United States, always drawing crowds far above average. He was a draw, he was a name, known—if not for his soccer brilliance—then for the fact that he was reputed to be the highest-paid athlete in the world. He was the man who could provide the glamour that major league soccer must have, concluded Toye and Woosnam as they peered presumptuously into their rosy-hued crystal ball.

Slowly, circumstances began to arrange themselves more and more favorably. The NASL rebuilt its strength and began to attract some substantially wealthy backers. Among them was Warner Communications, which owned the New York Cosmos. The Turkish-born brothers Ahmet and Nesuhi Ertegun, recording industry magnates and keen soccer fans, ran the club, and chose Clive Toye to be their general manager. They did not need much convincing on the idea to sign Pelé.

Starting in 1971 hints were dropped to Pelé that, after he retired from playing with his club Santos in 1974, he might think about joining the New York Cosmos. His response was a grin, a nod, and an inscrutability that meant neither yes nor no. Toye, ever the optimist, took it to mean that Pelé was interested. By June 1974 he was talking directly to Pelé about the opportunities that awaited him in the United States if he played with the Cosmos.

Pelé played his last game for Santos in October 1974. Eight months later he was in New York, at the fashionable "21" Club, signing a three-year, $4.5-million contract with the Cosmos.

The arrival of Pelé immediately proved to be everything that Toye and Woosnam had dreamed of in terms of bringing soccer into the limelight. His first game with the Cosmos was nationally televised by CBS.

The Cosmos were still playing at the rundown Randall's Island Stadium in New York (CBS had to paint the muddy patches green), but suddenly the austere press box at Cosmos games was jammed, full of people who could not pronounce Pelé's name, whose conversation made it painfully clear that they knew nothing of soccer, but well-heeled people who moved with a swagger not seen before in soccer press boxes and who made a fuss if they didn't get a good seat.

Articles on Pelé began to appear in all the chic magazines; Pelé was on the Johnny Carson show, Pelé was at the White House showing President Ford what a soccer ball looked like. And everywhere the fans poured out: capacity crowds in Boston (where the Boston Minutemen billed their game against the Cosmos as Minutemen vs. Pelé), St. Louis, San Jose, New York, Los Angeles, and Seattle, a league record 35,000 in Washington.

What Lamar Hunt had done for the financial end of the NASL, Pelé now did for the on-the-field side. Other top players began to arrive— Johan Cruyff, George Best, Giorgio Chinaglia, and Franz Beckenbauer.

In 1977 the Cosmos moved from Yankee Stadium to Giants Stadium in New Jersey, and suddenly the crowds poured in, climaxing with nearly 78,000 for the playoff game against Fort Lauderdale. The celebrities, too. The postgame scene in the Cosmos locker room was always likely to be a frantic mixture of half-naked athletes, struggling journalists, hordes of autograph hunters, and the likes of Mick Jagger, Rod Stewart, or Dr. Henry Kissinger.

An ABC TV contract came in 1979. It seemed like the crowning touch, the proof that soccer was now on a level with football and baseball. In reality, it marked the beginning of the end. In 1981, the NASL lost three franchises, and the following year ABC, dissatisfied with soccer's ratings, did not renew its contract. That same year, the NASL lost seven more clubs; one of them was the Dallas Tornado. Lamar Hunt's faith in soccer no longer outweighed the financial losses.

Everyone was losing money—indeed, no one had ever made any money—and panic surfaced. Phil Woosnam, the only commissioner the NASL had ever had, was fired; he was blamed for expanding the NASL too far, too fast. But none of it had been done without the owners' approval. And the Cosmos were accused of bankrupting the league as the other clubs tried to match their spending.

Leadership of the NASL was handed over to Howard Samuels, a New York politician who had successfully launched the state's Off Track Betting program. It was felt that he had the necessary business sense to save the league.

Samuels looked at all the figures, the clubs' income and expenditure, and exclaimed, "These guys are crazy!" The way he figured it, no one could make any money, the income just wasn't there. The maximum roster size was reduced from twenty-eight to nineteen, and a salary-cap agreement was worked out with the NASL Players Association.

Band-Aids for a hemorrhaging league. It was down to twelve clubs in 1983, nine in 1984. When Samuels died suddenly in October 1984, no move was made to replace him. Already there was a feeling that the NASL was without a future.

In March, the NASL, or what was left of it, announced officially that it would not operate in 1985. It also threw the Cosmos out for not posting its letter of credit. Warner Communications had sold out, but the new Cosmos owners—a group put together by former goal-scoring ace Giorgio Chinaglia—put on a brave face and announced a series of exhibition games in the summer.

On Father's Day, the Cosmos played Lazio of Italy in Giants Stadium. No huge crowds now, just 9,000 fans. "The money is nearly zero, the outlook isn't bright," said Chinaglia. "Nobody wants to invest in soccer in this country."

The sad ending to the Lazio game, and to the shining Cosmos adventure, was the spectacle of both teams in an all-out brawl on the field. The Cosmos were finished, they would never play again.

The collapse of the NASL meant the end of professional soccer in the United States—real soccer, the outdoor game, that is. There was always the six-a-side indoor game, as played by the thriving Major Indoor Soccer League (MISL). Spurned by the purists as an unspeakable corruption of their game, indoor soccer had what proved to be a fatal attraction for many of the NASL owners.

Various forms of indoor soccer had been played in Europe and South America since the 1930s. It was not a new sport, but what appealed to the NASL owners was that it enabled them to get more use out of players on twelve-month contracts. To the short twenty-four-game summer season, they could now add a winter season. Indoor soccer also allowed them to do something that FIFA would not permit with the outdoor game. They could tinker with the rules, they could get on with the Americanization process that we have encountered before.

So in 1975 and 1976 the NASL ran a winter indoor season. It was a divisive experiment. Not all of the clubs joined in. The Cosmos didn't take part because, said Nesuhi Ertegun, "We play *soccer*. That is what our fans want." While the NASL clubs argued and dithered over the merits of the indoor game, a Philadelphia lawyer, Earl Foreman, jumped in and formed the MISL. The MISL said it was playing "a truly American sport, the human pinball game," and suddenly soccer had penalty boxes and massive substitution, to say nothing of laser-beam light shows and screaming announcers and dancing girls. "This is the game Americans want," crowed Foreman.

The NASL had hatched a soccer cuckoo. The MISL gained in strength; the NASL weakened. As the NASL tried to peg back its salaries, the MISL lured away its best players with higher offers. The defection of Rick Davis—captain of the US national team, the leading American player of the day—came as the cruelest blow in the fall of 1983. When the Cosmos offered to renew his contract, but without a raise, Davis jumped to the St. Louis Steamers of the MISL.

Soccer had found yet another internal division—indoor vs. outdoor—with which to wound itself. Neither side triumphed. The NASL had lasted eighteen years, during which one of its biggest problems had been to find stable ownership. Only once in that period did it field the same lineup of clubs in consecutive seasons. It was to be no different for the MISL, which lasted only fourteen years before it withered to five teams and folded in 1992, with Commissioner Earl Foreman declaring that it was "unable to attract new owners."

Luckily, the cuckoo-sport of indoor soccer was not the only legacy of the NASL. It left behind much more positive influences, not least in the way that it acted as a catalyst to growth in other areas of the game—college soccer, for instance.

During the roughly fifty years of USSFA-controlled soccer in the United States, there had always been college soccer. Ironically, it was strongest in those Ivy League schools that had rejected it in the 1870s. Harvard, for instance, had taken up soccer in 1905, and when the Intercollegiate Soccer Association was formed in 1926, it included both Princeton and Yale among its twelve members.

USSFA and the colleges showed little interest in each other's activities. That was fine with the colleges, who went their own way, unburdened by interference from USSFA, which would have obliged it to stick the internationally accepted FIFA rules.

Surprise, surprise, the collegians made some Americanizing changes to the sport. They played the game in four quarters instead of two halves, they used two referees instead of one, they replaced the throw-in with a kick-in. And they permitted liberal use of substitutes, where FIFA rules did not permit any.

College soccer grew slowly until the 1960s, when it was hit by the same groundswell for the sport that was to give rise to the NASL. There were two special circumstances working in favor of soccer in the colleges: As college basketball and football became increasingly specialized, soccer was recognized as an ideal sport for the average-sized athlete, and it was a cheap team sport to organize, an attraction to budget-conscious colleges.

In 1959 the National Collegiate Athletic Association (NCAA) inaugurated a national championship for college soccer. By 1972 the sport had a national ratings system and a Senior Bowl game, and scholarships were increasingly available, something that further encouraged an already formidable growth in the game at the high school level. Soccer could now offer American boys the same thing as basketball and football, a high school and college career leading to the pros.

It looked that way, but the reality was something different.

By 1972 the NASL was coming under criticism for its reliance on foreign players. The Non-American Soccer League, said its critics, who pointed out that there were virtually no ex-college players at all in the league (although a substantial exception must be made in the case of the St. Louis Stars, which drew heavily on graduates from St. Louis University, at that time the strongest team in college soccer).

Phil Woosnam, the NASL's Welsh commissioner, had the answer: a college draft. A baffling experience for the eight NASL coaches, all of them foreign-born, who knew very little of college soccer. The draft was a farce, as the eight clubs picked thirty-five players they knew very little about. Eight of them were signed; only two made it as first-team starters.

All that could be put down to teething problems, and certainly the subsequent drafts were much more meaningful occasions. From 1972 on, NASL coaches were seen regularly at college games, and Phil Woosnam stated that the aim of the NASL was to field all-American teams. As the NASL increased the number of its teams, the number of players drafted went up—forty-four in 1973, seventy-six in 1975—but the signings remained pitifully small, six in 1973, twenty-four in 1975.

Disillusion came quickly. The college players were not good enough. In 1977 the Cosmos signed a promising young forward, Gary Etherington, straight out of high school. The following year they plucked Rick Davis away from his junior year in college. The message was clear: The colleges could not be relied on to develop talent. Indeed, how could they, with a short season of only around twenty games. Worse yet, there was a widespread feeling among NASL coaches that the colleges *retarded* the growth of players. It was a very awkward message for a league that was trying to Americanize itself.

A league regulation was introduced requiring a quota for North Americans.* By 1981, over 50 percent of the league's players were Americans, and during the NASL's final 1984 season each team had to have five Americans on the field at all times.

By then, the cost-cutting owners were embracing Americanization with a vengeance. It was cheaper to sign Americans. Money was saved, but the flood of young, inexperienced Americans, many of them straight out of college, brought with it a sharp lowering of the playing standards. The college players were still not good enough.

Strangely, very strangely, the quality of their product did not come up for discussion among the businessmen who were busy trying to bring financial sanity to the league. It was an extraordinary oversight, but one that was to become a hidden, destructive theme of subsequent events in U.S. soccer.

The game on the field was pushed aside, almost forgotten it seemed, as short-term monetary considerations took over. For those with sensitive ears for this sort of thing, the signs had been there for some

---

* The definition included Canadians, naturalized citizens, and resident-alien green-card holders.

time that the NASL, having at last brought American methods and American accents into soccer, was placing increasing emphasis on the commercial aspects of its operation.

Announcing a league expansion in 1970, Commissioner Phil Woosnam had welcomed "the addition of such great soccer centers as New York and Toronto." By 1974 there was no more talk of soccer centers—NASL franchises were now being awarded to "markets" like Tampa, "the twentieth largest market in the country," said Woosnam, adding that the league was "examining the possibility of expanding into another four of the eight markets that have indicated interest."

It was precisely to avoid this rampant obsession with money that the founders of soccer in England had insisted that the ultimate control of the sport be left in the hands of amateurs. And that, in theory anyway, was still the case in the United States.

The USSFA remained in the picture, too—the same USSFA that had all the trouble sorting out the surplus of pro leagues in 1967. Fifty years of vegetation as the champion of small-time hyphenated-American soccer had left USSFA singularly ill-equipped to deal with that situation, and the result was a tangle that ended with everyone in court.

But just as the NASL held on to rise again, USSFA, too, survived, but not as the USSFA of old. As the NASL gained strength, it dragged USSFA forward. The dreadful old office on Fifth Avenue was abandoned for a new one, just a few blocks farther north. But what a difference! The USSFA now had a suite in the Empire State Building. Even the name was altered, the word *football* was finally dropped, and the United States Soccer Federation (USSF) was born.

The game was exploding, especially at the youth level. All that NASL missionary work, all those clinics, were beginning to bear fruit. In 1979, the USSF's youth (under-nineteen) enrollment hit half a million for the first time. A year later it was 625,000, and increasing at the rate of over 200 kids a day, boys and girls.

Hordes of kids wanted to play, but who was to coach them? Most of them came from middle-class American families with no previous involvement with soccer. Yet it was these parents who were being pressed into service as coaches. The USSF started up its own coaching schools, with a range of licenses for anyone from absolute beginners to professionals.

But the USSF was still an amateur organization that hadn't gotten used to thinking big. The ambitious ideas came from the NASL, in particular, the one about the 1986 World Cup. That had been awarded to Colombia, but by 1982, it was common knowledge that Colombia was going to renege.

Then the USSF should make a bid, said the NASL leaders. They had their own interests very much in mind, of course. Their league was tottering, but they felt that the promise of the World Cup in 1986 could save it.

USSF president Gene Edwards was against the idea, so he was bypassed. The NASL turned to Werner Fricker, a USSF vice president, and conducted all the negotiations with FIFA through him. The bid was made—and brutally rejected by FIFA in 1983, who gave the tournament to Mexico.

In 1984, Fricker became the new president of USSF. He was backed by former NASL commissioner Phil Woosnam, who masterminded his campaign with electioneering and careful vote-counting, something that had never been seen before at a USSF convention.

A new realism, a modern approach, had arrived for the USSF. Within hours of his election, Fricker ordered the USSF to disband the amateur team that it was preparing for the Los Angeles Olympics, and to use professional players instead. This was something that every other nation was doing but which Gene Edwards had steadfastly resisted.

Fricker's hardheaded realism also dictated that the USSF would have to get out of New York. The collapse of the NASL put a big dent in the USSF's income, and it fled to Colorado Springs, there to nestle comfortably—and for free—in office space provided by the United States Olympic Committee.

The tranquility and obscurity of Colorado Springs did nothing to dampen Fricker's ambitions. Who would not be optimistic as those numbers continued to increase? Between 1974 and 1984, the number of colleges with men's teams had climbed from 415 to 544. At the beginning of the seventies, some 70,000 boys played high school soccer; by 1984 the figure was 180,000. Figures kept going up as the number of USSF under-nineteen youth registrations went on climbing. By 1987 the figure was 1.2 million.

A new phenomenon was on the horizon, too: women's soccer. In 1981 there was no such thing in the colleges. Just three years later, 165 colleges were fielding women's soccer teams.

At the end of the 1970s, when the NASL was at its peak, it had used a slogan "Soccer—the Sport of the '80s." The NASL wasn't around to see it, but soccer was certainly becoming the youth sport of the eighties.

Another set of figures had an enormous effect on soccer thinking. Fricker's use of professionals in the Los Angeles Olympics had not been successful—the United States was bounced out in the first round. But the crowds at the Rose Bowl had astonished everyone: 97,451 for France vs. Yugoslavia, 100,374 for Yugoslavia vs. Italy, and 101,799 for the final between Brazil and France.

Even FIFA, which runs the Olympic Soccer Tournament, had to be impressed. When the USSF, led by Fricker, went back to them in 1987, making a bid for the 1994 World Cup, the atmosphere was all sweetness and light. The other countries bidding were Chile, Morocco, and Brazil. Chile soon dropped out, and the United States seemed to be FIFA's preferred candidate.

The announcement was made on July 4, 1988: World Cup 1994 would be staged in the United States. A triumph for Fricker, but he was already in the process of undermining his own good work. He exposed his lack of knowledge of international soccer by appointing a college coach, Bob Gansler, to head the national team. Against weak opposition in the qualifying round, Gansler's supercautious tactics squeaked the Americans into the final round of Italia-90, the first time an American team had got that far since 1950, but the achievement turned to ashes in Italy. Gansler's lack of experience of World Cup soccer caught up with him. His team performed poorly and lost all three of its games.

Soon after that debacle, Fricker had to face reelection. His dour, hard-driving methods had made him a lot of enemies. He had accomplished a great deal in six years, and he might have survived had his enemies been solely within the USSF. But he had badly overplayed his hand in dealing with FIFA over the 1994 World Cup.

By 1990, FIFA had had enough of his stubbornness, of his refusing to take their advice, of his insistence on involving partners of whom FIFA did not approve. Working behind the scenes, FIFA persuaded Alan Rothenberg to run against Fricker. Rothenberg, a Los Angeles lawyer, was known to FIFA from his work during the 1984 Olympic Soccer Tournament.

Rothenberg decided to run only two weeks before the election. The extent of FIFA's involvement was revealed on the morning of the election, when the third candidate—USSF treasurer Paul Stiehl—received a 6:20 A.M. call from FIFA suggesting he should step aside and not split the anti-Fricker vote. Stiehl, appalled, stood anyway.

Said Rothenberg: "FIFA is concerned with the USSF leadership; it's just not up to the task. The 1994 World Cup is the last chance for soccer in the United States. FIFA officials have told me if a change isn't made, that chance will be lost."

A change was made. Rothenberg swept to victory. Later he was to say: "People didn't realize how precarious it was. FIFA was prepared to take the World Cup away from us. They told me that. I believed them."

With the World Cup secured, Rothenberg set about revitalizing the USSF. He brought in Hank Steinbrecher as secretary general, the first time in nearly 50 years that the USSF had had an American-born as secretary and one with business experience, at that. And it was made known that the USSF offices would soon be moved from their Colorado Springs backwater. In 1992, they would go to Chicago.

Eventually—it took eight months—Bob Gansler was replaced as national team coach by Bora Milutinovic, the Serbian who had been so successful in getting Costa Rica into the second round in Italia-90.

Change was long overdue at the USSF, but the most remarkable aspect of the process remained the way in which the USSF membership had voted so solidly for Rothenberg. For the USSF is a cumbersome, volunteer organization, not known for imaginative thinking, and with a considerable suspicion of outsiders.

Nominally, it is governed by a national council in which voting strength is divided equally between three groups: the amateurs, the youth, and the professionals. Other members of the council include representatives from the colleges, the high schools, the referees, the coaches, and from affiliated organizations such as the American Youth Soccer Organization (an independent national youth soccer organization with some 400,000 members).

The full council of over 300 delegates meets only once a year. In practice, most of the decisions are taken by the smaller National Board of Directors (twenty-nine members) or the nine-member Executive Committee. This consists of the elected officers: the president, four vice-presidents, and the treasurer, plus the immediate past president, and two Olympic representatives. Plus the secretary-general, the only full-time salaried member. All of the officers must be American citizens. There is also the usual collection—over thirty of them—of specialist committees and subcommittees.

For decades the USSF's constitution set out its aim as "supreme control and representation of soccer football in the United States of America." This sweeping claim was an attempt by USSF to invest itself with the same sort of undisputed authority that the national soccer organizations of other countries enjoyed. But other countries do not have the strong antitrust laws of the United States.

In the 1960s the USSF was taken to court three times as a result of its attempts to withhold recognition from leagues and teams of which it did not approve. All three cases were settled out of court: The USSF backed down in one by agreeing to recognize the NPSL in 1968, while in the other two it made financial settlements of $25,000 and $30,000.

Since that time, the wording of the USSF constitution has been altered to eliminate all talk of "supreme control"; the aim of USSF is now much more modest, not to say realistic: "to promote soccer in the United States of America."

The ways in which USSF now promotes soccer are as follows:

• It serves as a central registering authority for leagues, teams, and players. For each of these functions, a fee is paid to the USSF. Thus, a national Division II professional league (there are no Division I leagues) pays annual dues of $10,000, plus $5,000 for each team. Professional players pay annual dues of between $20 and $30, amateurs $3, and youth (under-nineteen) players $1.

• In the event of disputes between clubs over player registration or eligibility it acts as the final arbitrator, as it does on questions of discipline that the state associations cannot, or will not, enforce.

• It attempts to enforce uniformity in the rules throughout the United States (not easy—the colleges and the high schools are only associate members of the USSF, and have always published their own versions of the rules).

• It organizes eleven national cup competitions: men's open, amateur, and over-thirty; women's open and over-thirty; plus under-nineteen, under-seventeen, and under-sixteen for both boys and girls. These are strictly for USSF-registered players.

• It organizes and finances the national teams' programs. It appoints and pays the coaches, and arranges the teams' schedules. It also has, under full-time contract at the national team training center in Mission Viejo, California, some twenty players who form the nucleus of the national team.

• As the FIFA-affiliated body it grants permission for the playing of international games between American clubs, amateur and pro, and those from foreign countries. From every international club game, USSF takes a cut of the gate, ranging from 5 percent to 10 percent.

• It conducts regular courses, and refresher courses, for the licensing of coaches and referees.

Never a dull moment, then, for the USSF. It is an imposing list of duties, made much more so when you consider the numbers involved. With over 1.8 million youths registered (30 percent of them girls), USSF membership is now approaching 2 million players.

That's the official total, anyway. The Soccer Industry Council of America (SICA, the group that represents the interests of soccer equipment manufacturers) does its own surveys and has revealed that, whatever may be the USSF figure, the number of people who play soccer in the United States is closer to 14.6 million.

Just how the USSF has failed to recruit 12.6 million potential members is not explained. Possibly because the SICA definition of a soccer player includes all those who "played at least once" in 1991, the survey year.

Most of the players are pretty young—the SICA figures have 5.9 million of them under age 12, making soccer the number two sport, behind basketball's 7.8 million, for that age group.

However the numbers are viewed, they add up to something short of ideal for the USSF. They show a bottom-heavy organization, a pyramid with an enormous base of youngsters and amateurs, but that narrows into nothingness without the crowning glory of a pro league.

The idea of soccer as nothing more than a massive recreational sport for tots offends the sport's promoters. Indeed, it offends logic.

How can this be for the world's most popular game, played before huge crowds by highly paid professionals all over world, the game that dominates global television sports coverage, the game that FIFA has described as a $200 billion worldwide industry?

Two hundred *billion* dollars? Is that mere hype? Hardly. The proof lies in that most widely and closely and passionately followed of all man's sporting activities: the four-yearly extravaganza known as the World Cup. For one month in the summer of 1990, World Cup soccer dominated the world's television. Fifty two games were broadcast to 167 countries. The average was 500 million viewers per game. The final was watched by 1.06 billion fans. The cumulative total of viewers for the whole tournament was 26.7 billion.

The month-long party will soon be starting again. World Cup '94 will be right here in the United States. Surely this is the stimulus that will take the sport to that final level of a pro league. Will it work?

CHAPTER 9

American Soccer:
The Present and the Future

Alan Rothenberg, the man whom FIFA maneuvered into the president's chair at the United States Soccer Federation, is also the man running World Cup USA '94. Naturally enough. FIFA's machinations were designed to ensure the success of the tournament. Its own regulations required that, in organizing the World Cup, FIFA deal with the USSF. It could not get along with the then president, Werner Fricker, so he had to go.

Rothenberg moved in and appointed his own choice, Chuck Cale, to run the tournament. Cale lasted barely a year, before he, too, proved unsatisfactory to FIFA. Rothenberg, obliged to fire him, then gathered all the reins into his own hands, festooning himself with the titles of chairman, president, and chief executive officer of World Cup USA 1994.

The tournament, says Rothenberg, will be the best ever, and it will make a nice profit—$20 million is the figure he uses—for the USSF. Extravagant claims? Not at all. Routine, really. Every World Cup has been the "best ever," and every World Cup has made a profit. The figure of $20 million is reasonable, an underestimate if anything.

What is much more debatable is the matter of the national professional league that is supposed to follow in the euphoric wake of the World Cup. When it made the United States the host nation for the 1994 World Cup, FIFA was taken to task by many critics for having nothing but commercial motives on its mind. FIFA countered that by insisting that its aims were to spread the gospel of soccer, to welcome the Americans into the worldwide brotherhood of the sport . . . and to lay the groundwork for an American pro league.

Ironic, that. Only six years earlier it had been FIFA's rejection of the American bid to stage the 1986 World Cup that had helped to kill off the North American Soccer League. Now a new league was to be conjured into existence. "Soccer in the USA cannot stop with the World Cup," said the FIFA general secretary Sepp Blatter. "It must go on. This is only a step toward the formation of a professional league."

Soccer leagues do exist in the United States, plenty of them. The vast majority are regional loops, at best semipro. There are many local leagues in big cities like New York, Los Angeles, and Chicago, direct descendants of the old ethnic leagues. And, for those who like indoor soccer, there is the thirteen-team National Professional Soccer League, and the newly formed Continental Indoor Soccer League.

There are two outdoor leagues with some claim to national status. The largest is the United States Inter-regional Soccer League (USISL), a nationwide agglomeration of forty clubs in five regional leagues. A league of modest ambitions that openly declares that it "has no intention of becoming" major league.

The American Professional Soccer League (APSL) has only seven clubs, three of which are in Canada. It nevertheless claims to be "the benchmark for the continent's ultimate level of professional play . . . the only professional league in North American sanctioned by the USSF."

The second part of that claim is true enough, but there is a catch to it. The USSF has a master plan for pro soccer, which allows for one first division league and four second division leagues. The APSL fills one of the second division slots, the other three are vacant. And there is no first division league. This is the one that FIFA and the USSF so ardently desire.

Is there a chance that the APSL could grow to become a major league? Highly unlikely. Over the years soccer has never been short of minor leagues, many of them with large-sized ambitions. None of them has ever made the big step up. Says Rothenberg: "Even to the extent that the APSL is successful, it is not at the level of quality needed. It is not a major league in U.S. terms."

If a pro league is to come, it will come—as did the NASL—from the top, fully formed and financed at a major league level right from the start. That is the big bang theory, the one favored by Rothenberg: "How do you sustain the energy of '94? How do you structure and capitalize a league pretty quickly if not immediately into a major league? The structuring will be toward the big bang theory."

That is realistic thinking, a sharp contrast to Rothenberg's naive enthusiasm during his early days as the USSF president, when all the talk was of a pro league being in place *before* the World Cup. This was also the time when Rothenberg formed a committee to look into the matter of an outdoor pro league and named as its Chairman the high-priest of *indoor* soccer, Earl Foreman—the very same Earl Foreman who had recently announced to the world that "I don't give two shits about outdoor soccer."

The committee quietly evaporated after one meeting, and Rothenberg learned very quickly of the barriers that lie in the way of pro soccer. By 1993, there was acceptance that the league could not be in place until after the World Cup, and a realization that financing was not the only difficulty. There was the awkward fact that there was nowhere to play. No soccer stadiums. The NASL had made do with a mishmash of adapted football and baseball facilities. Many of the football fields were too narrow, or were of the widely disliked artificial turf; the baseball stadiums were the wrong shape and were likely to cause scheduling conflicts.

What a pro soccer league needs are middle-sized, custom-built soccer stadiums. "It's clear to me that the single biggest impediment to success," says Rothenberg, "is the stadium situation. But if people are going to invest in soccer, they ought to be willing to create first-class, 30,000-seat stadiums. It pencils out at $30 million. If we have the stadium situation corrected and if we're sufficiently capitalized, it'll work."

The flaw in this argument is that it does not address the soccer aspect of the project. It ignores the game on the field as though that will automatically take care of itself and be of the highest level.

That is a dangerously fanciful assumption. When asked whether some attention ought not to be paid to the caliber of soccer to be presented, Rothenberg says that times have changed. FIFA will now permit what they wouldn't countenance back in the NASL days: rule changes to produce a more offense-oriented game. Rule changes to Americanize the sport.

Just how far FIFA would go in that direction, no one knows. Probably not too far. Americanization could so quickly become bastardization. In any case, the approach has an air of defeatism about it right from the start, a surrender to those who believe that Americans will never take to soccer unless it is dressed up to resemble hockey or football.

As we have seen, FIFA is already modifying soccer's rules. But when Rothenberg talks of special rule changes for the USA, he is talking about gimmicks. Is that the way it has to be? Not at all. There is another approach, the only one that will give long-term success. An approach based on a careful, and knowledgeable, monitoring of the type of soccer, the style of soccer, to be played in the new league.

It is really quite extraordinary that with sponsors and marketing types swarming all over American soccer, so little thought is given to the "product": the sport itself. Most of these people know very little about soccer, so that it is no doubt asking too much of them to make sophisticated distinctions between various styles. But how can they not recognize that there is good soccer, and there is bad soccer?

Astoundingly, the question rarely comes up. Soccer, it seems, is soccer. A homogeneous, inert material that is presumably always acceptable and therefore always marketable. If only that were so.

The history, the anecdotes, the characters, the incidents described in this book make it crystal clear: Soccer is a perverse, eccentric, *living* activity. It comes in many different shapes. It is the best of sports, it is the worst of sports, it is the most exciting of sports, it is the dullest, it is the fastest, it is the slowest, it is the most difficult of sports to play, it is the easiest, it is the most intelligent, it is the most brainless of sports.

It belongs to everyone, and because of that it belongs to no one. It is not a German sport, any more than it is Argentine or English or Brazilian. Virtually every country in the world has taken to it, without the necessity for gimmicky rule changes. The Germans have Germanized it a bit, the English have Anglicized it, the Brazilians have Brazilianized it. All done within the sport's rules.

Soccer, no point in denying it, deals in extremes. When it is good, it is a breathtaking sport. But when it is bad, oh dear, what a bore it can be. Soccer people often find it difficult to admit that, but it is a confession that is, or should be, at the heart of American soccer's quest for a pro league.

It must be acknowledged that soccer is not just soccer and that the game, even at the top professional level, can be of poor quality. Once that admission has been made, a sharply focused aim for the pro league is revealed: to banish, or reduce to a minimum, the bad soccer. Nor is it that difficult to define bad soccer. Bad soccer is boring soccer. Soccer in which not much happens. People who pay money to watch professional sports expect to be entertained. Good soccer is entertaining soccer.

You get entertaining soccer from players who know how to play . . .

entertaining soccer. A platitude, but one that gets us to where any discussion of soccer on the field must begin: with the players. It is a given that any pro league in the USA must be largely populated by American players. It is the qualities of the American player that will determine its success. We need to know what those qualities are.

Each of the major soccer countries has its own style of playing, one that has developed over many years. So that you can, in broad terms, spell out the characteristics of the German, or the Brazilian, or the Italian player. You cannot do that with American players, for this country has not developed a recognizable soccer style.

Not everyone will agree with that. There are plenty of soccer experts who insist that there is, too, an American style. They point to college soccer where there is, admittedly, a certain uniformity. It is the same sort of game that St. Louis University used to play back in the 1960s and early 1970s when it regularly won the NCAA Division I title, and when the city of St. Louis was thought of as the soccer capital of the United States.

St. Louis was the one city in the America that had a long soccer tradition, dating back to before World War II, of well-organized youth programs for American kids. The players produced—most of the top ones went on to St. Louis University—did have a specific St. Louis way of playing. It involved a good deal of movement and off-the-ball running and first-time passing. St. Louis players did not dwell on the ball, they rarely dribbled. They tended to be well built and gluttons for work. Teamwork was excellent, the pace of the game high, with the accent on offense.

An impressive array of talents, but one that produced a strangely unsatisfactory sort of soccer. Too straightforward, with the emphasis on physical things like running and stamina, and tactically predictable. Soccer without individuality, flair, and inventiveness.

Yet today's college soccer is bursting with teams that play in this way. The style has its proponents, possibly because it contains elements of football. It is inevitable that, in the United States, soccer's merits and demerits will be measured against American sports, that people will try to find suggestions of football or hints of hockey or shades of basketball in the game. But the comparisons can be highly misleading.

Ironically, it is football—soccer's brother in the family of sports— that causes the most problems. At a superficial level the two sports resemble each other: outdoor games played by teams of eleven men on large rectangular fields. But that is about all that remains of their common origin. Beyond that, they diverge so completely that they are comparable only in terms of absolute opposites.

Football is a game of disciplined plays, highly specialized roles, massive substitution, and incessant coaching from the sidelines. Soccer is a fluid game that makes the planning of elaborate plays virtually impossible, that needs players with all-around skills, that permits only limited substitution, and in which the international rules impose limits on coaching from the sidelines.

But the most important difference between the two sports lies in the matter of body contact. Football is a sport that is built around the idea of players colliding with one another, of trying to knock opponents off their feet.

To try to play soccer with that mentality is to destroy the sport. But the trouble is that soccer *can* be played under a semifootball mentality that seeks to emphasize the physical aspects of the sport. For example, the one form of body contact that soccer does specifically permit is shoulder-charging, with the proviso that it not be done "in a violent or dangerous manner." This is a tactic that can be used within broad limits. It can get as violent as the referee allows, and, particularly at the high school level, many referees have a football background that makes them far too lenient in punishing rough charging.

Soccer played with a semifootball mentality is high on body contact; running, speed, and that good old coach's panacea, hustle, are preeminent. The existence of this type of soccer at the college level depends to a considerable extent on the fact that youth league and high school soccer permit free substitution, á la football. Substitution is more restricted in college soccer, but not restricted enough. Up to eighteen players (and more if both teams agree) can be used in a game.

Nowhere else in the world is anything like that permitted; most countries limit substitution to two or three players and do not allow a player to be sent back into the game once he has been removed.

Massive substitution strikes at the roots of skillful soccer because it allows, or encourages, a more physical game. Players can be sent into a game to run like mad for ten or fifteen minutes, taken out for a breather, then sent back in. Such players are hardly likely to bother with learning the skills and finesse of the game. Yet, particularly at the youth level, the physical, hustling teams can win. And, naturally enough, if you're going to rely on a power game, then the bigger the players, the better it is.

The ability to substitute repeatedly also greatly expands the importance of the coach *during the game*. He becomes, in effect, a twelfth player, constantly making decisions that affect the flow of the game. Very much like a football coach.

The worldwide trend toward an enhanced role for the coach in soccer has fallen on disturbingly fertile ground in the United States, where coaching is regarded with almost religious awe.

There is no reason to doubt that the aims of the coaching fraternity are constructive and well meaning: to produce better players and better soccer and, of course, to win games. But in practice, much of what they do runs counter to the spirit of soccer, which has traditionally been a players' game.

For soccer to be true to its roots, the game must be controlled by the players on the field. A constant stream of decisions by every player at every moment of the game: whether to stay put or to advance or to retreat, whether to run for a pass or not, or to fake a run, whether to challenge an opponent, whether to tackle or to delay, whether to dribble or to pass or to shoot, and so on, and so on. A game of constant innovation and improvisation, of ever-changing action and reaction.

Can a coach ever hope to control all of that? Of course not, but he can greatly interfere with the process. By imposing carefully worked-out tactics, by assigning specific roles to his players, he can reduce their responsibilities on the field. When that sort of thing happens at the youth level, the resourcefulness of the players is stunted. They grow up accepting that the coach makes a lot of the important decisions. They grow up as unenterprising players who, logically enough, play an unenterprising brand of soccer. But the football-type coach will praise that sort of player, the player who follows instructions.

The USSF's coaching schools turn out scores of newly licensed coaches each year. No doubt, in technical and theoretical terms, these are knowledgeable people. But the curse of the coaching schools is that they impose orthodoxy. It is like that purported ideal of German military training in which all the cadets, posed a problem, come up with the same answer. In 1987, Walt Chyzowych, who was then in charge of the schools, sent a letter to the teaching staff stating that "it is imperative that the teaching does not deviate from the prepared curriculum . . . it is important that the staff follow the syllabus religiously."

Religiously. No room for original thinking here. The utter stupidity of this rigid approach had been exposed earlier that year when the ex-Peruvian World Cup star Teófilo Cubillas, one of the game's great players, had taken the USSF's "A" license exams. The examiners were three college coaches, theoreticians with little knowledge of the game at its highest level. They failed Cubillas because he did not perform some artificial coaching drill in the way that they wanted. Teófilo Cubillas, who at that time stood in fifth place in the World Cup's all-time scoring table, was adjudged not good enough to coach in the United States.

Former FIFA president Sir Stanley Rous was the man who introduced coaching courses to England in the 1930s. Some forty-five years later, he was asked if he had any regrets about that. He replied: "Yes—it's developed into so much *instruction*. Players who have an instinctive way of playing, or wanting to play, have their mind divided; they're thinking, 'Now, what did he tell me to do in this circumstance?' with the result that their ability is impaired."

Football-influenced soccer is still prevalent in the colleges. Watching it is rather like being given a reading program of endless prose, and monotonous prose at that. One's heart cries out for a little poetry now and then. Surely, it protests, a game like this could never, never in a million years, have captured the imagination of the whole world? Surely there has to be more to soccer than this?

Yes, there is more to soccer, a hell of a lot more. What is missing is the very soul of the sport: ball skill. The off-the-ball side of the game, the running and the hustling, has been developed at the expense of the on-the-ball side. There is a lack of players with individual ball skills, players who have the confidence to hold on to the ball, who can take opponents on and dribble past them, who can change the pace of the game, who can do the unexpected. When players with ball skills are lacking, soccer becomes a pedestrian game enveloped in an atmosphere of mechanical predictability.

Sadly, it is this incomplete game that is pushed forward as the American style. It is, of course, no such thing. It is not a style at all, merely a sterile copy of how the northern Europeans play, or used to play.

It would be unfair and downright inaccurate to blame this physical approach to soccer on football. The ultimate responsibility for it lies with the soccer people themselves. Historically, soccer in the United States has always looked to Europe for its models, especially toward northern Europe: Britain, Germany, Scandinavia—a very important area, soccer-wise, one that has produced many great teams and players, but an area noted for a robust, manly approach to the game (though Germany now has a more sophisticated view of the sport).

The United States Soccer Federation, throughout its eighty-year history, has always been a relentlessly Eurocentric organization. British and German ideas and attitudes permeated the sport in this country right from the beginning. They received a further boost in the 1960s from the NASL, which needed English-speaking coaches and players to carry out its missionary and PR work. Thus a new wave of British influence arrived.

The United States is not England or Germany or Denmark, countries that developed their styles in days when they had little ethnic diversity. The American style, when it comes, will be a reflection of what the American player has to offer. It will be a style that allows the full development of all the talent that is available in this huge, ethnically complex nation. At the moment, American soccer is an overwhelmingly middle-class, white sport. There is minimal black involvement, and there has been no great effort on the part of the USSF and other soccer bodies to recruit blacks.

An unsatisfactory state of affairs, but one that might be expected to change as soccer's popularity widens. Then again, maybe not, because the experience of another minority, the Hispanics, is anything but encouraging.

Here we have a rapidly growing ethnic group that is already passionately devoted to soccer. In the New York–New Jersey area, for instance, there are eighteen Hispanic soccer *leagues*, involving over 200 clubs and some 3,000 players, to say nothing of the youth teams that many clubs run.

Where once the ethnic leagues in the area were German or Italian or Greek, they are now predominantly Hispanic, a reflection of new immigration patterns. Most of the leagues operate outside the jurisdiction of the USSF. Both sides seem to prefer it that way: The Hispanics can get on with running their own affairs in their own language; the soccer authorities do not have to be bothered with troublesome foreigners.

But the split goes much deeper than that. The rise of Hispanic soccer within the United States represents a major challenge to the traditional attitudes of American soccer leaders, because the Hispanics look to Latin America rather than to Europe for their inspiration.

The Latin game, on the field, is very different from the vigorous running game that is so dear to the hearts of the vast majority of American coaches. Greatly simplified, the difference is this: Latin soccer emphasizes technique, European soccer stresses physical power.

(For the moment, let us not argue over which is *better*, we shall come to that shortly.) These are two different approaches to the game, each with its pros and cons. Yet the American soccer leaders have chosen the European style, at the expense of the Latin.

When the USSF appointed Bora Milutinovic as national coach in 1991, there was hope that a change of attitudes might follow. But the Serbian-born Milutinovic, who lived and coached for many years in Mexico, has had little effect. His job has been carefully limited to producing a team for World Cup '94. The overall philosophy of the national team program—usually a key part of a national team coach's work—has been left with the same tired old admirers of size, strength, and stamina.

The prejudice against the Latin players comes close to racism. It will be argued that it is not the players but the style that is rejected. Which adds up to a distinction without a difference. And clearly there is economic racism at work. For boys to travel to the various district, state and regional tryouts that may lead to national team selection is an expensive business, it can cost several thousand dollars a year.

The USSF professes to be aware of the problem. In 1991 its secretary-general, Hank Steinbrecher, said: "The Hispanics are a phenomenal resource, but we're not using them. We must have a system that can identify the Hispanic player."

Two and a half years later there was no such system, nor was there a system of providing financial aid for players whose families could not afford to send them to tryouts. Nor was there any Hispanic representation in the upper echelons of the USSF. It is an ironic U-turn for the federation, once so ethnic and anti-American, now so pro-American, that its definition of the "American player" virtually excludes Latins.

In purely soccer terms, does this matter? That depends on your viewpoint. If you are satisfied with soccer as a massive recreational sport, if you can live with the suggestion of bias, then things can roll merrily along as they are. But if you feel that a pro league is the goal—and both FIFA and the USSF have made it clear that this is what they feel—then the current direction of American soccer is a disaster.

The European domination, plus the football mentality, has saddled American soccer with an unsophisticated, coach-dominated, hard-running athletic game that has a long track record of failure when offered to the American sports fan as a spectator attraction. A version of soccer that features large-sized players indulging in much running and physical contact. Why on earth *would* it appeal to Americans? They can get all that, and get it better, in football.

If the projected pro league is based on that style, it will fail. The soccer will be mindlessly tedious. It will not be entertaining. We are back to that. To face the stark realization that the "American player," as defined by the colleges and the USSF, is not capable of producing the attractive soccer that the pro league will need.

A generalization, of course. Over the past ten years, individual American players have risen above the mediocrity and have proved themselves good enough to play professionally in Europe. Players like Tab Ramos in Spain, John Harkes in England, and Eric Wynalda in Germany.

But they are the exceptions.* How to change the approach?

Indeed, *can* it be changed? It can, but it won't be easy. There is no logical reason at all why American soccer should be patterned on that of England or Germany, or any European country. If we are looking for a role model, then how about Brazil? An ex-colony like the United States, a huge country with a vast, ethnically mixed population.

Why not? Using Brazilian soccer as the yardstick would immediately solve the entertainment problem. If there is one thing that soccer fans worldwide agree on, it is that Brazil is always worth watching. Brazilian players are recognized as the supreme artists of the sport.

The point about Brazilian soccer—and Latin American soccer in general—is that it is based on ball skills. It does not exclude anyone, whatever their size or shape. It is an equal-opportunity style for any player who has taken the trouble to learn and refine the game's skills. Something that cannot be said of the current American "style" that places a premium on size and strength and regularly rejects good players because they don't run enough or are considered too small.

Can Americans play like Brazilians? The standard response from American coaches is to dismiss the idea as a pipe dream that doesn't correspond to the "characteristics of the American player." That is, to *their* definition of the American player's characteristics. It is a mean-spirited response. Probably also self-serving, for would these coaches, these products of the European-oriented USSF coaching schools,

* An exception to the college norm has given an exciting glimpse of what the future could hold. Coach Bruce Arena's University of Virginia won the NCAA 1992 Division I championship with a mixture of white, black, and Hispanic players and a skillful, entertaining style of soccer.

know how to coach Brazilian style? Indeed, one of the problems with any style based on ball skills is that so much of the player's development is outside the reach of the coach. The player teaches himself the skills and tricks of the game.

There is no wand to wave that will have Americans playing like Brazilians tomorrow. Maybe they never will. Maybe they will end up playing more like the Argentines, a skill-based South American style without the flamboyance of the Brazilians.

The crucial thing is to shift the emphasis in training to skill rather than strength, to self-learning rather than coach-imposed drills and tactics. That will set off fundamental changes in the identikit of the American player. For a start, it will give the Hispanics the influence that their passion for the game merits. This is not a matter of them dominating; they will become part of the mix that will bring a true American style.

The change in emphasis *must* result in a more skillful, more intelligent, more attractive, more exciting game—essential qualities for American soccer if there is to be a professional league.

An intriguing final note: The Japanese, who have a habit of getting things right, have put in a bid to stage the 2002 World Cup. They have also set up a brand-new pro soccer league. It contains a fair sprinkling of Brazilian players (over fifty of them) and coaches.

Glossary

Soccer, like every other sport, has its own language—in fact, it has a whole host of languages. Soccer terms come in Spanish and Portuguese and German and French and Italian and Arabic and, of course, English. British English, that is. Which poses a problem for Americans, for some of the terms are likely to get confused with similar or identical terms that have slightly or totally different meanings in American sports.

For example, "to tackle" in football (and therefore in American English) conjures up the picture of a player grabbing another player around the waist and bringing him crashing to the ground. That sort of action is strictly prohibited in soccer, where "to tackle" means using the feet to take the ball away from an opponent's feet.

In soccer we have to accept the British definition. But it is not the purpose of this section to extol the British way of saying things. I happen to believe that the British soccer vocabulary is one of the least imaginative in the world. In this it is a fairly accurate reflection of the way the British play soccer. Brazilian soccer terms, as anyone who has seen Brazilian soccer might expect, are playful, colorful, and generally delightful.

What can be said in favor of the British soccer vocabulary is that it is in English and it is there. It provides the basis of fundamental terms on which Americans, with their gift for lively language, will build an American English soccer vocabulary.

There follows a list of selected soccer terms, with some personal comments on their meaning, their use, and their acceptability. This is not meant to be a comprehensive glossary. It is limited to those terms that—often because of confusion with similar terms in other sports—seem to present problems to American fans.

ADVANTAGE RULE: The referee does not have to stop play every time he detects a foul. If the offending team gains an advantage from the offense, he will certainly do so. But sometimes it is penalizing the innocent team to stop play: if, for instance, a defender deliberately handles the ball to bring it under control but only succeeds in deflecting it to an opponent who is well placed for a shot at goal. To stop play at this moment would penalize the attacking team. In such a case, the referee would apply the so-called advantage rule and allow play to go on.

ASSIST: An American term that is gaining acceptance throughout the soccer world. The Italians regularly use the word, while the official FIFA World Cup statistics now include a list of assists. The English find every reason not to use the word. The idea of an American contribution to soccer is evidently more than they can bear.

BALL IN AND OUT OF PLAY: For the ball to pass out of play, *all* of it must be outside *all* of the sideline or goal line (the lines can be up to five inches wide). Thus, a ball on the line is in play. Even a ball resting on the ground just outside the line is in play if any part of it is projecting over the line. Similarly, a goal is not scored until all the ball has passed over all the goal line. The position of the player controlling or dribbling the ball does not matter—he can be standing or running with both feet outside the touchline, but as long as the ball is in play the game goes on.

BICYCLE KICK: A volley in which the player kicks the ball over his own head. This is not just a simple overhead kick, which can be accomplished keeping one foot on the ground. In the true bicycle kick, the player has both feet off the ground. With his body "floating" horizontally he uses a rapid pedaling motion of both legs (hence the bicycle reference) to kick the ball backward. The player is, in effect, performing a somersault as he kicks. This allows him to get his feet above the level of his head so that the trajectory of the ball can be kept down, essential for one of the bicycle kick's most spectacular uses as a shot on goal. The bicycle kick should not be confused with the Scissor Kick (q.v.).

BOOTER: Ugh! This, I suspect, is the invention of some deservedly obscure headline writer looking for an easy way of identifying soccer players. The word has an aura of heavy clumsiness about it, and no self-respecting soccer enthusiast should be caught dead using it. In any case, "to boot" has a more specific soccer meaning and should not be used as though it means simply "to kick." To boot the ball in soccer is to kick it hard and long and usually high; an aimless, thoughtless sort of wallop that is the very antithesis of good soccer.

BOX: The box means the penalty area. Sometimes called the eighteen-yard box, to distinguish it from the goal area, which is the six-yard box (for those with a metric turn of mind, the corresponding measurements are 16.5 meters and 5.5 meters).

CLEAR: To kick or head the ball away from the goalmouth, thus killing an immediate threat to the goal. In theory, there ought to be two types of clearance: good, in which the ball is passed to a teammate to start an attack, or bad, in which the ball is hoofed anywhere. In practice, the first, good, type of clearance is always referred to as a pass or as starting an attack. The words *clear* and *clearance* almost always describe those panic situations in which a defender is under pressure and is quite happy to boot the ball aimlessly upfield or out of play.

DEAD BALL: When play is stopped and the ball is not moving, it is a dead ball. All free kicks, including penalty kicks, have to be taken from a dead—i.e., stationary—ball.

FIELD: Soccer fields are by no means all the same size. International rules allow substantial variation, but the length (from 100 to 130 yards) must always be greater than the width (50 to 100 yards). Excessively narrow fields are a major problem in this country. Many soccer fields are modified football fields, whose playing width of just over fifty-three yards can rarely be sufficiently enlarged to give the minimum seventy yards that a satisfactory soccer field needs. In college soccer, the NCAA allows a length of between 110 and 120 yards, and a width from 65 to 80 yards, with a stipulation that newly constructed facilities must be at least 110 by 65. The recommended optimum size is 120 by 75 yards (109.73m x 68.58m). See also Pitch.

FIFTY-FIFTY BALL: A loose ball, or a badly placed pass, that is as near to a player of one team as it is to a player of the opposing team, allowing both an equal chance of controlling it. Bad soccer, in which players lack the technique to control the ball properly, is often a succession of ugly little tackling battles for possession of fifty-fifty balls.

GOAL: All goals, under international rules, must be *scored*—they cannot be awarded by the referee. If a defender (other than the goalkeeper) punches the ball out of the goal, the referee cannot award a goal, even though the ball was clearly going into the net and even though the defender's action was flagrantly illegal. The referee will eject the player who handled the ball and give the attacking team a penalty kick.

GOALKEEPER: This is the soccer term, sometimes shortened to goalie, or 'keeper. Beware of imitations, especially one labeled "goal tender." The trouble with goal tender is that it is a hockey term and it is likely to bring with it ideas that cannot be applied to soccer. A hockey goal tender is frequently credited with having "registered a shutout," and with a small goal (six feet by four feet) to guard, it is possible for him to single-handedly defy a barrage of shots. It is theoretically possible for a soccer goalkeeper to do the same—possible, but rare. His goal is *eight* times as large (twenty-four feet by eight feet) and to remain unbeaten for ninety minutes he needs a lot of help from the defenders playing in front of him.

In fact, it is probably not an exaggeration to say that in most soccer shutouts, thanks to his teammates' superior defensive play, the goalkeeper has relatively little to do.

GOAL TENDER: See Goalkeeper.

GUARD: See Mark.

HAND BALL: An offense in soccer, obviously. What is not so obvious is that the term "hand" includes any part of the arm below the armpit.

HEAD: To head the ball is to play it with the forehead, whether the intention is a clearance, a pass, or a shot at goal. The British describe all three under the general term "header," but the American term "head-shot" to describe a header that is intended as a scoring effort is a useful addition to soccer's vocabulary (and, more than likely, another term of American origin that the English will shun).

KICKER: Like the odious "booter" (q.v.), sometimes used to identify a soccer player. It should be shunned. It is not a particularly pleasant word and it already has a specific soccer meaning. A kicker is a player who tends to kick opponents more than he kicks the ball—a dirty player.

LINESMAN: See Referee.

MARK: In man-to-man coverage the defender is said to mark (rather than guard) the attacker. The closer he plays to him, the tighter the marking; the farther away, the looser the marking.

NATIONAL TEAM: An all-star team that represents a country in the various international tournaments—e.g., the World Cup, the Olympic Games, the under-twenty World Cup, etc. National teams are supposed to consist of the very best players in the country, regardless of which club they play for. They are not permanent teams; they are assembled only to play in specific games or tournaments, like the Dream Team that represented the United States in basketball in the 1992 Olympic Games. The clubs are expected to cooperate by releasing the players for the required period (it may be just two or three days, or a month or more for the World Cup). All of the top soccer nations in the world now have a full-time national team coach. Playing for the national team— i.e., representing one's country—was once considered such an honor that clubs rarely refused to release their players. Nowadays, release is less certain. For the World Cup, yes, pro clubs will release their players. But for other national team games, especially for exhibition games, clubs are not so keen to release their highly paid players, who run the risk of injury or who may miss vital club games while away on national team duty.

OFFSIDE: The word is singular. Offside. The origin of the term (see Chapter 6, page 150) explains why. How or why the plural version "offsides" arose I have no idea, but it is incorrect.

OWN GOAL: It is, obviously, possible for a player to kick, or head, or deflect, the ball into his own goal. If he does so, the score counts for his opponents; and if the ball clearly would *not* have gone in without his intervention, then he, unlucky soul, is listed as the scorer with the letters o.g. (for "own goal") after his name.

PENALTY: Beware! The word *penalty* has a very specific (and very dramatic) meaning in soccer. It should be applied *only* to the award of a penalty kick—i.e., the twelve-yard direct free kick taken from the penalty spot with only the goalkeeper to beat. It should never be used in connection with any other offense or free kick situation.

PERIOD: Soccer games are (or should be) divided into two halves: a first half and a second half. The term "period" belongs in games like football and hockey that are played in quarters or thirds. See also Time.

PITCH: An English word for a sports field. It is *not* specific to soccer—there are cricket and field hockey pitches as well. It has come into vogue in the United States, mouthed by those who feel they are showing some special inside knowledge when they use it. They are merely being pretentious. The American term "field" is all that is required.

PROMOTION and RELEGATION: Soccer leagues throughout the world usually feature a number of divisions. In England, for instance, there are Premier, First, Second, and Third divisions; in Italy Serie A, B, and C. The weakest clubs are in the lower divisions, the big pro clubs are in the top division. The composition of the divisions changes each season. The top clubs in each lower division (usually the first three or four) are promoted to the division above, whose bottom three or four clubs are relegated (demoted) to replace them. Thus each division features two competitions: one at the top to decide the championship and promotion places, the other at the bottom to avoid relegation.

PUNT: A useful way of measuring the sophistication of a soccer crowd is to listen to their reaction to a long punt by the goalkeeper. If they ooh and aah as the ball arcs downfield for forty or fifty yards, chances are that they don't know too much about soccer. A long punt, assessed by football criteria, is impressive. By soccer standards it is next to useless. As a pass, the high towering punt has two major drawbacks: The ball is in the air too long, allowing opponents plenty of time to cover the intended receiver, and when the ball finally does come down, the angle and the speed of its descent make it extremely difficult for a forward to control. The defender, of course, doesn't have to control it—he merely heads or hoofs it back whence it came. To the reader who asks why, then, do goalkeepers constantly punt the ball, I can only reply that it is something of a mystery to me, too.

REFEREE: The man in charge. His decisions on the field are final. He starts the game and, because under international rules he is also the official timekeeper, he (and not the scoreboard clock, should there be one) says when it is over. No player can enter or leave the field without his consent. He calls the fouls and has the power to caution players or to eject them from the game. He is also responsible for seeing that the ball and the players' equipment conform to the rules. He is assisted by two linesmen, but their function is strictly advisory. If a linesman, for example, waves his flag to indicate offside, the referee does not have to whistle for the infraction—he is entitled to overrule the linesman and allow play to continue.

RELEGATION: See Promotion and Relegation.

SCISSOR KICK: The side volley. The ball is kicked in the direction that the player is facing. The player leans sideways, throws his legs upward, and volleys the ball forward with a scissorlike motion as the kicking leg passes forward over the other leg. Not to be confused with the Bicycle Kick (q.v.).

SCORELINES: The convention used throughout the soccer world is to name the home team first. Thus, a scoreline of AC Milan 3 Lazio 2, tells you not only that Milan won the game, but also that the game was played in Milan. A scoreline of AC Milan 0 Lazio 1 indicates an away win for Lazio at Milan. The American convention of listing the winning team first is an annoying one to soccer fans, as it fails to indicate the home team. This is often vital information. There are certain two-leg cup ties (e.g., in the various European cup competitions, see pages 296–99), in which goals scored on an opponent's field may count double. (Soccer, however, does use the American system for tournaments such as the World Cup that are played at a fixed site and where there is in effect only one home team, the host nation.)

SHUTOUT: See Goalkeeper.

SIDELINES: Also called touchlines. A ball that goes out of play over the sidelines is said to have gone into touch.

SPOT-KICK: A penalty kick, so called because the ball is placed on the penalty spot, twelve yards in front of goal.

STATISTICS: Inevitably, Americans have brought statistics to soccer, a sport in which, traditionally, records have not been particularly plentiful. The theory behind most of the statistics—to plot the shape and progress of a game with figures—is excellent. But soccer is a game that is proving stubbornly resistant to having its portrait drawn in columns of numbers. I can only say that soccer statistics, particularly those such as shots on goal, or saves, should be viewed with caution. Many of them will be judgment calls by the scorekeeper, who may or may not be reliable. Also, special soccer considerations must be taken into account when assessing the figures (see the discussion of shutouts under Goalkeeper).

TACKLE: To use the feet in attempting to take the ball from an opponent's feet. A tackle may be accompanied by a legitimate shoulder charge, but there must be no holding, pushing, tripping, elbowing, or hip-checking. Clean tackling—the ability to strip the ball from an opponent without fouling—requires considerable skill. Unfortunately, the leniency shown to defenders during the 1970s and 1980s has meant that many defenders are not good tacklers. They simply clatter into the guy with the ball, often from behind, and if called for a foul protest, "But I got the ball, ref!" Possibly, but only by demolishing the opponent as well. Trends are changing, and it seems that referees are getting tougher on unfair tackling. There is even the probability of a long overdue rule change: the outlawing of the tackle from behind.

TIME: Traditionally, soccer games have always been divided into two halves: forty-five minutes per half in professional games, less (thirty or thirty-five minutes) for youth games.

TIME-OUT: The referee alone can stop the clock in soccer. Coaches are not permitted to call time-outs.

WALL-PASS: The give-and-go. So called because in soccer games played by boys in streets, the ball is bounced off a wall rather than passed to a teammate.

The Rules of Soccer

These are the 1993 rules of soccer as authorized by the International Football Association Board and published by the Fédération Internationale de Football Association. Their official title is Laws of the Game. They are the basis for the playing of soccer all over the world.

LAW I

The Field of Play

The field of play and appurtenances shall be as shown in the following plan:

(N. B. All measurements are in yards and inches unless otherwise marked)

(1) Dimensions. The field of play shall be rectangular, its length being not more than 130 yards nor less than 100 yards and its breadth not more than 100 yards nor less than 50 yards. (In international matches the length shall be not more than 120 yards nor less than 110 yards and the breadth not more than 80 yards nor less than 70 yards.) The length shall in all cases exceed the breadth.

(2) Marking. The field of play shall be marked with distinctive lines, not more than 5 inches in width (not by a V-shaped rut) in accordance with the plan, the longer boundary lines being called the touch-lines and the shorter the goal-lines. A flag on a post not less than 5 ft. high and having a non-pointed top, shall be placed at each corner; a similar flag-post may be placed opposite the half-way line on each side of the field of play, not less than 1 yard outside the touch-line. A halfway-line shall be marked out across the field of play. The centre of the field of play shall be indicated by a suitable mark and a circle with a 10 yards radius shall be marked round it.

(3) The Goal-Area. At each end of the field of play two lines shall be drawn at right-angles to the goal-line, 6 yards from each goal-post. These shall extend into the field of play for a distance of 6 yards and shall be joined by a line drawn parallel with the goal-line. Each of the spaces enclosed by these lines and the goal-line shall be called a goal-area.

(4) The Penalty-Area. At each end of the field of play two lines shall be drawn at right-angles to the goal-line, 18 yards from each goal-post. These shall extend into the field of play for a distance of 18 yards and shall be joined by a line drawn parallel with the goal-line. Each of the spaces enclosed by these lines and the goal-line shall be called a penalty-area. A suitable mark shall be made within each penalty-area, 12 yard from the mid-point of the goal-line, measured along an undrawn line at right-angles thereto. These shall be the penalty-kick marks. From each penalty-kick mark an arc of a circle, having a radius of 10 yards, shall be drawn outside the penalty-area.

(5) The Corner-Area. From each corner-flag post a quarter circle, having a radius of 1 yard, shall be drawn inside the field of play.

(6) The Goals. The goals shall be placed on the centre of each goal-line and shall consist of two upright posts, equidistant from the corner-flags and 8 yards apart (inside measurement), joined by a horizontal cross-bar the lower edge of which shall be 8 ft. from the ground. The width and depth of the cross-bars shall not exceed 5 inches (12 cm). The goal-posts and the cross-bars shall have the same width.

Nets may be attached to the posts, cross-bars and ground behind the goals. They should be appropriately supported and be so placed as to allow the goalkeeper ample room.

Footnote:

Goal nets. The use of nets made of hemp, jute or nylon is permitted. The nylon strings may, however, not be thinner than those made of hemp or jute.

LAW I

DECISIONS OF THE INTERNATIONAL F.A. BOARD

(1) In international matches the dimensions of the field of play shall be: maximum 110 x 75 metres; mimimum 100 x 64 metres.

(2) National Associations must adhere strictly to these dimensions. Each National Association organising an international match must advise the visiting Association, before the match, of the place and the dimensions of the field of play.

(3) The Board has approved this table of measurements for the Laws of the Game:

130 yards	....	120 Metres
120 yards	....	110
110 yards	....	100
100 yards	....	90
80 yards	....	75
70 yards	....	64
50 yards	....	45
18 yards	....	16,50
12 yards	....	11
10 yards	....	9,15
8 yards	....	7,32
6 yards	....	5,50
1 Yard	....	1
8 feet	....	2,44
5 feet	....	1,50
28 inches	....	0,71
27 inches	....	0,68
9 inches	....	0,22
5 inches	....	0,12
3/4 inch	....	0,019
1/2 inch	....	0,0127
3/8 inch	....	0,010
14 ounces	....	396 grams
16 ounces	....	453 grams
8.5 lb./sq.in.	....	600 gr/cm^2
15.6 lb./sq.in.	....	1100 gr/cm^2

(4) The goal-line shall be marked the same width as the depth of the goal-posts and the cross-bar, so that the goal-line and goal-posts will conform to the same interior and exterior edges.

(5) The 6 yards (for the outline of the goal-area) and the 18 yards (for the outline of the penalty-area) which have to be measured along the goal-line, must start from the inner sides of the goal-posts.

(6) The space within the inside areas of the field of play includes the width of the lines marking these areas.

(7) All Associations shall provide standard equipment, particularly in international matches, when the Laws of the Game must be complied with in every respect and especially with regard to the size of the ball and other equipment which must conform to the regulations. All cases of failure to provide standard equipment must be reported to FIFA.

(8) In a match played under the rules of a competition if the cross-bar becomes displaced or broken, play shall be stopped and the match abandoned unless the cross-bar has been repaired and replaced in position or a new one provided without such being a danger to the players. A rope is not considered to be a satisfactory substitute for a cross-bar.

In a friendly match, by mutual consent, play may be resumed without the cross-bar provided it has been removed and no longer constitutes a danger to the players. In these circumstances, a rope may be used as a substitute for a cross-bar. If a rope is not used and the ball crosses the goal-line at a point which, in the opinion of the referee is below where the cross-bar should have been, he shall award a goal.

The game shall be restarted by the referee dropping the ball at the place where it was when play was stopped, unless it was within the goal-area at that time, in which case it shall be dropped on that part of the goal-area line which runs parallel to the goal-line, at the point nearest to where the ball was when play was stopped.

(9) National Associations may specify such maximum and minimum dimensions for the cross-bars and goal-posts, within the limits laid down in Law I, as they consider appropriate.

(10) Goal-posts and cross-bars must be made of wood, metal or other approved material as decided from time to time by the International F.A. Board. They may be square, rectangular, round, half-round or elliptical in shape.

Goal-posts and cross-bars made of other materials and in other shapes are not permitted. The goal-posts must be of white colour.

(11) 'Curtain-raisers' to international matches should only be played following agreement on the day of the match, and taking into account the condition of the field of play, between representatives of the two Associations and the referee (of the international match).

(12) National Associations, particularly in international matches, should

— restrict the number of photographers around the field of play,

— have a line (photographers' line) marked behind the goal-lines at least two metres from the corner flag going through a point situated at least 3.5 metres behind the intersection of the goal-line with the line marking the goal-area to a point situated at least six metres behind the goal-posts,

— prohibit photographers from passing over these lines,

— forbid the use of artificial lighting in the form of "flashlights".

LAW II

The Ball

The ball shall be spherical; the outer casing shall be of leather or other approved materials. No material shall be used in its construction which might prove dangerous to the players.

The circumference of the ball shall not be more than 28 in. and not less than 27 in. The weight of the ball at the start of the game shall not be more than 16 oz. nor less than 14 oz. The pressure shall be equal to 0.6-1.1 atmosphere ($=600$-$1,100$ gr/cm^2) at sea level. The ball shall not be changed during the game unless authorised by the referee.

DECISIONS OF THE INTERNATIONAL F.A. BOARD

(1) The ball used in any match shall be considered the property of the Association or Club on whose ground the match is played, and at the close of play it must be returned to the referee.

(2) The International Board, from time to time, shall decide what constitutes approved materials. Any approved material shall be certified as such by the International Board.

(3) The Board has approved these equivalents of the weights specified in the Law: 14 to 16 ounces — 396 to 453 grammes.

(4) If the ball bursts or becomes deflated during the course of a match, the game shall be stopped and restarted by dropping the new ball at the place where the first ball became defective, unless it was within the goal-area at that time, in which case it shall be dropped on that part of the goal-area line which runs parallel to the goal-line, at the point nearest to where the ball was when play was stopped.

(5) If this happens during a stoppage of the game (place-kick, goal-kick, corner-kick, free-kick, penalty-kick or throw-in), the game shall be restarted accordingly.

Number of Players

(1) A match shall be played by two teams, each consisting of not more than eleven players, one of whom shall be the goalkeeper.

(2) Substitutes may be used in any match played under the rules of an official competition under the jurisdiction of FIFA, Confederations or National Associations, subject to the following conditions:

(a) that the authority of the international association(s) or National Association(s) concerned has been obtained.

(b) that, subject to the restriction contained in the following paragraph (c), the rules of a competition shall state how many, if any, substitutes may be nominated and how many of those nominated may be used.

(c) that a team shall not be permitted to use more than two substitutes in any match who must be chosen from not more than five players whose names may (subject to the rules of the competition) be required to be given to the referee prior to the commencement of the match.

(3) Substitutes may be used in any other match, provided that the two teams concerned reach agreement on a maximum number, not exceeding five, and that the terms of such agreement are intimated to the referee, before the match. If the referee is not informed, or if the teams fail to reach agreement, no more than two substitutes shall be permitted. In all cases the substitutes must be chosen from not more than five players whose names may be required to be given to the referee prior to the commencement of the match.

(4) Any of the other players may change places with the goalkeeper, provided that the referee is informed before the change is made, and provided also that the change is made during a stoppage of the game.

(5) When a goalkeeper or any other player is to be replaced by a substitute, the following conditions shall be observed:

(a) The referee shall be informed of the proposed substitution, before it is made.

(b) The substitute shall not enter the field of play until the player he is replacing has left, and then only after having received a signal from the referee.

(c) He shall enter the field during a stoppage in the game, and at the halfway line.

(d) A player who has been replaced shall not take any further part in the game.

(e) A substitute shall be subject to the authority and jurisdiction of the referee whether called upon to play or not.

f) The substitution is completed when the substitute enters the field of play, from which moment he becomes a player and the player whom he is replacing ceases to be a player.

Punishment:

(a) Play shall not be stopped for an infringement of paragraph 4. The players concerned shall be cautioned immediately the ball goes out of play.

(b) If a substitute enters the field of play without the authority of the

LAW III

referee, play shall be stopped. The substitute shall be cautioned and removed from the field or sent off according to the circumstances. The game shall be restarted by the referee dropping the ball at the place where it was when play was stopped, unless it was within the goal-area at that time, in which case it shall be dropped on that part of the goal-area line which runs parallel to the goal-line, at the point nearest to where the ball was when play was stopped.

(c) For any other infringement of this Law, the player concerned shall be cautioned, and if the game is stopped by the referee to administer the caution, it shall be restarted by an indirect free-kick, to be taken by a player of the opposing team from the place where the ball was when play was stopped, subject to the overriding conditions imposed in Law XIII.

(d) If a competition's rules require the names of substitutes to be given to the referee prior to the commencement of the match, then failure to do so will mean that no substitutes can be permitted.

DECISIONS OF THE INTERNATIONAL F.A. BOARD

(1) The minimum number of players in a team is left to the discretion of National Associations.

(2) The Board is of the opinion that a match should not be considered valid if there are fewer than seven players in either of the teams.

(3) A player who has been ordered off before play begins may only be replaced by one of the named substitutes. The kick-off must not be delayed to allow the substitute to join his team.

A player who has been ordered off after play has started may not be replaced.

A named substitute who has been ordered off, either before or after play has started, may not be replaced.

(This decision only relates to players who are ordered off under Law XII. It does not apply to players who have infringed Law IV.)

Players' Equipment

(1) (a) The basic compulsory equipment of a player shall consist of a jersey or shirt, shorts, stockings, shinguards and footwear.

(b) A player shall not wear anything which is dangerous to another player.

(2) Shinguards, which must be covered entirely by the stockings, shall be made of a suitable material (rubber, plastic, polyurethane or similar substance) and shall afford a reasonable degree of protection.

(3) The goalkeeper shall wear colours which distinguish him from the other players and from the referee.

Punishment:

For any infringement of this Law, the player at fault shall be instructed to leave the field of play by the referee, to adjust his equipment or obtain any missing equipment, when the ball next ceases to be in play, unless by then the player has already corrected his equipment. Play shall not be stopped immediately for an infringement of this Law. A player who is instructed to leave the field to adjust his equipment or obtain missing equipment shall not return without first reporting to the referee, who shall satisfy himself that the player's equipment is in order. The player shall only re-enter the game at a moment when the ball has ceased to be in play.

DECISIONS OF THE INTERNATIONAL F.A. BOARD

(1) In international matches, international competitions, international club competitions and friendly matches between clubs of different National Associations, the referee, prior to the start of the game, shall inspect the players' equipment and prevent any player whose equipment does not conform to the requirements of this Law from playing until such time as it does comply. The rules of any competition may include a similar provision.

(2) If the referee finds that a player is wearing articles not permitted by the Laws and which may constitute a danger to other players, he shall order him to take them off. If he fails to carry out the referee's instruction, the player shall not take part in the match.

(3) A player who has been prevented from taking part in the game or a player who has been sent off the field for infringing Law IV must report to the referee during a stoppage of the game and may not enter or re-enter the field of play unless and until the referee has satisfied himself that the player is no longer infringing Law IV.

(4) A player who has been prevented from taking part in a game or who has been sent off because of an infringement of Law IV, and who enters or re-enters the field of play to join or re-join his team, in breach of the conditions of Law XII, (j), shall be cautioned.

If the referee stops the game to administer the caution, the game shall be restarted by an indirect free-kick, taken by a player of the opposing side, from the place where the ball was when the referee stopped the game, subject to the overriding conditions imposed in Law XIII.

LAW V

Referees

A referee shall be appointed to officiate in each game. His authority and the exercise of the powers granted to him by the Laws of the Game commence as soon as he enters the field of play.

His power of penalising shall extend to offences committed when play has been temporarily suspended, or when the ball is out of play. His decision on points of fact connected with the play shall be final, so far as the result of the game is concerned. He shall:

(a) enforce the Laws.

(b) refrain from penalising in cases where he is satisfied that, by doing so, he would be giving an advantage to the offending team.

(c) keep a record of the game; act as timekeeper and allow the full or agreed time, adding thereto all time lost through accident or other cause.

(d) have discretionary power to stop the game for any infringement of the Laws and to suspend or terminate the game whenever, by reason of the elements, interference by spectators, or other cause, he deems such stoppage necessary. In such a case he shall submit a detailed report to the competent authority, within the stipulated time, and in accordance with the provisions set up by the National Association under whose jurisdiction the match was played. Reports will be deemed to be made when received in the ordinary course of post.

(e) from the time he enters the field of play, caution and show a yellow card to any player guilty of misconduct or ungentlemanly behaviour. In such cases the referee shall send the name of the offender to the competent authority, within the stipulated time, and in accordance with the provisions set up by the National Association under whose jurisdiction the match was played.

(f) allow no person other than the players and linesmen to enter the field of play without his permission.

(g) stop the game if, in his opinion, a player has been seriously injured; have the player removed as soon as possible from the field of play, and immediately resume the game. If a player is slightly injured, the game shall not be stopped until the ball has ceased to be in play. A player who is able to go to the touch- or goal-line for attention of any kind, shall not be treated on the field of play.

(h) send off the field of play and show a red card to any player who, in his opinion, is guilty of violent conduct, serious foul play, the use of foul or abusive language or who persists in misconduct after having received a caution.

(i) signal for recommencement of the game after all stoppages.

(j) decide that the ball provided for a match meets with the requirements of Law II.

LAW V

DECISIONS OF THE INTERNATIONAL F.A. BOARD

(1) Referees in international matches shall wear a blazer or blouse the colour of which is distinct from the colours worn by the contesting teams.

(2) Referees for international matches will be selected from a neutral country unless the countries concerned agree to appoint their own officials.

(3) The referee must be chosen from the official List of International Referees. This need not apply to amateur and youth international matches.

(4) The referee shall report to the appropriate authority misconduct or any misdemeanour on the part of spectators, officials, players, named substitutes or other persons which take place either on the field of play or in its vicinity at any time prior to, during, or after the match in question so that appropriate action can be taken by the authority concerned.

(5) Linesmen are assistants of the referee. In no case shall the referee consider the intervention of a linesman if he himself has seen the incident and from his position on the field, is better able to judge. With this reserve, and the linesman neutral, the referee can consider the intervention, and if the information of the linesman applies to that phase of the game immediately before the scoring of a goal, the referee may act thereon and cancel the goal.

(6) The referee, however, can only reverse his first decision so long as the game has not been restarted.

(7) If the referee has decided to apply the advantage clause and to let the game proceed, he cannot revoke his decision if the presumed advantage has not been realised, even though he has not, by any gesture, indicated his decision. This does not exempt the offending player from being dealt with by the referee.

(8) The Laws of the Game are intended to provide that games should be played with as little interference as possible, and in this view it is the duty of referees to penalise only deliberate breaches of the Law. Constant whistling for trifling and doubtful breaches produces bad feeling and loss of temper on the part of the players and spoils the pleasure of spectators.

(9) By par. (d) of Law V the referee is empowered to terminate a match in the event of grave disorder, but he has no power or right to decide, in such event, that either team is disqualified and thereby the loser of the match. He must send a detailed report to the proper authority who alone has power to deal further with this matter.

(10) If a player commits two infringements of a different nature at the same time, the referee shall punish the more serious offence.

(11) It is the duty of the referee to act upon the information of neutral linesmen with regard to incidents that do not come under the personal notice of the referee.

(12) The referee shall not allow any person to enter the field of play until play has stopped, and only then if he has given him a signal to do so.

(13) The coach may convey tactical instructions to players during the match.

The coach and other officials, however, must remain within the confines of the technical area* where such an area is provided and they must conduct themselves, at all times, in a responsible manner.

(14) In tournaments or competitions where a fourth official is appointed, his role and duties shall be in accordance with the guide-lines approved by the International Football Association Board.

---

*For top-level football, the technical area may be defined in terms of the length of the bench plus one metre at each side of the bench, and the area in front of the bench up to one metre parallel to the touch-line.

LAW VI

Linesmen

Two linesmen shall be appointed, whose duty (subject to the decision of the referee) shall be to indicate:

(a) when the ball is out of play,

(b) which side is entitled to a corner-kick, goal-kick or throw-in,

(c) when a substitution is desired.

They shall also assist the referee to control the game in accordance with the Laws. In the event of undue interference or improper conduct by a linesman, the referee shall dispense with his services and arrange for a substitute to be appointed. (The matter shall be reported by the referee to the competent authority.) The linesmen should be equipped with flags by the club on whose ground the match is played.

DECISIONS OF THE INTERNATIONAL F.A. BOARD

(1) Linesmen, where neutral, shall draw the referee's attention to any breach of the Laws of the Game of which they become aware if they consider that the referee may not have seen it, but the referee shall always be the judge of the decision to be taken.

(2) National Associations are advised to appoint official referees of neutral nationality to act as linesmen in international matches.

(3) In international matches linesmen's flags shall be of a vivid colour, bright reds and yellows. Such flags are recommended for use in all other matches.

(4) A linesman may be subject to disciplinary action only upon a report of the referee for unjustified interference or insufficient assistance.

Duration of the Game

The duration of the game shall be two equal periods of 45 minutes, unless otherwise mutually agreed upon, subject to the following:

(a) Allowance shall be made in either period for all time lost through substitution, the transport from the field of injured players, time-wasting or other cause, the amount of which shall be a matter for the discretion of the referee.

(b) Time shall be extended to permit a penalty-kick being taken at or after the expiration of the normal period in either half.

At half-time the interval shall not exceed five minutes except by consent of the referee.

DECISIONS OF THE INTERNATIONAL F.A. BOARD

(1) If a match has been stopped by the referee, before the completion of the time specified in the rules, for any reason stated in Law V, it must be replayed in full unless the rules of the competition concerned provide for the result of the match at the time of such stoppage to stand.

(2) Players have a right to an interval at half-time.

LAW VIII

The Start of Play

(a) **At the beginning of the game,** choice of ends and the kick-off shall be decided by the toss of a coin. The team winning the toss shall have the option of choice of ends or the kick-off. The referee having given a signal, the game shall be started by a player taking a place-kick (i.e. a kick at the ball while it is stationary on the ground in the centre of the field of play) into his opponents' half of the field of play. Every player shall be in his own half of the field and every player of the team opposing that of the kicker shall remain not less than 10 yards from the ball until it is kicked-off; it shall not be deemed in play until it has travelled the distance of its own circumference. The kicker shall not play the ball a second time until it has been touched or played by another player.

(b) **After a goal has been scored,** the game shall be restarted in like manner by a player of the team losing the goal.

(c) **After half-time;** when restarting after half-time, ends shall be changed and the kick-off shall be taken by a player of the opposite team to that of the player who started the game.

Punishment

For any infringement of this Law, the kick-off shall be retaken, except in the case of the kicker playing the ball again before it has been touched or played by another player; for this offence an indirect free-kick shall be taken by a player of the opposing team from the place where the infringement occurred, subject to the overriding conditions imposed in Law XIII.

A goal shall not be scored direct from a kick-off.

(d) **After any other temporary suspension;** when restarting the game after a temporary suspension of play from any cause not mentioned elsewhere in these Laws, provided that immediately prior to the suspension the ball has not passed over the touch- or goal-lines, the referee shall drop the ball at the place where it was when play was suspended, unless it was within the goal-area at that time, in which case it shall be dropped on that part of the goal-area line which runs parallel to the goal-line, at the point nearest to where the ball was when play was stopped. It shall be deemed in play when it has touched the ground; if, however, it goes over the touch- or goal-lines after it has been dropped by the referee, but before it is touched by a player, the referee shall again drop it. A player shall not play the ball until it has touched the ground. If this section of the Laws is not complied with, the referee shall again drop the ball.

DECISIONS OF THE INTERNATIONAL F.A. BOARD

(1) If, when the referee drops the ball, a player infringes any of the Laws before the ball has touched the ground, the player concerned shall be cautioned or sent off the field according to the seriousness of the offence, but a free-kick cannot be awarded to the opposing team because the ball was not in play at the time of the offence. The ball shall therefore be again dropped by the referee.

(2) Kicking-off by persons other than the players competing in a match is prohibited.

LAW IX

Ball in and out of Play

The ball is out of play:

(a) when it has wholly crossed the goal-line or touch-line, whether on the ground or in the air.

(b) when the game has been stopped by the Referee.

The ball is in play at all other times from the start of the match to the finish including:

(a) if it rebounds from a goal-post, cross-bar or corner-flag post into the field of play.

(b) if it rebounds off either the Referee or Linesmen when they are in the field of play.

(c) in the event of a supposed infringement of the Laws, until a decision is given.

DECISIONS OF THE INTERNATIONAL F.A. BOARD

(1) The lines belong to the areas of which they are the boundaries. In consequence, the touch-lines and the goal-lines belong to the field of play.

Method of Scoring

Except as otherwise provided by these Laws, a goal is scored when the whole of the ball has passed over the goal-line, between the goal-posts and under the cross-bar, provided it has not been thrown, carried or intentionally propelled by hand or arm, by a player of the attacking side, except in the case of a goalkeeper, who is within his own penalty-area.

The team scoring the greater number of goals during a game shall be the winner; if no goals or an equal number of goals are scored, the game shall be termed a "draw".

DECISIONS OF THE INTERNATIONAL F.A. BOARD

(1) Law X defines the only method according to which a match is won or drawn; no variation whatsoever can be authorised.

(2) A goal cannot in any case be allowed if the ball has been prevented by some outside agent from passing over the goal-line. If this happens in the normal course of play, other than at the taking of a penalty-kick: the game must be stopped and restarted by the referee dropping the ball at the place where the ball came into contact with the interference, unless it was within the goal-area at that time, in which case it shall be dropped on that part of the goal-area line which runs parallel to the goal-line, at the point nearest to where the ball was when play was stopped.

(3) If, when the ball is going into goal, a spectator enters the field before it passes wholly over the goal-line and tries to prevent a score, a goal shall be allowed if the ball goes into goal unless the spectator has made contact with the ball or has interfered with play, in which case the referee shall stop the game and restart it by dropping the ball at the place where the contact or interference occurred, unless it was within the goal-area at that time, in which case it shall be dropped on that part of the goal-area line which runs parallel to the goal-line, at the point nearest to where the ball was when play was stopped.

LAW XI

Off-side

1. A player is in an off-side position if he is nearer to his opponents' goal-line than the ball, unless:

(a) he is in his own half of the field of play, or

b) he is not nearer to his opponents' goal-line than at least two of his opponents.

2. A player shall only be declared off-side and penalised for being in an off-side position, if, at the moment the ball touches, or is played by, one of his team, he is, in the opinion of the referee

(a) interfering with play or with an opponent, or

(b) seeking to gain an advantage by being in that position.

3. A player shall not be declared off-side by the referee

(a) merely because of his being in an off-side position, or

b) if he receives the ball direct from a goal-kick, a corner-kick or a throw-in.

4. If a player is declared offside, the referee shall award an indirect free-kick, which shall be taken by a player of the opposing team from where the infringement occurred, unless the offence is committed by a player in his opponents' goal area, in which case the free-kick shall be taken from any point within the goal area.

DECISIONS OF THE INTERNATIONAL F.A. BOARD

---

(1) Off-side shall not be judged at the moment the player in question receives the ball, but at the moment when the ball is passed to him by one of his own side. A player who is not in an off-side position when one of his colleagues passes the ball to him or takes a free-kick, does not therefore become off-side if he goes forward during the flight of the ball.

2. A player who is level with the second last opponent or with the last two opponents is not in an off-side position.

Fouls and Misconduct

A player who intentionally commits any of the following nine offences:

(a) kicks or attempts to kick an opponent;

(b) trips an opponent, i.e. throwing or attempting to throw him by the use of the legs, or by stooping in front of or behind him;

(c) jumps at an opponent;

(d) charges an opponent in a violent or dangerous manner;

(e) charges an opponent from behind unless the latter is obstructing;

(f) strikes or attempts to strike an opponent or spits at him;

(g) holds an opponent;

(h) pushes an opponent;

(i) handles the ball, i.e. carries, strikes, or propels the ball with his hand or arm; (this does not apply to the goalkeeper within his own penalty area;

shall be penalised by the award of a **direct free-kick** to be taken by the opposing team from the place where the offence occurred, unless the offence is committed by a player in his opponents' goal area, in which case the free-kick shall be taken from any point within the goal area.

Should a player of the defending team intentionally commit one of the above nine offences within the penalty area, he shall be penalised by a **penalty-kick.**

A penalty-kick can be awarded irrespective of the position of the ball, if in play, at the time an offence within the penalty area is committed.

A player committing any of the five following offences:

1. playing in a manner considered by the referee to be dangerous, e.g. attempting to kick the ball while held by the goalkeeper;

2. charging fairly, i.e. with the shoulder, when the ball is not within playing distance of the players concerned and they are definitely not trying to play it;

3. when not playing the ball, intentionally obstructing an opponent, i.e. running between the opponent and the ball, or interposing the body so as to form an obstacle to an opponent;

4. charging the goalkeeper except when he

(a) is holding the ball;

(b) is obstructing an opponent;

(c) has passed outside his goal area;

5. when playing as a goalkeeper and within his own penalty area:

(a) from the moment he takes control of the ball with his hands, he takes more than 4 steps in any direction whilst holding, bouncing or throwing the ball into the air and catching it again, without releasing it into play, or

(b) having released the ball into play before, during or after

the 4 steps, he touches it again with his hands, before it has been touched or played by a player of the opposing team either inside or outside of the penalty area, or by a player of the same team outside the penalty area, subject to the overriding conditions of 5(c), or

(c) touches the ball with his hands after it has been deliberately kicked to him by a team-mate, or

LAW XII

(d) indulges in tactics, which in the opinion of the referee, are designed to hold up the game and thus waste time and so give an unfair advantage to his own team,

shall be penalised by the award of an **indirect free-kick** to be taken by the opposing side from the place where the infringement occurred, subject to the overriding conditions imposed in Law XIII.

A player shall be **cautioned and shown the yellow card** if:

(j) he enters or re-enters the field of play to join or rejoin his team after the game has commenced, or leaves the field of play during the progress of the game (except through accident) without, in either case, first having received a signal from the referee showing him that he may do so.

If the referee stops the game to administer the caution, the game shall be restarted by an indirect free-kick taken by a player of the opposing team from the place where the ball was when the referee stopped the game, subject to the overriding conditions imposed in Law XIII.

If, however, the offending player has committed a more serious offence, he shall be penalised according to that section of the law he infringed.

(k) he persistently infringes the Laws of the Game;

(l) he shows, by word or action, dissent from any decision given by the referee;

(m) he is guilty of ungentlemanly conduct.

For any of these last three offences, in addition to the caution, an indirect free-kick shall also be awarded to the opposing side from the place where the offence occurred, subject to the overriding conditions imposed in Law XIII, unless a more serious infringement of the Laws of the Game was committed.

A player shall be **sent off the field of play and shown the red card,** if, in the opinion of the referee, he:

(n) is guilty of violent conduct;

(o) is guilty of serious foul play;

(p) uses foul or abusive language;

(q) is guilty of a second cautionable offence after having received a caution.

If play is stopped by reason of a player being ordered from the field for an offence without a separate breach of the Law having been committed, the game shall be resumed by an **indirect free-kick** awarded to the opposing side from the place where the infringement occurred, subject to the overriding conditions imposed in Law XIII.

DECISIONS OF THE INTERNATIONAL F.A. BOARD

(1) If the goalkeeper either intentionally strikes an opponent by throwing the ball vigorously at him or pushes him with the ball while holding it, the referee shall award a penalty-kick, if the offence took place within the penalty-area.

(2) If a player deliberately turns his back to an opponent when he is about to be tackled, he may be charged but not in a dangerous manner.

(3) In case of body contact in the goal-area between an attacking player and the opposing goalkeeper not in possession of the ball, the referee, as sole judge of intention, shall stop the game if, in his opinion, the action of the attacking player was intentional, and award an indirect free-kick.

(4) If a player leans on the shoulders of another player of his own team in order to head the ball, the referee shall stop the game, caution the player for ungentlemanly conduct and award an indirect free-kick to the opposing side.

(5) A player's obligation when joining or rejoining his team after the start of the match to 'report to the referee' must be interpreted as meaning 'to draw the attention of the referee from the touchline'. The signal from the referee shall be made by a definite gesture which makes the player understand that he may come into the field of play; it is not necessary for the referee to wait until the game is stopped (this does not apply in respect of an infringement of Law IV), but the referee is the sole judge of the moment in which he gives his signal of acknowledgement.

(6) The letter and spirit of Law XII do not oblige the referee to stop a game to administer a caution. He may, if he chooses, apply the advantage. If he does apply the advantage, he shall caution the player when play stops.

(7) If a player covers up the ball without touching it in an endeavour not to have it played by an opponent, he obstructs but does not infringe Law XII para. 3 because he is already in possession of the ball and covers it for tactical reasons whilst the ball remains within playing distance. In fact, he is actually playing the ball and does not commit an infringement; in this case, the player may be charged because he is in fact playing the ball.

(8) If a player intentionally stretches his arms to obstruct an opponent and steps from one side to the other, moving his arms up and down to delay his opponent, forcing him to change course, but does not make "bodily contact" the referee shall

caution the player for ungentlemanly conduct and award an indirect free-kick.

(9) If a player intentionally obstructs the opposing goalkeeper, in an attempt to prevent him from putting the ball into play in accordance with Law XII, 5 (a), the referee shall award an indirect free-kick.

(10) If, after a referee has awarded a free-kick, a player protests violently by using abusive or foul language and is sent off the field, the free-kick should not be taken until the player has left the field.

(11) Any player, whether he is within or outside the field of play, whose conduct is ungentlemanly or violent, whether or not it is directed towards an opponent, a colleague, the referee, a linesman or other person, or who uses foul or abusive language, is guilty of an offence, and shall be dealt with according to the nature of the offence committed.

(12) If, in the opinion of the referee a goalkeeper intentionally lies on the ball longer than is necessary, he shall be penalised for ungentlemanly conduct and

(a) be cautioned and an indirect free-kick awarded to the opposing team;

(b) in case of repetition of the offence, be sent off the field.

(13) The offence of spitting at officials and other persons, or similar unseemly behaviour shall be considered as violent conduct within the meaning of section (n) of Law XII.

(14) If, when a referee is about to caution a player, and before he has done so, the player commits another offence which merits a caution, the player shall be sent off the field of play.

(15) If, in the opinion of the referee, a player who is moving toward his opponent's goal with an obvious opportunity to score a goal is intentionally impeded by an opponent, through unlawful means, i.e. an offence punishable by a free kick (or a penalty kick), thus denying the attacking player's team the aforesaid goal-scoring opportunity, the offending player shall be sent off the field of play for serious foul play in accordance with Law XII (n).

(16) If, in the opinion of the referee, a player, other than the goalkeeper within his own penalty area, denies his opponents a goal, or an obvious goal-scoring opportunity, by intentionally handl-

LAW XII

ing the ball, he shall be sent off the field of play for serious foul play in accordance with Law XII (n).

(17) The International F.A. Board is of the opinion that a goalkeeper, in the circumstances described in Law XII 5 (a), will be considered to be in control of the ball by touching it with any part of his hands or arms. Possession of the ball would include the goalkeeper intentionally parrying the ball, but would not include the circumstances where, in the opinion of the referee, the ball rebounds accidentally from the goalkeeper, for example after he has made a save.

(18) Subject to the terms of Law XII, a player may pass the ball to his own goalkeeper using his head or chest or knee, etc. If, however, in the opinion of the referee, a player uses a deliberate trick in order to circumvent article 5(c) of Law XII, the player will be guilty of ungentlemanly conduct and will be punished accordingly under the terms of Law XII; that is to say, the player will be cautioned and shown the yellow card and an indirect free-kick will be awarded to the opposing team from the place where the player committed the offence.

In such circumstances, it is irrelevant whether the goalkeeper subsequently touches the ball with his hands or not. The offence is committed by the player in attempting to circumvent both the text and the spirit of Law XII.

Free-kick

Free-kicks shall be classified under two headings: "direct" (from which a goal can be scored direct against the offending side), and "indirect" (from which a goal cannot be scored unless the ball has been played or touched by a player other than the kicker before passing through the goal).

When a player is taking a direct or an indirect free-kick inside his own penalty-area, all of the opposing players shall be at least ten yards (9.15 m) from the ball and shall remain outside the penalty-area until the ball has been kicked out of the area. The ball shall be in play immediately it has travelled the distance of its own circumference and is beyond the penalty-area. The goalkeeper shall not receive the ball into his hands, in order that he may thereafter kick it into play. If the ball is not kicked direct into play, beyond the penalty-area, the kick shall be retaken.

When a player is taking a direct or an indirect free-kick outside his own penalty-area, all of the opposing players shall be at least ten yards from the ball, until it is in play, unless they are standing on their own goal-line, between the goalposts. The ball shall be in play when it has travelled the distance of its own circumference.

If a player of the opposing side encroaches into the penalty-area, or within ten yards of the ball, as the case may be,

before a free-kick is taken, the referee shall delay the taking of the kick, until the Law is complied with.

The ball must be stationary when a free-kick is taken, and the kicker shall not play the ball a second time, until it has been touched or played by another player.

Notwithstanding any other reference in these Laws to the point from which a free-kick is to be taken:

1. Any free-kick awarded to the defending team, within its own goal-area, may be taken from any point within the goal-area.

2. Any indirect free-kick awarded to the attacking team within its opponent's goal-area shall be taken from the part of the goal-area line which runs parallel to the goal-line, at the point nearest to where the offence was committed.

Punishment:

If the kicker, after taking the free-kick, plays the ball a second time before it has been touched or played by another player, an indirect free-kick shall be taken by a player of the opposing team from the spot where the infringement occurred, unless the offence is committed by a player in his opponent's goal-area, in which case the free-kick shall be taken from any point within the goal-area.

LAW XIII

DECISIONS OF THE INTERNATIONAL F.A. BOARD

(1) In order to distinguish between a direct and an indirect free-kick, the referee, when he awards an indirect free-kick, shall indicate accordingly by raising an arm above his head. He shall keep his arm in that position until the kick has been taken and retain the signal until the ball has been played or touched by another player or goes out of play.

(2) Players who do not retire to the proper distance when a free-kick is taken must be cautioned and on any repetition be ordered off. It is particularly requested of referees that attempts to delay the taking of a free-kick by encroaching should be treated as serious misconduct.

(3) If, when a free-kick is being taken, any of the players dance about or gesticulate in a way calculated to distract their opponents, it shall be deemed ungentlemanly conduct for which the offender(s) shall be cautioned.

Penalty-kick

A penalty-kick shall be taken from the penalty-mark and, when it is being taken, all players with the exception of the player taking the kick, properly identified, and the opposing goalkeeper, shall be within the field of play but outside the penalty-area, and at least 10 yards from the penalty-mark. The opposing goalkeeper must stand (without moving his feet) on his own goal-line, between the goal-posts, until the ball is kicked. The player taking the kick must kick the ball forward; he shall not play the ball a second time until it has been touched or played by another player. The ball shall be deemed in play directly it is kicked, i.e. when it has travelled the distance of its circumference. A goal may be scored directly from a penalty-kick. When a penalty-kick is being taken during the normal course of play, or when time has been extended at half-time or full-time to allow a penalty-kick to be taken or retaken, a goal shall not be nullified if, before passing between the posts and under the cross-bar, the ball touches either or both of the goal-posts, or the cross-bar, or the goal-keeper, or any combination of these agencies, providing that no other infringement has occurred.

Punishment:

For any infringement of this Law:

(a) by the defending team, the kick shall be retaken if a goal has not resulted.

(b) by the attacking team other than by the player taking the kick, if a goal is scored it shall be disallowed and the kick retaken.

(c) by the player taking the penalty-kick, committed after the ball is in play, a player of the opposing team shall take an indirect free-kick from the spot where the infringement occurred, subject to the overriding conditions imposed in Law XIII.

LAW XIV

DECISIONS OF THE INTERNATIONAL F.A. BOARD

(1) When the referee has awarded a penalty-kick, he shall not signal for it to be taken, until the players have taken up position in accordance with the Law.

(2) (a) If, after the kick has been taken, the ball is stopped in its course towards goal, by an outside agent, the kick shall be retaken.

(b) If, after the kick has been taken, the ball rebounds into play, from the goalkeeper, the cross-bar or a goal-post, and is then stopped in its course by an outside agent, the referee shall stop play and restart it by dropping the ball at the place where it came into contact with the outside agent, unless it was within the goal-area at that time, in which case it shall be dropped on that part of the goal-area line which runs parallel to the goal-line, at the point nearest to where the ball was when play was stopped.

(3) (a) If, after having given the signal for a penalty-kick to be taken, the referee sees that the goalkeeper is not in his right place on the goal-line, he shall, nevertheless, allow the kick to proceed. It shall be retaken, if a goal is not scored.

(b) If, after the referee has given the signal for a penalty-kick to be taken, and before the ball has been kicked, the goal-keeper moves his feet, the referee shall, nevertheless, allow the kick to proceed. It shall be retaken, if a goal is not scored.

(c) If, after the referee has given the signal for a penalty-kick to be taken, and before the ball is in play, a player of the defending team encroaches into the penalty-area, or within ten yards of the penalty-mark, the referee shall, nevertheless, allow the kick to proceed. It shall be retaken, if a goal is not scored.

The player concerned shall be cautioned.

(4) (a) If, when a penalty-kick is being taken, the player taking the kick is guilty of ungentlemanly conduct, the kick, if already taken, shall be retaken, if a goal is scored.

The player concerned shall be cautioned.

(b) If, after the referee has given the signal for a penalty-kick to be taken, and before the ball is in play, a colleague of the player taking the kick encroaches into the penalty-area or within ten yards of the penalty-mark, the referee shall, neverthe-

less, allow the kick to proceed. If a goal is scored, it shall be disallowed, and the kick retaken.

The players concerned shall be cautioned.

(c) If, in the circumstances described in the foregoing paragraph, the ball rebounds into play from the goalkeeper, the cross-bar or a goal-post, and a goal has not been scored, the referee shall stop the game, caution the player and award an indirect free-kick to the opposing team from the place where the infringement occurred, subject to the over-riding conditions imposed in Law XIII.

(5) (a) If, after the referee has given the signal for a penalty-kick to be taken, and before the ball is in play, the goalkeeper moves from his position on the goal-line, or moves his feet, and a colleague of the kicker encroaches into the penalty-area or within 10 yards of the penalty-mark, the kick, if taken, shall be retaken.

The colleague of the kicker shall be cautioned.

(b) If, after the referee has given the signal for a penalty-kick to be taken, and before the ball is in play, a player of each team encroaches into the penalty-area, or within 10 yards of the penalty-mark, the kick, if taken, shall be retaken.

The players concerned shall be cautioned.

(6) When a match is extended, at half-time or full-time, to allow a penalty-kick to be taken or retaken, the extension shall last until the moment that the penalty-kick has been completed, i.e. until the referee has decided whether or not a goal is scored, and the game shall terminate immediately the referee has made his decision.

After the player taking the penalty-kick has put the ball into play, no player other than the defending goalkeeper may play or touch the ball before the kick is completed.

(7) When a penalty-kick is being taken in extended time:

(a) the provisions of all of the foregoing paragraphs, except paragraphs (2) (b) and (4) (c) shall apply in the usual way, and

(b) in the circumstances described in paragraphs (2) (b) and (4) (c) the game shall terminate immediately the ball rebounds from the goalkeeper, the cross-bar or the goal-post.

Throw-in

When the whole of the ball passes over a touch-line, either on the ground or in the air, it shall be thrown in from the point where it crossed the line, in any direction, by a player of the team opposite to that of the player who last touched it. The thrower at the moment of delivering the ball must face the field of play and part of each foot shall be either on the touch-line or on the ground outside the touch-line. The thrower shall use both hands and shall deliver the ball from behind and over his head. The ball shall be in play immediately it enters the field of play, but the thrower shall not again play the ball until it has been touched or play-ed by another player. A goal shall not be scored direct from a throw-in.

Punishment:

(a) If the ball is improperly thrown in the throw-in shall be taken by a player of the opposing team.

(b) If the thrower plays the ball a second time before it has been touched or played by another player, an indirect free-kick shall be taken by a player of the opposing team from the place where the infringement occurred, subject to the overriding conditions imposed in Law XIII.

DECISIONS OF THE INTERNATIONAL F.A. BOARD

(1) If a player taking a throw-in plays the ball a second time by handling it within the field of play before it has been touched or played by another player, the referee shall award a direct free-kick.

(2) A player taking a throw-in must face the field of play with some part of his body.

(3) If, when a throw-in is being taken, any of the opposing players dance about or gesticulate in a way calculated to distract or impede the thrower, it shall be deemed ungentlemanly conduct, for which the offender(s) shall be cautioned.

(4) A throw-in taken from any position other than the point where the ball passed over the touch-line shall be considered to have been improperly thrown in.

LAW XVI

Goal-kick

When the whole of the ball passes over the goal-line excluding that portion between the goal-posts, either in the air or on the ground, having last been played by one of the attacking team, it shall be kicked direct into play beyond the penalty-area from any point within the goal-area by a player of the defending team. A goalkeeper shall not receive the ball into his hands from a goal-kick in order that he may thereafter kick it into play. If the ball is not kicked beyond the penalty-area, i.e. direct into play, the kick shall be retaken. The kicker shall not play the ball a second time until it has touched or been played by another player. A goal shall not be scored direct from such a kick. Players of the team opposing that of the player taking the goal-kick shall remain outside the penalty-area until the ball has been kicked out of the penalty-area.

Punishment:

If a player taking a goal-kick plays the ball a second time after it has passed beyond the penalty-area, but before it has touched or been played by another player, an indirect free-kick shall be awarded to the opposing team, to be taken from the place where the infringement occurred, subject to the overriding conditions imposed in Law XIII.

DECISIONS OF THE INTERNATIONAL F.A. BOARD

(1) When a goal-kick has been taken and the player who has kicked the ball touches it again before it has left the penalty-area, the kick has not been taken in accordance with the Law and must be retaken.

Corner-kick

When the whole of the ball passes over the goal-line, excluding that portion between the goal-posts, either in the air or on the ground, having last been played by one of the defending team, a member of the attacking team shall take a corner-kick, i.e. the whole of the ball shall be placed within the quarter circle at the nearest corner-flagpost, which must not be moved, and it shall be kicked from that position. A goal may be scored direct from such a kick. Players of the team opposing that of the player taking the corner-kick shall not approach within 10 yards of the ball until it is in play, i.e. it has travelled the distance of its own circumference, nor shall the kicker play the ball a second time until it has been touched or played by another player.

Punishment:

(a) If the player who takes the kick plays the ball a second time before it has been touched or played by another player, the referee shall award an indirect free-kick to the opposing team, to be taken from the place where the infringement occurred, subject to the overriding conditions imposed in Law XIII.

(b) For any other infringement the kick shall be retaken.

The Members of FIFA

The controlling body for soccer worldwide is:

Fédération Internationale de Football Association
Hitzigweg 11
8030 Zurich
Switzerland

In 1993 the membership of the Fédération Internationale de Football Association stood at 178 countries, plus 9 associate members.

For ease of administration, the member nations are grouped into six regional confederations.

AFRICA
Confédération
  Africaine de Football
  (CAF)
5 Shareh Gabalaya
Guezira, Cairo
AR Egypt

Algeria
Angola
Benin
Botswana
Burkina Faso
Burundi
Cameroon
Cape Verde Islands
Central Africa
Chad

Congo
Egypt
Equatorial Guinea
Ethiopia
Gabon
Gambia
Ghana
Guinea
Guinea-Bissau
Ivory Coast
Kenya
Lesotho
Liberia
Libya
Madagascar
Malawi
Mali
Mauritania

Mauritius
Morocco
Mozambique
Namibia
Niger
Nigeria
Rwanda
São Tome e Principe
Senegal
Seychelles
Sierra Leone
Somalia
South Africa
Sudan
Swaziland
Tanzania
Togo
Tunisia

Uganda
Zaire
Zambia
Zimbabwe

**AMERICA—NORTH,
CENTRAL, and
CARIBBEAN**
*Confederación
Norte/Centro-
americana y del
Caribe de Fútbol
(CONCACAF)*
*725 Fifth Avenue, 17th
floor*
New York, NY 10022

Antigua and Barbuda
Aruba
Bahamas
Barbados
Belize
Bermuda
Canada
Cayman Islands
Costa Rica
Cuba
Dominica*
Dominican Republic
El Salvador
Grenada
Guatemala
Guyana
Haiti
Honduras
Jamaica
Mexico
Netherlands Antilles
Nicaragua
Panama
Puerto Rico

St. Kitts and Nevis
St. Lucia
St. Vincent and the
Grenadines
Suriname
Trinidad and Tobago
United States
Virgin Islands*

AMERICA—SOUTH
*Confederación
Sudamericana de
Fútbol (CSF, or
CONMEBOL)*
*Ed. Banco do Brasil—
Piso 4*
*Nuestra Señora de la
Asunción 540*
Asunción
Paraguay

Argentina
Bolivia
Brazil
Chile
Colombia
Ecuador
Paraguay
Peru
Uruguay
Venezuela

ASIA
*Asian Football Confed-
eration (AFC)*
*Wisma Olympic Coun-
cil of Malaysia*
*1st floor, Jalan Hang
Jebat*
*50150 Kuala Lumpur
Malaysia*

Afghanistan
Bahrain
Bangladesh
Brunei
Cambodia**
China PR
Chinese Taipei
(Taiwan)
Guam†
Hong Kong
India
Indonesia
Iran
Iraq
Japan
Jordan
Korea DPR (North)
Korea Republic (South)
Kuwait
Laos
Lebanon
Macao
Malaysia
Maldives Republic
Myanmar
Nepal
Oman
Pakistan
Philippines
Qatar
Saudi Arabia
Singapore
Sri Lanka
Syria
Thailand
United Arab Emirates
Vietnam
Yemen

* Associate members.
** FIFA member, not currently affiliated to AFC.
† Associate member.

EUROPE

*Union of European
Football Associa-
tions (UEFA)*
Jupiterstrasse 33
P.O. Box 16
CH-3000 Berne 15
Switzerland

Albania
Armenia
Austria
Belgium
Bulgaria
Belarus
Croatia
Cyprus
Denmark
England
Estonia
Faroe Islands
Finland
France
Georgia
Germany
Greece
Hungary
Iceland
Ireland, Northern
Ireland, Republic of
Israel*
Italy
Latvia
Lichtenstein
Lithuania
Luxembourg
Malta
Netherlands
Norway
Poland
Portugal
Representation of
    Czechs and Slovaks
Romania
Russia
San Marino
Scotland
Slovenia
Spain
Sweden
Switzerland
Turkey
Ukraine
Wales
Yugoslavia

OCEANIA

*Oceania Football Con-
federation (OFC)*
Mt Smart Stadium
P.O. Box 62-586
Central Park
Auckland 6
New Zealand

American Samoa*
Australia
Cook Islands*
Fiji
New Caledonia*
New Zealand
Niue Island*
Northern Marianas*
Papua New Guinea
Solomon Islands
Tahiti
Tonga†
Vanuatu
Western Samoa

* Independent FIFA member. Geographically, Israel belongs to the Asian region, but for political reasons it plays its games, both national team and club, within the European region.
† Associate members.

Worldwide Winners

NATIONAL TEAM COMPETITIONS
I. Global

The World Cup
Official Title: The FIFA World Cup.
Eligible: National teams from all member nations of FIFA (see pages 279–81).
Frequency: Every four years, between the Olympic Games cycle, in a predetermined host nation.
Format: 24 teams take part in the final tournament. They are made up as follows: 13 teams from Europe; 3 teams from South America; 3 teams from Africa; 2 teams from Asia; 2 teams from North and Central America. The twenty-fourth berth is decided by a three-team playoff involving the winner of the Oceania qualifying group and one team each from South America and CONCACAF.

A series of regional elimination games is played, starting about two years before the finals, to reduce the huge number of entries. For the 1994 World Cup, 144 nations entered. When the elimination rounds are over, 22 nations have survived. These join the host nation and the reigning champions, which qualify automatically, to make up the final 24.

At the World Cup draw, which is staged about six months before the final tournament, the 24 nations are drawn into six groups of four. Within each group, each team plays the other three once. First and second place in each group, plus the four best third-place finishers advance to a knock-out stage, the pairings having been decided in advance.

FIRST WORLD CUP, URUGUAY, 1930
13 finalists, 13 nations entered

Group 1
France 4 Mexico 1
Argentina 1 France 0
Chile 3 Mexico 0
Chile 1 France 0
Argentina 6 Mexico 3
Argentina 3 Chile 1
   Qualifier: Argentina

Group 2
Yugoslavia 2 Brazil 1
Yugoslavia 4 Bolivia 0
Brazil 4 Bolivia 0
   Qualifier: Yugoslavia

Group 3
Romania 3 Peru 1
Uruguay 1 Peru 0
Uruguay 4 Romania 0
   Qualifier: Uruguay

Group 4
USA 3 Belgium 0
USA 3 Paraguay 0
Paraguay 1 Belgium 0
   Qualifier: USA

Semifinals
Argentina 6 USA 1
Uruguay 6 Yugoslavia 1

Final
Uruguay 4 Argentina 2
   Champion: URUGUAY

SECOND WORLD CUP, ITALY, 1934
16 finalists, 32 nations entered

First round
Italy 7 USA 1
Czechoslovakia 2 Romania 1
Germany 5 Belgium 2
Austria 3 France 2
Switzerland 3 Netherlands 2
Sweden 3 Argentina 2
Hungary 4 Egypt 2

Second round
Germany 2 Sweden 1
Austria 2 Hungary 1
Italy 1 Spain 1
(Italy 1 Spain 0, replay)
Czechoslovakia 3 Switzerland 2

Semifinals
Czechoslovakia 3 Germany 1
Italy 1 Austria 0

3rd Place Game
Germany 3 Austria 2

Final
Italy 2 Czechoslovakia 1 (o/t)
   Champion: ITALY

THIRD WORLD CUP, FRANCE, 1938
16 finalists, 25 nations entered

First round
Switzerland 1 Germany 1
(Switzerland 4 Germany 2, replay)
Cuba 3 Romania 3
(Cuba 2 Romania 1, replay)
Hungary 6 Dutch East Indies 0
France 3 Belgium 1
Czechoslovakia 3 Netherlands 0
Brazil 6 Poland 5
Italy 2 Norway 1

Second round
Sweden 8 Cuba 0
Hungary 2 Switzerland 0
Brazil 1 Czechoslovakia 1
(Brazil 2 Czechoslovakia 1, replay)

Semifinals
Italy 2 Brazil 1
Hungary 5 Sweden 1

3rd Place Game
Brazil 4 Sweden 2

Final
Italy 4 Hungary 2
Champion: ITALY

FOURTH WORLD CUP, BRAZIL, 1950
13 finalists, 24 nations entered

Pool 1
Brazil 4 Mexico 0
Yugoslavia 3 Switzerland 0
Yugoslavia 4 Mexico 1
Brazil 2 Switzerland 2
Brazil 2 Yugoslavia 0
Switzerland 2 Mexico 1
    Qualifier: Brazil

Pool 2
Spain 3 USA 1
England 2 Chile 0
USA 1 England 0
Spain 2 Chile 0
Spain 1 England 0
Chile 5 USA 2
    Qualifier: Spain

Pool 3
Sweden 3 Italy 2
Sweden 2 Paraguay 2
Italy 2 Paraguay 0
    Qualifier: Sweden

Pool 4
Uruguay 8 Bolivia 0
    Qualifier: Uruguay

Final pool
Uruguay 2 Spain 2
Brazil 7 Sweden 1
Uruguay 3 Sweden 2
Brazil 6 Spain 1
Sweden 3 Spain 1
Uruguay 2 Brazil 1
    Champion: URUGUAY

FIFTH WORLD CUP,
SWITZERLAND, 1954
16 finalists, 41 nations entered

Group 1
Yugoslavia 1 France 0
Brazil 5 Mexico 0
France 3 Mexico 2
Brazil 1 Yugoslavia 1
    Qualifiers: Brazil, Yugoslavia

Group 2
Hungary 9 Korea 0
West Germany 4 Turkey 1
Hungary 8 West Germany 3
Turkey 7 Korea 0
West Germany 7 Turkey 2 (playoff)
    Qualifiers:
    Hungary, West Germany

Group 3
Austria 1 Scotland 0
Uruguay 2 Czechoslovakia 0
Austria 5 Czechoslovakia 0
Uruguay 7 Scotland 0
    Qualifiers: Uruguay, Austria

Group 4
England 4 Belgium 4
England 2 Switzerland 0
Switzerland 2 Italy 1
Italy 4 Belgium 1
Switzerland 4 Italy 1 (playoff)
    Qualifiers: England, Switzerland

Quarterfinals
West Germany 2 Yugoslavia 0
Hungary 4 Brazil 2
Austria 7 Switzerland 5
Uruguay 4 England 2

Semifinals
West Germany 6 Austria 1
Hungary 4 Uruguay 2

3rd Place Game
Austria 3 Uruguay 1

Final
West Germany 3 Hungary 2
    Champion: WEST GERMANY

SIXTH WORLD CUP, SWEDEN, 1958
16 finalists, 52 nations entered

Group 1
West Germany 3 Argentina 1
Northern Ireland 1 Czechoslovakia 0
West Germany 2 Czechoslovakia 2
Argentina 3 Northern Ireland 1
West Germany 2 Northern Ireland 2
Czechoslovakia 6 Argentina 1
Northern Ireland 2 Czechoslovakia 1
   (playoff)
   Qualifiers:
   West Germany, Northern Ireland

Group 2
France 7 Paraguay 3
Yugoslavia 1 Scotland 1
Yugoslavia 3 France 2
Paraguay 3 Scotland 2
France 2 Scotland 1
Yugoslavia 3 Paraguay 3
   Qualifiers: France, Yugoslavia

Group 3
Sweden 3 Mexico 0
Hungary 1 Wales 1
Wales 1 Mexico 1
Sweden 2 Hungary 1
Sweden 0 Wales 0
Hungary 4 Mexico 0
Wales 2 Hungary 1 (playoff)
   Qualifiers: Sweden, Wales

Group 4
England 2 USSR 2
Brazil 3 Austria 0
England 0 Brazil 0
USSR 2 Austria 0
Brazil 2 USSR 0
England 2 Austria 2
USSR 1 England 0 (playoff)
   Qualifiers: Brazil, USSR

Quarterfinals
France 4 Northern Ireland 0
West Germany 1 Yugoslavia 0

Sweden 2 USSR 0
Brazil 1 Wales 0

Semifinals
Brazil 5 France 2
Sweden 3 West Germany 1

3rd Place Game
France 6 West Germany 3

Final
Brazil 5 Sweden 2
   Champion: BRAZIL

SEVENTH WORLD CUP, CHILE, 1962
16 finalists, 49 nations entered

Group 1
Uruguay 2 Colombia 1
USSR 2 Yugoslavia 0
Yugoslavia 3 Uruguay 1
USSR 4 Colombia 4
USSR 2 Uruguay 1
Yugoslavia 5 Colombia 0
   Qualifiers: USSR, Yugoslavia

Group 2
Chile 3 Switzerland 1
West Germany 0 Italy 0
Chile 2 Italy 0
West Germany 2 Switzerland 1
West Germany 2 Chile 0
Italy 3 Switzerland 0
   Qualifiers: West Germany, Chile

Group 3
Brazil 2 Mexico 0
Czechoslovakia 1 Spain 0
Brazil 0 Czechoslovakia 0
Spain 1 Mexico 0
Brazil 2 Spain 1
Mexico 3 Czechoslovakia 1
   Qualifiers: Brazil, Czechoslovakia

Group 4
Argentina 1 Bulgaria 0
Hungary 2 England 1
England 3 Argentina 1

Hungary 6 Bulgaria 1
Argentina 0 Hungary 0
England 0 Bulgaria 0
  Qualifiers: Hungary, England

Quarterfinals
Yugoslavia 1 West Germany 0
Brazil 3 England 1
Chile 2 USSR 1
Czechoslovakia 1 Hungary 0

Semifinals
Brazil 4 Chile 2
Czechoslovakia 3 Yugoslavia 1

3rd Place Game
Chile 1 Yugoslavia 0

Final
Brazil 3 Czechoslovakia 1
  Champion: BRAZIL

EIGHTH WORLD CUP, ENGLAND, 1966
16 finalists, 70 nations entered, 51 played

Group 1
England 0 Uruguay 0
France 1 Mexico 1
Uruguay 2 France 1
England 2 Mexico 0
Uruguay 0 Mexico 0
England 2 France 0
  Qualifiers: England, Uruguay

Group 2
West Germany 5 Switzerland 0
Argentina 2 Spain 1
Spain 2 Switzerland 1
Argentina 0 West Germany 0
Argentina 2 Switzerland 0
West Germany 2 Spain 1
  Qualifiers: West Germany,
    Argentina

Group 3
Brazil 2 Bulgaria 0
Portugal 3 Hungary 1

Hungary 3 Brazil 1
Portugal 3 Bulgaria 0
Portugal 3 Brazil 1
Hungary 3 Bulgaria 1
  Qualifiers: Portugal, Hungary

Group 4
USSR 3 North Korea 0
Italy 2 Chile 0
Chile 1 North Korea 1
USSR 1 Italy 0
North Korea 1 Italy 0
USSR 2 Chile 1
  Qualifiers: USSR, North Korea

Quarterfinals
England 1 Argentina 0
West Germany 4 Uruguay 0
Portugal 5 North Korea 3
USSR 2 Hungary 1

Semifinals
West Germany 2 USSR 1
England 2 Portugal 1
3rd Place Game
Portugal 2 USSR 1

Final
England 4 West Germany 2 (o/t)
  Champion: ENGLAND

NINTH WORLD CUP, MEXICO, 1970
16 finalists, 71 nations entered

Group 1
Mexico 0 USSR 0
Belgium 3 El Salvador 0
USSR 4 Belgium 1
Mexico 4 El Salvador 0
USSR 2 El Salvador 0
Mexico 1 Belgium 0
  Qualifiers: USSR, Mexico

Group 2
Uruguay 2 Israel 0
Italy 1 Sweden 0
Uruguay 0 Italy 0
Israel 1 Sweden 1

Sweden 1 Uruguay 0
Israel 0 Italy 0
   Qualifiers: Italy, Uruguay

Group 3
England 1 Romania 0
Brazil 4 Czechoslovakia 1
Romania 2 Czechoslovakia 1
Brazil 1 England 0
Brazil 3 Romania 2
England 1 Czechoslovakia 0
   Qualifiers: Brazil, England

Group 4
Peru 3 Bulgaria 2
West Germany 2 Morocco 1
Peru 3 Morocco 0
West Germany 5 Bulgaria 2
West Germany 3 Peru 1
Bulgaria 1 Morocco 1
   Qualifiers: West Germany, Peru

Quarterfinals
Uruguay 1 USSR 0
Italy 4 Mexico 1
Brazil 4 Peru 2
West Germany 3 England 2 (o/t)

Semifinals
Italy 4 West Germany 3 (o/t)
Brazil 3 Uruguay 1

3rd Place Game
West Germany 1 Uruguay 0

Final
Brazil 4 Italy 1
   Champion: BRAZIL

TENTH WORLD CUP,
WEST GERMANY, 1974
*16 finalists, 95 nations entered, 89
played*

Group 1
West Germany 1 Chile 0
East Germany 2 Australia 0
West Germany 3 Australia 0
East Germany 1 Chile 1

East Germany 1 West Germany 0
Australia 0 Chile 0
   Qualifiers:
   East Germany, West Germany

Group 2
Brazil 0 Yugoslavia 0
Scotland 2 Zaire 0
Brazil 0 Scotland 0
Yugoslavia 9 Zaire 0
Scotland 1 Yugoslavia 1
Brazil 3 Zaire 0
   Qualifiers: Yugoslavia, Brazil

Group 3
Netherlands 2 Uruguay 0
Sweden 0 Bulgaria 0
Netherlands 0 Sweden 0
Bulgaria 1 Uruguay 1
Netherlands 4 Bulgaria 1
Sweden 3 Uruguay 0
   Qualifiers: Netherlands, Sweden

Group 4
Italy 3 Haiti 1
Poland 3 Argentina 2
Argentina 1 Italy 1
Poland 7 Haiti 0
Argentina 4 Haiti 1
Poland 2 Italy 1
   Qualifiers: Poland, Argentina

Semifinal Group A
Brazil 1 East Germany 0
Netherlands 4 Argentina 0
Netherlands 2 East Germany 0
Brazil 2 Argentina 1
Netherlands 2 Brazil 0
Argentina 1 East Germany 1
   Winner: Netherlands
   Runner-up: Brazil

Semifinal Group B
Poland 1 Sweden 0
West Germany 2 Yugoslavia 0
Poland 2 Yugoslavia 1
West Germany 4 Sweden 2
Sweden 2 Yugoslavia 1

West Germany 1 Poland 0
    Winner: West Germany
    Runner-up: Poland

3rd Place Game
Poland 1 Brazil 0

Final
West Germany 2 Netherlands 1
    Champion: WEST GERMANY

ELEVENTH WORLD CUP,
ARGENTINA, 1978
16 finalists, 101 nations entered

Group 1
Italy 2 France 1
Argentina 2 Hungary 1
Italy 3 Hungary 1
Argentina 2 France 1
Italy 1 Argentina 0
France 3 Hungary 1
    Qualifiers: Italy, Argentina

Group 2
Poland 0 West Germany 0
Tunisia 3 Mexico 1
Poland 1 Tunisia 0
West Germany 6 Mexico 0
Tunisia 0 West Germany 0
Poland 3 Mexico 1
    Qualifiers: Poland, West Germany

Group 3
Brazil 1 Sweden 1
Austria 2 Spain 1
Austria 1 Sweden 0
Brazil 0 Spain 0
Brazil 1 Austria 0
Spain 1 Sweden 0
    Qualifiers: Austria, Brazil

Group 4
Netherlands 3 Iran 0
Peru 3 Scotland 1
Netherlands 0 Peru 0
Iran 1 Scotland 1
Scotland 3 Netherlands 2

Peru 4 Iran 1
    Qualifiers: Peru, Netherlands

Semifinal Group A
Italy 0 West Germany 0
Netherlands 5 Austria 1
Netherlands 2 West Germany 2
Italy 1 Austria 0
Netherlands 2 Italy 1
Austria 3 West Germany 2
    Winner: Netherlands
    Runner-up: Italy

Semifinal Group B
Brazil 3 Peru 0
Argentina 2 Poland 0
Poland 1 Peru 0
Argentina 0 Brazil 0
Brazil 3 Poland 1
Argentina 6 Peru 0
    Winner: Argentina
    Runner-up: Brazil

3rd Place Game
Brazil 2 Italy 1

Final
Argentina 3 Netherlands 1 (o/t)
    Champion: ARGENTINA

TWELFTH WORLD CUP, SPAIN, 1982
24 finalists, 109 nations entered

Group 1
Italy 0 Poland 0
Cameroon 0 Peru 0
Italy 1 Peru 1
Cameroon 0 Poland 0
Poland 5 Peru 1
Cameroon 1 Italy 1
    Qualifiers: Poland, Italy

Group 2
Algeria 2 West Germany 1
Austria 1 Chile 0
West Germany 4 Chile 1
Austria 2 Algeria 0
Algeria 3 Chile 2

West Germany 1 Austria 0
  Qualifiers: West Germany, Austria

Group 3
Belgium 1 Argentina 0
Hungary 10 El Salvador 1
Argentina 4 Hungary 1
Belgium 1 El Salvador 0
Belgium 1 Hungary 1
Argentina 2 El Salvador 0
  Qualifiers: Belgium, Argentina

Group 4
England 3 France 1
Czechoslovakia 1 Kuwait 1
England 2 Czechoslovakia 0
France 4 Kuwait 1
Czechoslovakia 1 France 1
England 1 Kuwait 0
  Qualifiers: England, France

Group 5
Honduras 1 Spain 1
Northern Ireland 0 Yugoslavia 0
Spain 2 Yugoslavia 1
Honduras 1 Northern Ireland 1
Yugoslavia 1 Honduras 0
Northern Ireland 1 Spain 0
  Qualifiers: Northern Ireland,
  Spain

Group 6
Brazil 2 USSR 1
Scotland 5 New Zealand 2
Brazil 4 Scotland 1
USSR 3 New Zealand 0
Scotland 2 USSR 2
Brazil 4 New Zealand 0
  Qualifiers: Brazil, USSR

Semifinal Group A
Poland 3 Belgium 0
USSR 1 Belgium 0
Poland 0 USSR 0
  Winner: Poland

Semifinal Group B
England 0 West Germany 0

West Germany 2 Spain 1
England 0 Spain 0
  Winner: West Germany

Semifinal Group C
Italy 2 Argentina 1
Brazil 3 Argentina 1
Italy 3 Brazil 2
  Winner: Italy

Semifinal Group D
France 1 Austria 0
Austria 2 Northern Ireland 2
France 4 Northern Ireland 1
  Winner: France

Semifinals
Italy 2 Poland 0
West Germany 3 France 3 (o/t)
(West Germany win 5–4 on PKs)

3rd Place Game
Poland 3 France 2

Final
Italy 3 West Germany 1
  Champion: ITALY

THIRTEENTH WORLD CUP,
MEXICO, 1986
24 finalists, 121 nations entered

Group A
Bulgaria 1 Italy 1
Argentina 3 South Korea 1
Argentina 1 Italy 1
Bulgaria 1 South Korea 1
Argentina 2 Bulgaria 0
Italy 3 South Korea 2
  Qualifiers:
  Argentina, Italy, Bulgaria

Group B
Mexico 2 Belgium 1
Paraguay 1 Iraq 0
Mexico 1 Paraguay 1
Belgium 2 Iraq 1
Belgium 2 Paraguay 2

Mexico 1 Iraq 0
  Qualifiers:
  Mexico, Paraguay, Belgium

Group C
France 1 Canada 0
USSR 6 Hungary 0
France 1 USSR 1
Hungary 2 Canada 0
France 3 Hungary 0
USSR 2 Canada 0
  Qualifiers: USSR, France

Group D
Brazil 1 Spain 0
Algeria 1 Northern Ireland 1
Brazil 1 Algeria 0
Spain 2 Northern Ireland 1
Brazil 3 Northern Ireland 0
Spain 3 Algeria 0
  Qualifiers: Brazil, Spain

Group E
West Germany 1 Uruguay 1
Denmark 1 Scotland 0
West Germany 2 Scotland 1
Denmark 6 Uruguay 1
Denmark 2 West Germany 0
Scotland 0 Uruguay 0
  Qualifiers: Denmark,
  West Germany, Uruguay

Group F
Morocco 0 Poland 0
Portugal 1 England 0
England 0 Morocco 0
Poland 1 Portugal 0
England 3 Poland 0
Morocco 3 Portugal 1
  Qualifiers:
  Morocco, England, Poland

Second Round
Mexico 2 Bulgaria 0
Belgium 4 USSR 3 (o/t)
Brazil 4 Poland 0
Argentina 1 Uruguay 0
France 2 Italy 0

West Germany 1 Morocco 0
England 3 Paraguay 0
Spain 5 Denmark 1

Quarterfinals
France 1 Brazil 1 (o/t)
(France won 4–3 on PKs)
West Germany 0 Mexico 0 (o/t)
(West Germany won 4–1 on PKs)
Argentina 2 England 1
Belgium 1 Spain 1 (o/t)
(Belgium won 5–4 on PKs)

Semifinals
West Germany 2 France 0
Argentina 2 Belgium 0

3rd Place Game
France 4 Belgium 2 (o/t)
Final
Argentina 3 West Germany 2
  Champion: ARGENTINA

FOURTEENTH WORLD CUP,
ITALY, 1990
24 finalists, 109 nations entered

Group A
Italy 1 Austria 0
Czechoslovakia 5 USA 1
Italy 1 USA 0
Czechoslovakia 1 Austria 0
Italy 2 Czechoslovakia 0
Austria 2 USA 1
  Qualifiers: Italy, Czechoslovakia

Group B
Cameroon 1 Argentina 0
Romania 2 USSR 0
Argentina 2 USSR 0
Cameroon 2 Romania 1
USSR 4 Cameroon 0
Argentina 1 Romania 1
  Qualifiers:
  Cameroon, Romania, Argentina

Group C
Brazil 2 Sweden 1

Costa Rica 1 Scotland 0
Brazil 1 Costa Rica 0
Scotland 2 Sweden 1
Costa Rica 2 Sweden 1
Brazil 1 Scotland 0
    Qualifiers: Brazil, Costa Rica

Group D
Colombia 2 UAE 0
West Germany 4 Yugoslavia 1
Yugoslavia 1 Colombia 0
West Germany 5 UAE 1
Colombia 1 West Germany 1
Yugoslavia 4 UAE 1
    Qualifiers: West Germany,
    Yugoslavia, Colombia

Group E
Belgium 2 South Korea 0
Spain 0 Uruguay 0
Spain 3 South Korea 1
Belgium 3 Uruguay 1
Spain 2 Belgium 1
Uruguay 1 South Korea 0
    Qualifiers: Spain, Belgium,
    Uruguay

Group F
England 1 Ireland 1
Egypt 1 Netherlands 1
England 0 Netherlands 0
Egypt 0 Ireland 0
England 1 Egypt 0
Netherlands 1 Ireland 1

Qualifiers: England, Ireland,
Netherlands

Second Round
Cameroon 2 Colombia 1
Czechoslovakia 4 Costa Rica 1
Argentina 1 Brazil 0
West Germany 2 Netherlands 1
Ireland 0 Romania 0 (o/t)
(Ireland won 5–4 on PKs)
Italy 2 Uruguay 0
Yugoslavia 2 Spain 1 (o/t)
England 1 Belgium 0 (o/t)

Quarterfinals
Argentina 0 Yugoslavia 0 (o/t)
(Argentina won 3–2 on PKs)
Italy 1 Ireland 0
West Germany 1 Czechoslovakia 0
England 3 Cameroon 2 (o/t)

Semifinals
Argentina 1 Italy 1 (o/t)
(Argentina won 4–3 on PKs)
West Germany 1 England 1 (o/t)
(West Germany won 4–3 on PKs)

3rd Place Game
Italy 2 England 1

Final
West Germany 1 Argentina 0
    Champion: WEST GERMANY

Olympic Soccer Tournament

Eligible: All member nations of FIFA. Originally for amateurs, the Olympic Game qualifications have been modified to admit professionals. An age restriction now applies. Participants must be age 23 or under, but each team is allowed to field a maximum of three over-age players.

Frequency: Every four years, between the World Cup cycle.

Format: Host nation qualifies automatically. There is no automatic qualification for the reigning champion. Regional qualifying rounds establish the other 15 finalists. Places allocated as follows: Europe 6, South America 2, Africa 3, Asia 3, CONCACAF 2.

Winners:

1908	Great Britain	1956	USSR
1912	Great Britain	1960	Yugoslavia
1916	No competition	1964	Hungary
1920	Belgium	1968	Hungary
1924	Uruguay	1972	Poland
1928	Uruguay	1976	East Germany
1932	No competition	1980	Czechoslovakia
1936	Italy	1984	France
1948	Sweden	1988	USSR
1952	Hungary	1992	Spain

The Under-20 World Cup

Official Title: The World Youth Championship for the FIFA/Coca-Cola Cup
Eligible: All member nations of FIFA. Players must be 19 years old or younger.
Frequency: Every two years, in predetermined host nation.
Format: Host nation qualifies automatically. There is no automatic qualification for the reigning champion. Regional qualifying games establish the other 15 finalists. Places are allocated as follows: Europe 6, South America 3, Asia 2, CONCACAF 2, Africa 2, Oceania 1.

1977	USSR	1987	Yugoslavia
1979	Argentina	1989	Portugal
1981	West Germany	1991	Portugal
1983	Brazil	1993	Brazil
1985	Brazil		

The Under-17 World Cup

Official Title: U-17 World Championship for the FIFA/JVC Cup.
Eligible: All member nations of FIFA. Players must be 16 years old or younger.
Frequency: Every two years, in predetermined host nation.
Format: Host nation qualifies automatically. There is no automatic qualification for the reigning champion. Regional qualifying games establish the other 15 finalists. Places are allocated as follows: Europe 3, South America 3, Africa 3, Asia 3, CONCACAF 3, Oceania 1.

1985	Nigeria	1991	Ghana
1987	USSR	1993	Nigeria
1989	Saudi Arabia		

Women's World Cup

Official Title: FIFA World Championship for Women's Football for the M&M's Cup.
Eligible: All member nations of FIFA.

Frequency: Every four years.
Format: For the first, 1991, edition, qualifying games were played in each continent. Twelve teams participated in the final tournament, with berths allocated as follows: Europe 5, South America 1, Asia 3, CONCACAF 1, Africa 1, Oceania 1.

1991   United States

Indoor World Cup
Official Title: FIFA Indoor (Five-a-Side) Football World Championship.
Eligible: All member nations of FIFA.
Frequency: Every four years.
1989   Brazil
1992   Brazil

2. Europe

European Championship
Formerly the European Nations Cup. The trophy itself is officially known as the Henri Delaunay Cup.
Eligible: National teams from all the member nations of UEFA (see page 280).
Frequency: Every four years, between the World Cup cycle.
Format: Since 1980, the final tournament has been played in a predetermined host nation. The host nation qualifies automatically; there has been no automatic qualification for the reigning champion. Qualifying games, starting some two years before the tournament, establish the other 7 finalists. Final tournament: the 8 finalists are drawn into two groups of 4. Group winners play the second-place team from the other group in the semifinals. Semifinal winners play in the final. There is no third-place game. In the 1996 final tournament, to be staged in England, the number of finalists will be increased to 16, with automatic qualification for the reigning champion (Denmark).

Winners:

1960	USSR	1980	West Germany
1964	Spain	1984	France
1968	Italy	1988	Netherlands
1972	West Germany	1992	Denmark
1976	Czechoslovakia		

3. South America

Copa America
Championship for South American national teams.
Eligible: National teams from all the member nations of the South American

Football Confederation (see page 280).

Frequency: Every two years.

Format: Has been changed repeatedly over the years. Most recently, the tournament has been staged in a predetermined host nation. Within two five-team groups, each team plays the other four once. The top two teams from each group advance to a final group of four, the winner of which is the champion.

Winners:

1917	Uruguay	1946	Argentina
1919	Brazil	1947	Argentina
1920	Uruguay	1949	Brazil
1921	Argentina	1953	Paraguay
1922	Brazil	1955	Argentina
1923	Uruguay	1956	Uruguay
1924	Uruguay	1957	Argentina
1925	Argentina	1959	Argentina
1926	Uruguay	1963	Bolivia
1927	Argentina	1967	Uruguay
1929	Argentina	1975	Peru
1935	Uruguay	1979	Paraguay
1937	Argentina	1983	Uruguay
1939	Peru	1987	Uruguay
1941	Argentina	1989	Brazil
1942	Uruguay	1991	Argentina
1945	Argentina	1993	Argentina

4. OTHER CONTINENTAL CHAMPIONSHIPS

Africa

1957	Egypt	1976	Morocco
1959	Egypt	1978	Ghana
1961	Ethiopia	1980	Nigeria
1963	Ghana	1982	Ghana
1965	Ghana	1984	Cameroon
1968	Zaire	1986	Egypt
1970	Sudan	1988	Cameroon
1972	Congo	1990	Algeria
1974	Zaire	1992	Ivory Coast

Asia

1956	South Korea	1980	Kuwait
1960	South Korea	1984	Saudi Arabia
1964	Israel	1988	Saudi Arabia
1968	Iran	1992	Japan
1972	Iran		
1976	Iran		

CONCACAF

1963	Costa Rica	1977	Mexico
1965	Mexico	1981	Honduras
1967	Guatemala	1991	United States
1969	Costa Rica	1993	Mexico
1971	Mexico		
1973	Haiti		

CLUB COMPETITIONS
I. Global

World Club Championship (Toyota Cup)

Eligible: Winners of previous year's European Cup and Libertadores Cup (see below for details of both Cups).

Frequency: Yearly.

Format: Single game. Since 1980, it has been played in December, in Tokyo.

1960	Real Madrid (Spain)	1976	Bayern Munich (West Germany)
1961	Peñarol (Uruguay)	1977	Boca Juniors (Argentina)
1962	Santos (Brazil)	1978	Not played
1963	Santos (Brazil)	1979	Olimpia (Paraguay)
1964	Inter-Milan (Italy)	1980	Nacional (Uruguay)
1965	Inter-Milan (Italy)	1981	Flamengo (Brazil)
1966	Peñarol (Uruguay)	1982	Peñarol (Uruguay)
1967	Racing Club (Argentina)	1983	Gremio (Brazil)
1968	Estudiantes de la Plata (Argentina)	1984	Independiente (Argentina)
1969	AC Milan (Italy)	1985	Juventus (Italy)
1970	Feyenoord (Netherlands)	1986	River Plate (Argentina)
1971	Nacional (Uruguay)	1987	FC Porto (Portugal)
1972	Ajax (Netherlands)	1988	Nacional (Uruguay)
1973	Independiente (Argentina)	1989	AC Milan (Italy)
1974	Atletico Madrid (Spain)	1990	AC Milan (Italy)
1975	Not played	1991	Red Star (Yugoslavia)
		1992	São Paulo (Brazil)

2. Intercontinental

Copa Interamericana

Eligible: Winners of the CONCACAF American Airlines Cup and the Libertadores Cup (see below for details of both Cups). The winner is the champion club of the Americas.

Frequency: Intended as an annual event, there have been many years when the fixture has not been played.

Format: Home-and-home series.

1969	Estudiantes de la Plata (Argentina)	1980	Olimpia (Paraguay)
		1981	UNAM (Mexico)
1972	Nacional (Uruguay)	1986	Argentinos Juniors
1973	Independiente (Argentina)		(Argentina)
		1987	River Plate (Argentina)
1974	Independiente (Argentina)	1989	Nacional (Uruguay)
		1990	Nacional (Colombia)
1976	Independiente (Argentina)	1991	Club America (Mexico)
		1992	Colo Colo (Chile)
1978	Club America (Mexico)		

3. Europe

European Cup

Eligible: The reigning champion, plus the champion clubs from all the member nations of UEFA (see page 280). The 1993–1994 edition featured 42 teams.

Frequency: Yearly.

Dates: Played during the regular European season, starting in October, with the final in May. Games are played midweek, under floodlights.

Format: Knock-out competition, with the names of the clubs drawn in pairs. The two clubs drawn together play each other on a home-and-home basis, the two scores being added together to produce a winner. If, after full-time in the second game, the aggregate scores are level, the winner is the club that scored the greater number of away goals (i.e. goals scored on the opponent's field). If the score is also level on away goals, 30 minutes of overtime (*not* sudden death) are played. If the score is still tied after overtime, the winner is decided by a penalty kick shoot-out.

When only 8 teams remain, the format is changed. The 8 are divided into two groups of 4, with each team playing the other 3 in its group on a home-and-home basis. Two points are awarded for a win, one for a tie. In 1992 and 1993, the two group winners advanced to meet in the single-game final, played at a predetermined site. In 1994 a semifinal stage was introduced, with the group winners playing the second-place teams from the other group.

The semifinal winners went on to the single-game final played at a predetermined site.

1956	Real Madrid (Spain)	1977	Liverpool (England)
1957	Real Madrid (Spain)	1978	Liverpool (England)
1958	Real Madrid (Spain)	1979	Nottingham Forest
1959	Real Madrid (Spain)		(England)
1960	Real Madrid (Spain)	1980	Nottingham Forest
1961	Benfica (Portugal)		(England)
1962	Benfica (Portugal)	1981	Liverpool (England)
1963	AC Milan (Italy)	1982	Aston Villa (England)
1964	Inter-Milan (Italy)	1983	SV Hamburg
1965	Inter-Milan (Italy)		(West Germany)
1966	Real Madrid (Spain)	1984	Liverpool (England)
1967	Celtic (Scotland)	1985	Juventus (Italy)
1968	Manchester United	1986	Steaua Bucharest
	(England)		(Romania)
1969	AC Milan (Italy)	1987	FC Porto (Portugal)
1970	Feyenoord (Netherlands)	1988	PSV Eindhoven
1971	Ajax (Netherlands)		(Netherlands)
1972	Ajax (Netherlands)	1989	AC Milan (Italy)
1973	Ajax (Netherlands)	1990	AC Milan (Italy)
1974	Bayern Munich	1991	Red Star Belgrade
	(West Germany)		(Yugoslavia)
1975	Bayern Munich	1992	Barcelona (Spain)
	(West Germany)	1993	Marseille (France)
1976	Bayern Munich		
	(West Germany)		

European Cup Winners' Cup

Eligible: The reigning champion, plus the cup winners from all the member nations of UEFA (see page 280). The 1993–1994 edition featured 43 teams.

Frequency: Yearly.

Dates: Played during the regular European season—starting in October, with the final in May. Games are played midweek, under floodlights.

Format: Knock-out competition, played as in the early rounds of the European Cup (q.v.), until only two teams remain. These then meet in the one-game final, at a predetermined site.

1961	Fiorentina	1965	West Ham United
1962	Atlético Madrid (Spain)		(England)
1963	Tottenham Hotspur	1966	Borussia Dortmund
	(England)		(West Germany)
1964	Sporting Lisboa	1967	Bayern Munich
	(Portugal)		(West Germany)

1968	AC Milan (Italy)	1979	Barcelona (Spain)
1969	Slovan Bratislava (Czechoslovakia)	1980	Valencia (Spain)
		1981	Dynamo Tbilisi (USSR)
1970	Manchester City (England)	1982	Barcelona (Spain)
		1983	Aberdeen (Scotland)
1971	Chelsea (England)	1984	Juventus (Italy)
1972	Rangers (Scotland)	1985	Everton (England)
1973	AC Milan (Italy)	1986	Dynamo Kiev (USSR)
1974	FC Magdeburg (East Germany)	1987	Ajax (Netherlands)
		1988	Mechelen (Belgium)
1975	Dynamo Kiev (USSR)	1989	Barcelona (Spain)
1976	RSC Anderlecht (Belgium)	1990	Sampdoria (Italy)
		1991	Manchester United (England)
1977	SV Hamburg (West Germany)	1992	Werder Bremen (Germany)
1978	RSC Anderlecht (Belgium)	1993	Parma (Italy)

UEFA Cup

(From its beginning in 1958 until 1971, this was known as the Fairs Cup.)
Eligible: 64 top clubs from all member nations of UEFA (see page 280), other than the champions or Cup winners. Places are allocated to each country according to the country's previous showing in the tournament. Thus, strong countries like Germany and Italy have more places than Norway or Switzerland.
Frequency: Yearly.
Dates: During the regular European season, from October through May. Games are played midweek under floodlights.
Format: As for the Cup Winners Cup (q.v.), except that the final is played as a two-leg home-and-home series.

1958	Barcelona (Spain)	1968	Leeds United (England)
1959	Not played	1969	Newcastle United (England)
1960	Barcelona (Spain)		
1961	Roma (Italy)	1970	Arsenal (England)
1962	Valencia (Spain)	1971	Leeds United (England)
1963	Valencia (Spain)	1972	Tottenham Hotspur (England)
1964	Real Zaragoza (Spain)		
1965	Ferencvaros (Hungary)	1973	Liverpool (England)
1966	Barcelona (Spain)	1974	Feyenoord (Netherlands)
1967	Dynamo Zagreb (Yugoslavia)	1975	Borussia Moenchengladbach (West Germany)

1976	Liverpool (England)	1984	Tottenham Hotspur
1977	Juventus (Italy)		(England)
1978	PSV Eindhoven	1985	Real Madrid (Spain)
	(Netherlands)	1986	Real Madrid (Spain)
1979	Borussia Moenchenglad-	1987	IFK Gothenburg
	bach (West Germany)		(Sweden)
1980	Eintracht Frankfurt	1988	Bayer Leverkusen
	(West Germany)		(West Germany)
1981	Ipswich Town (England)	1989	Napoli (Italy)
1982	IFK Gothenburg	1990	Juventus (Italy)
	(Sweden)	1991	Inter-Milan (Italy)
1983	RSC Anderlecht	1992	Ajax (Netherlands)
	(Belgium)	1993	Juventus (Italy)

European Super Cup
Eligible: Winners of previous season's European Cup and Cup Winners' Cup.
Frequency: Yearly.
Format: Home-and-home series.

1972	Ajax (Netherlands)	1982	Aston Villa (England)
1973	Ajax (Netherlands)	1983	Aberdeen (Scotland)
1974	Not played	1984	Juventus (Italy)
1975	Dynamo Kiev (USSR)	1985	Not played
1976	RSC Anderlecht	1986	Steaua Bucharest
	(Belgium)		(Romania)
1977	Liverpool (England)	1987	FC Porto (Portugal)
1978	RSC Anderlecht	1988	Mechelen (Belgium)
	(Belgium)	1989	AC Milan (Italy)
1979	Nottingham Forest	1990	AC Milan (Italy)
	(England)	1991	Manchester United
1980	Valencia (Spain)		(England)
1981	Not played	1992	Barcelona (Spain)

4. CONCACAF

American Airlines Cup
CONCACAF club championship
Eligible: The top two clubs from all member nations of CONCACAF (see page 279).
Frequency: Yearly, though the competition suffered from an erratic schedule in its early years.
Format: Knock-out competition. Clubs, drawn in pairs, play each other home-and-home.

1962	Guadalajara (Mexico)	1981	Transvaal (Surinam)
1963	Racing (Haiti)	1982	UNAM (Mexico)
1967	Alianza (El Salvador)	1983	Atlante (Mexico)
1968	Toluca (Mexico)	1984	Violette (Haiti)
1969	Cruz Azul (Mexico)	1985	Defence Force
1971	Cruz Azul (Mexico)		(Trinidad & Tobago)
1972	Olimpia (Honduras)	1986	Liga Deportiva Alajue-
1973	Transvaal (Surinam)		lense (Costa Rica)
1974	Municipal (Guatemala)	1987	Club América (Mexico)
1975	Atlético Espanol (Mexico)	1988	Olimpia (Honduras)
1976	Aguila (El Salvador)	1989	UNAM (Mexico)
1977	Club América (Mexico)	1990	Club América (Mexico)
1979	FAS (El Salvador)	1991	Puebla (Mexico)
1980	UNAM (Mexico)	1992	Club América (Mexico)

5. South America

Copa Libertadores

Eligible: The reigning champion, plus the top two teams from each member nation of the South American Football Confederation (see page 280).

Frequency: Yearly.

Format: First round of minileague play (four groups of four teams, one of five teams) eliminates five teams. Remaining sixteen then play knock-out competition; teams are drawn in pairs, which play home-and-home series.

1960	Peñarol (Uruguay)	1973	Independiente (Argentina)
1961	Peñarol (Uruguay)		
1962	Santos (Brazil)	1974	Independiente (Argentina)
1963	Santos (Brazil)		
1964	Independiente (Argentina)	1975	Independiente (Argentina)
1965	Independiente (Argentina)	1976	Cruzeiro (Brazil)
		1977	Boca Juniors (Argentina)
1966	Peñarol (Uruguay)	1978	Boca Juniors (Argentina)
1967	Racing Club (Argentina)	1979	Olimpia (Paraguay)
1968	Estudiantes de la Plata (Argentina)	1980	Nacional (Uruguay)
		1981	Flamengo (Brazil)
1969	Estudiantes de la Plata (Argentina)	1982	Peñarol (Uruguay)
		1983	Gremio (Brazil)
1970	Estudiantes de la Plata (Argentina)	1984	Independiente (Argentina)
1971	Nacional (Uruguay)	1985	Argentinos Juniors (Argentina)
1972	Independiente (Argentina)		
		1986	River Plate (Argentina)

1987	Peñarol (Uruguay)	1990	Olimpia (Paraguay)
1988	Nacional (Uruguay)	1991	Colo Colo (Chile)
1989	Nacional Medellin	1992	São Paulo (Brazil)
	(Colombia)	1993	São Paulo (Brazil)

SuperCopa

Winners are awarded the João Havelange trophy.
Eligible: Previous winners of the Copa Libertadores.
Frequency: Yearly.
Format: Knock-out competition. Clubs are drawn in pairs and play each other in a home-and-home series. There were sixteen entries for the 1992 edition: six clubs from Argentina, five from Brazil, two from Uruguay, one each from Chile, Paraguay, and Colombia.

1988	Racing Club (Argentina)	1991	Cruzeiro (Brazil)
1989	Boca Juniors (Argentina)	1992	Cruzeiro (Brazil)
1990	Olimpia (Paraguay)		

INDIVIDUAL AWARDS
I. Global

FIFA World Player of the Year

	Winner	Club	National Team
1991	Lothar Matthäus	Inter-Milan	West Germany
1992	Marco Van Basten	AC Milan	Netherlands

2. Europe

European Player of the Year

	Winner	Club	National Team
1956	Stanley Matthews	Blackpool	England
1957	Alfredo di Stéfano	Real Madrid	Argentina/Spain
1958	Raymond Kopa	Real Madrid	France
1959	Alfredo di Stéfano	Real Madrid	Argentina/Spain
1960	Luis Suarez	Barcelona	Spain
1961	Enrique Sivori	Juventus	Argentina/Italy
1962	Josef Masopust	Dukla Prague	Czechoslovakia
1963	Lev Yashin	Dynamo Moscow	USSR
1964	Denis Law	Manchester United	Scotland
1965	Eusebio	Benfica	Portugal
1966	Bobby Charlton	Manchester United	England
1967	Florian Albert	Ferencvaros	Hungary
1968	George Best	Manchester United	Northern Ireland
1969	Gianni Rivera	AC Milan	Italy

1970	Gerd Müller	Bayern Munich	West Germany
1971	Johan Cruyff	Ajax	Netherlands
1972	Franz Beckenbauer	Bayern Munich	West Germany
1973	Johan Cruyff	Barcelona	Netherlands
1974	Johan Cruyff	Barcelona	Netherlands
1975	Oleg Blokhin	Dynamo Kiev	USSR
1976	Franz Beckenbauer	Bayern Munich	West Germany
1977	Allan Simonsen	B. Moenchengladbach	Denmark
1978	Kevin Keegan	SV Hamburg	England
1979	Kevin Keegan	SV Hamburg	England
1980	Karl Heinz Rummenigge	Bayern Munich	West Germany
1981	Karl Heinz Rummenigge	Bayern Munich	West Germany
1982	Paolo Rossi	Juventus	Italy
1983	Michel Platini	Juventus	France
1984	Michel Platini	Juventus	France
1985	Michel Platini	Juventus	France
1986	Igor Belanov	Dynamo Kiev	USSR
1987	Ruud Gullit	AC Milan	Netherlands
1988	Marco Van Basten	AC Milan	Netherlands
1989	Marco Van Basten	AC Milan	Netherlands
1990	Lothar Matthäus	Inter-Milan	West Germany
1991	Jean-Pierre Papin	Marseille	France
1992	Marco Van Basten	AC Milan	Netherlands

3. South America

South American Player of the Year

	Winner	Club	National Team
1971	Tostão	Cruzeiro	Brazil
1972	Teofilo Cubillas	Alianza Lima	Peru
1973	Pelé	Santos	Brazil
1974	Elias Figueroa	Internacional	Chile
1975	Elias Figueroa	Internacional	Chile
1976	Elias Figueroa	Internacional	Chile
1977	Zico	Flamengo	Brazil
1978	Mario Kempes	Valencia	Argentina
1979	Diego Maradona	Argentinos Juniors	Argentina
1980	Diego Maradona	Boca Juniors	Argentina
1981	Zico	Flamengo	Brazil
1982	Zico	Flamengo	Brazil
1983	Socrates	Corinthians	Brazil

1984	Enzo Francescoli	River Plate	Uruguay
1985	Julio Cesar Romero	Fluminense	Paraguay
1986	Antonio Alzamendi	River Plate	Uruguay
1987	Carlos Valderrama	Deportivo Cali	Colombia
1988	Ruben Paz	Racing Buenos Aires	Uruguay
1989	Bebeto	Vasco Da Gama	Brazil
1990	Raul Amarilla	Olimpia	Paraguay
1991	Oscar Ruggeri	Velez Sarsfield	Argentina
1992	Rai	São Paulo	Brazil

4. Africa

African Player of the Year

	Winner	National Team
1970	Salif Keita	Mali
1971	Ibrahim Sunday	Ghana
1972	Cherif Souleymane	Guinea
1973	Tshimimu Bwanga	Zaire
1974	Paul Moukila	Congo
1975	Ahmed Faras	Morocco
1976	Roger Milla	Cameroon
1977	Dhiab Tarak	Tunisia
1978	Abdul Razak	Ghana
1979	Thomas N'Kono	Cameroon
1980	Jean Manga Onguene	Cameroon
1981	Lakhdar Belloumi	Algeria
1982	Thomas N'Kono	Cameroon
1983	Mahmoud Al-Khatib	Egypt
1984	Theophile Abega	Cameroon
1985	Mohamed Timoumi	Morocco
1986	Badou Zaki	Morocco
1987	Rabah Madjer	Algeria
1988	Kalusha Bwalya	Zambia
1989	George Weah	Liberia
1990	Roger Milla	Cameroon
1991	Abedi Pele	Ghana
1992	Abedi Pele	Ghana

The United States

The controlling body for soccer in the United States is:

United States Soccer Federation
U.S. Soccer House
1801-1811 S. Prairie Avenue
Chicago, IL 60616

UNITED STATES OLYMPIC TEAM

1924—Paris—Final Tournament:

USA 1	Estonia 0
USA 0	Uruguay 3

1928—Amsterdam—Final Tournament:

USA 2	Argentina 11

1936—Berlin—Final Tournament:

USA 0	Italy 1

1948—London—Final Tournament:

USA 0	Italy 9

1952—Helsinki—Final Tournament:

USA 0	Italy 8

1960—Qualifying Round

Mexico 2	USA 0
USA 1	Mexico 1

USA failed to qualify for final tournament in Rome.

1964—Qualifying Round

USA 0	Suriname 1
USA 4	Panama 2
USA 1	Mexico 2

USA failed to qualify for final tournament in Tokyo.

1968—Qualifying Round

USA 1	Bermuda 1
Bermuda 1	USA 0

USA failed to qualify for the final tournament in Mexico City.

1972—Qualifying Round, 1st Preliminary

USA 1	El Salvador 1
USA 3	Barbados 0
El Salvador 1	USA 1
Barbados 1	USA 3

2nd Preliminary

Jamaica 1	USA 1
Mexico 1	USA 1

Guatemala 3	USA 2
USA 2	Guatemala 1
USA 2	Mexico 2
USA 2	Jamaica 1

USA qualified for the final tournament in Munich:

USA 0	Morocco 0
USA 0	Malaysia 3
USA 0	West Germany 7

1976—Qualifying Round

Bermuda 3	USA 2
USA 2	Bermuda 0
Mexico 8	USA 0
USA 2	Mexico 4

USA failed to qualify for final tournament in Montreal.

1980—Qualifying Round

USA 5	Bermuda 0
Bermuda 0	USA 3
USA 1	Costa Rica 1
Costa Rica 0	USA 1
USA 2	Suriname 1
Suriname 4	USA 2

USA qualified for final tournament in Moscow, but did not compete because of U.S. boycott.

1984—As host nation, USA qualified automatically for final tournament:

USA 3	Costa Rica 0
USA 0	Italy 1
USA 1	Egypt 1

1988—Qualifying Round

Canada 2	USA 0
USA 3	Canada 0
USA 4	Trinidad and Tobago 1
Trinidad and Tobago	0 USA 1
El Salvador 2	USA 4
USA 4	El Salvador 1

USA qualified for final tournament in Seoul:

USA 1	Argentina 1
USA 0	South Korea 0
USA 2	USSR 4

1992—Qualifying Round

USA 8	Haiti 0
Panama 1	USA 1
USA 7	Panama 1
Haiti 0	USA 2
Mexico 1	USA 2
USA 4	Honduras 3
Honduras 3	USA 4
USA 3	Mexico 0
USA 3	Canada 1
Canada 2	USA 1

USA qualified for final tournament in Barcelona:

USA 1	Italy 2
USA 3	Kuwait 1
USA 2	Poland 2

UNITED STATES NATIONAL TEAM: WORLD CUP RECORD

1930—Final Tournament in Uruguay:

USA 3	Belgium 0
USA 3	Paraguay 0

Semifinal

USA 1	Argentina 6

1934—Qualifying Round:

USA 4	Mexico 2

USA qualified for final tournament in Italy:

USA 1	Italy 7

1938—USA did not enter tournament

1950—Qualifying Round:

USA 0	Mexico 6
USA 1	Cuba 1
USA 2	Mexico 6
USA 5	Cuba 2

USA qualified for final tournament in Brazil:

USA 1	Spain 3
USA 1	England 0
USA 2	Chile 5

1954—Qualifying Round:

Mexico 4	USA 0
Mexico 3	USA 1
Haiti 2	USA 3
Haiti 0	USA 3

USA failed to qualify for final tournament in Switzerland.

1958—Qualifying Round:

Mexico 6	USA 0
USA 2	Mexico 7
Canada 5	USA 1
USA 2	Canada 3

USA failed to qualify for final tournament in Sweden.

1962—Qualifying Round:

USA 3	Mexico 3
Mexico 3	USA 0

USA failed to qualify for final tournament in Chile.

1966—Qualifying Round:

USA 2	Mexico 2
Mexico 2	USA 0
Honduras 0	USA 1
Honduras 1	USA 1

USA failed to qualify for final tournament in England.

1970—Qualifying Round:

Canada 4	USA 2
USA 1	Canada 0
USA 6	Bermuda 2
Bermuda 0	USA 2
Haiti 2	USA 0
USA 0	Haiti 1

USA failed to qualify for final tournament in Mexico.

1974—Qualifying Round:

Canada 3	USA 2
USA 2	Canada 2
Mexico 3	USA 1
USA 1	Mexico 2

USA failed to qualify for final tournament in West Germany.

1978—Qualifying Round:

Canada 1	USA 1
USA 0	Mexico 0
Mexico 3	USA 0
USA 2	Canada 0
Canada 3	USA 0

USA failed to qualify for final tournament in Argentina.

1982—Qualifying Round:

USA 0	Canada 0
Canada 2	USA 1
Mexico 5	USA 1
USA 2	Mexico 1

USA failed to qualify for final tournament in Spain.

1986—Qualifying Round:

Netherlands Antilles 0	USA 0
USA 4	Netherlands Antilles 0
Trinidad and Tobago 1	USA 2

USA 1	Trinidad and Tobago 0
Costa Rica 1	USA 1
USA 0	Costa Rica 1

USA failed to qualify for final tournament in Mexico.

1990—Qualifying Round:

Jamaica 0	USA 0
USA 5	Jamaica 1
Costa Rica 1	USA 0
USA 1	Costa Rica 0
USA 1	Trinidad and Tobago 1

USA 2	Guatemala 1
El Salvador 0	USA 1
Guatemala 0	USA 0
USA 0	El Salvador 0
Trinidad and Tobago 0	USA 1

USA qualified for final tournament in Italy:

USA 1	Czechoslovakia 5
USA 0	Italy 1
USA 1	Austria 2

1994—As host nation, USA qualifies automatically for final tournament.

UNITED STATES NATIONAL TEAM
ALL-TIME APPEARANCE RECORDS*

		Games Played	Years Active
1	Bruce Murray	92	1985–
2	Marcelo Balboa	73	1988–
3	Tony Meola	72	1988–
4	Peter Caligiuri	71	1984–
5	Desmond Armstrong	67	1987–
6	Peter Vermes	65	1988–
7	Michael Windischmann	58	1984–1990
8	John Doyle	56	1987–
9	Hugo Perez	55	1984–
10	Chris Henderson	54	1990–
11	Fernando Clavijo	52	1990–
	John Harkes	52	1987–
13	Tab Ramos	50	1988–
	Eric Wynalda	50	1990–
15	Steve Trittschuh	45	1987–1991

UNITED STATES NATIONAL TEAM
ALL-TIME LEADING GOAL SCORERS*

		Goals	Games	Years
1	Bruce Murray	21	92	1985–
2	Eric Wynalda	14	50	1990–

* As of September 8, 1993.

3	Hugo Perez	11	55	1984–
	Peter Vermes	11	65	1988–
5	Rick Davis	9	43	1977–1988

COLLEGE SOCCER

NCAA DIVISION I—MEN

1959	St. Louis	1976	San Francisco
1960	St. Louis	1977	Hartwick
1961	West Chester	1978	San Francisco
1962	St. Louis	1979	Southern Illinois
1963	St. Louis	1980	San Francisco
1964	Navy	1981	Connecticut
1965	St. Louis	1982	Indiana
1966	San Francisco	1983	Indiana
1967	St. Louis and Michigan State (co-champions)	1984	Clemson
		1985	UCLA
1968	Michigan State and Maryland (co-champions)	1986	Duke
		1987	Clemson
1969	St. Louis	1988	Indiana
1970	St. Louis	1989	Virginia and Santa Clara (co-champions)
1971	Howard		
1972	St. Louis	1990	UCLA
1973	St. Louis	1991	Virginia
1974	Howard	1992	Virginia
1975	San Francisco		

NCAA DIVISION I—WOMEN

1982	North Carolina	1988	North Carolina
1983	North Carolina	1989	North Carolina
1984	North Carolina	1990	North Carolina
1985	George Mason	1991	North Carolina
1986	North Carolina	1992	North Carolina
1987	North Carolina		

INDIVIDUAL AWARDS

HERMANN TROPHY
Awarded to the best player of the year. Voted on yearly by Division I college coaches and journalists.

1967	Dov Markus	Long Island University
1968	Manuel Hernandez	San José State
1969	Al Trost	St. Louis
1970	Al Trost	St. Louis
1971	Mike Seerey	St. Louis
1972	Mike Seerey	St. Louis
1973	Dan Counce	St. Louis
1974	Farrukh Quraishi	Oneonta State
1975	Steve Ralbovsky	Brown
1976	Glenn Myernick	Hartwick
1977	Billy Gazonas	Hartwick
1978	Angelo Di Bernardo	Indiana
1979	Jim Stamatis	Penn State
1980	Joe Morrone Jr	Connecticut
1981	Armando Betancourt	Indiana
1982	Joe Ulrich	Duke
1983	Mike Jeffries	Duke
1984	Amr Aly	Columbia
1985	Tom Kain	Duke
1986	John Kerr	Duke
1987	Bruce Murray	Clemson
1988	Ken Snow	Indiana
1989	Tony Meola	Virginia
1990	Ken Snow	Indiana
1991	Alexi Lalas	Rutgers
1992	Brad Friedel	UCLA

WOMEN'S HERMANN TROPHY
Awarded to the best player of the year. Voted on by Division I coaches and journalists.

1988	Michelle Akers	Central Florida
1989	Shannon Higgins	North Carolina
1990	April Kater	Massachusetts
1991	Kristine Lilly	North Carolina
1992	Mia Hamm	North Carolina

MISSOURI ATHLETIC CLUB (MAC) AWARD
Awarded to best player of the year. The recipient must be an American citizen, either by birth or naturalization. Voted on by 1,100 college and junior college coaches.

1986	John Kerr	Duke
1987	John Harkes	Virginia
1988	Ken Snow	Indiana
1989	Tony Meola	Virginia
1990	Ken Snow	Indiana
1991	Alexi Lalas	Rutgers
1992	Claudio Reyna	Virginia

Index